Recent Advances in Intelligent Technologies and Information Systems

Vijayan Sugumaran
Oakland University, USA & Sogang University, Seoul, Korea

A volume in the Advances in Computational
Intelligence and Robotics (ACIR) Book Series

Managing Director:	Lindsay Johnston
Managing Editor:	Austin DeMarco
Director of Intellectual Property & Contracts:	Jan Travers
Acquisitions Editor:	Kayla Wolfe
Production Editor:	Christina Henning
Development Editor:	Erin O'Dea
Typesetter:	Cody Page
Cover Design:	Jason Mull

Published in the United States of America by
Information Science Reference (an imprint of IGI Global)
701 E. Chocolate Avenue
Hershey PA, USA 17033
Tel: 717-533-8845
Fax: 717-533-8661
E-mail: cust@igi-global.com
Web site: http://www.igi-global.com

Library of Congress Cataloging-in-Publication Data

CIP Data
Recent advances in intelligent technologies and information systems / Vijayan
Sugumaran, editor.
    pages cm
 Includes bibliographical references and index.
  ISBN 978-1-4666-6639-9 (hardcover) -- ISBN 978-1-4666-6640-5 (ebook) -- ISBN 978-1-4666-6642-9 (print & perpetual access) 1. Data mining. 2. Big data. 3. Semantic computing. 4. Intelligent agents (Computer software) I. Sugumaran, Vijayan, 1960-
 QA76.9.D343R425 2015
 006.3'12--dc23
                          2014029058

This book is published in the IGI Global book series Advances in Computational Intelligence and Robotics (ACIR) (ISSN: 2327-0411; eISSN: 2327-042X)

British Cataloguing in Publication Data
A Cataloguing in Publication record for this book is available from the British Library.

All work contributed to this book is new, previously-unpublished material. The views expressed in this book are those of the authors, but not necessarily of the publisher.

For electronic access to this publication, please contact: eresources@igi-global.com.

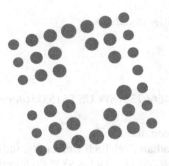

Advances in Computational Intelligence and Robotics (ACIR) Book Series

ISSN: 2327-0411
EISSN: 2327-042X

MISSION

While intelligence is traditionally a term applied to humans and human cognition, technology has progressed in such a way to allow for the development of intelligent systems able to simulate many human traits. With this new era of simulated and artificial intelligence, much research is needed in order to continue to advance the field and also to evaluate the ethical and societal concerns of the existence of artificial life and machine learning.

The **Advances in Computational Intelligence and Robotics (ACIR) Book Series** encourages scholarly discourse on all topics pertaining to evolutionary computing, artificial life, computational intelligence, machine learning, and robotics. ACIR presents the latest research being conducted on diverse topics in intelligence technologies with the goal of advancing knowledge and applications in this rapidly evolving field.

COVERAGE

- Add/Edit Topics Covered
- Automated Reasoning
- Pattern Recognition
- Cognitive Informatics
- Artificial Life
- Evolutionary Computing
- Algorithmic Learning
- Neural Networks
- Computer Vision
- Fuzzy Systems

IGI Global is currently accepting manuscripts for publication within this series. To submit a proposal for a volume in this series, please contact our Acquisition Editors at Acquisitions@igi-global.com or visit: http://www.igi-global.com/publish/.

Titles in this Series

For a list of additional titles in this series, please visit: www.igi-global.com

Handbook of Research on Advancements in Robotics and Mechatronics
Maki K. Habib (The American University in Cairo, Egypt)
Engineering Science Reference ● copyright 2015 ● 953pp ● H/C (ISBN: 9781466673878) ● US $515.00 (our price)

Handbook of Research on Advanced Intelligent Control Engineering and Automation
Ahmad Taher Azar (Benha University, Egypt) and Sundarapandian Vaidyanathan (Vel Tech University, India)
Engineering Science Reference ● copyright 2015 ● 795pp ● H/C (ISBN: 9781466672482) ● US $335.00 (our price)

Handbook of Research on Artificial Intelligence Techniques and Algorithms
Pandian Vasant (Universiti Teknologi Petronas, Malaysia)
Information Science Reference ● copyright 2015 ● 873pp ● H/C (ISBN: 9781466672581) ● US $495.00 (our price)

Recent Advances in Ambient Intelligence and Context-Aware Computing
Kevin Curran (University of Ulster, UK)
Information Science Reference ● copyright 2015 ● 376pp ● H/C (ISBN: 9781466672840) ● US $225.00 (our price)

Emerging Research on Swarm Intelligence and Algorithm Optimization
Yuhui Shi (Xi'an Jiaotong-Liverpool University, China)
Information Science Reference ● copyright 2015 ● 341pp ● H/C (ISBN: 9781466663282) ● US $225.00 (our price)

Face Recognition in Adverse Conditions
Maria De Marsico (Sapienza University of Rome, Italy) Michele Nappi (University of Salerno, Italy) and Massimo Tistarelli (University of Sassari, Italy)
Information Science Reference ● copyright 2014 ● 480pp ● H/C (ISBN: 9781466659667) ● US $235.00 (our price)

Computer Vision and Image Processing in Intelligent Systems and Multimedia Technologies
Muhammad Sarfraz (Kuwait University, Kuwait)
Information Science Reference ● copyright 2014 ● 312pp ● H/C (ISBN: 9781466660304) ● US $215.00 (our price)

Mathematics of Uncertainty Modeling in the Analysis of Engineering and Science Problems
S. Chakraverty (National Institute of Technology - Rourkela, India)
Information Science Reference ● copyright 2014 ● 441pp ● H/C (ISBN: 9781466649910) ● US $225.00 (our price)

Global Trends in Intelligent Computing Research and Development
B.K. Tripathy (VIT University, India) and D. P. Acharjya (VIT University, India)
Information Science Reference ● copyright 2014 ● 601pp ● H/C (ISBN: 9781466649361) ● US $235.00 (our price)

www.igi-global.com

701 E. Chocolate Ave., Hershey, PA 17033
Order online at www.igi-global.com or call 717-533-8845 x100
To place a standing order for titles released in this series, contact: cust@igi-global.com
Mon-Fri 8:00 am - 5:00 pm (est) or fax 24 hours a day 717-533-8661

Table of Contents

Section 1
Semantic Technologies and Applications

Detailed Table of Contents

Section 1
Semantic Technologies and Applications

Chapter 1
Strategies and Methods for Ontology Alignment 1
Hayden Wimmer, Bloomsburg University, USA
Victoria Yoon, Virginia Commonwealth University, USA
Roy Rada, University of Maryland Baltimore County, USA

The concept of ontologies has been around for millennia and spans many domains and disciplines. Ontologies are a powerful concept when applied to intelligent computing. Ontologies are the backbone of intelligent computing on the World Wide Web and crucial in many decision-support situations. Many sophisticated tools have been developed to support working with ontologies, including prominently exploiting the vast array of existing ontologies. Systems have been developed to automatically generate, match, and integrate ontologies in a process called ontology alignment. This chapter extends the current literature by presenting a system called ALIGN, which demonstrates how to use freely available tools to develop and facilitate ontology alignment. The first two ontologies are built with the ontology editor Protégé and represented in OWL. ALIGN then accesses these ontologies via Java's JENA framework and SPARQL queries. The efficacy of the ALIGN prototype is demonstrated on a drug-drug interaction problem. The prototype could readily be applied to other domains or be incorporated into decision-support tools.

Chapter 2
A Novel E-Learning Management System for Appropriate Recommendations on the Learning
Contents 16
Jegatha Deborah Lazarus, Anna University, India
Baskaran Ramachandran, Anna University, India
Kannan Arputharaj, Anna University, India

Educational organizations are able to bridge organizational gaps due to the rapid advances in science and technology. Specifically, e-learning drastically reduces the learning time compared to the traditional classroom setting. The challenges in e-learning are the organization of learning contents, characteristics of the learning individual, technological constraints, and performance evaluation. Moreover, the success of the e-learning environment is greatly influenced by the factors like appropriate recommendations of learning contents, content delivery, performance evaluation, and the maintenance of the psychological level through identification of the learning styles of the learners. The continual process of performance evaluation is commonly attributed by the challenging issues of Ontology Construction and Alignment in order to enhance the semantics of the evaluation documents. In the rest of the chapter, a novel rule-based e-learning management system is discussed as a solution for appropriate recommendations of the learning contents based on the psychological understanding of the learners for learning using fuzzy logic and the subsequent evaluation of the learners using Ontology Construction and Ontology Alignment technique using deontic logic. The experiments have been carried out on evaluating the learning of C programming language using an e-learning framework.

In the World Wide Web, users are an important information source for companies or institutions. People use the communication platforms of Web 2.0, for example Twitter, in order to express their sentiments of products, politics, society, or even private situations. In 2014, the Twitter users worldwide submitted 582 million messages (tweets) per day. To process the mass of Web 2.0's data (e.g. Twitter data) is a key functionality in modern IT landscapes of companies or institutions, because sentiments of users can be very valuable for the development of products, the enhancement of marketing strategies, or the prediction of political elections. This chapter's aim is to provide a framework for extracting, preprocessing, and analyzing customer sentiments in Twitter in all different areas.

Chapter 4

Modeling topic distributions over documents has become a recent method for coping with the problematic of huge amounts of unstructured data. Especially in the context of Web communities, topic models can capture the zeitgeist as a snapshot of people's communication. However, the problem that arises from that static snapshot is that it fails to capture the dynamics of a community. To cope with this problem, dynamic topic models were introduced. This chapter makes use of those topic models in order to capture dynamics in user behavior within microblog communities such as Twitter. However, only applying topic models yields no interpretable results, so a method is proposed that compares different political parties over time using regression models based on DTM output. For evaluation purposes, a Twitter data set divided into different political communities is analyzed and results and findings are presented.

Chapter 5

The recent technological advancements have significantly redefined the context in which organizations do business processes including the processes used to acquire, process, and share information. The transformations that emerged across the organizational and institutional landscapes have led to the emergence of new organizational forms of design and new business models. Within this context, the new business patterns, platforms, and architectures have been developed to enable for the maximization of benefits from data through the adoption of collaborative work practices. The main focus of such practices is oriented towards the improvement of responsiveness, building of alliances, and enhancing organizational reach. The use of global networks and Web-based systems for the implementation of collaborative work has been accompanied with a wide range of computer-supported collaborative systems. This chapter examines the context of collaboration, collaborative work, and the development of agent-supported collaborative work system. It also examines the implications of the ontological positions of sociomateriality on agent-supported collaborative work domains in terms of the multi-agent architecture and multi-agent evaluation.

US images are a commonly used tool for renal calculi diagnosis, although they are time consuming and tedious for radiologists to manually detect and calculate the size of the renal calculi. It is very difficult to properly segment the US image to detect interested area of objects with the correct position and shape due to speckle formation and other artifacts. In addition, boundary edges may be missing or weak and usually incomplete at some places. With that point of view, the proposed method is developed for renal calculi segmentation. A new segmentation method is proposed in this chapter. Here, new region indicators and new modified watershed transformation are utilized. The proposed method is comprised of four major processes, namely preprocessing, determination of outer and inner region indictors, and modified watershed segmentation with ANFIS performance. The results show the effectiveness of proposed segmentation methods in segmenting the kidney stones and the achieved improvement in sensitivity and specificity measures.

Section 2
Soft Computing and Decision Support

This chapter describes soft computing approaches for human-agent communications in the context of influencing decision-making behavior for health-related actions. Several methods are illustrated including using a person's predispositions and generalization techniques that allow issues to be viewed in a more favorable light with social interaction persuasion tendencies modeled with soft computing. The context of a robotic assistant for the elderly is used to illustrate the various communication techniques. Hierarchical generalization is introduced as a technique for generating potential alternatives in choices that might be more broadly acceptable to an individual who is being motivated towards a better choice. Finally, the related topic of negotiations using some the developed techniques is presented.

Chapter 8
S. Uma, Hindusthan Institute of Technology, India
J. Suganthi, Hindusthan College of Engineering and Technology, India

The design of a dynamic and efficient decision-making system for real-world systems is an essential but challenging task since they are nonlinear, chaotic, and high dimensional in nature. Hence, a Support Vector Machine (SVM)-based model is proposed to predict the future event of nonlinear time series environments. This model is a non-parametric model that uses the inherent structure of the data for forecasting. The dimensionality of the data is reduced besides controlling noise as the first preprocessing step using the Hybrid Dimensionality Reduction (HDR) and Extended Hybrid Dimensionality Reduction (EHDR) nonlinear time series representation techniques. It is also used for subsequencing the nonlinear time series data. The proposed SVM-based model using EHDR is compared with the models using Symbolic Aggregate approXimation (SAX), HDR, SVM using Kernel Principal Component Analysis (KPCA), and SVM using varying tube size values for historical data on different financial instruments. A comparison of the experimental results of the proposed model with other models taken for the experimentation has proven that the prediction accuracy of the proposed model is outstanding.

Chapter 9
Tim Pidun, Technische Universität Dresden, Germany

The supply of adequate information is one of the main functions of Performance Measurement Systems (PMS), but also one of its drawbacks and reason for failure. Not only the collection of indicators is crucial, but also the stakeholders' understanding of their meaning, purpose, and contextual embedding. Today, companies seek a PMS without a way to express the goodness of a solution, indicating its ability to deliver appropriate information and to address these demands. The goal of this chapter is to explore the mechanisms that drive information and knowledge supply in PMS in order to model a way to express this goodness. Using a grounded theory approach, a theory of visibility of performance is developed, featuring a catalog of determinants for the goodness of PMS. Companies can conveniently use them to assess their PMS and to improve the visibility of their performance.

Chapter 10

In the 21st century, the awareness of applying recent advanced intelligent technologies to promote a firm's brand image is the key to the success of expanding its business. Such implication demands efforts in strategic planning and massive investment from the top management team. However, most researches on branding strategies are narrowed to advertisement or classical marketing. Insufficient research on the backbone of making key successful branding strategies to effectively apply the intelligent technologies hinders the development of branding strategies. This chapter identifies three aspects: innovation in design technology, decision making on product quality, and collaborative communications to be the critical elements of the backbone. The methodology utilizes the power of the advanced computational technologies to generate innovative designs in a collaborative communication framework. Decision making on the quality of designs is monitored with EG-Kano reference models. Four case studies demonstrate that the backbone has potentials leading to ever-greater economic benefits.

Chapter 11

A novel Artificial Neural Network (ANN) dimension expansion-based framework that addresses the demand for privacy preservation of low dimensional data in clustering analysis is discussed. A hybrid approach that combines ANN with Linear Discriminant Analysis (LDA) is proposed to preserve the privacy of data in mining. This chapter describes a feasible technique for privacy preserving clustering with the objective of providing superior level of privacy protection without compromising the data utility and mining outcome. The suitability of these techniques for mining has been evaluated by performing clustering on transformed data and the performance of the proposed method is measured in terms of misclassification and privacy level percentage. The methods are further validated by comparing the results with traditional Geometrical Data Transformation Methods (GDTMs). The results arrived at are significant and promising.

Chapter 12

Walid Moudani, Lebanese University, Lebanon
Ahmad Shahin, Lebanese University, Lebanon
Fadi Chakik, Lebanese University, Lebanon
Dima Rajab, Lebanese University, Lebanon

The health industry collects huge amounts of health data, which, unfortunately, are not mined to discover hidden information. Information technologies can provide alternative approaches to the diagnosis of the osteoporosis disease. In this chapter, the authors examine the potential use of classification techniques on a huge volume of healthcare data, particularly in anticipation of patients who may have osteoporosis disease through a set of potential risk factors. An innovative solution approach based on dynamic reduced sets of risk factors using the promising Rough Set theory is proposed. An experimentation of several classification techniques have been performed leading to rank the suitable techniques. The reduction of potential risk factors contributes to enumerate dynamically optimal subsets of the potential risk factors of high interest leading to reduce the complexity of the classification problems. The performance of the model is analyzed and evaluated based on a set of benchmark techniques.

Preface

INTRODUCTION

Business Intelligence (BI) encompasses a wide range of business supporting analytical tools that are used to process increasing amounts of corporate data. The interpretation of output produced by BI applications, however, continues to be performed manually, as does the determination of appropriate actions to be taken based on that output. Knowledge surrounding these interpretations and actions builds within the members of an organization. When employees depart an organization, they take that knowledge with them, creating a vacuum. New members of the organization must rebuild such knowledge through experience.

Consider the following scenario. A business analyst has been on the job for six months. He or she finishes an analysis, pulling a complex query from her company's Business Intelligence (BI) enterprise application. The primary insight the analyst uncovers is a spike in year over year sales for last month. The analyst communicates to his or her manager and several executives that the interpretation of this points to sales being on an up-swing. The analyst recommends the company order more inventory.

However, the analyst was not aware that the company had a strike at that time last year, so the spike isn't nearly as encouraging as it looks. The previous analyst would have known this. A solution to this problem could be augmenting her company's BI applications with a tool to collect the type of knowledge that builds up in individuals over time. This tool would grow and learn about the individual aspects of your organization. It would be adapted to work specifically with her firm's BI environment to assist her in making key, often subtle, insights that only someone with years of experience could make. Further research is needed to develop design guidelines for that tool, and a methodology for implementing and using it.

The need to accurately interpret the output of BI applications becomes more critical as businesses come to rely on that output as a competitive advantage in the age of Big Data. According to a 2011 McKinsey Global Institute study, "15 out of 17 US sectors have more data per company than the Library of Congress" and over 140,000 more analysts are needed to take advantage of that data.

Analysts currently develop the knowledge needed to perform these tasks through experience over time. The resulting interpretations can be detached from their proper context if a given analyst's experience is not sufficient to provide that context. No analyst can be expected to have all of the contextual knowledge needed for the massive amounts of data companies are analyzing today. Semantic technologies, such as ontologies, should provide a means for storing the knowledge of organization members so it can be retained and effectively used and reused.

The volume of data is growing at a rapid rate and the phrase 'Big data' is being used to describe the exponential growth in both structured and unstructured data. It is becoming more and more difficult to manage and analyze this large volume of data. Big data analytics help companies make better decisions by enabling users to analyze large volume of transaction data as well as other data sources that may not have been considered otherwise. Existing technologies such as Natural Language Processing (NLP) can be of great help in big data analytics. Extracting meaningful information from any part of human language is a challenging problem. There is a wealth of information which can be extracted from natural language, but the complexity of the analysis and the need for scalable, parallel processing increases since extracting actionable knowledge from large volumes of unstructured human language is a non-trivial problem.

There have been major advancements in recent years, including textual and semantic analysis, cluster analysis, similarity matching, probabilistic latent semantic indexing, natural language processing, and other powerful tools, which promise to leverage human data in many new ways. The rapid advancement of technology has changed the way the world operates and has given rise to intelligent tools and technologies. We can use the available technology to manage the big data analytics issue appropriately, particularly with the help of domain knowledge and semantics. Much work is needed to explore and analyze the existing information available on different new tools and the role of natural language processing in big data analytics. Several open source software tools exist; however, small and medium size organizations (SMEs) do not have the necessary expertise or manpower to use these tools. Moreover, these tools are meant for specific purpose and they may have to be combined to carry out some meaningful activity. Hence, further research is needed to: a) develop architectures for integrated environments that use different open source tools that facilitate big data analytics, including NLP, and b) implement proof-of-concept prototypes and demonstrate their usefulness.

The existing literature has been surveyed to analyze the current state of affairs on big data analytics and has been summarized below. Considerable strides have been made in processing large volumes of unstructured data with the help of various technologies including natural language processing. Progress is being made in developing integrated environments that facilitate big data analytics even by novice users.

BIG DATA ANALYTICS

Big data analytics deals with processing large and complex data sets. These data sets are difficult to process and require advanced and unique data management, storage, analysis, and visualization techniques. With the current computing capability, a user can process easily exabytes of data in a reasonable amount of time. On the other hand, there is exponential growth in the data sets due to the continuous collection of data by ubiquitous information-sensing mobile devices, aerial sensory technologies, software logs, cameras, microphones and wireless sensor networks. Traditional database technologies such as relational databases and desktop statistical packages and visualization tools are not sufficient to process Big Data. It requires massively parallel software running on tens, hundreds, or even thousands of servers. Organizations have achieved varying degrees of success in being able to undertake big data analytics initiatives, depending upon the capabilities of the organization and the applications that are used. For some organizations, processing hundreds of gigabytes of data may be problematic while for others it may be that terabytes of data provide considerable opportunities.

Semantics can play greater role in big data analytics. Domain knowledge can help in bringing together very large, diverse data sets that often include varied data types and streaming data. Semantic technologies refer to a range of tools used to store and retrieve knowledge. They are intended to help capture some of the real world meaning associated with data, a notion proposed by the Semantic Web. Ontologies are often cited as a surrogate for capturing the meaning of terms and the relationships among them. Semantic technologies are intended to address questions of interoperability, recognition and representation of terms and concepts, categorization, and meaning, which are very useful in big data analytics. Further research is needed for using ontologies, specifically, as a semantic technology that could improve the interpretation of BI application output, especially for novice users.

A targeted ontology can be built to contain the knowledge of the organization being analyzed (not necessarily the organization to which an analyst belongs). A targeted ontology is defined as one that captures and represents organization-specific knowledge in a format that provides direct, formal relationships to the organization's BI environment. This is done through defining a special class of ontology objects called targeted objects. These objects directly mirror objects in the BI environment, thus easing automation of connecting ontological knowledge to BI output. A systematic methodology is needed for using targeted ontologies in the interpretation of BI application output. The ontology for this solution should be targeted to the organization because "Representing knowledge for the purpose of solving some problem is strongly affected by the nature of the problem and the inference strategy to be applied to the problem".

Big data analytics has two major aspects: a) how to manage extra ordinarily large volumes of unstructured and structured data, and b) how to process this data to generate meaningful information. How best to combine these two aspects to gain competitive advantage is the current focus as well as how the two can be paired up to create one of the most profound trends in Business Intelligence (BI) domain. Big data analytics explores the details of business operations and customer interactions that typically don't find their way into a data warehouse or standard report. The data can comprise unstructured data coming from sensors, devices, third parties, Web applications, and social media, much of it generated in real time on a large scale. Advanced analytics techniques such as predictive modeling, data mining, statistics, and natural language processing can be used by organizations to analyze the data to understand the current state of the business and track evolving aspects such as customer behavior and patterns in the market. New methods of working with big data, such as Hadoop and MapReduce, also offer alternatives to traditional data warehousing techniques.

As stated earlier, semantic technologies can be very useful in managing, analyzing and interpreting the results of big data analytics. Semantic technology uses the concept of associative indexing and establishing relationships. The Semantic Web relies on adding machine-readable metadata about the web page, including relationships across many web pages. This metadata and the relationships can be used by software agents to process the hyperlinks automatically. The Semantic Web describes the Web contents through annotations and metadata, which can be processed by applications or software agents to locate and reason over Web resources. The semantic web relies on ontologies as a way to represent the metadata and the domain knowledge that will be used by the application in reasoning about the resources. Ontologies are one of the main artifacts used to leverage the current Web to the Semantic Web.

There are several technologies that are used by the Semantic Web to make it a reality. Semantic Web Services facilitate the packaging of useful services that can be utilized by agents and applications on demand. These services can be provided by third party vendors and can be published, searched, and integrated into an application on the fly. These services can be composed to form useful applications without having to invest heavily in designing and building these applications. Several standards such as Extensible Markup Language (XML), Simple Object Access Protocol (SOAP), Universal Description,

Discovery and Integration (UDDI), and Web Services Description Language (WSDL) help operational-ize the Web services paradigm. In addition, there are other standards to implement the Semantic Web, such as Web Ontology Language (OWL), Resource Description Framework (RDF), Rule Interchange Format (RIF). OWL ontology is based on Description Logics, which are both expressive and decidable, and provide a foundation for developing precise models about various domains of knowledge. Ontologies provide the memory index that enables searches across vast amounts of data to return relevant, actionable information. Using Big Data, the appropriate content can be delivered to any device any time any place. Thus, users can get the data they need when and where they need it. Semantic technologies provide the necessary mechanisms to index crucial information and be able to recall them in a given context.

The "Cloud" technology is another major contributor to the up take in big data analytics. Since we are dealing with very large volumes of data, storing and managing it becomes a problem for small and medium sized enterprises since they do not have the necessary technology infrastructure. However, they can use the cloud based solutions which provide ample storage and processing capabilities without having to make heavy investments in technology infrastructure. Applications can be deployed in the cloud with their own set of essential elements. Organizations can use private, public, and hybrid clouds to consume great volumes of data and apply cloud-based analytics that can work through structured, semi-structured, or unstructured data. Cloud technologies can be used to create strong analytics platforms and as data continues to grow at rapid rates, cloud provides the platform to support the increasing data volume efficiently.

Natural Language Processing (NLP) can also play a great role in big data analytics. For example, it could be used to mine facts from unstructured textual data. NLP uses linguistic concepts such as part-of-speech (noun, verb, adjective, etc.) and grammatical structure (represented as phrases) to draw out a fuller meaning represented in free text. NLP technique makes use of various knowledge sources, such as a lexicon of words and their meanings and grammatical properties and a set of grammar rules and often other resources such as ontology of entities and actions, or a thesaurus of synonyms or abbreviations. The ultimate goal of NLP is to make computers understand statements written in human languages. There are commercial and open source NLP software, some of which can also be deployed in cloud. Some of these tools and packages are very accurate in extracting key entities, events, and relationships from un-structured text. Some can even extract to RDF (Resource Description Framework) and OWL (semantic technology standards) levels. Gathering structured data from unstructured text allows cloud-based analytics to work across all data in the organization.

Big Data often contains unstructured data, which has fueled the resurgence in Natural Language Processing research. Other than the data stored in structured databases, there is now a dearth of mas-sively unstructured data and text coming from several sources such as social media, automatic content generation, etc. Big Data technology will help to improve natural language processing technology as it will allow greater volumes of written works to be processed and algorithmically understood. So, Big Data will become easier to use. Semantic technology is a key asset in the analysis of Big Data. Semantic technologies brings structure, meaning and accessibility to previously unused or underused data

OPEN SOURCE TOOLS FOR BIG DATA ANALYTICS

Several technologies have emerged as key technologies to enable storage of large amounts of unstructured data. For example, technologies such as Hadoop and Map/Reduce have become the corner stone for storing and processing very large amounts of data. Various organizations may combine their traditional data warehouses containing structured enterprise data with unstructured piles of external data and store the results in the cloud (using services such as Amazon AWS/EC2, Rackspace, Microsoft Azure, or Google App Engines or other services).

Several algorithms can be applied to the data to extract useful and valuable information from it. Traditional data mining and statistical software as well as software/tools created specifically for large scale data manipulation can perform different types of processing on large data-sets (e.g., regression, classification, natural language processing, clustering, collaborative filtering, and machine learning). These software can be enhanced with toolkits (such as Rapidminer, Protégé, OpenNLP, NLTK, etc.) and evolved into entire frameworks for analyzing Big Data, finding and analyzing patterns, reducing uncertainties, and helping critical decisions and actions.

Hadoop was initially in-spired by papers published by Google outlining its approach to handling an avalanche of data, and has since become the standard for storing, processing and analyzing hundreds of terabytes, and even petabytes of data. Hundreds of enterprises have adopted it over the past three or so years to manage fast-growing volumes of structured, semi-structured and unstructured data. It is a free, Java-based programming framework and supports the processing of large data sets in a distributed computing environment. Hadoop makes it possible to run applications on systems with thousands of nodes involving thousands of terabytes and is the core platform for structuring Big Data, and serves useful for analytics purposes. Data from multiple sources can be joined and aggregated in arbitrary ways enabling deeper analyses than any one system can provide. Hadoop clusters are remarkably fault tolerant, so if a node is lost, the system redirects work to another location of the data and continues processing without losing time.

MapReduce is useful for big data analysis is 'MapReduce' which is a software framework that allows developers to write programs that process massive amounts of unstructured data in parallel across a distributed cluster of processors or stand-alone computers. MapReduce and Hadoop can be used for distributed big data processing that may deliver speed, cost, and flexibility advantages over just using massively parallel processing database options.

Graphlab is an open source project to produce free implementations of scalable machine learning algorithms on multicore machine and clusters. Designing and implementing efficient, error free parallel and distributed algorithms can be very challenging. Map-Reduce exposes a simple computational pattern that isolates users from the complexities of large-scale parallel and distribute system design. Unfortunately, many important computational tasks are not inherently data-parallel and cannot be efficiently or intuitively expressed in data-parallel abstractions. GraphLab is a high-level graph-parallel abstraction that efficiently and intuitively expresses computational dependencies. Unlike Map-Reduce where computation is applied to independent records, computation in GraphLab is applied to dependent records which are stored as vertices in a large distributed data-graph.

Dremel is a scalable, interactive, ad-hoc query system for analysis of read-only nested data. By combining multi-level execution trees and columnar data layout, it is capable of running aggregation queries over trillion-row tables in seconds. The system scales to thousands of CPUs and petabytes of data, and has thousands of users at Google.

RapidMiner is a free open source analytics tool and an excellent prototyping platform due to its flexibility and robustness. It is primarily Java based so can run on any platform smoothly. Models based on Sentiment analysis can be built in RapidMiner very easily. Sentiment analysis is an application of natural language processing and other analytic techniques to identify and extract subjective information from source text material. In order to improve the accuracy of the sentiment analysis, it is important to properly identify the semantic relationships between the sentiment expressions and the subject. Examples of applications include companies applying sentiment analysis to analyze social media to determine how different customer segments and stakeholders are reacting to their products and actions.

The Apache OpenNLP library is a machine learning based toolkit for the processing of natural language text. It is a java based toolkit and supports the common NLP tasks, such as tokenization, sentence segmentation, part-of-speech tagging, named entity extraction, chunking, parsing, and coreference resolution. These tasks are usually required to build more advanced text processing services. The toolkit also includes maximum entropy and perceptron based machine learning. This is a great toolkit to analyze and make sense of the data.

NLTK is a leading platform for building Python programs to work with human language data. It provides easy-to-use interfaces to over 50 corpora and lexical re-sources such as WordNet, along with a suite of text processing libraries for classification, tokenization, stemming, tagging, parsing, and semantic reasoning.

NLP research has been driven by naturally occurring language data instead of using purely knowledge-based or rule-based methods that are generally not as robust and are expensive to build. Data-driven NLP techniques have become more and more sophisticated by relying heavily on the fields of Statistics and Machine Learning. These techniques now require large amounts of data in order to build a reasonably good model of what human language looks like. The language data sets are typically extremely large and we need tools such as Hadoop to manage these datasets. Natural Language Toolkit or NLTK is also a useful tool in conjunction with Hadoop to process language datasets. NLTK ships with real-world data in the form of more than 50 raw as well as annotated corpora. In addition, it also includes useful language processing tools like tokenizers, part-of-speech taggers, parsers as well as interfaces to machine learning libraries.

Mavuno, a scalable and robust, Hadoop-based toolkit was developed specially for acquiring paraphrases from large corpora. It supports basic natural language processing tasks (e.g., part of speech tagging, chunking, parsing, named entity recognition) and is capable of large-scale distributional similarity computations (e.g., synonym, paraphrase, and lexical variant mining) and also has great information extraction capabilities.

Protégé: Protégé is a free, open source ontology editor and knowledge base frame-work. The Protégé platform supports two main ways of modeling ontologies via the Protégé-Frames and OWL editors. Protégé ontologies can be exported into a variety of formats including RDF(S), OWL, and XML Schema. It is based on Java, is extensible, and provides a plug-and-play environment that makes it a flexible base for rapid prototyping and application development.

Stanbol: A set of reusable components is provided by Apache Stanbol for semantic content management. Its intended use is to extend traditional content management systems with semantic services. Other feasible uses include, direct usage from web applications (e.g. for tag extraction/suggestion; or text completion in search fields), 'smart' content workflows or email routing based on extracted entities, topics, etc.

Hadoop streaming is a utility that comes with the Hadoop distribution and allows the user to create and run map/reduce jobs with any executable or script as the mapper and/or the reducer. Dumbo is an open source tool that can be used to do the NLP task of automatic word association with a very large corpus by using Hadoop on Amazon EC2. Word association is a very common task in psycholinguistics and having a computer do it is both entertaining and informative.

ORGANIZATION OF THE BOOK

This book is organized into two sections. The first section discusses semantic technologies and their applications as well as automated reasoning for Semantic Web services composition and knowledge management. The second section discusses issues related to intelligent agent and multi-agent systems and their use. A brief description of each of the chapters is provided below.

Section 1: Semantic Technologies and Applications

The first chapter of the book is titled "Strategies and Methods for Ontology Alignment," written by Hayden Wimmer, Victoria Yoon, and Roy Rada. The authors point out that the concept of ontologies has been around for millennia and spans many domains, and that ontologies are a powerful concept when applied to intelligent computing. Ontologies are the backbone of intelligent computing on the World Wide Web and crucial in many decision support situations. Many sophisticated tools have been developed to support working with ontologies, including prominently exploiting the vast array of existing ontologies. Systems have been developed to automatically generate, match, and integrate ontologies in a process called ontology alignment. This chapter extends the current literature by presenting a system called ALIGN, which demonstrates how to use freely available tools to develop and facilitate ontology alignment. The first two ontologies are built with the ontology editor Protégé and represented in OWL. ALIGN then accesses these ontologies via Java's JENA framework and SPARQL queries. The efficacy of the ALIGN prototype is demonstrated on a drug-drug interaction problem. The prototype could readily be applied to other domains or be incorporated into decision-support tools.

The second chapter of the book is titled "A Novel E-Learning Management System for Appropriate Recommendations on the Learning Contents," written by Jegatha Deborah Lazarus, Baskaran Ramachandran, and Kannan Arputharaj. Educational organizations are able to bridge organizational gaps due to the rapid advances in science and technology. Specifically, e-learning drastically reduces the learning time compared to the traditional classroom setting. The challenges in e-learning are the organization of learning contents, characteristics of the learning individual, technological constraints, and performance evaluation. Moreover, the success of the e-learning environment is greatly influenced by the factors like appropriate recommendations of learning contents, content delivery, performance evaluation, and the maintenance of the psychological level through identification of the learning styles of the learners. The continual process of performance evaluation is commonly attributed by the challenging issues of Ontology Construction and Alignment in order to enhance the semantics of the evaluation documents. In the rest of the chapter, a novel rule-based e-learning management system is discussed as a solution for appropriate recommendations of the learning contents based on the psychological understanding of the learners for learning using fuzzy logic and the subsequent evaluation of the learners using Ontology Construction and Ontology Alignment technique using deontic logic. The experiments have been carried out on evaluating the learning of C programming language using an e-learning framework.

The third chapter is titled "Evaluation of Topic Models as a Preprocessing Engine for the Knowledge Discovery in Twitter Datasets," written by Stefan Sommer, Tom Miller, and Andreas Hilbert. In the World Wide Web, users are an important information source for companies or institutions. People use the communication platforms of Web 2.0, for example Twitter, in order to express their sentiments of products, politics, society, or even private situations. In 2014, the Twitter users worldwide submitted 582 million messages (tweets) per day. To process the mass of Web 2.0's data (e.g. Twitter data) is a key functionality in modern IT landscapes of companies or institutions, because sentiments of users can be very valuable for the development of products, the enhancement of marketing strategies, or the prediction of political elections. This chapter's aim is to provide a framework for extracting, preprocessing, and analyzing customer sentiments in Twitter in all different areas.

The fourth chapter is titled "Welcome to the Party: Modeling the Topic Evolution of Political Parties in Microblogs Using Dynamic Topic Models," written by Kai Heinrich. Modeling topic distributions over documents has become a recent method for coping with the problematic of huge amounts of unstructured data. Especially in the context of Web communities, topic models can capture the zeitgeist as a snapshot of people's communication. However, the problem that arises from that static snapshot is that it fails to capture the dynamics of a community. To cope with this problem, dynamic topic models were introduced. This chapter makes use of those topic models in order to capture dynamics in user behavior within microblog communities such as Twitter. However, only applying topic models yields no interpretable results, so a method is proposed that compares different political parties over time using regression models based on DTM output. For evaluation purposes, a Twitter data set divided into different political communities is analyzed and results and findings are presented in this chapter.

The fifth chapter of the book is titled "Design Consideration of Sociomaterial Multi-Agent CSCW Systems," by Tagelsir Mohamed Gasmelseid. The recent technological advancements have significantly redefined the context in which organizations do business processes including the processes used to acquire, process, and share information. The transformations that emerged across the organizational and institutional landscapes have led to the emergence of new organizational forms of design and new business models. Within this context, the new business patterns, platforms, and architectures have been developed to enable for the maximization of benefits from data through the adoption of collaborative work practices. The main focus of such practices is oriented towards the improvement of responsiveness, building of alliances, and enhancing organizational reach. The use of global networks and Web-based systems for the implementation of collaborative work has been accompanied with a wide range of computer-supported collaborative systems. This chapter examines the context of collaboration, collaborative work, and the development of agent-supported collaborative work system. It also examines the implications of the ontological positions of sociomateriality on agent-supported collaborative work domains in terms of the multi-agent architecture and multi-agent evaluation.

The sixth chapter is titled "Segmentation of Renal Calculi in Ultrasound Kidney Images Using Modified Watershed Method," which is contributed by P. R. Tamilselvi. Ultrasound (US) images are a commonly used tool for renal calculi diagnosis, although they are time consuming and tedious for radiologists to manually detect and calculate the size of the renal calculi. It is very difficult to properly segment the US image to detect interested area of objects with the correct position and shape due to speckle formation and other artifacts. In addition, boundary edges may be missing or weak and usually incomplete at some places. With that point of view, the proposed method is developed for renal calculi segmentation. A new segmentation method is proposed in this chapter. Here, new region indicators and new modified watershed transformation are utilized. The proposed method is comprised of four major processes, namely preprocessing, determination of outer and inner region indictors, and modified watershed segmentation with ANFIS performance. The results show the effectiveness of proposed segmentation methods in segmenting the kidney stones and the achieved improvement in sensitivity and specificity measures. Furthermore, the performance of the proposed technique is evaluated by comparing with the other segmentation methods.

Section 2: Soft Computing and Decision Support

The second section of the book deals with soft computing and how soft computing and other relevant technologies can be used for decision support. To start this section. The seventh chapter is titled "Influencing Actions-Related Decisions Using Soft Computing Approaches," written by Frederick E. Petry and Ronald R. Yager. This chapter describes soft computing approaches for human-agent communications in the context of influencing decision-making behavior for health-related actions. Several methods are illustrated including using a person's predispositions and generalization techniques that allow issues to be viewed in a more favorable light with social interaction persuasion tendencies modeled with soft computing. The context of a robotic assistant for the elderly is used to illustrate the various communication techniques. Hierarchical generalization is introduced as a technique for generating potential alternatives in choices that might be more broadly acceptable to an individual who is being motivated towards a better choice. Finally, the related topic of negotiations using some the developed techniques is presented.

The eighth chapter of the book is titled "A Smart and Dynamic Decision Support System for Nonlinear Environments," written by S. Uma, and J. Suganthi. The design of a dynamic and efficient decision-making system for real-world systems is an essential but challenging task since they are nonlinear, chaotic, and high dimensional in nature. Hence, a Support Vector Machine (SVM)-based model is proposed to predict the future event of nonlinear time series environments. This model is a non-parametric model that uses the inherent structure of the data for forecasting. The dimensionality of the data is reduced besides controlling noise as the first preprocessing step using the Hybrid Dimensionality Reduction (HDR) and Extended Hybrid Dimensionality Reduction (EHDR) nonlinear time series representation techniques. It is also used for subsequencing the nonlinear time series data. The proposed SVM-based model using EHDR is compared with the models using Symbolic Aggregate approXimation (SAX), HDR, SVM using Kernel Principal Component Analysis (KPCA), and SVM using varying tube size values for historical data on different financial instruments. A comparison of the experimental results of the proposed model with other models taken for the experimentation has proven that the prediction accuracy of the proposed model is outstanding.

The ninth chapter of the book is titled "Determinants for the Goodness of Performance Measurement Systems: The Visibility of Performance," contributed by Tim Pidun. The supply of adequate information is one of the main functions of Performance Measurement Systems (PMS), but also one of its drawbacks and reason for *failure*. Not only the collection of *indicators* is crucial, but also the stakeholders' *understanding* of their *meaning*, *purpose,* and *contextual* embedding. Today, companies seek a PMS without a way to express the *goodness* of a solution, indicating its *ability* to deliver *appropriate* information and to address these demands. The goal of this chapter is to explore the mechanisms that drive information and knowledge supply in PMS in order to model a way to *express* this goodness. Using a grounded theory approach, a theory of *visibility of performance* is developed, featuring a catalog of *determinants* for the goodness of PMS. Companies can conveniently use them to assess their PMS and to *improve* the visibility of their performance.

The tenth chapter of the book is titled "The Backbone of Key Successful Branding Strategies in the 21st Century: Innovation in Design Technology, Decision Making on Product Quality, and Collaborative Communications," written by Ho Cheong Lee, Ahmad Noraziah, and Tutut Herawan. In the 21st century, the awareness of applying recent advanced intelligent technologies to promote a firm's brand image is the key to the success of expanding its business. Such implication demands efforts in strategic planning and massive investment from the top management team. However, most researches on branding strategies are narrowed to advertisement or classical marketing. Insufficient research on the backbone of making key successful branding strategies to effectively apply the intelligent technologies hinders the development of branding strategies. This chapter identifies three aspects: innovation in design technology, decision making on product quality, and collaborative communications to be the critical elements of the backbone. The methodology utilizes the power of the advanced computational technologies to generate innovative designs in a collaborative communication framework. Decision making on the quality of designs is monitored with EG-Kano reference models. Four case studies demonstrate that the backbone has potentials leading to ever-greater economic benefits.

The eleventh chapter of the book is titled "Hybrid Privacy Preservation Technique Using Neural Networks," written by R. VidyaBanu and N. Nagaveni. A novel Artificial Neural Network (ANN) dimension expansion-based framework that addresses the demand for privacy preservation of low dimensional data in clustering analysis is discussed. A hybrid approach that combines ANN with Linear Discriminant Analysis (LDA) is proposed to preserve the privacy of data in mining. This chapter describes a feasible technique for privacy preserving clustering with the objective of providing superior level of privacy protection without compromising the data utility and mining outcome. The suitability of these techniques for mining has been evaluated by performing clustering on transformed data and the performance of the proposed method is measured in terms of misclassification and privacy level percentage. The methods are further validated by comparing the results with traditional Geometrical Data Transformation Methods (GDTMs). The results arrived at are significant and promising.

The last chapter of the book, the twelfth chapter, is titled "Risk Prediction Model for Osteoporosis Disease Based on a Reduced Set of Factors," and contributed by Walid Moudani, Ahmad Shahin, Fadi Chakik, and Dima Rajab. The healthcare environment is generally perceived as informative yet with poor knowledge. The health industry collects huge amounts of health data which, unfortunately, are not mined to discover hidden information. However, there is a lack of effective analytical tools to discover hidden relationships and trends in data. Information technologies can provide alternative approaches to the diagnosis of the disease of osteoporosis. In this chapter, the authors examine the potential use of classification techniques on a huge volume of healthcare data, particularly in anticipation of patients who may have Osteoporosis Disease (OD) through a set of potential risk factors. They develop an innovative solution based on dynamic reduced sets of potential risk factors using the promising Rough Set theory which is a new mathematical approach to data analysis based on classification of objects. To identify cases of osteoporosis, experimentation of several classification techniques have been performed leading to rank the suitable techniques. The reduction of potential risk factors contributes to enumerate dynamically one or more optimal subsets of the potential risk factors of high interest which implicitly leads to reduce the complexity of the classification problems while maintaining the prediction classification quality. The performance of the proposed model is analyzed and evaluated based on set of benchmark techniques applied in this classification problem.

Big Data Analytics is becoming one of the most crucial issues in enterprise data centers nowadays. If correctly analyzed, the enormous amounts of business data can generate huge value. Uncovering that value and leveraging Big Data for analytics is quickly becoming one of the prime objectives of Business Analytics (BI). However, Big Data analytics can become an enormous challenge, if the correct tools and techniques are not used for the analysis. In order to overcome this challenge we have to identify and understand the value behind useful technologies such as Hadoop, MapReduce, NLP, and others that are designed to help organizations deal with huge amounts of data, both structured and unstructured. Semantic technology can provide mechanisms for identifying and establishing important concepts and maintain relationships between them, and provide indexing of these concepts. Cloud technology can be used to store and process large amounts of data with appropriate analytics tools and techniques to mine interesting nuggets of knowledge. Natural language processing can be used to create trusted, structured data from the rapidly expanding volume of unstructured emails, logs, and other documents as well as user generated content on social media. Thus, several enabling technologies are coming together to make Big Data Analytics possible and exciting times are ahead where Business Intelligence can be routinely generated from the massive amount of data being generated in this digital world. Leveraging Big Data Analytics to generate intelligence and gain competitive advantage will become a necessity in the not too distant future.

Vijayan Sugumaran
Oakland University, USA & Sogang University, South Korea

REFERENCES

McKinsey Global Institute. (2011). *Big data: The next frontier for innovation, competition, and productivity.* Retrieved from http://www.mckinsey.com/.../Big%20Data/MGI_big_data

Acknowledgment

Dr. Sugumaran's research has been partly supported by Sogang Business School's World Class University Program (R31-20002) funded by Korea Research Foundation and Sogang University Research Grant of 2011.

Vijayan Sugumaran
Oakland University, USA & Sogang University, South Korea

Section 1
Semantic Technologies and Applications

Chapter 1
Strategies and Methods for Ontology Alignment

Hayden Wimmer
Bloomsburg University, USA

Victoria Yoon
Virginia Commonwealth University, USA

Roy Rada
University of Maryland Baltimore County, USA

ABSTRACT

The concept of ontologies has been around for millennia and spans many domains and disciplines. Ontologies are a powerful concept when applied to intelligent computing. Ontologies are the backbone of intelligent computing on the World Wide Web and crucial in many decision-support situations. Many sophisticated tools have been developed to support working with ontologies, including prominently exploiting the vast array of existing ontologies. Systems have been developed to automatically generate, match, and integrate ontologies in a process called ontology alignment. This chapter extends the current literature by presenting a system called ALIGN, which demonstrates how to use freely available tools to develop and facilitate ontology alignment. The first two ontologies are built with the ontology editor Protégé and represented in OWL. ALIGN then accesses these ontologies via Java's JENA framework and SPARQL queries. The efficacy of the ALIGN prototype is demonstrated on a drug-drug interaction problem. The prototype could readily be applied to other domains or be incorporated into decision-support tools.

INTRODUCTION

The concept of ontologies has been widely applied as a means for providing a shared understanding of common domains. However, the generalized use of large distributed environments, such as WWW, has resulted in the proliferation of different ontolo-gies, even in the same or similar domain, calling for methods to align the diverse ontologies. As the number of ontologies available increases, the need to align these ontologies increases (Y. Kalfoglou & M Schorlemmer, 2003). A single ontology is not sufficient to support the distributed nature of the semantic web or the operations of many

DOI: 10.4018/978-1-4666-6639-9.ch001

businesses (Thomas, Redmond, & Yoon, 2009) or governments (Santos & Madeira, 2010). In order to effectively leverage knowledge represented in these overlapping ontologies, ontology alignment may be useful. Ontology alignment is achieved in part by mapping the concepts of one ontology to the concepts of another ontology. Ontology alignment may also be a step in the larger process of ontology integration or merging (Pinto, Gomez-Perez, & Martins, 1999).

Ontologies may be manually mapped by a knowledge engineer or domain expert; however, this process has shortcomings. Manual mapping is tedious, error prone, and hinders ontology maintenance (Ding & Foo, 2002). Automated mapping may occur at the schema-level or the instance-level. Schema-level mapping begins with two schemas as input producing output in the form of semantic links between the elements of the input schemas (Rahm & Bernstein, 2001). These links may range from simple one-to-one links to complex many-to-many, semantically labeled links (Embley, Xu, & Ding, 2004). Instance-level mapping occurs by using classified instance data in order to construct links between concepts based on the co-occurrences of the instances (Isaac, Van der Meij, Schlobach, & Wang, 2007). Finally, a hybrid approach employs schema and instance techniques.

This chapter presents a hybrid, ontology alignment system, called ALIGN. Two crucial steps in this system are:

- A schema-based method to determine the similarity between a concept in one ontology and a concept in another ontology based on the lexical match of the two. This is considered a schema-level method in that it employs the concept category of each ontology, although it does not make inferences based on larger structures in either ontology.

- An instance-based approach to determine the similarity between two concepts based on their instances using a Jaccard coefficient similarity measure.

Notably, this work illustrates how several, readily available Semantic Web technologies can be used for ontology alignment.

The system that is developed could be applied to any two ontologies that maintain the class-instance relationship. To demonstrate the system, the authors have constructed two adverse drug reaction ontologies. A set of tests were then conducted on the extent to which the system could successfully exploit the information in both ontologies through mapping. The following sections present related work, the system architecture, a detailed development methodology and an application, and the conclusions.

BACKGROUND

As previously noted, the interest in ontologies long predates the current interest in the World Wide Web and the power of ontologies to help people organize and retrieve information. Instead, one might go back, at least, three thousand years to the origins of metaphysics (see, for instance, Thales of Miletus, the pre-Socratic Greek philosopher) and see that philosophers were pondering the relations between particulars and universals, and those relations are the essence of ontologies. Jumping to the computerized world, one can find innumerable historical precedents to the interest in ontology alignment. One such path through the history is sketched next.

Ontologies are often equated with thesauri or taxonomic hierarchies of classes, class definitions, and the subsumption relation, although ontologies need not be limited to these forms (Gruber, 1995). Theories and software to align thesauri were initiated in part in the American National Library of Medicine (NLM) initiative to create a Unified Medical Language which had its beginnings in the 1980s. NLM is the creator and maintainer of one of the world's largest and most useful ontologies, and as early as the 1980s NLM was embarked on mapping and merging its ontology for the medical literature with other ontologies that had been developed specifically for medical patient records or for public health records (Lester & Rada, 1987). This work at NLM led to various theoretical (Mili & Rada, 1988) advances in mapping and merging ontologies. For instance, graph homomorphisms were used to represent and manipulate ontological hierarchies (Mili & Rada, 1992). Different tools were also explored; for instance, the role of user-interfaces (McMath, Tamaru, & Rada, 1989) in ontology manipulation were explored. The work at NLM also led to applications outside medicine. For instance, software reuse is a major challenge in the information technology industry and methods to support software reuse were shown to benefit from ontology mapping and merging (Mili et al., 1994).

Jumping forward to the 21st century, one finds a wide array of tools and theories for ontology alignment whose existence has, in part, been driven by the opportunities presented by the WWW. Prominent ontology alignment systems include GLUE, ONIONS, FCA-Merge, S-Match, PROMPT, IF-Map, and MIMapper. Each uses hybrid mapping and employs a wide range of techniques (Lambrix & Tan, 2006) to include:

- Linguistic matching that uses similar words or hyponyms to match concepts.
- Structure-matching that exploits the taxonomic structure of the ontologies.
- Constraint-based techniques that use domain knowledge outside the ontologies to guide or constrain matching.
- Instance-based matching that utilizes the patterns of matches among the instances of a class to decide whether or not the classes match.

Knowledge from outside the ontologies being aligned is typically employed. One of the most popular generic sources is Word Net.

GLUE uses probabilities and constraints to interpret global and local patterns in the ontologies that are being aligned. A distribution estimator computes joint probability distributions for multiple ontologies. A similarity estimator then computes the similarity of the results of the distribution estimator. Finally, a relaxation labeler makes mapping determinations with the support of domain constraints (Doan, Madhavan, Dhamankar, Domingos, & Halevy, 2003).

ONIONS (Mitra, Wiederhold, & Decker, 2001) takes, as input, terms in two ontologies and produces a set of rules as to how those ontologies are aligned. In the course of creating these rules, it uses a linguistic matcher and structure-based heuristics. The system has been applied in the medical domain to support the retrieval of medical documents (Noy & Klein, 2004).

The FCA-Merge system aligns and integrates ontologies by exploiting the knowledge in both the ontologies and in domain-relevant documents. It uses the Saarbrucken Message Extraction System (Neumann, Backofen, Baur, Becker, & Braun, 1997) and performs morphological analysis and part-or-speech tagging. Concepts are linked based on a variety of inferences (Stumme & Maedche, 2001).

The S-Match system takes two ontologies and provides semantic matches between them. A matrix is computed which indicates the degree of semantic match between concepts. Relationships, such as equality and intersection, are determined (Giunchiglia, Shvaiko, & Yatskevich, 2004).

PROMPT (Noy & Musen, 2003) is a semi-automatic tool and a plug-in for the open-source ontology editor PROTEGE. It determines string similarity and analyzes the structure of an ontology. It accepts OWL/RDF ontologies and provides the possible mapping of similar concepts to guide the user for merging ontologies. It also analyzes the conflicts in the ontology and suggests solutions for conflict resolution.

The IF-Map (Yannis Kalfoglou & Marco Schorlemmer, 2003) system identifies mappings between disparate ontologies based on the theory of information flow (Barwise & Seligman, 1997), string similarity, structure analysis (is-a hierarchy), and Horn logic. Given two local ontologies with instances, IF-Map generates a logic info-morphism —a subclass relationship between local ontologies and reference ontology without instances. Input of IF-Map is two local RDF ontologies and one reference ontology. Its output is concept-to-concept and relation-to-relation mapping.

The MIMapper developed by Kaza and Chen (2008) uses a two-step process to align different ontologies. The first step is lexicon based, which uses a string match approach to determine the similarities between the names of classes in disparate ontologies. The same or partially overlapping names of classes are considered similar classes. For example, the class 'City' is considered similar to the class 'CityName' due to a partial string match in those two names. Further, it uses WordNet to determine the synonymous names of the classes. The second step is data driven, which uses the class instances in the ontology to establish mappings between classes. This instance-based ontology alignment approach employs point-wise mutual information (Pantel, Philpot, & Hovy, 2005) to identify the common informative instances of classes in different ontologies; it is assumed that instances of equivalent classes in different ontologies are likely to include common informative instances.

Reviews of ontology alignment systems have suggested various dimensions along with examining these systems. For instance, systems may be viewed along these dimensions (Choi, Song, & Han, 2006): input, output, user interaction, mapping algorithm, structure knowledge, instance-based knowledge, lexical knowledge, and domain knowledge. Some authors focus on a formal approach. For instance, an ontology may be defined as a six-tuple to include Classes, Relationships, and ordering among Classes and Relationships (Stoutenburg, 2008), and from those six-tuple types of ontology mappings are defined and algorithms for identifying the types of mappings are developed.

A popular theme in the literature is the construction of ontologies. For instance, a tool for supporting the ready development of ontologies by domain experts rather than ontology experts has been developed (Dahlem, 2011). Another tool seeks to automate the generation of ontologies from existing information (Kim & Storey, 2011).

Ontological approaches are suited to the field of biomedicine (Ghazvinian, Noy, & Musen, 2011), (Yu, 2006). A biomedical ontology may be defined as a framework of concepts related to biology and medical knowledge that includes hierarchical relationships among concepts (Gottgtroy, Kasabov, & MacDonell, 2008). Biomedical ontologies are helpful for interoperability of information systems (Tan & Lambrix, 2007), (Gomez-Perez, Fernadez-Lopez, & Corcho, 2004). Many disparate but related ontologies span the field of biomedicine; however, exploiting this diversity of ontologies requires aligning them (Mukherjea, 2005). These ontologies may also support web applications (Yoshikawa, Satou, & Konagaya, 2004). This research explores drug interaction ontologies that might help prevent fatal drug interactions.

SYSTEM ARCHITECTURE

The ALIGN architecture for ontology alignment takes as input two or more ontologies (see Figure 1). The individual disparate ontologies are read into a working space and combined in order to facilitate the alignment process. The alignment process uses first a schema based subsystem and then an instance based subsystem.

The schema-based subsystem first performs a pairwise check of the similarity of all concepts in two different ontologies. If the two ontology instances are identical per a string comparison, ALIGN will generate an equivalence statement

Figure 1. Conceptual architecture for ALIGN

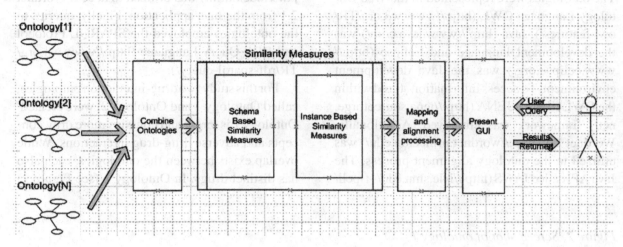

(i.e. owl:sameAs or owl:equivalentClass). If there is no direct string match, then the system will issue a query to Word Net to determine the concept's hyponyms. ALIGN then checks whether two concepts are hyponyms of each other. If the concepts are hyponyms, then the system treats creates a mapping link between them.

The instance-based similarity subsystem uses a Jaccard similarity index to rate the similarity of two classes based on instances of the classes. The instances of one concept form a set A, and the instances of another concept form a set B. These instances are pair-wise compared to each other to determine their lexical similarity. The Jaccard correlation coefficient is computed as

$$\frac{\left(A \bigcap B\right)}{A \bigcup B}$$

where the intersection of A and B includes only those instances which are lexically unique. Concepts whose Jaccard coefficient is below a specified threshold are mapped together. This threshold can be set on an application-by-application basis to correspond to the specifics of the problem.

The value employed in this experiment is design artifact is a Jaccard similarity index of '0' as

it is necessary to err on the side of caution when dealing with potentially fatal drug interactions. A higher metric could be set for other applications where a potential error is not as critical as in the case of fatal drug interactions.

CASE STUDY OF DRUG-DRUG INTERACTION

The Case Study for ALIGN is the heart of this chapter. This section will unfold in this sequence:

1. System tools,
2. Ontologies,
3. User interface,
4. Alignment process,
5. Negative interactions, and
6. Evaluation.

Multiple screen shots are provided of the ontology development and query interface to help readers appreciate the steps involved to implement such a system.

ALIGN has been applied to the domain of drug-drug interaction. Two ontologies were developed with the Protégé 3.4.4 (http://protege.stanford.edu/) ontology editor from Stanford University.

The ontologies were represented in the Web Ontology Language OWL (http://www.w3.org/TR/owl-features/). Java (http://www.java.com/) was the development language and Eclipse (http://www.eclipse.org/) was the Java development environment. To access information stored within the OWL files the JENA (http://jena.sourceforge.net/) framework was employed. Additionally, Wordnet 2.1 (http://wordnet.princeton.edu/) was utilized in the ontology alignment process. The Java API called JAWS (http://lyle.smu.edu/~tspell/jaws/index.html) was utilized to access Wordnet 2.1 from the Java application. Finally, queries to the ontologies employed the SPARQL Protocol and RDF Query Language (http://www.w3.org/TR/rdf-sparql-query/).

For this study two drug-interaction ontologies, called Ontology 1 and Ontology 2, were created. Ontology 1 is larger and contains more drug concepts and adverse drug-drug interactions. While overlap exists between the ontologies, each also has distinct drugs. In Ontology 1 (see Figure 2)

Figure 2. Screen shot of ontology 1

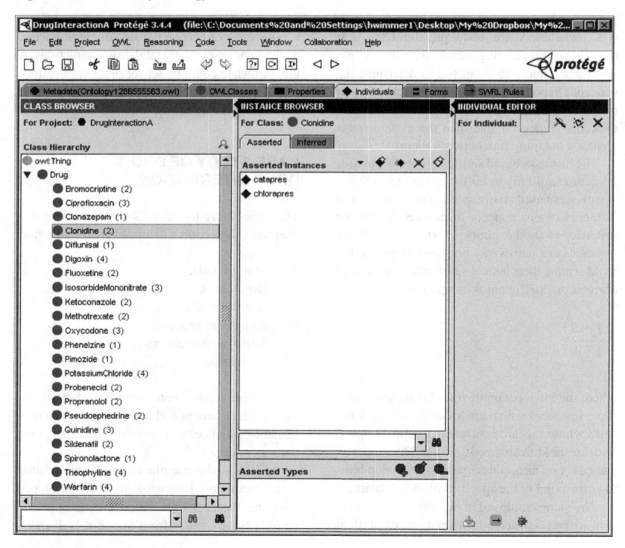

the parent class "Drug" has many subclasses of drugs such as "Bromocriptine", "Clondine". Each drug subclass has instances or individuals. In the case of "Clondine" the instances are "catapres" and "chlorapres."

In Ontology 1 the parent is named "Drug", while in Ontology 2 (see Figure 3) the parent is named "medications." Additionally, as highlighted in Ontology 2, cdine contains the instance "catapres." Ontology 1 also contains "catapres"; however, the parent is "Clondine." Information about adverse drug-drug interactions in also incorporated into the ontologies (see Figure 4).

Drugs in column A negatively react with drugs in column D, and drugs in column B negatively react with drugs in column E. Drugs in columns A and D are from Ontology 1, and columns B and E are from Ontology 2.

The user interface consists of two combo boxes, and each contains medications, also called drugs (see Figure 5). The user is to select a medication from each combo box and then select the "Click Here" button. The system will subsequently display whether a negative drug-drug interaction exists.

Once the application is launched it queries the two ontologies for all instances relating to drugs or medications. One ontology is loaded into both combo boxes, as the other ontology's instances are compared with the contents of the combo boxes to

Figure 3. Screen shot of ontology 2

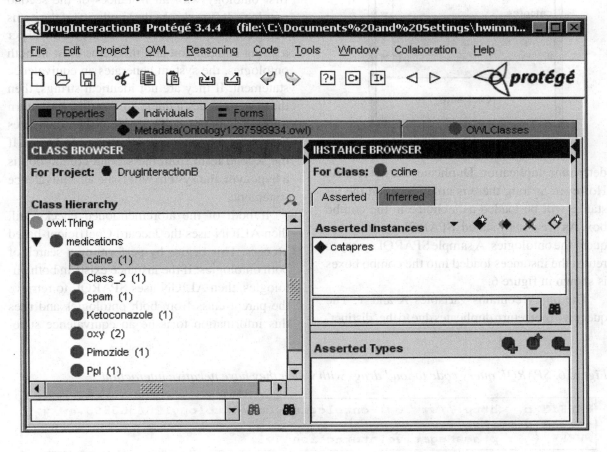

Figure 4. Negative drug-drug interactions

A	B	C	D	E	F
Drug - A	Drug - B	Names	Drug-A	Drug-B	Names
Fluoxetine		*Prozac, Sarafem*	Phenelzine		*Nardil*
Digoxin		*Digitek, Lanoxicaps, Lanoxin, Cardoxin*	Quinidine		*Quinidine Gluconate, Quinidine Sulfate*
Sildenafil		*Viagra, Revatio*	Isosorbide Mononitrate		*mdur, Ismo, Monoket*
Potassium Chloride		*K-Dur, K-Lor, K-Tab, Kaon CL*	Spironolactone		*Aldactone*
Clonidine	c-dine	*Catapres(a,b), Chlorpres(a)*	Propranolol	ppl	*Inderal(a,b), Inderal LA(a), Innopran XL(a)*
Warfarin		*Coumadin, Jantoven, Marevan, Lawarin*	Diflunisal		*Dolobid*
Theophylline		*Theo-Dur, Theo-24, Uniphyl, Theochron*	Ciprofloxacin		*Ciloxan, Cipro, CiproHC*
	Pimozide	*Orap*		Ketoco	*Kuric, Nizoral*
Methotrexate		*Rheumatrex, Trexall*	Probenecid		*Benemid , probalan*
Bromocriptine		*Parlodel, Cycloset*	Pseudoephedrine		*Allermed, Genaphed*
oxycodone	oxy	*Tylox(a), Percodan(b), OxyContin(b)*	clonazepam	c-pam	*Klonopin(a,b)*

Figure 5. User interface for negative drug-drug interactions

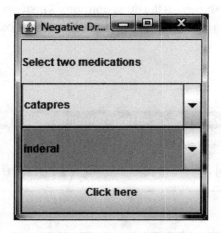

determine duplication. Duplicates are not loaded. However, as long there is no duplication the instance will be loaded as a choice in the combo box. As previously stated, SPARQL is utilized to query the ontologies. A sample SPARQL query to return the instances loaded into the combo boxes is shown in figure 6.

The query contains variables X and Y. The query will not return duplicates due to the 'distinct'

keyword in the 'select' statement. The query returns all instances that have a negative interaction with another instance.

The application opens the two ontologies as Jena models. The lexicon based alignment process begins by comparing all instances of the first ontology with all instances of the second ontology. It first checks the similarity of the items being compared. If the two items are identical per a string comparison and the items exist in both ontologies, the system generates an equivalence statement. If they are not identical strings, then the system issues a query to Word Net to return a list of hyponyms. The system then compares the returned hyponyms with the second term. If the second term from the second combo box is a hyponym, the system will issue an equivalence statement.

If both of the aforementioned checks fail, then ALIGN uses the Jaccard Coefficient-based process. This begins by performing a search of both ontologies. If the instance exists in both ontologies, then ALIGN uses SPARQL to retrieve the parent class from both ontologies and uses this information to issue an equivalence state-

Figure 6. SPARQL query code to load drugs with which they have negative interaction

```
PREFIX p: <http://www.owl-ontologies.com/Ontology1286555563.owl#>
select distinct ?y
WHERE { ?x p:hasNegativeInteraction ?y }
```

ment. The threshold for determining a negative interaction is that any two classes have a Jaccard coefficient greater than 0. This low threshold is due to the sensitivity of determining a negative drug interaction and a need to err on the side of caution. This threshold could be altered for other application areas.

Ontology1 has a property called 'hasNegativeInteraction'. This property has the domain of Drug and range of Drug. This indicates that a drug can have a negative interaction with another drug. Once the alignment process is complete, and the user has selected two drugs from the combo boxes, ALIGN calls a method to return whether a negative drug-drug interaction is expected.

A user tested ALIGN with eight scenarios:

- Both drugs come from the first ontology and have no negative interaction,
- Both drugs come from the first ontology and have negative interactions,
- Both drugs come from the second ontology and have no negative interaction,
- Both drugs come from the second ontology and have a negative interaction,
- One drug comes from the first ontology and one from the second ontology and no negative interaction is expected.
- One drug is from the first ontology and one from the second ontology and a negative interaction is expected,
- One drug is from the second ontology and one from the first ontology and no negative interaction is expected, and finally,
- One drug is from the second ontology and one from the first ontology and a negative interaction is expected.

The system was correct in its function for each of the eight scenarios.

FUTURE RESEARCH DIRECTIONS

Directions for future work would include experimenting with larger ontologies and integrating ALIGN into decision support systems. For instance, in the domain of drug-drug interactions various thesauri and databases exist which could be connected with ALIGN, and the very powerful biomedical ontology called the Unified Medical Language System could replace Word Net as a domain-specific reference. As an example of integrating ALIGN in a decision support system, a financial investing decision support system might map diverse industry classifications of companies in discovering meaningful groupings of companies. Additionally, future research may incorporate automated ontology creation methods or social media data (Wimmer & Zhou, 2013) in order to add features to ALIGN.

CONCLUSION

Ontologies, or the shared conceptualization of a domain, have existed for more than three thousand years. Ontologies can be found in various domains. One such example is the medical field with the Unified Medical Language (UML) or the International Classification of Diseases (ICD). Ontologies have been integrated into computing and are a cornerstone of intelligent systems. Ontology alignment occurs when relationships are defined between concepts in multiple ontologies and is sometimes referred to as ontology mapping or matching.

Great efforts have been made to develop the automatic approaches to align disparate ontologies. The ontology alignment methods described in the literature can be largely categorized into schema-based and instance-based methods. In addition, there is a wide array of standards, languages, compatible tools, and development methods that grew out of the vision of Semantic Web. Specifically, semantic web standards and technologies, such as RDF, OWL, JENA and SPARQL, permit ready manipulation of ontologies and may be useful tools for ontology alignment.

Although many efforts in ontology mapping have already been carried out, we have noticed that few of them present a method of using open-source tools for ontology alignment. This study developed a generic hybrid system for ontology alignment, called ALIGN, that relies heavily on freely available tools. The open-source tools used in ALIGN include Protégé, JENA, WordNet 2.1, and SPARQL. ALIGN was tested in the domain of drug-drug interaction and proved effective. The evaluation result shows that ALIGN is capable of mapping the classes in disparate ontologies, enabling the user to retrieve information from multiple, aligned ontologies. Furthermore, a system such as this could be readily integrated with larger systems for exploiting ontologies and supporting users in real-world problems.

REFERENCES

Barwise, J., & Seligman, J. (1997). The logic of distributed systems. *Cambridge Tracts in Theoretical Computer Science, 44.*

Choi, N., Song, I.-Y., & Han, H. (2006). A survey on ontology mapping. *SIGMOD Record, 35*(3), 34–41. doi:10.1145/1168092.1168097

Dahlem, N. (2011). OntoClippy: A user-friendly ontology design and creation methodology. *International Journal of Intelligent Information Technologies, 7*(1), 15–32. doi:10.4018/jiit.2011010102

Ding, Y., & Foo, S. (2002). Ontology research and development. Part I - A review of ontology generation. *Journal of Information Science*, 123–136.

Doan, A., Madhavan, J., Dhamankar, R., Domingos, P., & Halevy, A. (2003). Learning to match ontologies on the semantic web. *The VLDB Journal, 12*(4), 303–319. doi:10.1007/s00778-003-0104-2

Embley, D., Xu, L., & Ding, Y. (2004). Automatic direct and indirect schema mapping: Experiences and lessons learned. *SIGMOD Record, 33*(4), 14–19. doi:10.1145/1041410.1041413

Ghazvinian, A., Noy, N. F., & Musen, M. A. (2011). *From mappings to modules: Using mappings to identify domain-specific modules in large ontologies*. Paper presented at the K-CAP'11, Banff, Canada. doi:10.1145/1999676.1999684

Giunchiglia, F., Shvaiko, P., & Yatskevich, M. (2004). S-match: An algorithm and an implementation of semantic matching. *Semantic Web: Research and Applications*, 61-75.

Gomez-Perez, A., Fernadez-Lopez, M., & Corcho, O. (2004). *Ontological engineering with examples from the areas of knowledge management, e-commerce and the semantic web*. Berlin: Springer-Verlag.

Gottgtroy, P., Kasabov, N., & MacDonell, S. (2008). *An ontology driven approach for knowledge discovery in biomedicine*. Paper presented at the Trends in Artificial Intelligence.

Gruber, T. (1995). Toward principles for the design of ontologies used for knowledge sharing. *International Journal of Human-Computer Studies, 43*(5-6), 907–928. doi:10.1006/ijhc.1995.1081

Isaac, A., Van der Meij, L., Schlobach, S., & Wang, S. (2007). *An empirical study of instance-based ontology matching*. Paper presented at the ISWC/ASWC. doi:10.1007/978-3-540-76298-0_19

Kalfoglou, Y., & Schorlemmer, M. (2003). *IF-map: An ontology-mapping method based on information-flow theory*. Springer.

Kalfoglou, Y., & Schorlemmer, M. (2003). Ontology mapping: The state of the art. *The Knowledge Engineering Review*, *18*(1), 1–31. doi:10.1017/S0269888903000651

Kaza, S., & Chen, H. (2008). Evaluating ontology mapping techniques: An experiment in public safety information sharing. *Decision Support Systems*, *45*(4), 714–728. doi:10.1016/j.dss.2007.12.007

Kim, J., & Storey, V. (2011). Construction of domain ontologies: Sourcing the world wide web. *International Journal of Intelligent Information Technologies*, *7*(2), 1–24. doi:10.4018/jiit.2011040101

Lambrix, P., & Tan, H. (2006). SAMBO - A system for aligning and merging biomedical ontologies. *Journal of Web Semantics*, *4*(3), 196–206. doi:10.1016/j.websem.2006.05.003

Lester, S., & Rada, R. (1987). A method of medical knowledge base augmentation. *Methods of Information in Medicine*, *26*(1), 31–39. PMID:3550379

McMath, C., Tamaru, B., & Rada, R. (1989). Graphical interface to thesaurus-based information retrieval system. *International Journal of Man-Machine Studies*, *31*(2), 121–147. doi:10.1016/0020-7373(89)90024-2

Mili, H., & Rada, R. (1988). Merging thesauri: Principles and evaluation. *IEEE Transactions on Pattern Analysis and Machine Intelligence*, *10*(2), 204–220. doi:10.1109/34.3883

Mili, H., & Rada, R. (1992). A model of hierarchies based on graph homomorphisms. *Computers & Mathematics with Applications (Oxford, England)*, *23*(2), 343–361. doi:10.1016/0898-1221(92)90147-A

Mili, H., Rada, R., Wang, W., Strickland, K., Bolydreff, C., Olsen, L., & Elzer, P. et al. (1994). Practitioner and SoftClass: A comparative study of two software reuse research projects. *Journal of Systems and Software*, *25*(2), 147–170. doi:10.1016/0164-1212(94)90003-5

Mitra, P., Wiederhold, G., & Decker, S. (2001). *A scalable framework for interoperation of information sources*. Paper presented at the 1st International Semantic Web Working Symposium (SWWS'01), Stanford, CA.

Mukherjea, S. (2005). Information retrieval and knowledge discovery utilizing a biomedical semantic web. *Briefings in Bioinformatics*, *6*(3), 252–262. doi:10.1093/bib/6.3.252 PMID:16212773

Neumann, G., Backofen, R., Baur, J., Becker, M., & Braun, C. (1997). *An information extraction core system for real world German text processing*. Paper presented at the Fifth Conference on Applied Natural Language Processing, Washington, DC. doi:10.3115/974557.974588

Noy, N. F., & Klein, M. (2004). Ontology evolution: Not the same as schema evolution. *Knowledge and Information Systems*, *6*(4), 428–440. doi:10.1007/s10115-003-0137-2

Noy, N. F., & Musen, M. A. (2003). The PROMPT suite: Interactive tools for ontology merging and mapping. *International Journal of Human-Computer Studies*, *59*(6), 983–1024. doi:10.1016/j.ijhcs.2003.08.002

Pantel, P., Philpot, A., & Hovy, E. (2005). Data alignment and integration. *Computer*, *38*(12), 43–50. doi:10.1109/MC.2005.406

Pinto, H., Gomez-Perez, A., & Martins, J. (1999). *Some issues on ontology integration*. Paper presented at the IJCAI99 Conference on Ontologies and Problem Solving Methods: Lessons Learned and Future Trends.

Rahm, E., & Bernstein, P. A. (2001). A survey of approaches to automatic schema matching. *The VLDB Journal*, *10*(4), 334–350. doi:10.1007/s007780100057

Santos, I. J. G., & Madeira, E. R. M. (2010). A semantic-enabled middleware for citizen centric e-government services. *International Journal of Intelligent Information Technologies*, *6*(3), 34–55. doi:10.4018/jiit.2010070103

Stoutenburg, S. (2008). *Acquiring advanced properties in ontology mapping*. Paper presented at the PIKM'08, Napa Valley, CA. doi:10.1145/1458550.1458553

Stumme, G., & Maedche, A. (2001). *FCA-merge: Bottom-up merging of ontologies*. Paper presented at the International Joint Conference on Artificial Intelligence.

Tan, H., & Lambrix, P. (2007). *A method for recommending ontology alignment strategies*. Paper presented at the ISWC/ASWC 2007. doi:10.1007/978-3-540-76298-0_36

Thomas, M., Redmond, R., & Yoon, V. (2009). Using ontological reasoning for an adoptive e-commerce experience. *International Journal of Intelligent Information Technologies*, *5*(4), 41–52. doi:10.4018/jiit.2009080703

Wimmer, H., & Zhou, L. (Eds.). (2013). AMCIS. Chicago, IL: Academic Press.

Yoshikawa, S., Satou, K., & Konagaya, A. (2004). Drug interaction ontology (DIO) for inferences of possible drug-drug interactions. *Studies in Health Technology and Informatics*, *107*(1), 454–458. PMID:15360854

Yu, A. C. (2006). Methods in biomedical ontology. *Journal of Biomedical Informatics*, *39*(3), 252–266. doi:10.1016/j.jbi.2005.11.006 PMID:16387553

ADDITIONAL READING

Adam, P., Ian, N., & John, L. (2002). The Suggested Upper Merged Ontology: A Large Ontology for the Semantic Web and its Applications.

Ahmed, K. B. S., Toumouh, A., & Malki, M. (2012). Effective Ontology Learning: Concepts Hierarchy Building Using Plain Text Wikipedia. Paper presented at the ICWIT, Hawaii.

Antoniou, G., & Van Harmelen, F. (2004). *Web ontology language: Owl Handbook on ontologies* (pp. 67–92). Springer. doi:10.1007/978-3-540-24750-0_4

Apanovich, Z., & Vinokurov, P. (2010). Ontology based portals and visual analysis of scientific communities. Paper presented at the First Russia and Pacific Conference on Computer Technology.

Arabshian, K., Danielsen, P., & Afroz, S. (2012). LexOnt: A Semi-Automatic Ontology Creation Tool for Programmable Web. Paper presented at the AAAI Spring Symposium Series.

Benjamin, P. C., Menzel, C., Mayer, R. J., Fillion, F., Futrell, M. T., DeWitte, P. S., & Lingineni, M. (1994). *Ontology capture method (IDEF5)*. Knowledge Based Systems, Inc.

Bouaud, J., Bachimont, B., Carlet, J., & Zweigenbaum, P. (1994). Acquisition and Structuring of an Ontology within Conceptual Graphs. Paper presented at the ICCS Workshop on Knowledge Acquisition and Conceptual Graph Theory, College Park, MD.

Bouaud, J., Bachimont, B., Charlet, J., & Zweigenbaum, P. (1995). Methodological Principles for Structuring an Ontology. Paper presented at the IJCAI-95 Workshop on Basic Ontological Issues in Knowledge Sharing, Montreal, Canada.

Buitelaar, P., Olejnik, D., & Sintek, M. (2004). A Protégé Plug-In for ontology extraction from text based on linguistic analysis. Paper presented at the ESWS 2004.

Chen, Y., Zhou, L., & Zhang, D. (2006). Ontology-Supported Web Service Composition: An Approach to Service-Oriented Knowledge Management in Corporate Services. *Journal of Database Management, 17*(1), 67–84. doi:10.4018/jdm.2006010105

Choi, N., Song, I., & Han, H. (2006). A survey on ontology mapping. *SIGMOD Record, 35*(3), 34–41. doi:10.1145/1168092.1168097

Cocchiarella, N. (1991). *Formal Ontology Handbook of metaphysics and ontology* (pp. 640–647). Munich: Philosophia Verlag.

Deborah, L. M., Richard, F., James, R., & Steve, W. (2000). *An Environment for Merging and Testing Large Ontologies*. Morgan Kaufmann.

Dellschaft, K., & Staab, S. (2006). On how to perform a gold standard based evaluation of ontology learning. Paper presented at the ISWC 2006 LNCS 4273. doi:10.1007/11926078_17

Ding, Y., & Fensel, D. (2001). Ontology Library Systems: The key to successful Ontology Re-use. Paper presented at the Proceedings of the 1st Semantic Web Working Symposium, Stanford, CA.

Ding, Y., & Foo, S. (2002a). Ontology research and development. Part 2 - a review of ontology mapping and evolving. *Journal of Information Science*, 375–388.

Ding, Y., & Foo, S. (2002b). Ontology research and development. Part I - a review of ontology generation. *Journal of Information Science*, 123–136.

Doan, A., Madhavan, J., Dhamankar, R., Domingos, P., & Halevy, A. (2003). Learning to match ontologies on the Semantic Web. *The VLDB Journal, 12*(4), 303–319. doi:10.1007/s00778-003-0104-2

Drymonas, E., Zervanou, K., & Petrakis, Z. (2010). Unsupervised ontology acquisition from plain texts: The OntoGain system. Paper presented at the International Conference on Applications of Natural Language to Information Systems (NLDB). doi:10.1007/978-3-642-13881-2_29

Ehrig, M., & Sure, Y. (2004). Ontology mapping - An integrated approach. Semantic Web: Research and Applications, 76-91.

Embley, D., Xu, L., & Ding, Y. (2004). Automatic direct and indirect schema mapping: Experiences and lessons learned. *SIGMOD Record, 33*(4), 14–19. doi:10.1145/1041410.1041413

Fensel, D., van Harmelen, F., Horrocks, I., McGuinness, D., & Patel-Schneider, P. (2001). OIL: An ontology infrastructure for the Semantic Web. *IEEE Intelligent Systems & their Applications, 16*(2), 38–45. doi:10.1109/5254.920598

Fox, P., McGuinness, D. L., Cinquini, L., West, P., Garcia, J., Benedict, J. L., & Middleton, D. (2009). Ontology-supported scientific data frameworks: The virtual solar-terrestrial observatory experience. *Computers & Geosciences, 35*(4), 724–738. doi:10.1016/j.cageo.2007.12.019

Gil, K., & Martin-Bautista, M. J. (2011). An Ontology Learning Knowledge Support System to Keep E-Organizations Knowledge Up-to-Date: A University Case Study. *Lecture Notes in Computer Science, 6866*, 249–263. doi:10.1007/978-3-642-22961-9_20

Gottgtroy, P., Kasabov, N., & MacDonell, S. (2008). An ontology driven approach for knowledge discovery in Biomedicine. Paper presented at the Trends in Artificial Intelligence. Proc. VIII.

Gruber, T. R. (1993). A Translation Approach to Portable Ontology Specification. *Knowledge Acquisition*, *5*(2), 199–220. doi:10.1006/knac.1993.1008

Hiep, L., Susan, G., & Qiang, W. (2012). Ontology Learning Using Word Net Lexical Expansion and Text Mining.

Kalfoglou, Y., & Schorlemmer, M. (2003). *IF-Map: An ontology-mapping method based on information-flow theory Journal on data semantics I* (pp. 98–127). Springer.

Kalfoglou, Y., & Schorlemmer, M. (2003). Ontology mapping: The state of the art. *The Knowledge Engineering Review*, *18*(1), 1–31. doi:10.1017/S0269888903000651

Kavalec, M., Maedche, A., & Svatek, V. (2004). Discovery of lexical entries for non-taxonomic relations in ontology learning. Sofsem 2004: Theory and Practice of Computer Science, Proceedings, 249-256.

Kaza, S., & Chen, H. (2008). Evaluating ontology mapping techniques: An experiment in public safety information sharing. *Decision Support Systems*, *45*(4), 714–728. doi:10.1016/j.dss.2007.12.007

Kaza, S., & Chen, H. (2008). Evaluating ontology mapping techniques: An experiment in public safety information sharing. *Decision Support Systems*, *45*(4), 714–728. doi:10.1016/j.dss.2007.12.007

Kotis, K., & Papaslouros, A. (2011). Automated Learning of Social Ontologies. In I. G. I. Global (Ed.), *Ontology Learning and Knowledge Discovery Using the Web: Challenges and Recent Advances*. Hershey, PA: IGI Global. doi:10.4018/978-1-60960-625-1.ch012

Lambrix, P., Habbouche, M., & Perez, M. (2003). Evaluation of ontology development tools for bioinformatics. *Bioinformatics (Oxford, England)*, *19*(12), 1564–1571. doi:10.1093/bioinformatics/btg194 PMID:12912838

Maedche, A. (2001). *The Ontology Extraction & Maintenance Framework Text-to-Onto*. New Orleans, Louisiana.

Missikoff, M., Navigli, R., & Velardi, P. (2002). Integrated approach to Web ontology learning and engineering. *Computer*, *35*(11), 60–63. doi:10.1109/MC.2002.1046976

Navigli, R. (2003). Ontology Learning and its application to automated terminology translation. *IEEE Intelligent Systems*, *18*, 21–33.

Noy, F. (2001). Ontology development 101: A guide to creating your first ontology. Technical Report SMI-2001-0880.

Noy, N. F., & Musen, M. A. (2003). The PROMPT suite: Interactive tools for ontology merging and mapping. *International Journal of Human-Computer Studies*, *59*(6), 983–1024. doi:10.1016/j.ijhcs.2003.08.002

Oro, E., & Rullalo, M. (2009). Ontology based information extraction from PDF documents with XONTO. *International Journal of Artificial Intelligence Tools*, *18*(5), 673–695. doi:10.1142/S0218213009000354

Patrick, C., Pádraig, C., & Conor, H. (2001). Ontology discovery for the semantic web using hierarchical clustering.

Pinto, H., Gomez-Perez, A., & Martins, J. (1999). Some Issues on Ontology Integration. Paper presented at the IJCAI99 Conference on Ontologies and Problem Solving Methods: Lessons Learned and Future Trends.

Reimer, U., Maier, E., Streit, S., Diggelmann, T., & Hoffleisch, M. (2011). Learning a Lightweight Ontology for Semantic Retrieval in Patient-Centered Information Systems. *International Journal of Knowledge Management*, *7*(3), 11–26. doi:10.4018/jkm.2011070102

Sanchez, D., Batet, M., Isern, D., & Valls, A. (2012). Ontology-based semantic similarity: A new feature-based approach. *Expert Systems with Applications*, *39*(9), 7718–7728. doi:10.1016/j.eswa.2012.01.082

Shvaiko, P., & Euzenat, J. (2005). A survey of schema-based matching approaches. Journal on Data Semantics Iv, 146-171.

Wimmer, H., Forgionne, G., Rada, R., & Yoon, V. (2012). A Conceptual Model for Knowledge Marts for Decision Making Support Systems. [IJDSST]. *International Journal of Decision Support System Technology*, *4*(4), 24–38. doi:10.4018/jdsst.2012100102

Wimmer, H., & Rada, R. (2013). Applying Information Technology to Financial Statement Analysis for Market Capitalization Prediction. *Open Journal of Accounting*, *2*(1), 1–3. doi:10.4236/ojacct.2013.21001

Wimmer, H., Yoon, V., & Rada, R. (2012). Applying semantic Web technologies to ontology alignment. [IJIIT]. *International Journal of Intelligent Information Technologies*, *8*(1), 1–9. doi:10.4018/jiit.2012010101

Wimmer, H., Yoon, V., & Rada, R. (2013). Integrating Knowledge Sources: An Ontological Approach. [IJKM]. *International Journal of Knowledge Management*, *9*(1), 60–75. doi:10.4018/jkm.2013010104

Wimmer, H., & Zhou, L. (Eds.). (2013) AMCIS. Chicago, IL USA.

Zouaq, A., Gasevic, D., & Hatala, M. (2011). Towards Open Ontology Learning and Filtering. *Information Systems*, *36*(7), 1064–1081. doi:10.1016/j.is.2011.03.005

KEY TERMS AND DEFINITIONS

Attribute: A property of a class or individual.

Class: Concepts, sets, or collections of other concepts or instances.

Instance: Lowest level of an ontology which includes concrete entities such as people, places, or things.

Ontology: A shared conceptualization of a domain.

Ontology Mapping or Alignment: Mapping concepts or instances from one ontology to another (i.e. a class in ontology A is the same as a class in ontology B).

Ontology Merging: Combining two ontologies into a single ontology.

Ontology Schema: The structure of the ontology.

Triple: A subject, predicate, and object statement (i.e. John knows Sally).

Chapter 2
A Novel E–Learning Management System for Appropriate Recommendations on the Learning Contents

Jegatha Deborah Lazarus
Anna University, India

Baskaran Ramachandran
Anna University, India

Kannan Arputharaj
Anna University, India

ABSTRACT

Educational organizations are able to bridge organizational gaps due to the rapid advances in science and technology. Specifically, e-learning drastically reduces the learning time compared to the traditional classroom setting. The challenges in e-learning are the organization of learning contents, characteristics of the learning individual, technological constraints, and performance evaluation. Moreover, the success of the e-learning environment is greatly influenced by the factors like appropriate recommendations of learning contents, content delivery, performance evaluation, and the maintenance of the psychological level through identification of the learning styles of the learners. The continual process of performance evaluation is commonly attributed by the challenging issues of Ontology Construction and Alignment in order to enhance the semantics of the evaluation documents. In the rest of the chapter, a novel rule-based e-learning management system is discussed as a solution for appropriate recommendations of the learning contents based on the psychological understanding of the learners for learning using fuzzy logic and the subsequent evaluation of the learners using Ontology Construction and Ontology Alignment technique using deontic logic. The experiments have been carried out on evaluating the learning of C programming language using an e-learning framework.

DOI: 10.4018/978-1-4666-6639-9.ch002

1. INTRODUCTION

Learning environment focuses on increasing the individual performance, thereby increasing the organizational progress. E-learning is a terminology that represents an inventive shift in the field of learning, providing rapid and meaningful access to information and knowledge. An efficient E-learning management system is influenced by two major components, namely learning system and the subsequent evaluation system (Carver, Howard & Lane, 1999). The major goals of e-learning are reduction in the necessity for classroom training, constant progress monitoring of the target audience, track training effectiveness, bridge between training and knowledge management, time-management, cost-effective, improved task performance, high supported business objectives, flexible and convenient learning environment. E-learning is defined technically as "Anytime and Anywhere learning" thus reducing the performance factors with respect to time, effort and cost. The purpose of E-learning is fivefold namely flexibility, personalized learning, updated knowledge, intelligent tutoring system and continual assessment of learners' progress. Moreover, the success of e-learning environments is greatly influenced by the factors like learning objects, content delivery, relevant information retrieval, performance evaluation and the maintenance of the psychological level through identification of the individual learning styles of the learners. The psychological level of the learners in an e-learning environment is greatly attributed by the learning styles of the learners involved in learning. A deep understanding of one's own way of learning can lead to a great personal empowerment and self confidence. This kind of deep understanding can be known by analyzing the behavior of the learners involved in an e-learning environment (Sanders, & Suso, 2010). Since, the learner is independent of a tutor in e-learning, the learning style is absolutely vague in nature. An understanding of learning styles can be used to identify and implement best teaching and learning strategies. Learning styles have also been shown to have an impact on the effectiveness of online learning.

Semantic Web (Lee, Hendler, & Lassila, 2001) focuses on effective management of documents intelligently which are present in the Web by considering the properties of the entities (terms) and the relationships involved among them. This conceptual organization is facilitated by building ontology pertaining to a particular domain (Perez, Lopez, & Corcho, 2003). One of the major areas of research in retrieving the web information intelligently is the provision of learning course contents through online (E-learning) (Deborah, Baskaran, & Kannan, 2011; Bateman, 2010). The prerequisite of the semantic-driven resource management and content delivery in E-learning web service has been facilitated in such systems by building Ontology. Therefore, this kind of technique can be utilized for the performance evaluation component of the learning management system.

1.1 Impact of Learning Styles in Learning

Learning Style is defined as a particular way in which an individual learns. A deep understanding and analysis of the e-learners, learning styles can be used to implement better teaching–learning methodologies (Dunn, 1990; Budny, & Paul, 2003). Accordingly, learning styles are "characteristic, cognitive, affective, and psychological behaviors that serve as relatively stable indicators of how learners perceive, interact with and respond to the learning environment" (Carver et al., 1999). An understanding of learning styles can be used to identify and implement best teaching and learning strategies. Intelligent web-based systems, such as INSPIRE (Papanikolaou, Grigoriadou, Magoulas, & Kornilakis, 2002), ARTHUR (Gilbert, & Han, 1999), AES-CS (Triantafillou, Pomportsis, & Georgiadou, 2002), Tangow (Paredes, & Rodriguez, 2002) and AHA (Suso et al., 2005), have attempted to provide intelligent content adaptation based on learning style and previous knowledge, but these systems have to assess students learning styles offline and through simple questionnaires. iLessons was a novel set of tools that overcame the limitations of other web-based educational authoring tools by giving teachers the ability to reuse materials readily available on the WWW (Sanders et al., 2010). The Felder–Silverman dimensions of learning style model was a well-accepted model used in several adaptive hypermedia applications such as Tangow and the same has been selected for further study before fully coding the new systems because it provided four dimensions of learning style (Felder, & Silverman, 1988), that might be measured from data obtained from the computer systems namely timings, actions, locations, etc. In this E-learning management system, a new technique based on Felder-Silverman learning style model is discussed and implemented for learning style identification. Such learning style identification and suitable recommendations on the learning contents is helpful for increasing the self-efficacy of the self learning learners.

1.2 Need for Semantics

Automatic exchanging and reusing of data or information in the universal medium for information exchange (WWW) is very limited due to two main reasons, namely the heterogeneity problem prevailing in the information resources and the non-semantic nature of HTML and URL. Information heterogeneity occurs in syntax, structure and semantics. Though enhanced techniques are developed to solve syntactic and structural heterogeneity problems (Giunchiglia, Yatskevich, & Shvaiko, 2007), the problem of semantic heterogeneity is still prevailing to be a great challenge. When two contexts do not share the same interpretation of information, semantic heterogeneity occurs. Several approaches were proposed in the past (Doan,

Madhavan, Dhamankar, Domingos, & Haley, 2003) to solve semantic heterogeneity problems like synonym sets, concept lattices, features and constraints. However, all these existing approaches could solve this problem only partially.

1.3 Ontology Alignment

In the semantic web, Ontologies play a key role to solve the problem of semantic heterogeneity. Ontology Alignment aims to find semantic correspondences between similar elements of different Ontologies and has been the subject of research in various web domains and applications (Kim, & Storey, 2011). An ontology is an explicit formal specification of a shared conceptualization. In the ontology, a set of concept types and a set of formal axioms are explicitly defined with both human-readable and machine-readable text (Dahlem, 2011). The ontology is also widely used as an important component in many areas, such as knowledge management (Bateman, 2010), electronic commerce (Meng, & Chatwin, 2010), E-Learning (Deborah et al., 2011; Cristani, 2008), and information retrieval systems (Bateman, 2010).

Ontology alignment can be carried out either manually or using automated tools (Ehrig, & Staab, 2004). Such alignment becomes very critical when it is performed manually as the size and complexity of the ontology structure increases. Hence, automatic ontology alignment became a well-known technique in many practical applications including information transformation and data integration, query processing, E-commerce and E-Learning. Several categories of Ontology Alignment techniques exist in the literature which includes String-based, Language-based, Constraint-based and Semantic-based methodologies (De Marnee, & Manning, 2010). However, all these existing Ontology Alignment techniques suffer from two main limitations:

1. They have only limited expressivity,
2. Relationships between the entities in the existing systems are retrieved based on the occurrence of only dominant words in the input text documents (Ehrig et al., 2004). These shortcomings may lead to a reduction in the accuracy of evaluation in an E-Learning scenario. Therefore, it is necessary to provide intelligent techniques for effective Ontology Alignment.

In this chapter, we propose a new framework that derives deontic relations from the input text documents for identifying non-dominant words which helps to perform a better evaluation in an E-Learning environment. In addition, a measure of similarity/conflict resolution between two ontologies is also given. In this technique, deontic relationships are used to perform Ontology Alignment instead of propositional logic. The application of deontic logic allows us to use universal and existential quantifiers in rules. Moreover, it enhances the efficiency of Semantic Matching techniques through the use of additional predicates such as can, could, ought, each, every, any, before, after and when. This evaluation framework considers not only the predicate logic features, namely equals and partially equals, but also the newly added consistency checking deontic predicate 'conflicts' and hence it covers all the aspects of logic including unification, resolution, subsumption and conflict identification.

The main objective of this discussion work is to provide appropriate recommendations of the learning contents to the E-learner and to improve the accuracy of the performance evaluation of the students in E-Learning environments by developing Ontology Alignment techniques. The appropriate recommendations is provided by the learning styles identification and evaluating the learners accurately. Accurate performance evaluation is achieved by resolving the conflicts between two ontologies using the deontic relationships holding two sets of entities that belong to different discrete ontologies. There are many advantages of this deontic framework. First, the learners learning styles are identified using fuzzy logic that accommodates different kinds of learners. Second, it helps to evaluate the students in an E-Learning environment using not only the dominant words but also the non-dominant words in their input text documents. Third, it uses the rules from deontic logic. Therefore, the accuracy of evaluation is increased. Fourth, it not only considers the keywords, but also their relationships. Next, it performs semantic analysis in addition to syntax analysis. This work is advantageous in evaluating the performance of the learners effectively compared to other existing techniques since this work has increased the expressiveness through the construction of ontologies using axioms and the deontic relationships derived from the text documents. Finally, the learners learning styles are also considered as one of the main component for appropriate recommendations. Moreover, this integrated learning management system considers not only the dominant words but also the non-dominant words occurring in the text documents, thus resolves the semantic limitations present in the existing systems. In addition, appropriate learning contents are recommended to the learners based on learning styles and their performance evaluation.

The rest of this chapter is semantically organized as follows. The immediately following Section 2 elaborates the working of the learning style identification and Ontology Alignment in the e-learning framework mathematically by way of defining a Problem Statement. Section 3 provides the working of some of the related literature work. Section 4 offers the working of the proposed integrated E-learning management system. Section 5 presents the experimental results evaluation of several web data corpuses and performs a comparative study. This section depicts the evaluation of some of the well known performance metrics. Section 6 precisely concludes with the future scope of the work in progress. The chapter ends with the complete list of reference works that the authors had employed.

2. PROBLEM STATEMENT

In this integrated system, a fuzzy logic based learning style model is discussed by extending the classification provided by (Sanders et al., 2010). Therefore, the unknown groups in the existing model are further classified into reflective, medium reflective, medium active and active in this work. This new e-learning approach can handle the uncertainty in the inference found in the unknown category since it uses fuzzy rules for effective classification of learners. Uncertainty, in this context considers the degree or extent to which the learner is active or reflective. Queries based on the degree of activeness or reflectiveness is not addressed in the existing models. Moreover, this system considers only the first dimension of Felder-Silverman learning style model, namely active/reflective sense, this dimension is sufficient to identify the learning styles of the learners from the web usage pattern of any media namely text, audio and video.

Since, Ontology Alignment is useful for discovering similarities between two ontologies and to determine the relationships holding two sets of entities incorporated with the domain knowledge, it is necessary to provide effective techniques for semantic analysis in Ontology Alignment. Semantic techniques (Giunchiglia et al., 2007) attempt to map the elements (concepts) in the two ontologies according to their semantic interpretation. The main objective of the technique is to discover the similarities that exist between dominant and non-dominant terms associated with one concept. In this work, the alignment is represented in the form of axioms where each concept is converted into a propositional validity problem. Semantic relations

obtained from E-Learning evaluation documents are translated into propositional connectives using the rules, namely $a \leftrightarrow b$, $a \rightarrow b$, $b \rightarrow a$ and $\neg (a \vee b)$. There are three kinds of relationships that are identified in this work and the mathematical relationship is of the form –

$$\text{axiom:: rel(context}_1, \text{context}_2) \qquad (1)$$

where

context_1 = node elements in Ontology 1 constructed from a student document

context_2 = node elements in Ontology 2 constructed from a domain experts document

rel = relationship that exists between the concepts

The candidate axioms that are handled in this work are

$equals(c_1, c_2)$, *partial equals*(c_1, c_2) and *conflicts*(c_1, c_2).

Case 1: *Equals* (c_1, c_2)

As proposed by (Assawamekin, Sunetnanta, & Pluempitiwiriyawej, 2009), we have evaluated and obtained results for the equality conditions, where context_1 in Ontology 1 is exactly equal to context_2 in ontology 2. The above formula turns out to be unsatisfiable when they are evaluated using the SAT library (Berre, 2006). Therefore, the final relation for the given pair of concepts is *equivalence*.

Case 2: *Partial Equals* (c_1, c_2)

Similarly, the partial equals conditions have been evaluated based on the work proposed by (Assawamekin et al., 2009), where context_1 in Ontology 1 is only partially equal to the context_2

in ontology 2. Some examples of this matching are superset and subset analysis and the relation is *subsumption*.

Case 3: *Conflicts* (c_1, c_2)

Conflicts relationship is the relationship between two entities of different ontologies and is extracted by writing deontical relationships from the text documents using the Standard Deontic rules which have the unique facility of understanding the non-dominant words occurring in the text document (Lomuscio, & Sergot, 2003). Conflicts between documents are due to the enormous usage of non-dominant words, and are identified in this work by using deontic logic. In this evaluation framework, the conflicting documents are identified by using both the *dominant* and the *non-dominant* words in the text documents and hence considers relationships which are neither fully equal nor partially equal.

3. RELATED WORKS

This section gives an overview of the existing work related to the notion of learning styles identification and Semantic Analysis. Various kinds of techniques have been proposed in the past to solve the problem of Semantic analysis using Ontology Alignment techniques. Some of the well known systems for performing ontology alignment are GLUE (Doan et al., 2003), LILY (Wang, & Xu, 2007), ASMOV(Jean-Mary, & Kabuka, 2007), RIMOM (Tang, Li, Liang, Huang, Li, & Wang, 2006), S-Match (Giunchiglia, Autayeu, & Pane, 2010), Content-based techniques (Partyka, Alipanah, Khan, Thuraisingham, & Shekhar, 2008) and MUPRET (Assawamekin et al., 2009). Most of these works used S-Match, Content-based techniques and MUPRET framework for evaluating their contributions because they are considered as the standard techniques. The work discussed in

this chapter is an extension to the work proposed by Assawamekinet.alwho developed MUPRET framework for Ontology Alignment and this proposed framework has been evaluated and tested for an E-Learning system.

3.1 Works on Learning Styles Identification

Felder-Silverman learning style model (Felder et al., 1988) often used in technology-enhanced learning and that is designed for traditional learning. Moreover, Felder–Silverman learning style model describes the learning style of a learner in more detail, distinguishing between preferences on four dimensions. It was used by many researchers since this model provides four dimensions of learning based on psychological aspects of the learners which is found to be important in an e-learning environment. The learning styles proposed by Felder–Silverman for categorizing the learners are:

1. **Active–Reflective:** Active learners learn best by working actively with the learning material, by applying the material, and by trying things out. Reflective learners prefer to think about and reflect on the material.
2. **Sensing–Intuitive:** Learners who prefer a sensing learning style like to learn facts and concrete learning material. Intuitive learners prefer to learn abstract learning material, such as theories and their underlying meanings.
3. **Visual–Verbal:** Learners who remember best and therefore prefer to learn from what they have seen (e.g., pictures, diagrams and flow-charts), and learners who get more out of textual representations, regardless of whether they are written or spoken.
4. **Sequential–Global:** Sequential learners learn in small incremental steps and therefore have a linear learning progress. Global

learners use a holistic thinking process and learn in large leaps. They tend to absorb learning material almost randomly without seeing connections but after they have learned enough material they suddenly get the whole picture.

Since most learners fall in the category of either active or reflective for the first dimension, this model is more suitable to evaluating the learners in an e-learning environment. The iLessons system developed by Suso et al., (2005) overcame the limitations of the previous e-learning systems by providing two additional features namely Drag and Drop facility for reuse and an intelligent recommendation system that recommends relevant web pages to the learners based on their learning styles. Therefore, iLessons is an important contribution for e-learning through the identification of learners as active or reflective. The work done by the authors promptly followed an algorithm in identifying the first dimension and classified the users into two kinds as either Active or Reflective. From his works it is understood that the learners belonged to either of the dimensions crisply. It is evident from their experiments that the classification accuracy for identifying such learners was 71% when considering the first dimension of Felder-Silverman learning style model.

Sanders et al. (2010) proposed a new intelligent e-learning system with an effective user interface. The main advantage of this intelligent e-learning system is that it is capable of performing deductive inference to obtain the learning style of learners. They followed Felder-Silverman learning style model and developed an e-learning system that can infer the learning styles in real time and provided recommendations for selecting suitable e-learning contents. This is a significant achievement in the area of e-learning since, it uses Artificial Intelligent techniques for classifying the learners based on their learning style into three categories namely active or reflective or unknown. He categorized in such a way, since the users may not fall into one category virtually all the time and most learners tend towards a particular dimension in course of time, environmental factor, mood, need and psychological changes. The accuracy of classifying the learners Sander's et al has increased to 81% compared to the earlier work done by Bergasa-Suso. One of the important contributions of Sanders and Begrasa-Suso is the inclusion of unknown sets in addition to the active and reflective categories of learners.

3.2 Works on Ontology Alignment Using Taxonomy

GLUE (Doan et al., 2003) is the first ontology alignment framework proposed in the literatures. It is a system based on taxonomical structure and uses instance-based methodology for ontology alignment. Moreover, this system exploits the concepts of statistical computation analysis and then uses the taxonomical structure of applications for decision making. GLUE system is more suitable for applications like computer vision, natural language processing and hypertext classification which adopts relaxation labeling approach. LILY (Wang et al., 2007) framework is a generic ontology alignment framework based on extraction of semantic sub graphs. The system uses the concepts of both linguistic and structural information in semantic sub graphs to iterate initial alignments. Moreover, it combines all separate similarities iteratively using some weights assignments and hence it fails to consider ontology constraints directly. Later on, Tang et al.,proposed the Ontology Alignment technique called RiMOM which is based on Bayesian Networks decision theory. They used many kinds of taxonomical relationships like superClassOf, siblingClassOf, domain, etc are resolved using this system. All these systems are suitable only for situations where taxonomical classification is possible.

3.3 Works on Ontology Alignment Using Semantic Matching

ASMOV (Jean-Mary et al., 2007) is an ontology alignment tool which calculates the similarity between concepts recursively by analyzing textual description. The tool effectively identifies the semantic inconsistencies like crisscross mappings and many-to-one mappings. However, ontology alignment must focus on both matching for equality and also detection of inconsistencies. S-Match (Giunchiglia et al., 2010) is an open source semantic matching framework that tackles the semantic interoperability problem by transforming several data structures including web services descriptions into lightweight ontologies and establishes the semantic correspondences between them. The major limitation of the framework is that S-Match could identify only three kinds of XML relationships namely "is-a", "part-of" and "attribute-of", whereas there are numerous relationships that are existing between the ontology for effective matching of them semantically. Therefore, it is necessary to extend the light-weight ontologies with axioms in order to provide heavy-weight ontologies. Content-based techniques (Partyka et al., 2008) proposed by Jeffrey Partyka et.al for ontology matching deal with examining the associated instance data from the compared concepts and apply a content-matching strategy to measure similarity based on value types. The major limitation of the content-based framework is that, it uses only syntactic structure of the two types of ontology for analysis. Therefore, the system could not identify the major relationships like partial overlap, intersection and subsumption. This can be enhanced by introducing semantic axioms for enhancing the efficiency. MUPRET (Assawamekin et al., 2009) framework is another Ontology

alignment technique used in web applications. This framework actually uses a semantic matching procedure based on dominant words matching. The main advantage of MUPRET framework over the existing systems is that it considers relationships such as equivalence, subsumption, overlapping and mismatch. However, it is necessary to find inconsistencies in order to apply the resolution procedure.

Bodea, Dascalu, & Serbanati (2012) proposed a recommendation mechanism in order to enhance the managerial training Project-Oriented Organizations (POO). This innovative system is used for training and implementation services to support POO's. The recommender engine has an assessment system based on ontology construction and alignment technique. The inputs of the two ontology alignment are one from the management documents provided by POO's and the other from the training curriculum offered to the POO's. The engine is responsible for adapting the training curriculum by translating the ontology alignment results into a user friendly form. The developed system produces smart recommendations to personalize the training curriculum to POO's.

Jan, Maozhen Li, Al-Raweshidy, Mousavi, & Man Qi (2012) proposed a rough-set based approach to facilitate the exchange of knowledge among heterogeneous sources through ontology alignment. It helps in addressing the conflicting results on the similarity of the mapped entities during ontology alignment. The proposed framework achieves a high degree of accuracy in uncertainty situations during the emergence of conflicting results. This framework is also compared with several traditional similarity measures and achieved a high degree of precision. Wagatsum, & Cheng, (2012) Various cryptographic protocols are available for the establishment of several security applications. In most of the traditional approaches appropriate security analysis had not been accomplished through accurate reasoning. They proposed a framework to elaborate the reasoning approach of Needham-Schroeder Shared Key protocol using deontic relevant logic. The successful implementation of the framework could efficiently find out the vulnerabilities of the target cryptographic protocol and in the traditional approach.

Poernomo, Umarov, & Hajiyev (2011) addressed the problem of describing and analyzing data manipulations within business process workflow specifications. In the proposed framework a typical workflow description in Petri nets is augmented using ontologies. The ontological descriptions are written in Ontology Web Language and the constraints of the workflow are written in Deontic logic. The written workflow in submitted to the behavioral analysis and the analysis of data exchange is achieved using the B-based theorem prover. (Geesaman, Cordy, & Zouaq, 2013) Ontology alignment aims to find the similarities between two formal ontologies to recover the common relationships and concepts representing the same domain. In such a scenario, the description of the ontologies may be similar but there can be differences in the structure or vocabulary that makes similarity detection a critical task. They proposed a near-miss clone detection is used to address such problem of ontology alignment and the use of best-match clone detection achieves good results. Integrating several similarity measures into a single similarity metric during ontology alignment is a challenging problem. Marjit, & Mandal (2012) developed a swarm based algorithm to address the problem of optimality during ontology alignment using similarity measures. An optimal alignment is achieved using multiobjective particle swarm based algorithm and similarity aggregation function.

3.4 Analysis of Related Works

Application of these existing learning models to the modern web based e-learning leads to a lot of new challenges. First, all these models assume that the teacher and the learner meet frequently in the learning process so that the learning style of the learner will be known to the teacher easily. On the other hand, in e-learning, the learner-instructor interactions are not frequent. Moreover, most applications in the real world have incomplete and vague information. Therefore, in this e-learning framework self learning is supported through learning style identification and provision of suitable learning materials. Therefore, this work uses fuzzy rules for making decisions since it helps to make effective conclusions even from incomplete data understanding the learner characteristics. Finally, the existing models consider psychology as an important factor. In order to understand the learner's psychology, this system identifies behaviors from web interface information. This helps to identify the learning styles easily and to provide suitable learning materials in the e-learning environment.

From the analysis made on the related work, it has been observed that most of the existing works and the techniques used for Semantic Ontology Alignment were performed either by using light-weight ontologies or with axioms of propositional logic with limited expressivity. In such a scenario, the performance evaluation of the students in E-Learning might not produce accurate results. On the other hand, accurate results can be obtained only when all kinds of relationships like equivalence, subsumption, overlap, partial overlap and inconsistencies are resolved during ontology alignment. Hence, it is necessary to provide some effective techniques to identify and resolve all these kinds of relationships. The work discussed in this chapter derives deontic relationships with increased expressivity through the introduction of axioms from deontic logic, which helps in identifying all the above kinds of relationships and thus it increases the accuracy in evaluating the performance of the students in E-Learning.

4. INTEGRATED E-LEARNING MANAGEMENT SYSTEM

In this work, an integrated E-learning management system is discussed for appropriate recommendations of the learning contents to the learners using learning style identification and semantic matching for evaluation documents in E-Learning applications. This framework is based on Felder-Silverman learning style model using fuzzy logic and XML Path expressions where the input text is preprocessed and the output is written into an XML file for further processing. Using this output, ontology is created to evaluate the learning ability of the students in learning the C programming language electronically. Now, Ontology is done to identify the commonalities between the documents given by various students. A rule-based method is used to identify the conflicts among the documents produced by the learner and the domain expert. Unlike, the existing works where the non dominant keywords are rejected, in this work both the dominant and non-dominant words are considered for Ontology Alignment. The non dominant keywords addressed in this work are modal verbs, determiner words and adjectival time clauses where deontic rules are created. Separate ontologies, called A and B are constructed for two different input text documents provided by the learner and domain expert respectively. The deontic rules created in student ontology (A) are then matched with the dentist rules created in domain expert ontology (B). The integrated learning management system is shown in Figure 1. This framework consists of

Figure 1. Integrated e-learning management system

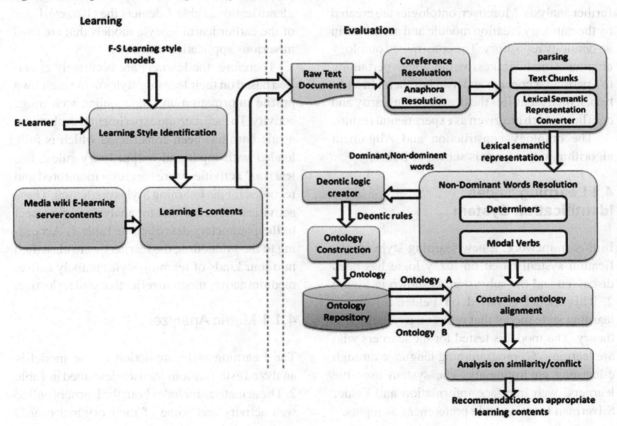

two major modules, namely learning and evaluation. The learning module concentrates on the learning activities and the evaluation module concentrates on the subsequent evaluation. The learning module consists of learning style identification subsystem and the learning activity using Media Wiki e-learning server contents. However, the learning styles of the e-learners are identified using fuzzy logic and Felder-Silverman learning style model. The evaluation modules consist of coreference resolution, parsing, dominant and non-dominant keywords resolution, deontic rule creator and constrained ontology alignment. The coreference resolution module takes a raw input text document and performs anaphora resolution. The parsing module performs lexical analysis and provides a lexical semantic representation. The dominant and non-dominant keywords resolution module extracts the respective keywords. The deontic rule creator extracts the deontic rules for further analysis. Moreover, ontologies are created by the ontology creation module and are stored in an ontology repository. The constrained ontology alignment module takes two ontologies pertaining to a particular concept and matches them. In addition, it then identifies the degree of similarity and conflicts which are given as experimental results.

The ontology construction and Alignment algorithm in this work is shown in Box 1.

4.1 Learning Styles Identification System

In this framework, a new learning style identification system based on fuzzy logic has been discussed and the subsystem is shown in Figure 2. This model is based on Felder Silverman learning style model that relies on psychological theory. The model is tested for the learners who are learning 'C' programming language through e-learning environments. The system uses the learners' web interface information and Felder Silverman learning style preferences as inputs.

The major features of this model are the introduction of metrics analyzer and fuzzy inference engine for effective learning style identification. The model uses mediawiki e-Learning servers for the e-Learning contents to be posted in various formats. This e-learning server consists of C programming language course contents in textual, audio, and video formats. The learner after proper authentication could access any type of contents. The major features of this model are the introduction of metrics analyzer and fuzzy inference engine for effective learning style identification. that are available in mediawiki e-Learning server. The target learners in this model tend towards textual format of the course contents, and therefore this model was evaluated and tested for identifying the first dimension of Felder Silverman learning style preferences. The learners' during the authentication are asked to provide their original profile information for the purpose of learning style identification. Table 1 depicts the characteristics of the earlier learning style models that are used in various application domains.

Therefore, the learners are accurately classified based on their learning styles using their own profile information and their online web usage activity. To facilitate the experimental evaluation, a rule base has been constructed which is fully loaded with input and output fuzzy rules. The learners' activities were carefully monitored and recorded for the Learning Styles prediction. These activities were recorded for analysis with respect to the parameters described in Table 1. According to the evaluation, the learners were classified into four kinds of learning styles namely active, medium active, medium reflective, and reflective.

4.1.1 Metric Analyzer

The Learning style prediction of the model is analyzed using various metrics described in Table 2. These metrics includes both the learners online web activity and some of their original profile

Box 1.

```
Algorithm: Ontology Visualization and Ontology Alignment
Input: Raw text Documents
Output: Similarity and Conflict percentage among the documents
Procedure
Begin
For each raw text document
Begin
                          Iterate Anaphora Resolution algorithm for he/she/it
                          kind of words
                          Reiterate Anaphora Resolution algorithm for who/where
                          kind of words
               End
For each pre-processed document
Begin
Split the document using sentence splitter algorithm
                    Compound words are identified
                    Perform lemmatization process to obtain the root words
                    Identification of non-dominant keywords
                    Obtain four ontological relationships for aiding the
                    ontology construction
                    Resolution of deontic relationships from the POS tags
                    Removal of redundant relationships by precedence
(Obligatory-high, forbidden-high, permissibility-low)
End
For any two processed documents
Begin
Formation of context-based propositional logic for sentence pair in the text
documents
[Checking for equals, partial equals and conflict relationships]
Evaluation of logic and checking for unsatisfiability using SAT solver
Calculation of degree of similarity/conflict between the documents.
End        End
```

Table 1. Parameters of learners web interface

Parameters List	Parameters Included	
	Deadband model	Fuzzy Logic based model
Number of mouse movement in the y-axis	Yes	Yes
Ratio of document length to the time spent on a page	Yes	Yes
Ratio of images area to document length and scroll distance	Yes	Yes
Number of visits to a document	No	Yes
Fuzzy Rules	No	Yes

Figure 2. Learning style identification subsystem

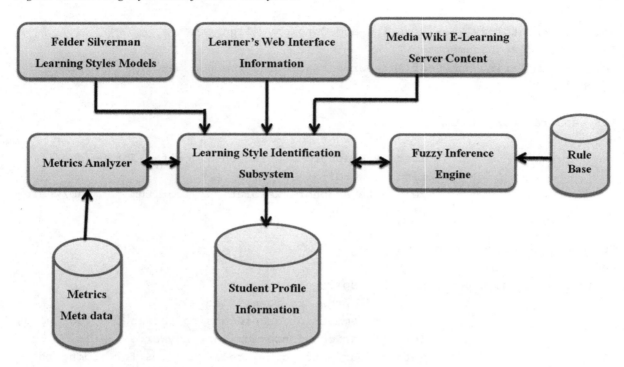

Table 2. Metrics for learning styles prediction

Online Web Information	Offline Profile Information
Number of mouse movement in the y-axis	Domain of Interest
Ratio of document length to the time spent on a page	Educational Background
Ratio of images area to document length and scroll distance	Professional Career
Number of visits to a document	

information. Using the information from Table 2, the metric analyzer present in the system analyzes the learners' behavior and aids in classifying the learners with respect to their learning styles.

4.1.2 Rule Base

A rule based approach is discussed in this work for the effective classification of learners which can handle uncertain information as well is used. Moreover, this model aids in recommending and providing suitable e-learning materials based on the identification of learning styles. The knowl-

edge editor rule base consists of approximately 30 fuzzy rules for the prediction of learners based on their learning styles using online web activity information and offline profile information. The sample set of 15 rules used in this system are shown in Table 3.

4.1.3 Fuzzy Inference Engine

The learners membership degrees for active/reflective type of dimensions were experimented using Engineering students of Anna University. On successfully providing the e-learning course

Table 3. Fuzzy rules in the integrated e-learning system

Rule No	Fuzzy Rules
1	If(mousemove is more) and (doclentime is more) and (imagedoclen is more) and (visitsdoc is more) then (student is reflective)
2	If(mousemove is less) and (doclentime is lesss) and (imagedoclen is less) and (visitsdoc is less) then (student is active)
3	If(mousemove is less) and (doclentime is less) and (imagedoclen is less) and (visitsdoc is more) then (student is mactive)
4	If(mousemove is less) and (doclentime is less) and (imagedoclen is more) and (visitsdoc is less) then (student is mactive)
5	If(mousemove is less) and (doclentime is more) and (imagedoclen is less) and (visitsdoc is less) then (student is mactive)
6	If(mousemove is more) and (doclentime is less) and (imagedoclen is less) and (visitsdoc is less) then (student is mactive)
7	If(mousemove is more) and (doclentime is more) and (imagedoclen is more) and (visitsdoc is less) then (student is mreflective)
8	If(mousemove is more) and (doclentime is more) and (imagedoclen is less) and (visitsdoc is more) then (student is mreflective)
9	If(mousemove is more) and (doclentime is less) and (imagedoclen is more) and (visitsdoc is more) then (student is mreflective)
10	If(mousemove is less) and (doclentime is more) and (imagedoclen is more) and (visitsdoc is more) then (student is mreflective)
11	If(mousemove is less) and (doclentime is less) then (student is active)
12	If (imagedoclen is more) and (visitsdoc is more) then (student is active)
13	If(mousemove is more) and (doclentime is more) then (student is reflective)
14	If(imagedoclen is more) and (visitsdoc is more) then (student is reflective)
15	If(mousemove is less) and (doclentime is more) then (student is mreflective)

materials of 'C' programming language, the symmetric Gaussian membership function for a fuzzy set A, that represents the learning styles of the learners is represented by,

$$f\left(x:\tilde{A},c\right) = e^{\dfrac{\left(x-c\right)^2}{2\tilde{A}^2}} \qquad (2)$$

The parameters σ (width) and c (center) alter the width of the membership function curve of the fuzzy set A, based on the input value x. This fuzzy set A represents the learning style, and the parameter c denotes the mean of the membership function curve in this function (Chen,&,Chang, 2011). The symmetric Gaussian fuzzy membership function used in the learning model for the four categories of the learners namely active, medium active, medium reflective and reflective is shown in Figure 3. Based on the rule base developed in the model, and on the application of the symmetric Gaussian fuzzy membership function described in equation (2), the learners could be predicted on their suitable learning styles.

4.2 Co-Reference Resolution

In linguistics, anaphora is an instance of an expression referring to another noun (Winograd, 1972). Anaphora resolution helps to resolve what a pronoun or a noun phrase refers to which was previously defined in the complete text document.

Figure 3. Symmetric gaussian fuzzy function

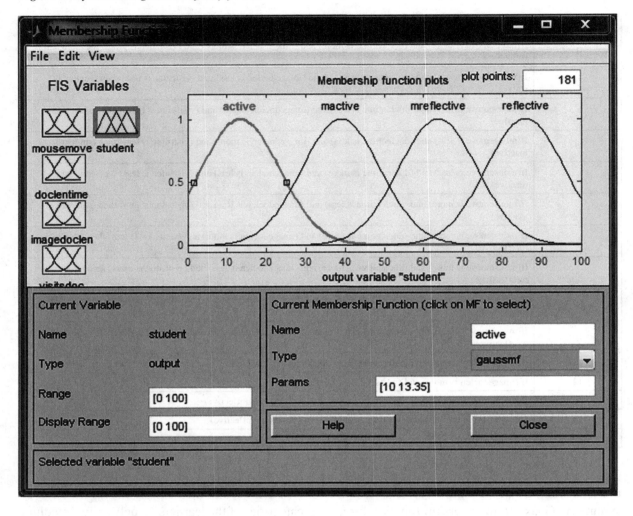

In other words, the referential entity is called as an anaphor and the entity to which it referred previously is called as an antecedent. The process of determining the antecedent of the anaphor is called as Anaphora Resolution. The existence of several anaphors in a document has a great impact in the construction of correct ontology. Several types of anaphora exists in documents which includes pronominal anaphora, definite noun-phrase anaphora and One-anaphora (Denis, & Baldridge, 2007; Markert, & Nissim, 2005). Therefore, in this framework a "Anaphora Resolution" module has been developed which concentrates on three categories of nouns that pertain to the gender, person and grammar resolution of the text. The main advantage of this module is that it can identify the pronouns such as he/she/it and also the who/where types of words for the replacement of nouns. In this work, coreference was performed individually on each student document and the domain expert Professor A document during the first experiment. In the subsequent experiments, these ontologies were compared with ontologies produced by other professors.

4.3 Document Parsing

The document is now ready for analysis after coreference resolution. Now, the documents are given to the parser module which uses the standard Stanford Parser for parsing the document (De Marnee et al., 2010). The parser generates a parse tree for each document. These parse trees are given as input to the typed dependencies generator module of the Stanford Parser. The complete typed dependencies of the documents are generated and stored in XML files. The compound words are also identified from this document. Once the compound words are identified the other words are lemmatized to resolve the root words. On successfully finding the compound nouns and root words by lemmatization, the entire documents are now cleaned by removing the existing prepositional dependencies. These compound words and the root words are replaced in all the original documents which provide the dominant words.

4.4 Recovery of Ontological Relationships

The output document obtained from the previous stage is converted to a lexical semantic representation in this module. Therefore, the exact hierarchy for the ontology construction is designed in this phase. The first-order logic implementation is used in this work in order to write the facts and rules to be applied on the document. Now, the query processor finds the different kinds of structural relationships among the dominant terms in the document. The results obtained are cleaned and the following four types of structural relationships are obtained. They are categorized based on the classifications done by Assawamekinet.al namely Aggregation relationship (partOf), Property relationship (propertyOf), Generalization/specialization relationship (isA), Equivalence relationship (sameAs). After these structural relationships have been identified, the connectives among the

terms were easily resolved and viewed. The rules extracted for identifying these structural relationships are as follows:

Extraction Rules

Noun RULE – Object: If x is a noun, then x is an object.

Verb RULE - Relationship: If r is a verb, then r is a relationship.

PartOf RULE - Aggregation: Let r be a special verb relation (e.g., part of, belong to or subdivision of). If a noun x participates in object y with r, then object x is a part of object y.

Includes RULE - Aggregation: Let r be a special verb relation (e.g., have, contain, comprise, include, define, consist of, compose of, denote by, identify by, make up of or record with). If a noun x participates in a noun y with r and a noun y also participates in a noun z with another r, then noun y is a part of noun x.

Generalization/Specialization RULE: Let r be a special verb relation (e.g., be, kind of, type of, classify into or consider as). If a noun x participates in noun y with r, then the noun x is a kind of the noun y.

Adjective RULE : If a noun x is a numeric modifier of another noun y, then the noun x is a property of the noun y.

Equivalence RULE : If a noun x is an abbreviation for another noun y, then the noun x is the same as another noun y.

4.5 Deontic Rule Creator

Deontic logic is the formal study of the normative concepts of obligation, permission, and prohibition (Lomuscio et al., 2003). In modern deontic logic, the notions of prohibition F, permission P are usually defined in terms of obligation O as shown in equations 2 and 3 and the basic ontology for deontic modalities are used .

$$F A = O \neg A \qquad (3)$$

$$P A = \neg F A \qquad (4)$$

In this discussion work, the deontic relations from the text documents are identified in order to resolve the conflicts between the documents. When there is a conflict, the algorithm indicates the positions of conflicting words. The text documents with no conflicts are identified as "Identical/ Similar Documents". For this purpose, we use the properties of negation, unification and resolution. Experimental works have been carried using a number of tools and algorithms. In this process, dominant keyword resolution was carried out using Stanford Part of Speech (POS) tagger. In addition, filtering of useless tags from POS tags was also performed. The structural relationships were identified using rules and hence the relationships such as isA, sameAs, PropertyOf and PartOf have been identified. Now, the resolution of deontic relationships from the POS tags were carried out using deontic rules. The detection of transitive relationships was also performed using deontic rules. Finally, the removal of redundant relationships such as obligatory-high, forbidden-high and permissibility-low were performed.

4.5.1 Rules for Detecting Deontic Relations

In the E-Learning experiments conducted in this work, the students were allowed to view the course contents from the service providers. In order to validate the understanding of the user on the E-learning content, the domain experts were also allowed to view the content. Both the user and the domain expert are asked to write a short description about the viewed course content. Separate ontologies are created and they are matched against each other. This is done in order to find out three kinds of relationships namely equals, partialequals and

conflicts. Based on the relationships obtained, the learner levels of understating are obtained. In order to obtain these relationships, special kinds of deontic relations shown below have been used in this work.

Rule 1: If x is a noun and x is related to y by attribute or part of relationship and there exists a determiner relationship between X and Y then OBLIGATORY (X HAS Y)

Rule 2: If x is a noun and x is related to Y by attribute or part of relationship and there is a modal relationship between X and Y then

Rule 2.1: If the modal relationship is MUST or SHOULD then OBLIGATORY (X HAS Y)

Rule 2.2: If the modal relationship is CAN then PERMITTED (X HAS Y)

Rule 3: If X is a noun and X is related to Y by part of or attribute relationship and consists of negative modal relationship

Rule 3.1: If the modal relationship is MUST NOT or SHOULD NOT then FORBIDDEN (X HAS Y)

Rule 3.2: If the modal relationship is CAN NOT then NOT_PERMITTED (X HAS Y)

Rule 4: If X and Y are nouns and are related with PropertyOf relationship OBLIGATORY (X is NOT NULL)

Rule 5: If X and Y are noun and are related by isA relationship OBLIGATORY (X has attribute TYPE)

4.5.2 Transitivity Rules Generation

Rule 6: If X and Y are related with isA relationship and Y is related to another Z with some Deontic relationship R then X is related to Z with deontic relationship R

Rule 7: If X and Y are related with sameAs relationship and Y is related to another Z with some Deontic relationship R then X is related to Z with deontic relationship R

Rule 8: If X and Y are related by a deontic relationship R and Y and Z are related by deontic relationship R then X and Z are also related with deontic relationship R

4.5.3 Mathematical Predicate Calculus for Deontic Rules

Rule 1: $\forall x, \exists y$ -> OBLIGATORY(x,y)

Rule 2.1: MUST(x,y)$\lor$ SHOULD (x,y) -> HAS_OBLIGATORY(x,y)

Rule 2.2: NOUN(x) $\land$ NOUN(y) $\land$ CAN(x,y) -> HAS_PERMITTED(x,y)

Rule 3.1: NOUN(x) $\land$ NOUN(y) $\land$ MUST_NOT(x,y) $\land$ SHOULD_NOT(x,y) -> HAS_FORBIDDEN(x,y)

Rule 3.2: NOUN(x) $\land$ NOUN(y) $\land$ CAN_NOT(x,y)-> HAS_NOT_PERMITTED(x,y)

Rule 4: NOUN(x) $\land$ NOUN(y) $\land$ PROPERTY_OF(x,y) -> OBLIGATORY(x, NOTNULL)

Rule 5: NOUN(x) $\land$ NOUN(y) $\land$ OBLIGATORY(x,y) -> HAS_ATTRIBUTE(x, TYPE)

Rule 6, 7: NOUN(x) $\land$ NOUN(y) $\land$ NOUN(z) $\land$ DEONTIC(y,z) -> DEONTIC(x,z)

whereDEONTIC(y,z) -> MUST(y,z) $\lor$ SHOULD(y,z) $\lor$ CAN_NOT(y,z) $\lor$ HAS_FORBIDDEN(y,z) $\lor$ HAS_NOT_PERMITTED(y,z)

Rule 8: NOUN(x) $\land$ NOUN(y) $\land$ NOUN(z) $\land$ DEONTIC(x,y) $\land$ DEONTIC(y,z) -> DEONTIC(x,z)

whereDEONTIC(x,y) -> MUST(x,y) $\lor$ SHOULD(x,y) $\lor$ CAN_NOT(x,y) $\lor$ HAS_FORBIDDEN(x,y) $\lor$ HAS_NOT_

PERMITTED(x,y) $\land$ DEONTIC(y,z) -> MUST(y,z) $\lor$ SHOULD(y,z) $\lor$ CAN_NOT(y,z) $\lor$ HAS_FORBIDDEN(y,z) $\lor$ HAS_NOT_PERMITTED(y,z)

4.6 Constrained Ontology Alignment

The relationships and rules identified are represented in the form of ontology. The relationships are arranged based on the base ontologies of deontic rules and the input documents. Semantic ontology matching using propositional logic is followed to identify the implicit relationship among the documents (Berre, 2006). Wordnet is used for matching the elements in the documents (Miller, 1995). Wordnet is a lexical database used to identify the synonym, antonym, hypernym and hyponym. Wordnet Similarity is used to find the similarity between two words. Wordnet distance measure returns 0 if both words are equal. The elements in the ontologies that have to be matched should be compared using wordnet and propositional logic is formed. Relationship between wordnet semantic relations and corresponding propositional logic for ontology alignment is shown in Table 4. The logic is then given to the SATsolver tool to solve the problem using the propositional logic. In table 4, the evaluated axioms for conflict resolution are also included in addition to the existing axioms. To make a decision on the satisfiability, the following rule is used. If the mathematical axiom given in equation (1) is said to be unsatisfiable, then the relationship holds.

The exact algorithm for ontology alignment is shown in Box 2.

Similarity Computation

The text documents are processed for the deontic relations obtained from the input documents. In the evaluation module, any two documents to be aligned are checked for similarity or conflicts. This kind of alignment is resolved as equivalence, partialoverlap and conflict relationships. This is

Table 4. Ontology alignment table

Semantic Relations	Input Keywords	Propositional Logic	Relationships	Semantic-Numeric Mapping	Translation into CNF
Synonym $a=b$	Dominant	$a \leftrightarrow b$	equals($=$)	1	Axioms$\land$(context$_1\land\neg$context$_2$) Axioms$\land$($\neg$context$_1\land$context$_2$)
Hyponym or Meronym $a \subseteq b$	Dominant	$a \rightarrow b$	partialequals ($\supseteq,\subseteq$)	0.5	Axioms$\land$(context$_1\land\neg$context$_2$)
Hypernym or holonym $a \supseteq b$	Dominant	$b \rightarrow a$	partialequals ($\supseteq,\subseteq$)	0.5	Axioms$\land$($\neg$context$_1\land$ context$_2$)
Deontic Conflict $a \mp b$ (New Relation)	*Dominant & Non-dominant*	$\neg (a \lor b)$	*Conflicts($\mp$)*	*-1*	*Axioms$\land$($\neg$context$_1\land\neg$context$_2$)*

Box 2.

```
Algorithm: Ontology Alignment
Input: Deontic statements obtained from Ontology A, Da
       Deontic statements obtained from Ontology B, Db
Output: rel
Output Domain Set: <equals, partial equals, conflicts>
Procedure
Begin
For each logic statement ls1 in Da
       For each logic statement ls2 in Db
              Pl <- FormPropositionalLogic(ls1,ls2)
              Rel<-SATSolver(pl)
       End        End         Return rel
```

achieved by calculating the similarity/conflict percentage in terms of the positive matches identified by the ontology alignment algorithm described in the above section. In this work, structural similarity is considered for semantic matching between two ontologies. The structural similarity between two ontologies O_1 and O_2 is given by

$$Structural\, Similarity\left(O_1, O_2\right) = \frac{\sum_{i=1}^{n} sim\left(a_i, b_i\right)}{max\left(n_1, n_2\right)}$$

(5)

Where $O_1=$ ontology constructed by the domain expert O_2 = ontology constructed by the student a_i = node entities present in O_1 b_i = node entities present in O_2 n_1 = Total number of nodes present in O_1 n_2 = Total number of nodes present in O_2

For this kind of similarity computation, the node entities and the total number of nodes in the ontologies constructed by the domain expert and the students are considered. The degree of similarity/conflicts of the constructed ontologies is found using the mathematical equations given below

$$sim\left(a_i, b_i\right) = 1 \text{ if } a_i = b_i = 1 \qquad (6)$$

$$sim\left(a_i, b_i\right) = 0 \text{ Otherwise} \qquad (7)$$

Several numbers of experiments were performed in order to identify the threshold values. The threshold for the similarity computation in this application is set to be 0.5. If sim (a_i, b_i) is equal to 1, then the documents written by the student after E-Learning and the domain expert are exactly equal. This indicates the equivalence relationship. In the opposite case, where sim (a_i, b_i) is equal to 0, the documents are exactly mismatched, which describes the conflicts relationship. However, the subsumption relationship of partialequals is obtained by the values ranging between 0 and 1.

5. PERFORMANCE EVALUATION

The applicability of this framework is tested in real problem applications. Since, the authors' domain of interest is concerned with E-Learning; in this work the students' level of understanding in learning the C programming language course electronically is tested. The objective of the developed framework is to obtain the degree of similarity/conflict after the text documents produced by the students and the domain experts are compared. This objective was also tested for other existing algorithms and the results are depicted in this section.

5.1 Experimental Set-Up: Preparation of Raw Text Documents

The text documents were collected from the students and domain experts. The students provide their documents based on their learning experience that is gained from E-Learning of the C programming language from the E-Learning serv-

ers namely MediaWiki, Moodle and Joomla. Our experiments are mainly based on the E-contents posted by various instructors on the MediaWiki E-Learning server and experiments were carried out using 120 First year Undergraduate students of 4 different departments namely Civil Engineering, Mechanical Engineering, Electronics and Communication Engineering and the Computer Science and Engineering. 30 students from each branch were considered as target students for the E-Learning of C programming language. The rule base included a set of 30 fuzzy rules for Learning Styles prediction. In this work, the inference for Learning Styles was done using Matlab R2009a 7.8.0.347. The experiments were repeated, analyzed and compared with the other existing models provided by Suso et al (2005), Sanders et al (2010). The model is also compared with the traditional Bayesian Classification algorithm to test the significant difference in the accuracy of the model. In all the repeated experiments, the Learning Styles of the learners were predicted based on their e-learning of 'C' programming language course contents. However, this work is an ongoing work. This work actually had its base from Felder Silverman learning style model preferences for Learning Style prediction and this work is limited to predicting the first dimension of learning styles only (Active/Reflective). For the purpose of performance evaluation, four professors from the Department of Computer Science and Engineering in Anna University were considered as experts in the C programming language and the ontology construction and alignment were based on the documents produced by these experts as well as the learners.

5.2 Results and Discussion: Learning Styles Identification

The experimental evaluation results shown in Figure 4 are obtained from the experiments conducted in this work on predicting the learning styles of

Figure 4. Three dimensional views of learners

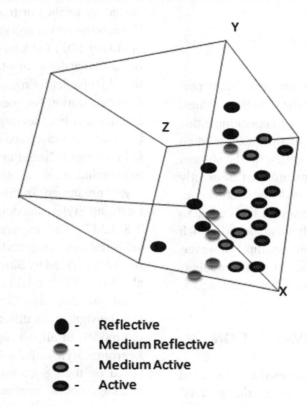

- ● - **Reflective**
- ● - **Medium Reflective**
- ◉ - **Medium Active**
- ◍ - **Active**

the learners through offline profile information and online web activity information. The learners provide their complete information through a web interface. Subsequent, they e-learn the 'C' programming language course contents in the textual format available in mediawiki e-learning servers. On successfully collecting and recording this information, the metric analyzer analyzes for the available metrics to be used for learning styles prediction.

In this experiment, the metrics include both the profile information and the online web activity information. With the help of these metrics, the fuzzy inference engine classifies the learners into four categories namely active, medium active, medium reflective and reflective. This fuzzy

inference engine makes use of a rule base fully loaded with 30 input and output fuzzy rules. The evaluation of the model was estimated in terms of percentage of accuracy. Figure 4 shows the three dimensional view of the different kinds of the categorized learners namely active, medium active, medium reflective, and reflective. The X, Y, Z axis represents the first three parameters described in Table 1.

5.3 Inference

The psychology of the learners may change periodically. Moreover, the learners tend towards a particular dimension depending on circumstances, mood and need. Therefore, tight coupling of learners to any of the two dimensions namely active or reflective may not be complete in e-contents recommendation to the learners. In such a scenario, the learners can be loosely categorized as more active and less reflective known as medium active and more reflective and less active known as medium reflective. Therefore, this work aims at resolving this 'unknown' category to be classified into any one of the four categories namely active, medium active, medium reflective and reflective, thereby increasing the accuracy percentage in predicting the learners based on their learning styles. The evaluation measure called accuracy is defined as the percentage of classified users belonging to a particular dimension. Table 5 shows the accuracy percentage of the various algorithms present in the literature.

From the Table 5 the accuracy in classifying the learners is found where the fuzzy logic based algorithm identifies four categories of learners namely active, medium active, medium reflective and reflective since fuzzy membership functions are used for refined classification. However, the other algorithms present in the literatures could identify only active and medium type of learners. The accuracy percentage of the other algorithms in comparison with the fuzzy logic algorithm is shown in Figure 5.

Hence, the objective of obtaining fine accuracy in the Learning Styles prediction of the uncertain learners who are learning through web environments has been achieved. The accuracy of the fuzzylogic algorithm is validated using precision performance measure.

5.4 Results and Discussion: Performance Evaluation

In this work, Ontology construction was carried out by using Jena programming toolkit in Java programming language. The experiments were repeated and tested with the approaches provided in S-Match, Content-match and MUPRET, in addition to the work discussed in this chapter. In all these experiments, documents were processed and Ontologies were constructed based on the E-Learning of C programming language concepts. The experimental results given below are obtained from the experiments conducted in this discussion works on evaluating the learning capability of students in learning the C language from e-contents. The students were made to learn the E-contents of the MediaWiki E-Learning server and are asked to produce a short written document on what they have learnt for the purpose ontology construction. Moreover, for the purpose of obtaining the degree of similarity/ conflict, a domain expert is also asked to produce a short written document on the same contents of C programming language. Separate ontologies were constructed for the documents produced by the students and domain experts. Following the ontology construction, these ontologies are aligned to check for the relationships indicated as equals, partialequals and conflicts. Subsequently, the degree of similarity/conflict was calculated. The experiments were carried out in several stages. In the first stage of experiments, the input documents from 30 students from each branch and 4 domain

Table 5. Accuracy of the classified users

Algorithms	Accuracy (%)			
	Active	Reflective	Medium Active	Medium Reflective
Bayesian	53	47	0	0
Bergasa	61	39	0	0
Deadband	65	35	0	0
Fuzzy logic	40	33	14	13

Figure 5. Learning style identification

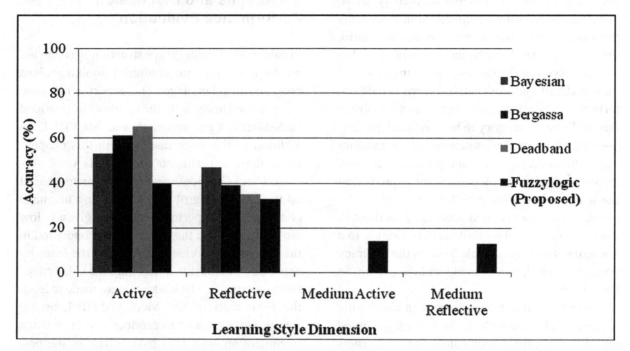

experts were tested and these experimental results alone are shown in this chapter. The evaluation of the framework was estimated in terms of the performance metrics namely precision, recall and specificity (Patel, Supekar, Lee, & Park, 2003). It is found that, the evaluation accuracy in terms of the above performance metrics given by the algorithm is better than the other existing algorithms and is shown in Figures 6-8. Subsequent experiments conducted with the rest of the students and domain experts also yielded the similar results.

The inference made by the authors from the experiments is that, the learners' level of understanding through E-Learning of C programming language is analyzed using Ontology Alignment techniques as indicated in the objectives of this chapter. In addition, the deontic rules derived from the documents aids in finding the degree of similarity/conflict of the documents produced by the students and domain experts is found by considering both the dominant and the non-dominant words occurring in the text documents. Hence, it is evident that almost all the concepts of the logic are covered namely equivalence, subsumption, unification and conflicts.

5.5 Inferences on Results

This work has been evaluated using Precision (PR), Recall (RE) andSpecificity (SP) metrics. Generally, Precision is the degree to which repeated experiments yield the same results under unchanged conditions. It is computed using the formula given in equation (8). In this work, Precision is measured as the ratio of the number of relationships correctly identified by the students to the total number of relationships present in the E-learning system considered for learning C language. Figure 6 shows the precision analysis for the results obtained from this work. From this figure, it can be observed that the precision of the Ontology Alignment technique is higher than

Figure 6. Precision evaluation

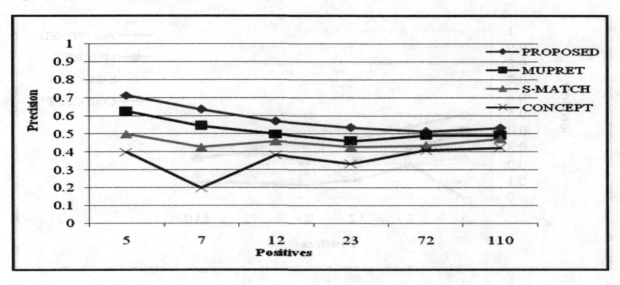

Figure 7. Recall evaluation

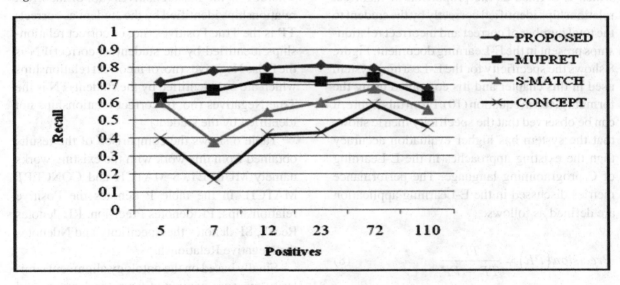

the other existing algorithms namely MUPRET, S-MATCH and CONCEPT-MATCH. This is due to the fact that the ontology alignment technique used in this work uses axioms from deontic logic for resolving the structural relationships in ontology construction and alignment. The second performance metric used in this chapter is Recall. In this work, recall is measured as the ratio of the

number of correctly identified relationships by the students to the total number of correct and incorrect relationships present in the E-Learning document and is computed using the formula given in equation (9). Figure 7 depicts the recall measure for the algorithm and compares it with the other existing algorithms. The third performance metric used in this work for analysis is specificity

Figure 8. Specificity evaluation

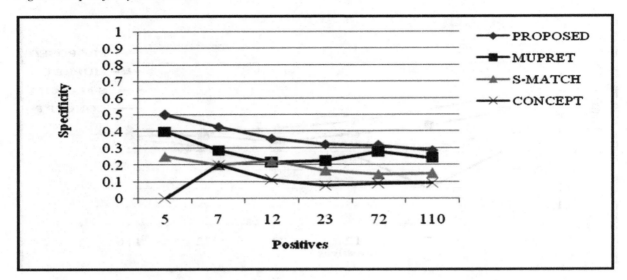

which is defined as the proportion of incorrect relationships identified correctly by the student to the total number of correct and incorrect relationships present in the E-Learning document. Figure 8 shows the specificity for the E-Learning system used in this chapter and it is computed using the formula given in equation (10). From this figure, it can be observed that the specificity metric shows that the system has higher evaluation accuracy than the existing approaches in the E-Learning of C programming language. The performance metrics discussed in the E-Learning application are defined as follows:

$$Precision\left(PR\right) = \frac{TP}{TP + FP} \qquad (8)$$

$$Recall\left(RE\right) = \frac{TP}{TP + FN} \qquad (9)$$

$$Specificity\left(SP\right) = \frac{TN}{TN + FP} \qquad (10)$$

where **FP** is the False Positives (no. of incorrect relationships identified by the student as correct) **TP** is the True Positives (no. of correct relationships identified by the student as correct) **FN** is the False Negatives (no. of incorrect relationships which are not identified by the student) **TN** is the True Negatives (no. of correct relationships not identified by the student)

Table 6 shows the comparison of the results obtained from this work with the existing works namely MURPET, S-MATCH and CONCEPT MATCH. In the table P denotes the Positive relationships, PR denotes Precision, RE denotes Recall, SP denotes the Specificity and **N** denotes the Negative Relationships.

Finally based on the ontology alignment similarity measure computed from the learners and domain expert ontology structure and the learners profile information the decisions are provided for the suitable recommendations on the methodology of learning to the learners. The metrics used for the decision making are ontology alignment similarity computation measure, learner profile information namely age, professional career, domain of interests and learning styles.

Table 6. Precision, recall and specificity evaluation results

P	N	PROPOSED							MUPRET							S-MATCH							CONCEPT-MATCH						
		TN	TP	FP	FN	PR	RE	SP	TN	TP	FP	FN	PR	RE	SP	TN	TP	FP	FN	PR	RE	SP	TN	TP	FP	FN	PR	RE	SP
5	3	2	5	2	2	0.71	0.71	0.5	2	5	3	3	0.62	0.62	0.4	1	3	3	2	0.5	0.6	0.25	0	2	3	3	0.4	0.4	0
7	4	3	7	4	2	0.63	0.77	0.42	2	6	5	3	0.54	0.66	0.28	1	3	4	5	0.42	0.37	0.2	1	1	4	5	0.2	0.16	0.2
12	6	5	12	9	3	0.57	0.8	0.35	3	11	11	4	0.5	0.73	0.21	2	6	7	5	0.46	0.54	0.22	1	5	8	7	0.38	0.41	0.11
23	9	9	22	19	5	0.53	0.81	0.32	6	18	21	7	0.46	0.72	0.22	4	15	20	10	0.42	0.6	0.16	2	12	24	16	0.33	0.42	0.077
72	18	31	71	67	18	0.51	0.79	0.31	27	68	70	24	0.49	0.73	0.27	12	55	71	26	0.43	0.67	0.14	7	50	72	35	0.41	0.58	0.08
110	25	37	105	92	50	0.53	0.67	0.28	31	95	98	55	0.49	0.63	0.24	16	82	91	65	0.47	0.55	0.15	9	64	87	75	0.42	0.46	0.09

6. CONCLUSION AND FUTURE WORKS

In this system, a new integrated E-learning management is discussed based on fuzzy logic and deontic logic for learning styles identification and ontology alignment technique for E-Learning of C Programming Language respectively. The main advantage of this approach is that recommendations of the learning contents to the e-learners are approrpiately provided. Moreover, it evaluates the learner performance based on both dominant and non-dominant words present in the documents produced by the learners. In addition, domain experts' advice is taken in the E-Learning evaluation for learning C programming language using E-Contents. The rules applied in this work considered comparison based on equals, partialequals and also conflicts which were not considered in the previous works. The performance accuracy in the evaluation of E-Learning of students obtained in this work is approximately 5% more than the existing systems and tools available in the current scenario.

The future work in the learning styles prediction system involves the implementation of a back propagation neural network algorithm in order to identify the learning style of a learner of an e-learning environment accurately. The current work in ontology construction provided a positive motivation and presents a wide research gap in the area of resolving cataphora in the raw text corpus which will be discussed in the future work. Moreover, the future work addresses the problem of resolving cataphora (twin domain of anaphora), where, the occurrence of the pronoun will be at an initial stage and the nouns (exact meaning of pronouns) shall be occurring later in a sentence. Future works in the direction of ontology alignment could be the provision of spatio-temporal extensions to the deontic logic in order to enhance the capability of the semantic analysis techniques.

REFERENCES

Assawamekin, N., Sunetnanta, T., & Pluempiti-wiriyawej, C. (2009). Ontology based multiple respective requirements traceability framework. *Knowledge and Information Systems Journal, 25*(3), 493-522.

Bateman, J.A. (2010). A linguistic ontology of space for natural language processing. *Journal of Artificial Intelligence, 174*(14), 1027-1071.

Berre, D. L. (2006). Monitoring and diagnosing software requirements. *Journal of Automated Software Engineering, 16*(1), 3–35.

Bodea, C., Dascalu, M., & Serbanati, L. D. (2012). An ontology-alignment based recommendation mechanism for improving the acquisition and implementation of managerial training services in project oriented organizations. In *Proceedings of IEEE International Conference and Workshops on Engineering of Computer Based Systems* (ECBS) (pp.257-266). Novi Sad, Serbia: ECBS. doi:10.1109/ECBS.2012.14

Budny, D. D., & Paul, C. (2003). Working with students and parents to improve the freshman retention. *Journal of Science, Mathematics, Engineering, and Technology Education, 4*(3&4), 45–53.

Carver, C. A., Howard, R. A., & Lane, W. D. (1999). Enhancing student learning through hypermedia courseware and incorporation of student learning styles. *IEEE Transactions on Education, 42*(1), 33–38. doi:10.1109/13.746332

Chen, S. M., & Chang, Y. C. (2011). Weighted fuzzy rule interpolation based on GA-based weight-learning techniques. *IEEE Transactions on Fuzzy Systems, 19*(4), 729–744. doi:10.1109/TFUZZ.2011.2142314

Cristani, M. (2008). Ontologies and e-learning: How to teach a classification. *Intelligent Information Technologies: Concepts, Methodologies, Tools, and Applications, 4*(2), 322–331. doi:10.4018/978-1-59904-941-0.ch017

Dahlem, N. (2011). OntoClippy: A user-friendly ontology design and creation methodology. *International Journal of Intelligent Information Technologies, 7*(1), 15–32. doi:10.4018/jiit.2011010102

De Marnee, M. C., & Manning, C. D. (2010). *Stanford typed dependencies manual*. Retrieved from http://www.mendeley.com/research/stanford-typed-dependencies-manual

Deborah, L. J., Baskaran, R., & Kannan, A. (2011). Ontology construction using computational linguistics for e-learning. In *Proceedings of the 2nd International Conference on Visual Informatics* (pp. 50-63). Kualalumpur, Malaysia: Springer.

Denis, P., & Baldridge, J. (2007). A ranking approach to pronoun resolution. In *Proceedings of IJCAI 2007* (pp.1588-1593). Hyderabad, India: IJCAI.

Doan, A., Madhavan, J., Dhamankar, R., Domingos, P., & Haley, A. Y. (2003). Learning to match ontologies on the semantic web. *The VLDB Journal, 12*(4), 303–319. doi:10.1007/s00778-003-0104-2

Dunn, R. (1990). Understanding the Dunn and Dunn learning styles model and needs for individual diagnosis and prescription, reading. *Writing and Learning Disabilities, 6*(3), 233–247.

Ehrig, M., & Staab, S. (2004). Efficiency of ontology mapping approaches. In *Proceedings of the International Workshop on Semantic Intelligent Middleware for the Web and the Grid* (pp.64-71). Valencia, Spain: Institute of Applied Informatics and Formal Description Methods.

Felder, R. M., & Silverman, L. K. (1988). Learning styles and teaching styles in engineering education. *English Education*, *78*(7), 674–681.

Geesaman, P. L., Cordy, J. R., & Zouaq, A. (2013). Light-weight ontology alignment using best-match clone detection. In *Proceedings of International Workshop on Software Clones* (pp.1-7). Antwerp, Belgium: IWSC. doi:10.1109/IWSC.2013.6613032

Gilbert, J. E., & Han, C. Y. (1999). Adapting instruction in search of a significant difference. *Journal of Network and Computer Applications*, *22*(3), 149–160. doi:10.1006/jnca.1999.0088

Giunchiglia, F., Autayeu, A., & Pane, J. (2010). *S-match: An open source framework for matching lightweight ontologies* (Technical Report # DISI-10-043). University of Trento.

Giunchiglia, F., Yatskevich, M., & Shvaiko, P. (2007). Semantic matching – Algorithms and implementation. *Journal on Data Semantics IX*, *4601*, 1–38. doi:10.1007/978-3-540-74987-5_1

Jan, S., Li, M., Al-Raweshidy, H., Mousavi, A., & Qi, M. (2012). Dealing With uncertain entities in ontology alignment using rough sets. *IEEE Transactions on Systems, Man and Cybernetics. Part C, Applications and Reviews*, *42*(6), 1600–1612. doi:10.1109/TSMCC.2012.2209869

Jean-Mary, Y. R., & Kabuka, M. R. (2007). AS-MOV: Results for OAEI 2008. In *Proceedings of ISWC 2007 Ontology Matching Workshop* (pp.132-139). Busan, Korea: OAEI.

Kim, J., & Storey, V. C. (2011). Construction of domain ontologies: Sourcing the world wide web. *International Journal of Intelligent Information Technologies*, *7*(2), 1–24. doi:10.4018/jiit.2011040101

Lee, T. B., Hendler, J., & Lassila, O. (2001). The semantic web. *Scientific American*, *284*(5), 34–43. doi:10.1038/scientificamerican0501-34 PMID:11396337

Lomuscio, A.R., & Sergot, M.J. (2003). Deontic interpreted systems. *The Dynamics of Knowledge*, *75*(1), 63-92.

Marjit, U., & Mandal, M. (2012). Multiobjective particle swarm optimization based ontology alignment. In *Proceedings of 2nd IEEE International Conference on Parallel Distributed and Grid Computing* (pp. 368-373). Himachal Pradesh, India: PDGC. doi:10.1109/PDGC.2012.6449848

Markert, K., & Nissim, M. (2005). Comparing knowledge sources for nominal anaphora resolution. *Association for Computational Linguistics*, *31*(3), 367–402. doi:10.1162/089120105774321064

Meng, S. K., & Chatwin, C. R. (2010). Ontology-based shopping agent for e-marketing. *International Journal of Intelligent Information Technologies*, *6*(2), 21–43. doi:10.4018/jiit.2010040102

Miller, G. A. (1995). WordNet: A lexical database for English. *Communications of the ACM*, *38*(11), 39–41. doi:10.1145/219717.219748

Papanikolaou, K. A., Grigoriadou, M., Magoulas, G. D., & Kornilakis, H. (2002). Towards new forms of knowledge communication: The adaptive dimension of a Web-based learning environment. *Computers & Education*, *39*(4), 333–360. doi:10.1016/S0360-1315(02)00067-2

Paredes, P., & Rodriguez, P. (2002). Considering sensing-intuitive dimension to exposition-exemplification in adaptive sequencing. In *Proceedings of AH2002 Conference* (pp. 556–559). Malaga, Spain: Adaptive Hypermedia and Adaptive Web-Based Systems. doi:10.1007/3-540-47952-X_83

Partyka, J., Alipanah, N., Khan, L., Thuraisingham, B., & Shekhar, S. (2008). Content-based ontology matching for GIS datasets. In *Proceedings of the International Conference on Advances in Geographic Information Systems* (pp.407-410). New York: Academic Press.

Patel, C., Supekar, K., Lee, Y., & Park, E. K. (2003). OntoKhoj: A semantic web portal for ontology searching, ranking and classification. In *Proceedings of the 5th ACM CIKM International Workshop on Web Information and Data Management* (pp. 58-61). ACM. doi:10.1145/956708.956712

Perez, A. G., Lopez, M. F., & Corcho, O. (2003). *Ontological engineering*. Retrieved from http://www.imamu.edu.sa/topics/IT/IT%206/Ontological%20/Engineering.pdf

Poernomo, I., Umarov, T., & Hajiyev, F. (2011). Formal ontologies for data-centric business process management. In *Proceedings of International Conference on Application of Information and Communication Technologies* (pp. 1-8). AICT. doi:10.1109/ICAICT.2011.6110897

Sanders, D. A., & Suso, J. B. (2010). Inferring learning style from the way students interact with a computer user interface and the WWW. *IEEE Transactions on Education*, *53*(4), 613–620. doi:10.1109/TE.2009.2038611

Suso, J. B., Sanders, D. A., & Tewkesbury, G. E. (2005). Intelligent browser-based systems to assist Internet users. *IEEE Transactions on Education*, *48*(4), 580–585. doi:10.1109/TE.2005.854570

Tang, J., Li, J., Liang, B., Huang, X., Li, Y., & Wang, K. (2006). Using Bayesian decision for ontology mapping. *Journal of Web Semantics: Science, Services and Agents on the World Wide Web, 4*(4), 243-262.

Triantafillou, E., Pomportsis, A., & Georgiadou, E. (2002). AES-CS: Adaptive educational system based on cognitive styles. In *Proceeding of AH2002 Workshop on Recommendation and Personalization in Ecommerce* (pp. 10–20). Malaga, Spain: Universidad de Málaga, Departamento de Lenguajes y Ciencias de la Computación.

Wagatsuma, K., Goto, Y., & Cheng, J. (2012). Formal analysis of cryptographic protocols by reasoning based on deontic relevant logic: A case study in Needham-Schroeder shared-key protocol. In *Proceedings of International Conference on Machine Learning and Cybernetics* (ICMLC) (pp. 1866-1871). ICMLC. doi:10.1109/ICMLC.2012.6359660

Wang, P., & Xu, B. (2007). LILY: The results for the ontology alignment contest OAEI 2007. In *Proceedings of ISWC 2007 Ontology Matching Workshop* (pp.167-175), Busan, Korea: OAEI.

Winograd, T. (1972). *Understanding natural language*. New York, NY: Academic Press.

KEY TERMS AND DEFINITIONS

Artificial Intelligence: Artificial intelligence is the branch of computer science concerned with making computers behave like humans. It is concerned with providing intelligence to machines.

Deontic Logic: Deontic logic is the field of logic that is concerned with expressions of obligation, permission, and forbidden concepts. A deontic logic is alternatively defined as a formal system that attempts to capture the essential logical features of these concepts and their relationships.

E-Learning Management System: E-learning management system is a software application that administers, documents, track information, report analysis and the delivery of e-learning education contents or learning materials.

Knowledge Representation: Knowledge representation is the subfield of artificial intelligence that is devoted to the representation and storage of information about the world in a comfortable form that a computer system can utilize to solve complex tasks such as medical diagnosis, natural language processing.

Learning Styles: Learning style is an individual's natural pattern of acquiring and processing information in learning situations.

Logic: The study of the principles of reasoning, especially of the structure of propositions as distinguished from their content and of method and validity in deductive reasoning.

Ontology Alignment: Ontology alignment also called as ontology matching, is the systematic process of determining correspondences between concepts. A set of various correspondences among the concepts, subconcepts, properties and instances is also called an alignment.

Ontology: An ontology is a formal description or a formal specification of a program or the entities in the form of concepts, subconcepts, properties, instances and relationships among them.

Chapter 3
Evaluation of Topic Models as a Preprocessing Engine for the Knowledge Discovery in Twitter Datasets

Stefan Sommer
Telekom Deutschland GmbH, Germany

Tom Miller
T-Systems Multimedia Solutions GmbH, Germany

Andreas Hilbert
Technische Universität Dresden, Germany

ABSTRACT

In the World Wide Web, users are an important information source for companies or institutions. People use the communication platforms of Web 2.0, for example Twitter, in order to express their sentiments of products, politics, society, or even private situations. In 2014, the Twitter users worldwide submitted 582 million messages (tweets) per day. To process the mass of Web 2.0's data (e.g. Twitter data) is a key functionality in modern IT landscapes of companies or institutions, because sentiments of users can be very valuable for the development of products, the enhancement of marketing strategies, or the prediction of political elections. This chapter's aim is to provide a framework for extracting, preprocessing, and analyzing customer sentiments in Twitter in all different areas.

INTRODUCTION

Twitter is one of the fastest growing social network platforms in the world. In 2014 the social network consists of over two billion users, which submit 582 million messages per day (Twopcharts, 2014). In comparison to 2011 the number of users increased by factor four and the amount of tweets per day increased by factor 5 (Stieglitz, Krüger, Eschmeier, 2011). By using Twitter people share news, information or sentiments in a short message, which is limited to 140 characters, named tweet. Twitter is

DOI: 10.4018/978-1-4666-6639-9.ch003

a so-called microblog, a special kind of a blog that combines an ordinary blog with features of social networks. The communication platforms of Web 2.0 gain in importance, as interaction increases between users through these media (Stephen & Toubia, 2010). Due to the positive development of microblogs and Twitter in particular, these services become a valuable source for companies or institutions (Pak & Paroubek, 2010; Barnes & Böhringer, 2011).

Today users are considered to be key communication partners for companies: providing relevant feedback, requests, and testimonials to the company's performance, a political party or an institution (Richter, Koch, Krisch, 2007; Tumasjan et al., 2010; Sommer et al., 2012). They share their sentiments with other users through the communication platforms of Web 2.0 (Jansen, Zhang, Sobel, Chowdury, 2009). By spreading their thoughts through platforms, such as blogs, communities, or social networks, users influence other users in the process of their own sentiment creation (O'Connor, Balasubramanyan, Routledge, Smith, 2010). But how to deal with this huge amount of unstructured or semi-structured data of social networks within a complex IT infrastructure?

Our research aim is to provide a preprocessing framework for Twitter data, which extracts, transforms and supplies the relevant tweets of a huge amount of data in order to make the data applicable for sentiment analysis. The framework can be used for different approaches and areas. On the one hand to enhance the company's products e.g. by adding mandatory features and finally involving users in the product development as so-called 'prosumers'. On the other hand to optimizing the company's marketing activities by analyzing which advertising is most discussed or referenced in the Web 2.0 platforms, especially in the case of viral marketing (Jansen et al., 2009; Lee, Jeong, Lee, 2008; Liu, Hu, Cheng, 2005). Other examples show the use of Twitter to predict the voters' opinion in political elections (Tumasjan et

al., 2010). In this chapter, we focus on the evaluation of our framework, which is based on topic models. Our Twitter dataset for the evaluation contains tweets covering the TV debate between the candidates for the election of the Deutsche Bundestag in Germany.

RELATED WORK

In the last five years many articles have been published in the area of Sentiment Analysis. Liu (2007) gives a broad overview of characteristics, tasks and methods of Sentiment Analysis and places them into the context of Web Data Mining. Next to the theoretical descriptions of Liu (2007) you can find various articles covering different existing Sentiment Analysis systems, which are systematically presented by Lee et al. (2008), as Table 1 shows.

A direct comparison of the performance of these systems is difficult, because the test datasets are not equal and the extraction methods are very different. Nevertheless, Lee et al. (2008) state that systems, which are using syntactic analysis tend to obtain better results regarding the extraction of sentiment expressions. Further information about the systems can be found in Lee et al. (2008) or in the research of authors of the different systems (Dave, Lawrence, & Pennock, 2003; Liu et al., 2005; Yi, Niblack, 2005; Popescu & Etzioni, 2007; Scaffidi et al., 2007).

Due to the popularity of microblogs and Twitter, in particular, there are many papers covering this research area. Böhringer & Gluchowski (2009) describe the microblogging service Twitter, and how users are able to communicate with each other by using this platform. Tweets can contain different content, for example short expressions about the user's personal situation, but also sentiments of or testimonials on products, services or even political parties and personal situations. It is interesting to analyze this content in order to get useful insights into users' sentiments. Hence,

Table 1. An overview of current Sentiment Analysis systems (modified by Lee et al., 2008)

System	Sentiment Resource	Syntactic Analysis	Extracting Sentiment Expression		Presentation
			Feature Extraction	**Sentiment Assignment**	
Review Seer (2003)	Thumbs up/down	No	Probabilistic model Naïve Bayes Classifier		List sentences containing the feature term
Red Opal (2007)	Star rating	No	Frequent noun and noun phrase	Average star rating	Order products by scoring each feature
Opinion Observer (2004)	Linguistic resource	Yes	CBA miner Infrequent feature selection	WordNet exploring the dominant polarity of each phrase	Bar graph
WebFountain (2005)	Linguistic resource	Yes	bBNP heuristic	Sentiment lexicon Sentiment pattern database	List sentences which bear a sentiment for a product
OPINE (2005)			Web PMI	Relaxation labeling	N/A

many researchers analyze Twitter posts and show their results: The objectives of this analysis reach from general insights to concrete extractions of sentiments and their application in a special area. Oulasvirta, Lehtonen, Esko, Kurvinen & Raento (2010) explain common findings, such as the characteristics of users' self-disclosures, and they explored the behavior of microblog users publishing current events and experiences. However, Golder & Macy (2011) show differences in the diurnal mood of Twitter users. They state that individual mood is an indicator for well-being, working memory, creativity and the immune system. With this knowledge they want to draw inferences about the health status of users. In contrast to these general insights, many researchers use Twitter in more specific case studies in order to reveal the sentiments of the tweet authors. In this context the most popular aim is to extract political sentiments (O'Connor, 2010; Tumasjan, Sprenger, Sandner, Welpe, 2010; Chung & Mustafaraj, 2011). For example, Tumasjan et al. (2010) want to answer the question, whether the expressed sentiments in Twitter are able to mirror the real sentiment of voters. They come to the conclusion that the content of Twitter entries can represent the political attitude of the users. The example shows that Twitter is a valuable resource for important insights into users' sentiments, not only for political expressions, but also for expressions about products or society topics.

Before we are able to analyze the different expressions in the tweets, we have to deal with the huge amount of tweets and the selection of relevant content which is required for sentiment analysis. In the first step we use our Twitter crawler, which accesses the Twitter API to select the relevant tweets by a keyword search. After different steps of data cleaning and data transformation, we secondly want to separate the posts into groups corresponding to specific topics. For this separation we use generative topic models. Blei & Lafferty (2009) give a fundamental explanation of topic models and their usage. In their work they adapt topic models to a digital archive of the journal 'Science', which contains articles from 1980 to 2002. Searching for interesting articles within this huge amount of information can be difficult. Therefore, they postulate the possibility of exploring this collection through the underlying topics in the articles. With probabilistic topic models they are able to automatically detect a structure of topics in this collection, even without manually constructed training data. In the case of the 'Science' archive Blei & Lafferty (2009) found 50 topics corresponding to the articles. So, while searching for documents, scientists are able to browse through a list of similar documents that deal with the same topic.

Since their publication, topic models have been successfully used by other authors in order to identify topics. There are also researchers who have used topic models to analyze tweets. Ramage, Dumais, & Liebling (2010) detect dimensions of content in Twitter entries with the help of topic models. They introduce five dimensions, in which Twitter content can be matched. For example, the dimension 'substance' contains expressions with generally interesting meanings; they have found words like 'president', 'American', and 'country' for this dimension. Another dimension is called 'status' and they have detected words like 'still', 'doing', and 'sleep', which express the current situation of the user. With this partially supervised approach Ramage et al. (2010) show the distribution of these five dimensions for specific Twitter users in order to get an idea of the user's tweeting behavior. However, Zhao et al. (2011) used unsupervised topic modeling on a Twitter dataset. They aim for an empiric comparison of Twitter content and a traditional news medium. They have adopted topic models on both the Twitter content and the New York Times news. Afterwards, they have compared the topics and have focused on the differences between them. As a result, Zhao et al. (2011) have found out that Twitter users actively and rapidly spread news of important or extraordinary events. Twitter is a popular data source, because of the great number of text posts and the heterogeneous audience (Pak & Paroubek, 2010). In addition to that, in Twitter, users express a certain sentiment about different topics, so it is possible to analyze their sentiments regarding those topics. In this context, Pak & Paroubek (2010) have shown examples of entries

with expressed sentiments in order to demonstrate the high potential of sentiment analysis in tweets. Tumasjan et al. (2010) have used 100,000 tweets for revealing political sentiment in Germany. They have figured out that the majority of the analyzed tweets reflect voter preferences and even come close to traditional election polls. Users not only express their sentiments, but also discuss them with other users. Beside the content-based analysis of a microblog, the social network structure of Twitter also yields valuable information about a person's behavior. Heinrich (2011), for example, have analyzed relationships in Twitter, which predict the reference potential of a person as a determinant of the grade of opinion leadership and social centrality. Filtering those important users, helps to reduce the amount of Twitter updates that one has to scan and monitor over time while researching dynamic effects in topic and sentiment trends. These approaches illustrate the capabilities that topic modeling offers for uncovering latent structure in text documents.

Our final step in preparing the Twitter dataset for sentiment analysis is to evaluate the performance of our topic modeling approach. The commonly used evaluation metric for topic models is the document held-out probability (Wallach et al., 2009). This metric measures the probability that a trained topic model could not classify an unseen document. In our work, this evaluation approach is called "extrinsic", because the evaluation is done on external objects – the unseen documents. On the one hand the extrinsic evaluation will be the right approach, if the topic models application domain is focused on the classification aspect of the topic model. On the other hand, if the application domain focuses the topics themselves, the evaluation will be done in an "intrinsic" way. In that case, "intrinsic" means that the evaluation focuses on the words of the topics and the topics semantic nature. Newman, Lau, Grieser, Baldwin (2010) "proposed the novel task of topic coherence evaluation as a form of intrinsic topic evaluation".

RESEARCH APPROACH

In this chapter we emphasize on the evaluation of our preprocessing framework for Twitter datasets. The basis of our preprocessing framework is our developed algorithm, which is able to identify microblog entries (tweets) containing sentiments in a particular context (Sommer, Schieber, Heinrich, Hilbert, 2012). The evaluation of the algorithm is mandatory as we need to be able to analyze the performance of our preprocessing approach. We follow in our research the design science approach by Hevner, March, Park, Ram (2004). The purpose of Hevner's approach is gaining new insights by developing an artifact that solves a specific problem. In our case the specific problem is the preprocessing of Twitter datasets in order to gain insights into the user's sentiments or testimonials in different areas. In this chapter we focus on the sentiments of users during the election of the Deutsche Bundestag in Germany. With our approach we give answers to the following research questions:

1.   How does the preprocessing framework for knowledge discovery in Twitter datasets works?
2.   What kinds of criteria or metrics exist to evaluate topic models as basis of the preprocessing framework?
3.   What are the results of the evaluation regarding to our example of the TV debate between the candidates for the election of the Deutsche Bundestag in Germany?

The first question covers the composition of the different components of our framework and how these work together. It describes a powerful technique, which is able to automatically create topic clusters out of a huge amount of textual data by analyzing terms that co-occur with other terms. The algorithm is the basis of our framework. The second and third question deals with the problem how to evaluate topic models in this special case.

We discuss different critiera and metrics for an evaluation and calculate them for our example of the TV debate.

PREPROCESSING FRAMEWORK FOR SENTIMENT ANALYSIS IN TWITTER

Knowledge Discovery in Databases

In order to build a framework to extract, transform and analyze Twitter datasets we align our approach to the process of Knowledge-Discovery-in-Databases (KDD), which is widely accepted by academics and practitioners. It was published by Fayyad (1996) and shows the nontrivial process of identifying patterns in huge amounts of data. Following Azevedo & Santos (2008), other approaches for pattern recognition in datasets such as SEMMA or CRISP-DM can be referred in the implementation of the KDD process by Fayyad (1996). The KDD process contains five stages: Selection, Preprocessing, Transformation, Data Mining, and Interpretation.

The first stage in the KDD process contains the selection of the target dataset, which can be an entire dataset, a subset of variables, or data samples. In the next two stages (Preprocessing and Transformation) the target data is prepared for the data-mining methods. Data cleaning and transformation algorithms provide consistent data for example by purging double entries, filtering outliers, reducing dimensionality or creating new variables. The fourth stage includes the analysis of the preprocessed and transformed data in order to gain patterns of interest in a particular form, depending on the analysis objective. These patterns have to be evaluated and interpreted for the purpose of generating knowledge in the last stage (Azevedo & Santos, 2008; Fayyad, 1996).

The KDD process is iterative. So if necessary, it is possible to improve the results by enhancing the activities within the earlier stages. The five stages in the KDD process lead the data analyst from the raw datasets to significant patterns and formerly unknown insights.

Knowledge Discovery in Twitter Datasets

To adopt the KDD process for the analysis of Twitter datasets we have to consider some changes referring to the special capabilities and challenges of the medium Twitter. Böhringer & Gluchowski (2009) introduce the microblogging service Twitter and its functionalities: First, Twitter users can communicate with each other by referencing the name of the communication partner with a prefixed '@'. For example, user A writes an entry containing '@userB' in order to address user B. In addition, users can distribute the entry of another user by forwarding this entry with the prefixed characters 'RT'. For example, in order to forward the origin entry 'tweet' of user A user B publishes the tweet with 'RT @userA tweet'. In this way, the range of an expression is increased, which ultimately will benefit the reputation of the original author. Finally, there is a very important function of microblogs: the tagging of the entries. Authors can tag their entries by adding keywords to the tweet. These keywords are called hashtags and can be recognized by the prefixed '#'. In summary, the technical functionalities of Twitter provide several possibilities for analysis. The character limitation of 140 characters leads to the main challenge in the analysis of microblogs. In order to write as much information as possible users tend to use abbreviations (for example, '4ever' is used as an abbreviation for 'forever'). In addition, the informal way of speaking in microblogs and syntactic errors complicate the mining procedure. In contrast, Bermingham & Smeaton (2010) consider the short length to be a strength of microblogs, because the limited text can contain compact and explicit sentiments. In their paper they have found classifying sentiments in microblogs easier to mine than in blogs.

Therefore, the brevity might be an advantage, too. The modified process for knowledge discovery in Twitter datasets is shown in figure 1.

The first stage in the knowledge discovery process for Twitter datasets contains the selection of the target data, as shown in figure 2. We have implemented a Twitter crawler as a prototype, which accesses the open Twitter API to select our target data of the complete raw Twitter data. With the crawler we are able to gather a huge analysis corpus of tweets. The crawler searches recursive via the Twitter API for user selected keywords and stores the raw Twitter data in a database.

The crawler can process several Twitter search jobs in a parallel operating mode, as shown in figure 3. We are also able to extract the relationship between Twitter users corresponding to the tweets. The job overview is divided into search jobs or relationship jobs.

After the selection of our target data, we have to perform some data cleaning and transformation tasks in the next two stages. We have to point out that our data cleaning and transformation tasks focus on the relevant task to perform the topic modeling for our preprocessing framework. For a sentiment analysis the additional transformation and tasks might be added to our process, which, for instance, has been already discussed by Kaufmann (2010), Parikh & Movassate (2009), Lee et al. (2008) and Lo, He, Ounis (2005). The dataset contains only textual content from tweets. Thus, we have only one variable. In order to obtain useful results, we process the data and filter some parts form each entry in the second stage of our preprocessing framework. The data cleaning tasks start in the first step with the tokenization of each tweet. We use the whitespace-tokenization to keep hashtags (e.g. #Merkel) and links with the URL as separate tokens. In the next step we filter these hashtags and links with regular expressions as discrete entities. These entities are removed from the dataset for the topic modeling, but we keep the entities as own variables stored in order to perform sentiment analysis in later stages. In

Figure 1. Preprocessing framework for Twitter datasets

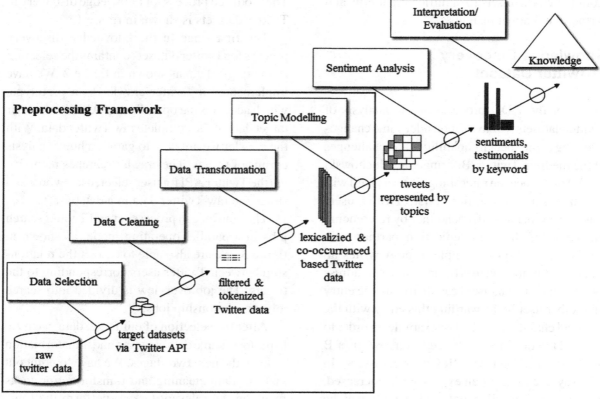

Figure 2. Prototype: Data selection for Twitter crawling job

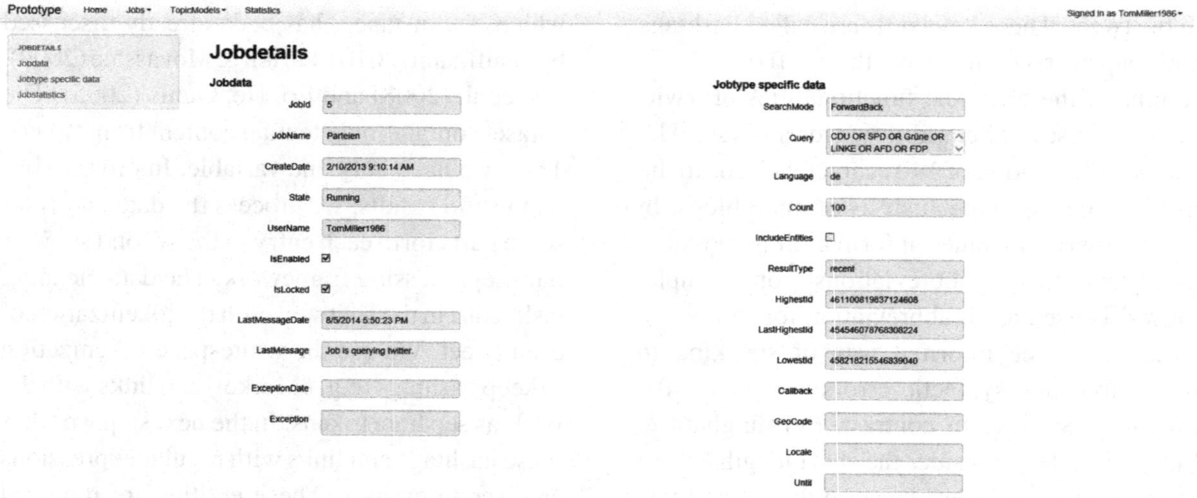

Figure 3. Prototype: Overview of Twitter crawling jobs

Prototype	Home	Jobs ▾	TopicModels ▾	Statistics				Signed in as TomMiller1986 ▾

Jobs
TwitterSearchJobs
TwitterRelationshipJobs

TwitterSearchJobs

JobName	State	IsEnabled	IsLocked	CreateDate	LastMessage	LastMessageDate	SearchMode	
Playstation	Running	True	True	12/18/2013 12:00:00 AM	Job is querying twitter.	8/5/2014 5:51:07 PM	ForwardBack	Actions▾
Xbox	Running	True	True	12/18/2013 5:15:05 PM	Job is querying twitter.	8/5/2014 5:50:38 PM	ForwardBack	Actions▾
Xbox_Playstation	Canceled	False	False	1/16/2014 12:00:00 AM	Job has been canceled.		None	Actions▾
BMW i3	Running	True	True	2/19/2014 12:00:00 AM	Job is querying twitter.	8/5/2014 5:51:03 PM	ForwardBack	Actions▾
Parteien	Running	True	True	2/10/2014 9:10:14 AM	Job is querying twitter.	8/5/2014 5:50:23 PM	ForwardBack	Actions▾
Daniela_Smileys	Running	True	True	4/8/2014 4:29:19 PM	Job is querying twitter.	8/5/2014 5:50:58 PM	ForwardBack	Actions▾
Daniela_VW	Running	True	True	4/8/2014 4:36:18 PM	Job is querying twitter.	8/5/2014 5:50:53 PM	ForwardBack	Actions▾
BMW	Running	True	True	4/30/2014 11:41:23 AM	Job sleeps now for 300 seconds.	8/5/2014 5:49:29 PM	Forward	Actions▾
Audi	Running	True	True	4/30/2014 11:42:20 AM	Job sleeps now for 300 seconds.	8/5/2014 5:50:04 PM	Forward	Actions▾
Mercedes	Running	True	True	4/30/2014 11:44:52 AM	Job sleeps now for 300 seconds.	8/5/2014 5:46:15 PM	Forward	Actions▾
News	Running	True	True	5/23/2014 9:50:09 AM	Job sleeps now for 300 seconds.	8/5/2014 5:46:24 PM	Forward	Actions▾

the next step we filter non-relevant text components such as stopwords, the keywords of our search string, single characters or numbers and cross-references to other users (e.g. @userA). The cross-references to other users are also stored separate for network analysis in posterior stages. In the last step of the data cleaning we eliminate spam and advertising tweets form our dataset. We use a combination of regular expressions together with duplicate detection to identify spam or advertising tweets. This approach filters some of the unwanted tweets, but there is still a potential for optimization. The result of this stage is an adjusted corpus collection of our previous Twitter dataset. In the transformation process we firstly apply our vocabulary automatically. Afterwards we transform our corpus by lexicalizing it to the vocabulary. The results of this stage are yield co-occurrence-based data in order to perform our algorithm for building the topic models.

The next step contains the topic modeling of the tweets. We implement the LDA algorithm by Blei, Ng and Jordan (2003) in order to identify topic clusters in our Twitter datasets. Sommer et al. (2012) successful implemented the LDA algorithm for preprocessing Twitter datasets. Figure 4 shows the results of the LDA algorithm in the frontend of our prototype. Blei et al. (2003) introduced

Figure 4. Prototype: Resulting topic models after the LDA

Prototype	Home	Jobs ▾	TopicModels ▾	Statistics	Signed in as TomMiller1986 ▾

Topics

Id	Alpha	TotalTokens	Titles	
0	1	47905	das ist ein so wie ja gut war sehr auch aber doch wäre schon ganz der klar da schön plakat	Actions▾
1	1	49073	in am heute piraten nach dem cdu in die und bayern piratenpartei im morgen mit auf beim infostand kommt forum wieder	Actions▾
2	1	42873	csu der aus mit dem cdu in die und bayern seehofer von sieht weg im raus über müssen hessen will	Actions▾
3	1	49721	nicht man sie die sich kann wenn dass wie muss sein das so werden dann wird nur cdu wählen sollte	Actions▾
4	1	47450	die wir sind haben piraten und sie uns alle auch werden viele wieder wollen plakate parteien können ihre schon machen	Actions▾
5	1	46301	die piraten bei wahl linke mir und partei wahllokal cdu mit mal wählen vor beim mein sagt ergebnis soll dann	Actions▾
6	1	45195	afd der auf die deutschland euro für lucke in über btw gegen via partei alternative wahlkampf nach vor chef griechenland	Actions▾
7	1	45735	die und den an für auf von sich spd grünen zu cdu macht danke der hat stimmen zwischen einen linken	Actions▾
8	1	41863	im grüne de ein und für zum auf mit at frage ins wollen an thema neue newsflash aws it hallo	Actions▾
9	1	49189	tvduell merkel cdu spd steinbrück hat tv vertrauen frau duell koalition peer btw angela spricht wird maut große zdf keine	Actions▾
10	1	43452	in für der grüne gegen linke syrien eine des ohne politiker cdu deutschland ab kein und von keine fordert krieg	Actions▾
11	1	44716	btw cdu spd grüne linke fdp für und csu zur wahlkampf ueberzeugtuns gute alle bahr gruene politik bundestagswahl arbeit menschen	Actions▾
12	1	43313	fdp und mit npd für der quark wahlkampf haben familie was spd gemeinsam fail ein via eine wirbt oh werben	Actions▾
13	1	50717	ich nicht mich piraten bin wählen aber habe auch mal ja hab mir dass würde da meine schon noch so	Actions▾
14	1	47627	die nicht als mehr ist auch zu nur aber noch ja sind das viel besser keine immer leider gar sondern	Actions▾
15	1	47878	die was hat das ist wer oder da doch eigentlich warum denn er nicht eine wählt alles nichts schon macht	Actions▾
16	1	45621	der von in mit bei den cdu einer einem unter wurde an wird hier gerade eine einen ein dem durch	Actions▾
17	1	44192	spd will rot vor der grün steinbrück grüne und nach berlin von schwarz mindestlohn programm tage des auf bundestagswahl dpa	Actions▾
18	1	44274	piraten der den auf im zu über von zur bei nsa zum om bundestag gegen video wegen des ein twitter	Actions▾
19	1	47054	es ihr du zu geht gibt um noch eine mal und dann wenn euch nur bitte hier liebe jetzt machen	Actions▾

Topic Models as a powerful technique for finding useful structure in an otherwise unstructured collection of data. Topic models are probabilistic models for unsupervised uncovering the underlying semantic structure of a document collection (e.g. Twitter). With the special characteristics of tweets in mind several approaches have to be validated for our purpose of analyzing sentiments in Twitter entries that are related to a certain topic. Therefore we have to assign a certain probability to those documents that are likely to represent such a topic. We therefore only discuss methods that are probabilistic in their approach. Well-known methods like 'tf-idf' are only suitable in a preprocessing manner because next to the fact that it is not probabilistic, it also holds a small amount of reduction which would lead to unsatisfying scaling behavior with the fast-growing database of Twitter streams. The 'pLSI' model by Hofmann (1999), while probabilistic in its nature, lacks a representation on a document level. This fact is quite important when looking at our research goal of not only exploring topics and filtering them according to our interests, but also using the method for representing those documents in terms of topics so that we can reduce the amount of data that is generated by the Twitter entries.

EVALUATION

Selection of Evaluation Criteria and Metrics

The first in the evaluation of our preprocessing is to select criteria and metrics that that divide "good" from "bad" topic models in sense of our intrinsic perspective. The selection of criteria for the intrinsic evaluation is done in an inductive way. Consequently, only a topic model with the most essential data transformation and data cleaning is required. We used the "MALLET topic modeling toolkit" by McCallum et al. (2002) generating the LDA model. The only preparation that we did beforehand was the transformation to lowercase-strings and the filtering of all non-latin-characters, except ß, ä, ü and ö.

The underlying data has been collected during the Bundestag elections in Germany in the week before the TV debate between chancellor Angela Merkel (CDU) and the challenger Peer Steinbrück (SPD). In the following table, three example topics of the generated model are represented:

The first criterion for the intrinsic evaluation is the interpretability. This is obvious by comparing topic one and topic three. Nearly all terms within topic one are forming a meaningful topic. E.g. "frau", "angela", "merkel" and "cdu" refer to the chancellor and "peer", "steinbrück" and "spd" apply to the challenger. The TV debate is characterized by "tvduell", "tv", "btw" and "zdf". The terms "keine", "maut", "große" and "koalition" referring to two of the main issues of the TV debate. In contrast, no combination of the words within topic three makes sense.

The second criterion is the importance of words. Topic three contains only meaningless, but frequently used words – so called stopwords. Those words have no importance for the topics, because they are not delivering any valuable input. Even worse, due to the limitation of representative words for a topic, those stopwords are wasted space. A good topic model would not contain any meaningless words. Thus, the importance of words is added to the criteria that should be evaluated.

The last criterion in this chapter is the separation of topics. A topic model that separates different contents to different topics is better than a topic model that mixes different contents. The second topic of our example (Table 2) contains content about a German party called "AFD – Alternative für Deutschland". This topic is clearly separated from the TV debate topic and also separated from the "stopwords" topic. If the content of topic two

Table 2. Topic model example

Topic	Terms of the Topics in Descending Order of Their Weight
1	tvduell merkel cdu spd steinbrück hat tv vertrauen frau duell koalition peer btw angela spricht wird maut große zdf keine
2	afd der auf die deutschland euro für lucke in über btw gegen via partei alternative wahlkampf nach vor chef griechenland
3	die nicht als mehr ist auch zu nur aber noch ja sind das viel besser keine immer leider gar sondern

mixed into topic one, misinterpretation of this mixed topic would happen, because the AFD was neither represented in the TV debate by a challenger nor an aspect of the debate. A model that avoids this type of misinterpretation is obviously a better one. Depending on the model being evaluated more or different criteria can be used.

Newman et al. (2010) evaluates various metrics for the measurement of "topic coherence", which is in substance the same as the interpretability in this paper. In their work the "best-performing method was term co-occurrence within Wikipedia based on pointwise mutual information" (Newman et al., 2010). Therefore, for each pairwise combination of the terms from one topic, the pointwise mutual information (PMI)-value is calculated. This calculation is done on the basis of all Wikipedia articles. If a combination of two terms occurs often within a sliding window of ten words, this combination gets a higher PMI-value than a combination that co-occurs rarely. Co-occurring terms tend to be a good indicator for interpretable combinations. To obtain a topic-level-value for the criterion interpretability the average over all combinations of that topic is formed. For the model-level-value all topic-values are calculated as the mean and as the average over all topic-values. For the criterion importance of words two possible metrics were proposed. The first one is the well-known "tf-idf" measure by Salton & McGill (1983). The second metric is an adapted form of the Kullback-Leibler-Divergence (KLD), which

was described by Lo et al. (2005). Both metrics had been applied to a Wikipedia basis, and a basis that has been formed of all crawled tweets. In the same way that the interpretability-value is calculated from word-level to model-level, the tf-idf-values and the KLD-values are calculated as the average from word- to topic-level and from topic-level to the model-level, the average and the mean is calculated. The separation of topics is measured by the inverse cosine similarity. The popular cosine similarity measures the similarity between two vectors, and since the topics of a topic model are word-vectors, this is a practicable option. The model-level-value for separation of topics is also calculated as the average, and the mean of the inverse cosine similarity values on topic-level.

The selection of the metrics is done in a procedure presented by Newman et al. (2010). Therefore, $N = 5$ users had to score 13 different LDA models, while each LDA model consists of 10 topics with 20 words. The users have scored the three identified criteria interpretability, importance of words and separation of topics on a three-point-scale from 1 … topic is not interpretable / word is unimportant / topics are not clearly separated to 3 … topic is interpretable / word is important for the topic / topics are clearly separated. On top of the user-scores the gold standard for the evaluation is built as the inter annotator agreement (IAA). The 13 topic models are different in the parameters stopword count and use white list. Stopword count sets the

Table 3. Parameterization of the user-evaluated LDA models

Id	1	2	3	4	5	6	7	8	9	10	11	12	13
#stop words	0	50	100	200	300	400	500	50	100	200	300	400	500
whitelist	☒	☒	☒	☒	☒	☒	☒	☑	☑	☑	☑	☑	☑

number of words that should be filtered by the stopword filter and the use white list parameter turns the white list on and off.

The 13 LDA models that have been scored by the users were also evaluated by the preselected metrics of section 6.2. For all criterion scores of each LDA model a spearman's rank correlation coefficient (RCC) was calculated. For each criterion the metric with the highest RCC between the IAA and the metric itself was selected as the preferred evaluation-metric.

For interpretability the PMI approach on Wikipedia basis with calculating the median, to get the interpretability value on model level, was selected. The "tf-idf" metric on Wikipedia basis with calculating the average over all topics was chosen for the importance of words criterion. This combination of metric, database and building the

model-value reaches nearly a perfect representation of the IAA. For separation of topics the average inverse cosine similarity values of all topic combinations within one model was selected.

Evaluation

The last part of the framework, besides the criteria and the metrics, is the topic model scorecard. The idea of the topic model scorecard is to aggregate the individual criteria to one meaningful value – the topic model score. Before the aggregation, all measurements within one criterion and over all evaluated topic models have to be normalized. This normalization is fundamental to the ability to compare the different criterion values. The topic model score is aggregated as the product of the weighted topic model criterion values. E.g. within

Table 4. Spearman's rank correlation coefficients between inter annotator agreement and the preselected metrics

Criterion	Databasis	Metric	Topic-Level to Model-Level	RCC
Interpretability	Wikipedia	PMI	Ø	0.4560
			Median	**0.6154**
Importance of words	Twitter	Tf-idf	Ø	-0.0055
			Median	0.1923
		KLD	Ø	0.0330
			Median	0.2637
	Wikipedia	Tf-idf	Ø	**0.9615**
			Median	0.9451
		KLD	Ø	0.4451
			Median	0.5385
Separation of topics	/	Inverse cosine similarity	Ø	**0.7777**
			Median	0.5960

a use case where the interpretability is the most important criterion and the importance of words is much more important than the separation of topics, a topic score could be aggregated by a 60/30/10 weighting. With this topic model score it is possible to compare different types of topic models or different parameter settings for topic models with an application-domain-fitted value.

For the evaluation 65 LDA-models have been created on the TV debate tweets. Those models differ in the parameters stopword count and use whitelist. The first model was not filtered for any stopwords. Models two to ten have a stopword count rising by ten stopwords. From the eleventh model the count rises by 50 stopwords. Model 29 filters 1000 stopwords. From this model the rise is 1000 stopwords until the 33rd model, which

filters 5000 stopwords. The models 2 to 33 are generated without a whitelist. The models 34 to 65 have been generated in the same way, but this time with the usage of a whitelist. For all models the topic count was set to 20, the dirichlet parameter α was set to 1 and the count of the gibbs sampling iterations was set to 2000. Figure 4 provide the normalized scores for each criterion and the overall topic model score.

The interpretability increases the more stopwords will be filtered – until 250 filtered stopwords. This results of the fact that in those models a lot of stopwords, without any interpretative value, are included. From 250 to 750 stopwords a plateau is formed, because from this point on only meaningful words are replaced by other meaningful words. The filtering of more than

Figure 5. Normalized scores for each criterion for the topic model evaluation

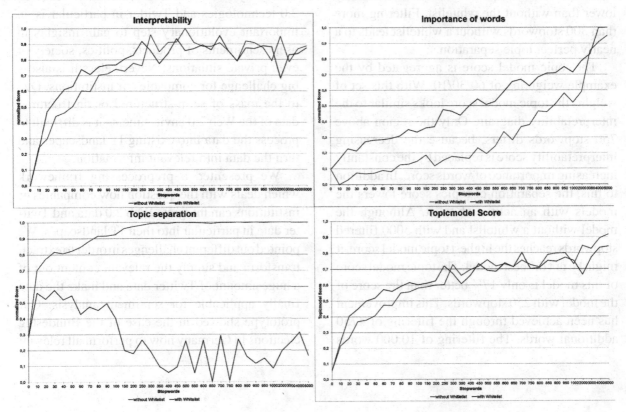

750 stopwords leads to poorer models, because now meaningful words will be replaced by very rare words and those words are more difficult to interpret and the chance of accidently filtering non-stopwords increases.

The criterion importance of words increases nearly constantly with a rising count of filtered stopwords. The more stopwords are filtered the more rare words are included in the models and this leads to a higher value of the underlying metric. Models that have been generated with the whitelist are always better than those without the whitelist. This is because the whitelist consists of words out of a political domain. Those words are very frequent in the TV-Debate-tweets, and therefore they are often included in the models. In contrast, those words are very rare in the Wikipedia and this leads to a better importance of words score. The usage of the whitelist has also a disadvantage – the separation of topics score will be constantly lower than without the whitelist. Filtering more than 300 stopwords without a whitelist leads to a nearly perfect topic separation.

The topic model score is aggregated by the example weighting of 60/30/10. With this set of weights the topic model score looks similar to the interpretability diagram. Only the region above 750 stopwords differs, because the decreasing interpretability score is replaced by the constantly increasing importance of words score. In addition to this, the separation of topics score lowers the models with an active whitelist. Although the model without a whitelist and with 5000 filtered stopwords reaches the highest topic model score, it might be not the best model. The topic model score of this model is only 17% better than the score of the model with 250 stopwords. This improvement has been achieved through the filtering of 4750 additional words. The filtering of 10,000 words

will lead to an even higher topic model score. With this in mind, it seems to be better to favor a model at the beginning of the plateau.

The following diagram shows that the topic model score is better suited to choose the right topic model variant instead of an extrinsic metric like the log document held-out probability. In the diagram a high document held-out probability value means that this model is good in classifying an unseen document. By choosing this metric as the basis for the model decision, the model with only 60 stopwords and without a whitelist would be taken. However, models with a higher stopword count are better application-domain-fitted than this model.

CONCLUSION

The analysis of user communication via Web 2.0 technologies and Twitter in particular is an important evolutionary step to gain insights in users sentiments of products, politics, society or even private situations. Nevertheless it is also a big challenge for companies or institutions. Due to the mass of semi-structured or unstructured data of the Web 2.0 environments it is difficult to process the data into existing IT landscapes and turn the data into relevant information.

We presented a preprocessing framework which deals with the question how companies or institutions can integrate Web 2.0 data and Twitter data in particular into their IT landscapes. We pointed out different challenges in order to extract, transform and supply the relevant content out of a huge amount of Twitter data and make the data finally applicable for sentiment analysis. Our prototype showed in the case of the Bundestag elections in Germany how to perform all relevant

Figure 6. Topic model scores vs. inverted document held-out probability

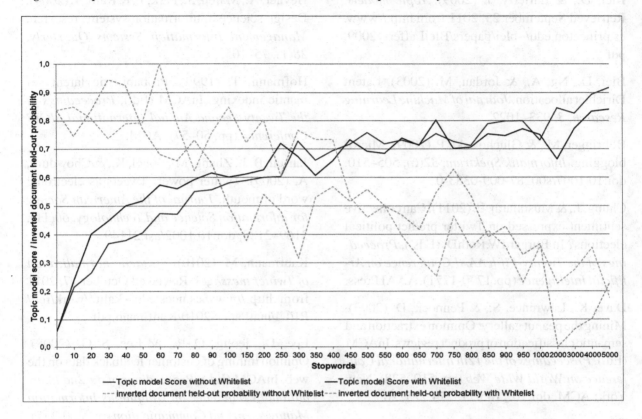

steps in the KDD process for Twitter datasets and how to gain the relevant topic models as the final result. Furthermore we discussed the evaluation of our framework in detail by detecting different criterions and metrics for the evaluation of our LDA algorithm.

Further research needs to verify that our evaluation methods will work also with English vocabulary and with more complex topic model structures. Our evaluation example focused only on German language which is a limitation in our work. But we already showed in other publications that the LDA algorithm works in for German or English Twitter datasets. We will extend our framework to German and English language support including the evaluation and also implement different LDA algorithms.

REFERENCES

Azevedo, A., & Santos, M. F. (2008). KDD, SEMMA and CRISP-DM: A parallel overview. In AbrahamA. (Ed.), *IADIS European conference on data mining* (pp. 182–185). IADIS.

Barnes, S. J., & Böhringer, M. (2011). Modeling Use continuance behavior in microblogging services: The case of Twitter. *Journal of Computer Information Systems, 51*(4), 1–13.

Bermingham, A., & Smeaton, A. F. (2010). Classifying sentiment in microblogs: Is brevity an advantage? In ACM (Ed.), *Proceedings of the 19th ACM International Conference on Information and Knowledge Management* (pp. 1833–1836). New York: ACM. doi:10.1145/1871437.1871741

Blei, D., & Lafferty, J. (2009). *Topic models.* Retrieved September 25, 2011 from http://www. cs.princeton.edu/~blei/papers/BleiLafferty2009. pdf

Blei, D., Ng, A., & Jordan, M. (2003). Latent Dirichlet allocation. *Journal of Machine Learning Research, 3,* 933–1022.

Böhringer, M., & Gluchowski, P. (2009). Microblogging. *Informatik Spektrum, 32*(6), 505–510. doi:10.1007/s00287-009-0383-0

Chung, J., & Mustafaraj, E. (2011). Can collective sentiment expressed on Twitter predict political elections? In BurgardW.RothD. (Eds.), *Proceedings of the Twenty-Fifth AAAI Conference on Artificial Intelligence* (pp. 1770-1771). AAAI Press.

Dave, K., Lawrence, S., & Pennock, D. (2003). Mining the peanut gallery: Opinion extraction and semantic classification of product reviews. In ACM (Ed.), *Proceedings of the 12th International Conference on World Wide Web* (pp. 519–528). New York: ACM. doi:10.1145/775224.775226

Fayyad, U. M. (1996). *Advances in knowledge discovery and data mining.* Menlo Park, CA: AAAI Press.

Golder, S. A., & Macy, M. W. (2011). Diurnal and seasonal mood vary with work, sleep, and daylength across diverse cultures. *Science, 333*(6051), 1878–1881. doi:10.1126/science.1202775 PMID:21960633

Heinrich, K. (2011). Influence potential framework: Eine Methode zur Bestimmung des Referenzpotenzials in microblogs. In P. Gluchowski, A. Lorenz, C. Schieder, & J. Stietzel (Eds.), *Tagungsband zum 14: Interuniversitären doktorandenseminar wirtschaftsinformatik* (pp. 26–36). Universitätsverlag Chemnitz.

Hevner, A., March, S., Park, J., & Ram, S. (2004). Design science in information systems research. *Management Information Systems Quarterly, 28*(1), 75–105.

Hofmann, T. (1999). Probabilistic latent semantic indexing. In ACM (Ed.), *Proceedings of the Twenty-Second Annual International SIGIR Conference* (pp. 50–57). ACM.

Jansen, B. J., Zhang, M., Sobel, K., & Chowdury, A. (2009). Twitter power: Tweets as electronic word of mouth. *Journal of the American Society for Information Science and Technology, 60*(11), 2169–2188. doi:10.1002/asi.21149

Kaufmann, M. (2010). *Syntactic normalization of Twitter messages.* Retrieved October 17, 2011 from http://www.cs.uccs.edu/~kalita/work/reu/ REUFinalPapers2010/Kaufmann.pdf

Lee, D., Jeong, O.-R., & Lee, S.-G. (2008). Opinion mining of customer feedback data on the web. In ACM (Ed.), *Proceedings of the 2nd International Conference on Ubiquitous Information Management and Communication* (pp. 230-235). New York: ACM. doi:10.1145/1352793.1352842

Liu, B. (2007). *Web data mining: Exploring hyperlinks, contents, and usage data.* Berlin: Springer.

Liu, B., Hu, M., & Cheng, J. (2005). Opinion observer: Analyzing and comparing opinions on the web. In ACM (Ed.), *Proceedings of the 14th International Conference on World Wide Web* (pp. 342–351). New York: ACM. doi:10.1145/1060745.1060797

Lo, R. T.-W., He, B., & Ounis, I. (2005). Automatically Building a stopword list for an information retrieval system. In *Proceedings of the Fifth Dutch-Belgian Information Retrieval Workshop* (pp. 17-24). Academic Press.

Newman, D., Lau, J. H., Grieser, K., & Baldwin, T. (2010). Automatic evaluation of topic coherence. In *Proceedings of Human Language Technologies. The 2010 Annual Conference of the North American Chapter of the Association for Computational Linguistics* (pp. 100-108). ACL.

O'Connor, B., Balasubramanyan, R., Routledge, B. R., & Smith, N. A. (2010). From Tweets to polls: Linking text sentiment to public opinion time series. In W. Cohen & S. Gosling (Eds.), *Proceedings of the Fourth International AAAI Conference on Weblogs and Social Media* (pp. 122–129). The AAAI Press.

Oulasvirta, A., Lehtonen, E., Kurvinen, E., & Raento, M. (2010). Making the ordinary visible in microblogs. *Personal and Ubiquitous Computing, 14*(3), 237–249. doi:10.1007/s00779-009-0259-y

Pak, A., & Paroubek, P. (2010). Twitter as a corpus for sentiment analysis and opinion mining. In Calzolari N. Choukri K. Maegaard B. Mariani J. Odijk J. Piperidis S. Rosner M. Tapias D. (Eds.), *Proceedings of the International Conference on Language Resources and Evaluation* (pp. 1320–1326). European Language Resources Association.

Parikh, R., & Movassate, M. (2009). *Sentiment analysis of user-generated Twitter updates using various classification techniques*. Retrieved October 17, 2011 from http://nlp.stanford.edu/courses/cs224n/2009/fp/19.pdf

Popescu, A.-M., & Etzioni, O. (2007). Extracting product features and opinions from reviews. In A. Kao & S. R. Poteet (Eds.), *Natural language processing and text mining* (pp. 9–28). London: Springer. doi:10.1007/978-1-84628-754-1_2

Ramage, D., Dumais, S., & Liebling, D. (2010). Characterizing microblogs with topic models. In W. Cohen & S. Gosling (Eds.), *Proceedings of the Fourth International AAAI Conference on Weblogs and Social Media* (pp. 130–137). The AAAI Press.

Richter, A., Koch, M., & Krisch, J. (2007). *Social commerce - Eine Analyse des Wandels im E-Commerce (technical report no. 2007-03)*. Munich: Faculty Informatics, Bundeswehr University Munich.

Salton, G., & McGill, M. (1983). *Introduction to modern information retrieval*. New York: McGraw-Hill.

Scaffidi, C., Bierhoff, K., Chang, E., Felker, M., Ng, H., & Chun, K. (2007). Red Opal: Product-feature scoring from reviews. In ACM (Ed.), *Proceedings of the 8th ACM Conference on Electronic Commerce* (pp. 182–191). New York: ACM.

Sommer, S., Schieber, A., Heinrich, K., & Hilbert, A. (2012). What is the conversation about? A topic-model-based approach for analyzing customer sentiments in Twitter. *International Journal of Intelligent Information Technologies, 8*(1), 10–25. doi:10.4018/jiit.2012010102

Stephen, A., & Toubia, O. (2010). Deriving value from social commerce networks. *Networks Journal of Marketing Research, 67*(2), 215–228. doi:10.1509/jmkr.47.2.215

Stieglitz, S., Krüger, N., & Eschmeier, A. (2011). Themenmonitoring in Twitter aus der Perspektive des Issue Managements. In K. Meißner & M. Engelien (Eds.), Virtual enterprises, communities & social networks (pp. 69–78). Dresden: TUDpress.

Tumasjan, A., Sprenger, T. O., Sandner, P. G., & Welpe, I. M. (2010). Predicting elections with Twitter: What 140 characters reveal about political sentiment. In W. Cohen & S. Gosling (Eds.), *Proceedings of the Fourth International AAAI Conference on Weblogs and Social Media* (pp. 178–185). The AAAI Press.

Twopcharts. (2014). *Twitter activity monitor*. Retrieved March 06, 2014, from http://twopcharts.com/twitteractivitymonitor

Wallach, H. M., Murray, I., Salakhutdinov, R., & Mimno, D. (2009). Evaluation methods for topic models. In *Proceedings of the 26th International Conference on Machine Learning* (pp. 1-8). ACM Press.

Yi, J., & Niblack, W. (2005). Sentiment mining in webfountain. In *Proceedings of the 21st International Conference on Data Engineering* (pp. 1073-1083). IEEE Computer Society.

Zhao, W., Jiang, J., Weng, J., He, J., Lim, E.-P., Yan, H., & Li, X. (2011). Comparing Twitter and traditional media using topic models. In P. Clough, C. Foley, C. Gurrin, G. Jones, W. Kraaij, H. Lee, & V. Mudoch (Eds.), *Advances in information retrieval* (pp. 338–349). Berlin: Springer. doi:10.1007/978-3-642-20161-5_34

KEY TERMS AND DEFINITIONS

Design Science: In the computer science the design science approach is a popular research method and follows the goal to gain new insights by developing an IT artifact that solves a specific problem.

Knowledge-Discovery-in-Databases (KDD): The KDD describes the iterative process of identifying patterns in huge amounts of data. The process is divided into five stages: Selection, Preprocessing, Transformation, Data Mining, and Interpretation.

Microblog: A microblog is a special kind of a blog that combines an ordinary blog with features of social networks, but with a limitation of characters for each entry. Twitter is the most popular microblog with a limitation of 140 characters for each entry.

Preprocessing: A Preprocessor is an engine that processes input data to a defined output data for other programs. In our case it performs different steps of data selection, cleaning and transformation for analysis purposes (sentiment analysis).

Sentiment Analysis: Sentiment Analysis (as a synonym for Opinion Mining) uses methods of natural language processing, linguistic and text analysis to extract sentiment patterns in structured or unstructured documents.

Topic Modeling: A topic model is a statistical model that discovers the occurrence of defined elements (topics) in a collection of documents. Topic modeling is mainly used in the areas of machine learning or natural language processing.

Web Data Mining: Web Data Mining (as a synonym for Web Mining) covers the application of data mining methods to discover different patterns in the web. It is divided into web usage mining (user behavior), web content mining (text analysis) and web structure mining (structure of linking).

Chapter 4
Welcome to the Party:
Modeling the Topic Evolution of Political Parties in Microblogs Using Dynamic Topic Models

Kai Heinrich
TU-Dresden, Germany

ABSTRACT

Modeling topic distributions over documents has become a recent method for coping with the problematic of huge amounts of unstructured data. Especially in the context of Web communities, topic models can capture the zeitgeist as a snapshot of people's communication. However, the problem that arises from that static snapshot is that it fails to capture the dynamics of a community. To cope with this problem, dynamic topic models were introduced. This chapter makes use of those topic models in order to capture dynamics in user behavior within microblog communities such as Twitter. However, only applying topic models yields no interpretable results, so a method is proposed that compares different political parties over time using regression models based on DTM output. For evaluation purposes, a Twitter data set divided into different political communities is analyzed and results and findings are presented.

INTRODUCTION

It is clear that every day, we are becoming increasingly enmeshed in the Web. Millions of individuals are communicating with each other using essentially a few clicks of a mouse. These discourses, supported by a growing number of on-line media–forums, Wikipedia, Twitter, Facebook and blogs–are engaging millions of individuals globally. Within the political and social realm, a recent study reports that close to a fifth of US

Internet users have posted online or used a social networking site for civic or political engagement (Dugan & Smith, 2013). Another study found that 55% of the adult US population went online in 2008 in order to get involved in the political process or to seek information about the last US election (Ha Thuc, 2011). A key characteristic of social data is that it is generated by a large number of people from different cultures, locations, age groups, religions, income categories etc. This is in contrast to the case of traditional media such as

DOI: 10.4018/978-1-4666-6639-9.ch004

newswire generated by a small group of journalists. Because of its popularity and diversity, social data is an excellent source for understanding the perspectives of large groups of people.

The Analysis of social data from Facebook, Twitter, LinkedIn or other sources is crucial in order to gain information about the social behavior of people in online communities (Aarts, Schraagen, van Maanen, & Ouboter, 2012). The research that is done here, while broadly applicable, will be focused on the microblogging platform Twitter. There are various information that can be gained by analyzing Twitter. Examples include demographic analysis, *social network analysis*, as well as message analysis. Focusing on the message characteristics, it is important to capture user behavior and the dynamics of topics within online social networks.

Along with the exponential growth of text data on the Web, particularly of the user-generated content, comes an increasing need for hierarchically organizing documents, retrieving documents accurately, and discovering evolutionary trends of various popular topics from the data. However, all of these are challenging due to the diversity, heterogeneity, noisiness and time-sensitivity of Web 2.0 data.

While there is a variety of tasks that can be dealt with when facing social media analysis, this chapter focuses on the message characteristics to reflect on the behavior of people within a social network. Other topics in this area of Twitter analysis include topological and geographical properties (Hong & Davison, 2010), novelty and opinion leader detection (e.g. Bi, Tian, Sismanis, Balmin, & Cho, 2014), this work aims to provide a framework for evolution monitoring in social networks. Therefore we will examine related work in the fields of Twitter analytics and *topic models* in the following background section. As an output of the literature review concerning topic modeling in Twitter, we define our research goal, as well as certain sub problems, that we have to deal with in order to reach that goal.

BACKGROUND

Social Behavior in Online Networks

In the research field of social behavior in online networks, (Aarts et al., 2012) found that three specific research tasks can be identified: actor characteristics, message characteristics and network characteristics.

Actor characteristics determine to what extent individuals are part of the network and how much influence the individual actor has to spread the information further. Evidently, actors form the building blocks of a social network. It is between these actors that communication or information exchange may or may not occur.

Message characteristics form a part of the explanation to the extent to which information circulates through the social network. Message characteristics play a role in the distribution and propagation of information. An attractive or stimulating message is more likely to spread to various individuals within the network. Unappealing or uninformative messages are likely to die out quickly.

Network characteristics give us insight in the relational features between actors instead of features confined to one actor only. The extent to which information spreads is not solely determined by either the characteristics of the actor or the message characteristics. The social context or network (who is connected to whom, and in which way) to a large extent determines the flow and diffusion of information. This relational approach is a distinctive feature of a social network approach.

The research in the area focusing on message characteristics includes topic trend research (Lau, Collier, & Baldwin, 2012; Perkiö, Buntine, & Sami Perttu, 2004; Wang & McCallum, 2006), as well as retweet mechanics (Liu, Niculescu-Mizil, & Gryc, 2009). The pure motivational aspects of posting tweets and dealing with social communication in Twitter, e.g. the spread of rumors have also been dealt with (Java, Song, Finin, & Tseng, 2007).

We are particularly interested in the field of *topic modeling* for Twitter corpora. Topic Modeling is a way to gather information on latent topics and examine the distribution of those topics. But to apply topic models onto a corpora of Twitter messages one has to understand the corpus first and more importantly the creation process of the corpus. In this case we are dealing with Twitter data, so we have to understand the mechanics and characteristics of Twitter first.

The Nature of Twitter

Twitter is a *microblogging* service and with social network characteristics. Users of Twitter share their opinions, thoughts or interesting information on Twitter in the form of short messages, also called tweets. Alongside that like in any other developed social network there is a lot of non-useful information in the form of advertising or spam. People can share interests by following each other. Before we investigate the implications of the properties of a Twitter message on topic modeling we first investigate the demographic of Twitter.

In order to gain information for any purpose, including social behavior, one has to define a certain sample group or object group to investigate. In order to infer from the sphere of Twitter onto a population, much larger, for example people who vote in a presidential election in a certain country, one has to familiarize with the demographic structure of Twitter.

In a recent study (Dugan & Smith, 2013), those demographic distributions were investigated. Figure 1 shows the overall usage of social networks.

Figure 1. Overall usage of social networks (Dugan & Smith, 2013)

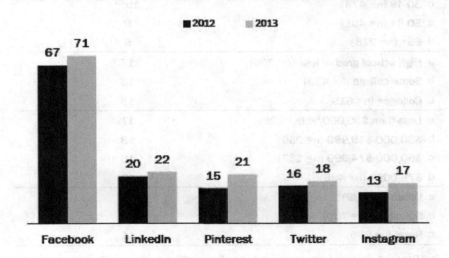

Social media sites, 2012-2013

% of online adults who use the following social media websites, by year

Pew Research Center's Internet Project Tracking Surveys, 2012 -2013. 2013 data collected August 07 –September 16, 2013. N=1,445 internet users ages 18+. Interviews were conducted in English and Spanish and on landline and cell phones. The margin of error for results based on all internet users is +/- 2.9 percentage points.

PEW RESEARCH CENTER

Figure 2 shows the percentages of different racial and ethnic groups, represented in Twitter (Smith & Brenner, 2012). The percentage of internet users who are on Twitter has doubled since November 2010, currently standing at 16%. Those under 50, and especially those 18-29, are the most likely to use Twitter. Urban-dwellers are significantly more likely than both suburban and rural residents to be on Twitter.

The latter statistics in *Table 1* show the importance of the information source Twitter. With an average 58 million tweets per day and increasing, the need for automated textual analytic methods is obvious.

Related work concerning demographic Twitter research includes (Java et al., 2007) alongside (Krishnamurthy, Gill, & Arlitt, 2008), who researched geographical properties of Twitter

Figure 2. Demographic distribution in Twitter (Smith & Brenner, 2012)

Twitter users

Among online adults, the % who use Twitter

	Use Twitter
All internet users (n= 1,445)	18%
a Men (n= 734)	17
b Women (n= 711)	18
a White, Non-Hispanic (n= 1,025)	16
b Black, Non-Hispanic (n= 138)	29[ac]
c Hispanic (n= 169)	16
a 18-29 (n= 267)	31[bcd]
b 30-49 (n= 473)	19[cd]
c 50-64 (n= 401)	9
d 65+ (n= 278)	5
a High school grad or less (n= 385)	17
b Some college (n= 433)	18
c College+ (n= 619)	18
a Less than $30,000/yr (n= 328)	17
b $30,000-$49,999 (n= 259)	18
c $50,000-$74,999 (n= 187)	15
d $75,000+ (n= 486)	19
a Urban (n= 479)	18[c]
b Suburban (n= 700)	19[c]
c Rural (n= 266)	11

Pew Research Center's Internet Project August Tracking Survey, August 07 –September 16, 2013. N=1,445 internet users ages 18+. Interviews were conducted in English and Spanish and on landline and cell phones. The margin of error for results based on all internet users is +/- 2.9 percentage points.

Note: Percentages marked with a superscript letter (e.g., [a]) indicate a statistically significant difference between that row and the row designated by that superscript letter, among categories of each demographic characteristic (e.g., age).

PEW RESEARCH CENTER

Table 1. Usage statistics of Twitter (Twitter, 2014)

Twitter Company Statistics	Data
Total number of active registered Twitter users	645,750,000
Number of new Twitter users signing up everyday	135,000
Number of unique Twitter site visitors every month	190 million
Average number of tweets per day	58 million
Number of Twitter search engine queries every day	2.1 billion
Percent of Twitter users who use their phone to tweet	43%
Percent of tweets that come from third party applicants	60%
Number of people that are employed by Twitter	2,500
Number of active Twitter users every month	115 million
Percent of Twitters who don't tweet but watch other people tweet	40%
Number of days it takes for 1 billion tweets	5 days
Number of tweets that happen every second	9,100
Twitter Annual Advertising Revenue	**Revenue**
2013	$405,500,000
2012	$259,000,000
2011	$139,000,000
2010	$45,000,000

messages. Spam research and influential user research is also on the top list of research fields.

It is important to point out that these findings are rather important to follow up research, since with 58 million tweets per day, the amount of spam that has to be detected and excluded from further analysis is not a small portion. With the interference of automated spam bots that even create follower-relationships with users and are therefore hard to isolate with simple methods, more advanced methods as proposed by (Benevenuto, Magno, Rodrigues, & Almeida, 2010) and (Wang, 2010) are needed.

Annotating the text corpora with useful dimensions such as demographics or geographical properties is in particular useful when you have to limit your findings to a certain subgroup, which will be the case in most behavioral research approaches (Aarts et al., 2012).

When analyzing microblogs we face the special issues which characterize these short posts. We shortly introduce the microblogging service Twitter and its functionalities: First, Twitter users can communicate with each other by referencing the name of the communication partner with a prefixed '@'. For example, userA writes an entry containing '@userB' in order to address userB. In addition, users can distribute the entry of another user by forwarding this entry with the prefixed characters 'RT'. For example, in order to forward the origin entry 'tweet' of userA userB publishes the tweet with 'RT @userA tweet'. In this way, the range of an expression is increased, which ultimately will benefit the reputation of the original author. Finally, there is a very important function of microblogs: the tagging of the entries. Authors can tag their entries by adding keywords to the tweet. These keywords are called hashtags and can be recognized by the prefixed '#'. In summary, the technical functionalities of Twitter provide several possibilities for analysis. Possible research areas are Social Network Analysis, Web Content Mining and Consumer Behavior Analysis.

The character limitation of 140 characters leads to the main challenge in the analysis of microblogs. In order to write as much information as possible users tend to use abbreviations (for example, '4ever' is used as an abbreviation for 'forever'). In addition, the informal way of speaking in microblogs and syntactic errors complicate the mining procedure. In contrast, (Bermingham & Smeaton, 2012) see the short length as a strength of microblogs because the limited text can contain compact and explicit sentiments. In their paper they found classifying sentiments in microblogs easier to mine than in blogs. Therefore, the brevity can also be an advantage. As mentioned before, several researchers have successfully analyzed microblog entries. Twitter is a popular data source because of the great number of text posts and the heterogeneous audience (Pak & Paroubek, 2010). In addition, in Twitter, users express a certain sentiment about different topics, so it is possible to analyze people's sentiments regarding those topics. In this context (Pak & Paroubek, 2010) show examples of entries with expressed sentiments in order to demonstrate the high potential of sentiment analysis in tweets. (Jungherr, Jurgens, & Schoen, 2012) used 100,000 tweets in order to reveal political sentiment in Germany.

They found that the majority of the analyzed tweets reflect voter preferences and even come close to traditional election polls. Users not only express their sentiments but also discuss them with other users. Beside the content-based analysis of a microblog, the social network structure of Twitter also yields valuable information about a person's behavior. (Heinrich, 2011) for example, analyzed relationships in Twitter in order to predict the reference potential of a person as a determinant of the grade of opinion leadership and social centrality. Filtering those important users helps to reduce the amount of Twitter updates one has to scan and monitor over time when researching dynamic effects in topics.

We conclude that Twitter offers a lot of data (both useful and noisy) in form of restricted textual observations called Tweets. In fact, too much to handle in a semi-automated way. In the next chapter we introduce topic models as a way of dealing with structuring those observations.

TOPIC MODELS

Before we are able to analyze the expressions in the tweets, we have to deal with the magnitude of textual data. In the first step, one may want to separate the posts into groups corresponding to specific topics. For this separation one can use generative topic models. (Blei, Ng, & Jordan, 2003) give a fundamental explanation of topic models and their usage. In their work they adapt topic models to a digital archive of the journal

'Science', which contains articles from 1980 to 2002. Searching for interesting articles within this huge amount of information can be difficult. Therefore, they postulate the possibility to explore this collection through the underlying topics in the articles. With probabilistic topic models they are able to automatically detect a structure of topics in this collection, even without manually constructed training data. In the case of the 'Science' archive (Blei et al., 2003) found 50 topics corresponding to the articles. So, when searching for documents, scientists are able to browse through a list of similar documents that deal with the same topic. Since their publication, topic models have been successfully used by other authors in order to identify topics. The main fields of topic model literature can be characterized by *models*, *inference*, *software* and *evaluation*.

While models introduce whole new variants of topic models, the inference subject proposes new methods for dealing with those complex models in order to get valid statistical estimates for the model parameters. In the software field, new tools based on known algorithms are introduced and described. The evaluation subject deals with interpreting and evaluation of topic coherence. Also algorithm evaluation is subsidized under this specific subject.

The following table (*Table 2*) shows scientific sources in the fields mentioned above based on literature review of topic models, that was systematically conducted based on the above mentioned subject keywords. The methodology for the literature review is based on (Kitchenham et al., 2009). We searched papers from 2003 to 2014 with the above mentioned keywords in combination with the term "topic model". We excluded duplicates and papers that gave no in-depth talk on the above mentioned fields, but rather just mentioned those terms. Especially in the field of *models* the mass of papers was greatly reduced. The results are presented in *Table 2*.

Since there are numerous advances in topic modeling, the subject of actual model formulation

Table 2. Number of publications in topic model research fields

Subject	# of Publications
Models	42
Inference	24
Software	14
Evaluation	12

gathers the most scientific publications. Notable findings include correlated topic models (Blei & Lafferty, 2007; Zhang, Song, Zhang, & Liu, 2010), topic random fields (Daumé III, 2009; Zhu & Xing, 2010) and dynamic topic models (Blei & Lafferty, 2006; Wang, Blei, & Heckerman, 2008). There are many more applications and modifications of the *latent dirichlet allocation* for special purposes like regression and classification (Mimno & McCallum, 2008; Zhu, Ahmed, & Xing, 2009) or semi-supervised or and supervised topic models (Ramage, Hall, Nallapati, & Manning, 2009; Blei & McAuliffe, 2007; Toutanova & Johnson, 2007).

Particularly the subject of dynamic topic models is important for our findings of evolutionary behavior in microblogs. We will explain and define a dynamic model for our purpose in the next section.

In the field of inference the main cause of action is the scalability of topic model parameter estimation, since in most cases we are dealing with streams of text data, often combined with Big Data infrastructures and vast amounts of text data. Subjects like on-line inference (Grant, George, Jenneisch, & Wilson, 2011; He, Lin, Gao, & Wong, 2012; Hoffman, Blei, & Bach, 2010), efficient parameter estimation (Asuncion, Welling, Smyth, & Teh, 2009, Mukherjee & Blei, 2008, Yao, Mimno, & McCallum, 2009), as well as parallel inference (Yan, Xu, & Qi, 2009) are the main subjects within the field of inference.

The software field includes various implementations of different algorithms, theoretically

discussed in the above mentioned papers (Mc-Callum, 2002, Ramage & Rosen, 2009, Steyvers & Griffiths, 2005).

The field of evaluation claims just a little amount of scientific research. Topics include performance evaluation (Musat, Velcin, Trausan-Matu, & Rizoiu, 2011, Newman, Han Lau, Grieser, & Baldwin, 2010), as well as interpretation of the results by humans, in order to assess the quality of the generated topic clusters (Wallach, Murray, Salakhutdinov, & Mimno, 2009, Newman, Karimi, & Cavedon, 2009, Chang, Boyd-Graber, Wang, Gerrish, & Blei, 2009).

We also conducted a semi-systematic literature search for through all research fields and noted the papers that include topic models in the methodology. Without limiting our search to the above mentioned four main subjects, we found that an increasing number of authors across multiple fields use topic models in their research (see *Figure 4*). Apart from information system, information retrieval and software engineering or pattern recognition, the research domains include humanistic research, medical research, as well as physics. A growing area of application for topic models is political research within the social science (Hong & Davison, 2010; Ramage, Rosen, Chuang, Manning, & McFarland, 2009).

We conduct our research within the area of social science, specifically the political subject of short term election politics. As stated in the introduction our goal is to develop a model to catch the evolutionary dynamics of topics over time before a national election. That will let us take a look into the dynamic probability distributions of topics from the angle of different political parties and there "adjustment" to certain political topics that arise during that time. Furthermore we limit our research to the microblogging platform of Twitter. Therefore we now specify further findings for topic modeling in Twitter.

Ramage, Dumais, & Liebling (2010) detect dimensions of content in Twitter entries with the

Figure 3. Number of publications in topic model research fields

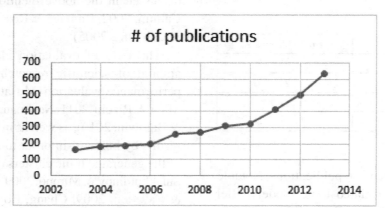

Figure 4. Analytical KDD process for topic modeling and sentiment analytics

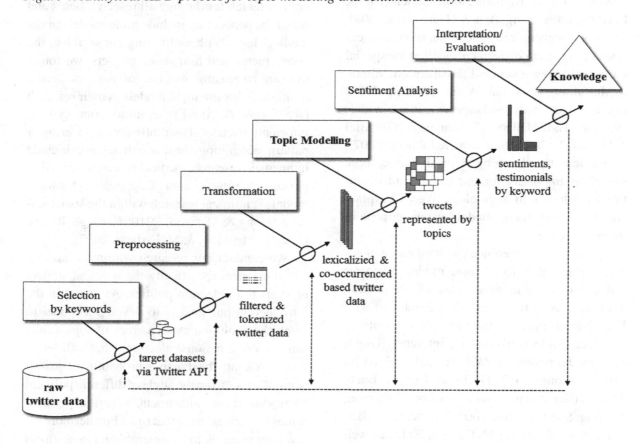

help of topic models. They introduce five dimensions in which tweet content can be matched. For example, the dimension 'substance' contains expressions with generally interesting meanings; they found words like 'president', 'American', and 'country' for this dimension. Another dimension is called 'status'; there, words like 'still', 'doing', and 'sleep' could be found which express the current situation of the user. With this partially supervised approach (Ramage et al., 2010) show the distribution of these five dimensions for specific Twitter users in order to get an idea of the user's tweeting behavior. However, Zhao et al. (2011) used unsupervised topic modeling on a Twitter dataset. The aim of their work is an empiric comparison of content of Twitter and a traditional news medium. They adopted topic models on both the Twitter content and the New York Times news. Afterwards they compared the topics and focused on the differences between them. As a result, Zhao et al. (2011) found that Twitter users actively and rapidly spread news of important or extraordinary events. These approaches illustrate the capabilities that topic modeling can offer for uncovering latent structure in text documents.

Other applications of topic models in Twitter include hashtag recommendation (Godin, Slavkovikj, Neve, Schrauwen, & de Walle, Rik Van, 2013) as well as trend analysis (Lau et al., 2012) and real time search algorithms (Grant et al., 2011).

In the next section we propose a modified dynamic topic model for the purpose of catching the dynamic distribution of political tweets prior to an election.

Dynamic Topic Models for Twitter

Data Situation and Analytical Process

Our research goal is to build a model for catching dynamic effects based on message characteristics of tweets. More specifically we collected tweets from sub-networks of different political parties prior to a national election in Germany. We wanted to see how their behavior changed around election day. Also we wanted to catch influences of daily events and political affairs that occurred during that time interval. In the end we compare the different dynamic topic distributions in order to reflect on the political behavior of those parties.

We bear in mind that without modifications those findings cannot be transformed to real world findings (Hong, Dom, Gurumurthy, & Tsioutsiouliklis, 2011) without limitations.

In order to analyze microblog datasets we align our approach to the process of Knowledge-Discovery-in-Databases (KDD) which is widely accepted by academics and practitioners. It was published by Fayyad, Piatetsky-shapiro, & Smyth (1996) and shows the nontrivial process of identifying patterns in huge amounts of data. Following Azevedo & Santos (2008), other approaches for pattern recognition in datasets such as SEMMA or CRISP-DM can be referred in the implementation of the KDD process by (Fayyad et al., 1996). The KDD process contains five stages: Selection, Pre-Processing, Transformation, Data Mining, and Interpretation.

The first stage in the KDD process contains the selection of the target dataset, which can be an entire dataset, a subset of variables, or data samples. In the next two stages (Pre-Processing and Transformation) the target data is prepared for the data-mining methods. Data cleaning and transformation algorithms provide consistent data for example by purging double entries, filtering outliers, reducing dimensionality or creating new variables. The fourth stage includes the analysis of the pre-processed and transformed data in order to gain patterns of interest in a particular form, depending on the analysis objective. These patterns have to be evaluated and interpreted for the purpose of generating knowledge in the last stage (Azevedo & Santos, 2008, Fayyad et al., 1996). The KDD process is iterative so if necessary, it is possible to improve the results by enhancing the activities within the earlier stages. The five stages in the KDD process lead the data analyst from the raw datasets to significant patterns and formerly unknown insights.

To adopt the KDD process for the analysis of Twitter datasets we have to consider some changes referring to the special capabilities and challenges of the medium Twitter, as mentioned before. The modified process for knowledge discovery in Twitter datasets is shown in Figure 4.

The first stage in the KDD process for Twitter datasets contains the selection of the target data. We use the Twitter search via the free accessible Twitter API to select our target data out of the complete raw Twitter data. By sending search strings with our selected keywords (e.g. Sony 3D) to the Twitter search API, we get back corresponding tweets which were tweeted within the last two weeks. At this stage in our research we decided to use the time-limited Twitter search stream because the amount of tweets is sufficient to show what insights can be gained by applying generative topic models to Twitter datasets.

Several authors emphasize the great potential of the Twitter API for future research (Pak & Paroubek, 2010). In addition we are about to access the Twitter search function automatically by a Twitter-specific crawler in order to gather an analysis corpus with more Twitter entries for user selected keywords. This is the basis to perform a large scale evaluation in the future to strengthen the validity of our model.

After the selection of our target data we have to perform some pre-processing and transformation tasks in the next two stages. We have to point out that our pre-processing and transformation tasks focus on the relevant task to perform the topic modeling. The dataset contains only textual content from Twitter entries as well as annotated meta data about the political party. In order to obtain useful results we process the data and filter some parts form each entry in the second stage in the KDD process.

The pre-processing tasks start in the first step with the tokenization of each Twitter entry. We use the whitespace-tokenization to keep hashtags and links with the URL as separate tokens. In the next step we filter these hashtags and links with regular expressions as discrete entities. These entities are removed from the dataset for the topic modeling but we keep the entities as own variables stored in order to perform Sentiment Analysis in later stages. In the next step we filter non-relevant text components such as stop words, the keywords of our search string, single characters or numbers and cross-references to other users (e.g. @userA). The cross-references to other users are also stored separate for Network Analysis in posterior stages. In the last step of the pre-processing we deal with spam and advertising tweets by eliminating these entries form our dataset. We use a combination of regular expressions together with duplicate detection to identify spam or advertising tweets. This approach filters some of the unwanted entries but there is still a potential for optimization. The result of this stage is an adjusted corpus collection of our previous Twitter dataset.

Afterwards we transform our corpus by lexicalizing it into vocabulary reference form (Blei et al., 2003). The results of this stage are yield co-occurrence-based data in order to perform the *Latent Dirichlet Allocation (LDA)*. The next section contains the standard topic model of the tweets, as well as the dynamic expansion based on (Blei & Lafferty, 2006). As you can see in *Figure 4* we included the next step of sentiment analysis and evaluation in our modified process model. However the sentiment analysis and the evaluation will not be part of this chapter, since they are subject to further research.

Model

With the special characteristics of Twitter entries in mind several approaches have to be validated for our purpose of analyzing sentiments in Twitter entries that are related to a certain topic. Therefore we have to assign a certain probability to those documents that are likely to represent such a topic. We therefore only discuss methods that are probabilistic in their approach. Well-known methods like 'tf-idf' (Salton & McGill, 1983) are only suitable in a pre-processing manner because other than the fact that it is not probabilistic, it also holds a small amount of reduction which would lead to unsatisfying scaling behavior in incremental load environments (Rahman, Burkhardt, & Hibray, 2010) considering the fast growing database of Twitter streams our research is based on. Other non-probabilistic models include fuzzy based clustering of documents (Thangamani & Thangaraj, 2011) or ontology based models for document segmentation (Sridevi & Nagaveni, 2011). The 'pLSI' model by (Hofmann, 1999), while probabilistic in its nature, lacks a representation on a document level. This fact is quite important when looking at our research goal of not only exploring topics and filtering them according to our interests, but also using the method for representing those documents in terms of topics so that we can reduce the amount of data that is generated by the Twitter entries.

The first approach of representing documents in terms of a topic mixture is given by the classic LDA algorithm developed by (Blei et al., 2003).

The LDA model is based on a three-level generative hierarchical Bayesian model. With respect to our Twitter problem there are three main components that this model considers:

- A word within a Twitter status update (entry) as the unit with the smallest granularity represented by an indexed part of a vocabulary Vector V, so that a word with index position v is represented by unit vector w, so that $w^v = 1$ with all other elements $w^u = 0$ for $u \neq v$.
- A Twitter entry or status update is simply defined by a sequence of N words $w = (w_1, w_2, ..., w_N)$.
- The whole data stream that is collected with respect to the search terms combines all M status updates within a corpus $C = (w_1, w_2, ..., w_M)$.

Figure 5 shows the plate notation of the LDA model as applied on Twitter data. The outer plate therefore represents a Twitter status update with a Dirichlet-distributed topic mixture θ while the inner plate represents the words w choosen from a certain topics z. The Dirichlet prior is parameterized by the vector α, while the word probabilities are parameterized by matrix β with $\beta_{ij} = (w^j = 1 | z^i = 1)$.

As stated in Blei et al. (2003) α and β are corpus-level parameters and therefore are estimated once for the corpus of our Twitter data streams. We assume the standard generative process of the LDA-Model for a Twitter document w:

1. Choose $N \sim \text{Poisson}(\xi)$.
2. Choose $\theta \sim \text{Dir}(\alpha)$.
3. For each of the N words w_n:

Figure 5. Graphical plate notation for the LDA model (Blei et al., 2003)

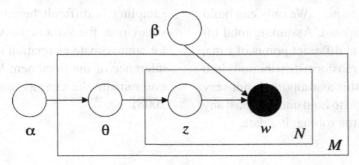

a.   Choose a topic $z_n \sim$ Multinomial$\left(\theta\right)$.

b.   Choose a word w_n from $p(w_n \mid z_n, \beta)$.

For our explorative approach we use this model to estimate the word probabilities associated with certain topics. This allows us to filter the documents we are interested in by probability mass distribution over the topics given by the topic probabilities.

As mentioned before, Ramage et al. (2010) also used topic modeling on Twitter datasets. They use a supervised approach in order to characterize Twitter posts into given categories. Zhao et al. (2011) suggest a multi-step approach to a topic comparison between real-world media and Twitter. In the first step classical LDA is used. But since they compare news and event cycles in Twitter vs. the real-world, they are using supervised AI-based methods on top of LDA to assign the topics explored by LDA into topic categories. Since our approach only features queries on a rather fine level of granularity, namely the product level, this step is not necessary in our case.

A problem that arises from using this model is that neither correlation nor topic trends can be directly derived from it. In the first case researcher could use the correlated topic model as described by (Blei & Lafferty, 2007), (Li & McCallum, 2006)). While we intend to discover correlation structures between topics in upcoming research, we cannot be sure about them now. With this fact in mind the use of correlated topic models cannot be justified because a correlation structure is required as input.

Another problem that occurs with standard LDA is the lack of dynamics. We only can build topic models for a snapshot. Assuming total independence of topics at different points of time, we could use LDA to transform distributions into time series. However this assumption is not very realistic, since it will fail to hold under almost any circumstances within microblogging data.

Therefore we expand our model to include topic dynamics based on the findings of (Blei & Lafferty, 2006).

Keeping the notation from the standard LDA the dynamic model for Twitter is presented in plate notion in *Figure 6*.

The generative process for slice t of a Twitter corpus is thus as follows:

1.   Draw topics $\beta_t \mid \beta_{t-1} \sim N\left(\beta_{t-1}, \sigma^2 I\right)$.

2.   Draw $\alpha_t \mid \alpha_{t-1} \sim N\left(\alpha_{t-1}, \delta^2 I\right)$.

3.   For each tweet:

    a.   Draw $\eta \sim N\left(\alpha_t, a^2 I\right)$.

    b.   For each word in the tweet:

        i.   Draw $Z \sim Mult\left(\pi\left(\eta\right)\right)$.

        ii.   Draw $W_{t,d,n} \sim Mult\left(\pi\left(\beta_{t,z}\right)\right)$.

Once again we have K-components (topics) over a vocabulary with V terms. Since the documents are not drawn exchangeably like in the standard LDA model, but with a certain structure presented by time slices, the model has to be modified.

Blei & Lafferty (2006) suggest chaining the parameters β_t in a state space model with Gaussian noise, since the former used Dirichlet distribution is not suitable for sequential modeling. The resulting model uses an extension of the logistic normal distribution for proportions α_t instead of a Dirichlet distribution for proportions θ. While Gibbs sampling is used in the classical model due to the conjugancy of the Dirichlet and the multinomial distribution, inference based on Gibbs sampling is difficult here. Instead of stochastic simulation, the authors use variational inference for approximate estimation of the posterior. The inference of the document-level-variables however remains the same as described in (Blei et al., 2003).

Figure 6. Dynamic topic model in plate notation (Blei & Lafferty, 2006)

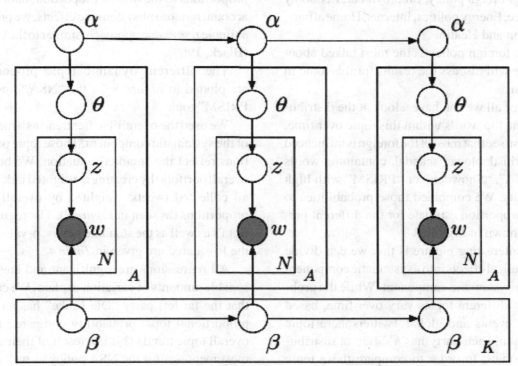

Results

For our approach to dynamically modeling text corpora we collected Tweets from different political German parties. In order to distinguish between parties we only used posts deeply connected to the Twitter accounts of those parties. The four main parties, as well as the collected number of tweets during the time period are listed in *Table 3*. This will help to model the associated topic evolution for each party and compare them in the end. We

Table 3. Number of Tweets within the research period

Political Party	# of Tweets
CDU	241249
SPD	442955
Die Linke	162148
FDP	3400975

collected tweets around the German national election, which was held on September 22, 2013. Our time window of five months therefore reached from August 2013 to December 2013.

As a first result we see the big spike on posts concerning the FDP in *Table 3*. This is easily explained by the surprising fact that the FDP did not achieve the 5% of votes needed in order to participate in the government ("Bundestag").

For topic model input we choose to divide the time period into 25 time slices in order to gain some stability considering the short-term-event-nature of Twitter.

We choose to delimit the number of topics to 20. After comparing the topic-word-vectors, we used a group of students to find "topic headings" and to agglomerate similar topics if necessary. This process was cross validated by another student group independently. We asked the students to classify the topics based on the following "heading" list: Foreign policy, Employment, Economy & Finance, Energy politics, Internet, Home affairs, Education and Health.

Since foreign policy is the most talked about topic, we will discuss the results for this topic in particular.

First of all we can have a look at the distribution of the top words within this topic over time.

We can see that most of the foreign is influenced by the whistleblower scandal, containing words like "NSA", "Snowden" or "PRISM" with high probability. We combined those probabilities to yield a proportion estimate for the different parties, as shown in *Figure 7*.

The interesting picture is that we can divide the dynamical effects into a systematic component and an unsystematic component. While the probability of different topics vary over time, based on news events and global Twittersphere topic distribution, each party has a different distribution of topics. In order to compare those topic

Figure 7. Topic distribution

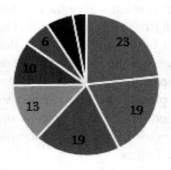

proportions to the overall proportion, taking into account random unsystematic effects, we propose a simple *regression* approach, similar to the CAPM (Black, 1969).

The different dynamic topic proportions are plotted in *Figure 8* for the "NSA/Snowden/PRISM" topic.

We used the overall Twitter trend as a measure of the systematic component. Those topic proportions reflect the "market" situation. We built an overall portfolio by creating a weighted index over all collected tweets, weighted by overall topic proportions (as seen in *Figure 7*). The regression Beta's as well as the standard errors, p-values and the R-squared are given in *Table 4*.

All regressions are significant and have reasonable amounts of variation explain. We can see that the far left party "Die Linke" has an over-proportional topic probability compared to the overall topic trend. This is a result of their strong movement against the NSA policy as well as the continuing fight for Snowden. All other parties are below this trend. Among this subject there are a few other topics within the subject of foreign politics, which would explain the Betas < 1. In general the messages posted in the networks around the Twitter accounts of the political parties seem to underestimate the public importance of some topics. This finding shows that politics, discussed online does not always align with the mass.

The close to "1" fit of the CDU is surprising, since they are not nearly as extreme as "Die Linke" and more likely to swim around with the other parties. An explanation is the impact of the news, that the German chancellor was also under surveillance from the NSA and the fact that the current chancellor is a member of the CDU. That shows that the event character is very persistent in the model. So on the one hand side the model does not fail to catch news dynamics. On the other hand high impact factor events tend to lead to a biased model.

Figure 8. DTM results for "NSA/Snowden/PRISM" topic

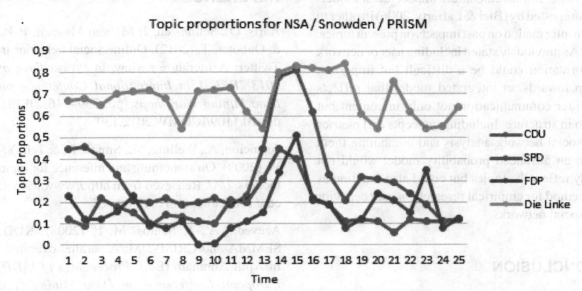

Table 4. DTM-regression results

	Beta	SE	t-Statistic	P-Value	R-Squared
CDU	0,8180	0,0466	17,5666	3,3267E-15	0,928
SPD	0,4049	0,0339	11,9333	1,4027E-11	0,856
FDP	0,3905	0,0463	8,4405	1,2064E-08	0,748
Die Linke	1,4496	0,1249	11,6095	2,4716E-11	0,849

A network based impact factor model may be a solution here. We will shortly discuss other methods and future research in the next section.

When interpreting these topic proportions however, we have to keep in mind the demographic distribution of Twitter defers from that of registered voters. It's a skewed distribution towards a younger generation of people such as digital natives (Dugan & Smith, 2013, Smith & Brenner, 2012).

FUTURE RESEARCH DIRECTIONS

The range of topic model application is rather small compared to other methods, but the number of applications grows rapidly. With this rapid growth more tasks and research ideas evolve.

As partly discussed previously, the evaluation of topics in terms of human understanding of words associated with a certain topic, is a crucial point when using topic modeling for modeling text corpora in order to yield message characteristics. Semiautomatic or automatic evaluation processes are needed for Big Data tasks like collecting and analyzing messages from social networks.

Another thing future research may deal with is the fact of adding and removing topics from the evaluation process. Until now the death of a topic or its birth is not specifically part of any model.

When managing topic life cycles or gathering information on the evolution of communities in terms of conversations via microblog postings those concepts play a crucial row and therefore this filed needs further research.

Other improvements are impact factor models as suggested by (Blei & Lafferty, 2006) in other to gain information on past impacts on present topics.

As previously stated including user or network information could be a difficult but important step towards an integrated model that reflects Twitter communication not only in content but also in structure. Including concepts and metrics of social network analysis and combining them into an advanced probability model would not only reflect the topics but could also function as a method for empirical research on user behavior in social networks.

CONCLUSION

In this chapter we presented an extension of topic models and applied it on Twitter corpora under the premises of political and social research. We found that dynamic topic models can reflect real world events over time. However since this is an automatic approach, further evaluation of the topics, the topic structure and the model is needed to formulate general findings. At this point topic models are a way of representing text corpora dynamically, therefore we are able to get an insight into large datasets of unstructured text data. This allows us for example to formulate simple *regression* models based on topic proportions and examine the difference of certain time series that reflect user behavior. In this chapter we conducted political research and compared the evolution of topics over a time period of 4 month and compared the different model outputs for different political parties.

Further steps include sentiment analysis and inclusion of network and user data in order to get a deeper inside into user behavior. With all the ongoing research on social media analysis and topic modeling, those approaches only mark the beginning of a research perspective that uses social media data to perform empirical research, in order to gain an understanding of people's behavior in the world of the Web 2.0.

REFERENCES

Aarts, O., Schraagen, J. M., van Maanen, P.-P., & Ouboter, T. (2012). Online social behavior in Twitter: A literature review. In *Proceedings of 2013 IEEE 13th International Conference on Data Mining Workshops* (pp. 739–746). IEEE. doi:10.1109/ICDMW.2012.139

Asuncion, A., Welling, M., Smyth, P., & Teh, Y.-W. (2009). On smoothing and inference for topic models. *UAI*. Retrieved from http://www.ics.uci.edu/ asuncion/pubs/UAI_09.pdf

Azevedo, A., & Santos, M. F. (2008). KDD, SEMMA and CRISP-DM: A parallel overview. In Ajith Abraham (Ed.), *Proceedings of IADIS European Conference on Data Mining* (pp. 182–185). IADIS.

Benevenuto, F., Magno, G., Rodrigues, T., & Almeida, V. (2010). Detecting spammers on Twitter. In *Proceedings of Collaboration, Electronic Messaging, Anti-Abuse and Spam Conference (CEAS)*. Retrieved from http://ceas.cc/2010/papers/Paper%2021.pdf

Bermingham, A., & Smeaton, A. F. (2012). Classifying sentiment in microblogs. In J. Huang, N. Koudas, G. Jones, X. Wu, K. Collins-Thompson, & A. An (Eds.), *Proceedings of the 19th ACM International Conference* (p. 1833). ACM. doi:10.1145/1871437.1871741

Bi, B., Tian, Y., Sismanis, Y., Balmin, A., & Cho, J. (2014). Scalable topic-specific influence analysis on microblogs. In B. Carterette, F. Diaz, C. Castillo, & D. Metzler (Eds.), *Proceedings of the 7th ACM International Conference* (pp. 513–522). ACM. doi:10.1145/2556195.2556229

Black, F. (1969). The capital asset pricing model: Some empirical tests. In *Studies in the theory of capital markets*. Academic Press.

Blei, D. M., & Lafferty, J. D. (2006). Dynamic topic models. *ICML*. Retrieved from http://portal.acm.org/citation.cfm?id=1143859

Blei, D. M., & Lafferty, J. D. (2007). A correlated topic model of science. *AAS*, *1*(1), 17–35.

Blei, D. M., & McAuliffe, J. D. (2007). Supervised topic models. *NIPS*. Retrieved from http://books. nips.cc/papers/files/nips20/NIPS2007_0893.pdf

Blei, D. M., Ng, A., & Jordan, M. (2003). Latent Dirichlet allocation. *JMLR*, *3*, 993–1022.

Chang, J., Boyd-Graber, J., Wang, C., Gerrish, S., & Blei, D. M. (2009). Reading tea leaves: How humans interpret topic models. *NIPS*. Retrieved from http://books.nips.cc/papers/files/nips22/NIPS2009_0125.pdf

Daumé, H., III. (2009). Markov random topic fields. Academic Press.

Dugan, M. & Smith, A. (2013). *Social media update 2013*. Academic Press.

Fayyad, U., Piatetsky-shapiro, G., & Smyth, P. (1996). From data mining to knowledge discovery in databases. *AI Magazine*, *17*, 37–54.

Godin, F., Slavkovikj, V., Neve, W. D., Schrauwen, B., & van de Walle, R. (2013). Using topic models for Twitter hashtag recommendation. In *Proceedings of International World Wide Web Conferences Steering Committee* (pp. 593–596). ACM. Retrieved from http://dblp.uni-trier.de/db/conf/www/www2013c.html#GodinSNSW13

Grant, C. E., George, C. P., Jenneisch, C., & Wilson, J. N. (2011). Online topic modeling for real-time Twitter search. In *TREC, National Institute of Standards and Technology NIST*. Retrieved from http://dblp.uni-trier.de/db/conf/trec/trec2011.html#GrantGJW11

Ha Thuc, V. (2011). Topic modeling and applications in web 2.0. Iowa City, IA: Academic Press.

He, Y., Lin, C., Gao, W., & Wong, K.-F. (2012). (in press). Dynamic joint sentiment-topic model. *ACM Transactions on Intelligent Systems and Technology*. Retrieved from http://oro.open.ac.uk/36255/

Heinrich, K. (2011). Influence potential framework: Eine Methode zur Bestimmung des Referenzpotenzials in Microblogs. In P. Gluchowski, A. Lorenz, C. Schieder, & J. Stietzel (Eds.), Tagungsband zum 14: Interuniversitären Doktorandenseminar Wirtschaftsinformatik (pp. 26–36). Chemnitz: Universitätsverlag Chemnitz. Retrieved from http://nbn-resolving.de/urn:nbn:de:bsz:ch1-qucosa-70640

Hoffman, M., Blei, D. M., & Bach, F. (2010). *Online learning for latent Dirichlet allocation*. NIPS.

Hofmann, T. (1999). Probabilistic latent semantic indexing. In F. Gey, M. Hearst, & R. Tong (Eds.), *Proceedings of the 22nd Annual International ACM SIGIR Conference* (pp. 50–57). ACM. doi:10.1145/312624.312649

Hong, L., & Davison, B. D. (2010). Empirical study of topic modeling in Twitter. In Proceedings of the First Workshop on Social Media Analytics (pp. 80–88). New York: ACM. Retrieved from http://doi.acm.org/10.1145/1964858.1964870 doi:10.1145/1964858.1964870

Hong, L., Dom, B., Gurumurthy, S., & Tsioutsiouliklis, K. (2011). A time-dependent topic model for multiple text streams. In C. Apte, J. Ghosh, & P. Smyth (Eds.), *Proceedings of the 17th ACM SIGKDD International Conference* (p. 832). ACM. doi:10.1145/2020408.2020551

Java, A., Song, X., Finin, T., & Tseng, B. (2007). Why we twitter. In H. Zhang, B. Mobasher, L. Giles, A. McCallum, O. Nasraoui, & M. Spiliopoulou (Eds.), *Proceedings of the 9th WebKDD and 1st SNA-KDD 2007 Workshop* (pp. 56–65). ACM. doi:10.1145/1348549.1348556

Jungherr, A., Jurgens, P., & Schoen, H. (2012). Why the pirate party won the German election of 2009 or the trouble with predictions: A response to Tumasjan, A., Sprenger, T. O., Sander, P. G., & Welpe, I. M. "Predicting Elections With Twitter: What 140 Characters Reveal About Political Sentiment". *Social Science Computer Review*, *30*(2), 229–234. doi:10.1177/0894439311404119

Kitchenham, B., Pearl Brereton, O., Budgen, D., Turner, M., Bailey, J., & Linkman, S. (2009). Systematic literature reviews in software engineering - A systematic literature review. *Information and Software Technology*, *51*(1), 7–15. doi:10.1016/j.infsof.2008.09.009

Krishnamurthy, B., Gill, P., & Arlitt, M. (2008). A few chirps about twitter. In C. Faloutsos, T. Karagiannis, & P. Rodriguez (Eds.), *Proceedings of the First Workshop on Online Social Networks* (p. 19). Academic Press. doi:10.1145/1397735.1397741

Lau, J. H., Collier, N., & Baldwin, T. (2012). Online trend analysis with topic models: \#twitter trends detection topic model online. In Martin Kay & Christian Boitet (Eds.), *COLING 2012, 24th International Conference on Computational Linguistics, Proceedings of the Conference: Technical Papers* (pp. 1519–1534). Indian Institute of Technology Bombay.

Li, W., & McCallum, A. (2006). *Pachinko allocation: DAG-structured mixture models of topic correlations*. ICML. doi:10.1145/1143844.1143917

Liu, Y., Niculescu-Mizil, A., & Gryc, W. (2009). Topic-link LDA. In A. Danyluk, L. Bottou, & M. Littman (Eds.), *ICML '09 Proceedings of the 26th Annual International Conference on Machine Learning* (pp. 1–8). ICML. doi:10.1145/1553374.1553460

McCallum, A. K. (2002). *MALLET: A machine learning for language toolkit*. Retrieved from http://mallet.cs.umass.edu

Mimno, D., & McCallum, A. (2008). Topic models conditioned on arbitrary features with Dirichlet-multinomial regression. *UAI*. Retrieved from http://www.cs.umass.edu/ mimno/papers/dmr-uai.pdf

Mukherjee, I., & Blei, D. (2008). Relative performance guarantees for approximate inference in latent Dirichlet allocation. *NIPS*. Retrieved from http://books.nips.cc/papers/files/nips21/NIPS2008_0434.pdf

Mukherjee, I., & Blei, D. (2008). Relative performance guarantees for approximate inference in latent Dirichlet allocation. *NIPS*. Retrieved from http://books.nips.cc/papers/files/nips21/NIPS2008_0434.pdf

Musat, C., Velcin, J., Trausan-Matu, S., & Rizoiu, M.-A. (2011). *Improving topic evaluation using conceptual knowledge*. IJCAI.

Newman, D., Han Lau, J., Grieser, K., & Baldwin, T. (2010). *Automatic evaluation of topic coherence*. NAACL.

Newman, D., Karimi, S., & Cavedon, L. (2009). External evaluation of topic models. In *Proceedings of Australasian Document Computing Symposium* (pp. 11–18). Sydney: Academic Press.

Pak, A., & Paroubek, P. (2010). Twitter as a corpus for sentiment analysis and opinion mining. In *Proceedings of the Seventh International Conference on Language Resources and Evaluation (LREC'10)*. Valletta, Malta: European Language Resources Association (ELRA).

Perkiö, J., Buntine, W. L., & Sami Perttu, S. (2004). Exploring independent trends in a topic-based search engine. In Proceedings of Web Intelligence (pp. 664–668). Academic Press. doi:10.1109/WI.2004.10053

Rahman, N., Burkhardt, P. W., & Hibray, K. W. (2010). Object migration tool for data warehouses. *International Journal of Strategic Information Technology and Applications*, *1*(4), 55–73. doi:10.4018/jsita.2010100104

Ramage, D., Dumais, S., & Liebling, D. (2010). Characterizing microblogs with topic models. *ICWSM*. Retrieved from http://www.stanford.edu/dramage/papers/twitter-icwsm10.pdf

Ramage, D., Hall, D., Nallapati, R., & Manning, C. D. (2009). Labeled LDA: A supervised topic model for credit attribution in multi-labeled corpora. EMNLP. doi:10.3115/1699510.1699543

Ramage, D., & Rosen, E. (2009). *Stanford topic modeling toolbox*. Retrieved from http://nlp.stanford.edu/software/tmt/tmt-0.3/

Ramage, D., Rosen, E., Chuang, J., Manning, C. D., & McFarland, D. A. (2009). Topic modeling for the social sciences. In *Proceedings of NIPS 2009 Workshop on Applications for Topic Models: Text and Beyond*. Whistler, Canada: NIPS. Retrieved from http://www.brokenurl#pubs/tmt-nips09.pdf

Salton, G., & McGill, M. J. (1983). *Introduction to modern information retrieval*. New York: McGraw-Hill.

Smith, A. & Brenner, J. (2012). *Twitter use 2012*. Academic Press.

Sridevi, U. K., & Nagaveni, N. (2011). An ontology based model for document clustering. *International Journal of Intelligent Information Technologies*, *7*(3), 54–69. doi:10.4018/jiit.2011070105

Steyvers, M., & Griffiths, T. (2005). *Matlab topic modeling toolbox*. Retrieved from http://psiexp.ss.uci.edu/research/programs_data/toolbox.htm

Thangamani, M., & Thangaraj, P. (2011). Effective fuzzy ontology based distributed document using non-dominated ranked genetic algorithm. *International Journal of Intelligent Information Technologies*, *7*(4), 26–46. doi:10.4018/jiit.2011100102

Toutanova, K., & Johnson, M. (2007). A Bayesian LDA-based model for semi-supervised part-of-speech tagging. NIPS. Retrieved from http://books.nips.cc/papers/files/nips20/NIPS2007_0964.pdf

Wallach, H., Murray, I., Salakhutdinov, R., & Mimno, D. (2009). Evaluation methods for topic models. *ICML*. Retrieved from http://www.cs.umass.edu/ mimno/papers/wallach09evaluation.pdf

Wang, A. H. (2010). Don't follow me - Spam detection in Twitter. In *Security and Cryptography (SECRYPT), Proceedings of the 2010 International Conference on* (pp. 142–151). Retrieved from http://dblp.uni-trier.de/db/conf/secrypt/secrypt2010.html#Wang10

Wang, C., Blei, D. M., & Heckerman, D. (2008). Continuous time dynamic topic models. *UAI*. Retrieved from http://uai2008.cs.helsinki.fi/UAI_camera_ready/wang.pdf

Wang, X., & McCallum, A. (2006). Topics over time: A non-Markov continuous-time model of topical trends. KDD. doi:10.1145/1150402.1150450

Yan, F., Xu, N., & Qi, Y. (2009). Parallel inference for latent Dirichlet allocation on graphics processing units. *NIPS*. Retrieved from http://books.nips.cc/papers/files/nips22/NIPS2009_0546.pdf

Yao, L., Mimno, D., & McCallum, A. (2009). Efficient methods for topic model inference on streaming document collections. *KDD*. Retrieved from http://www.cs.umass.edu/ mimno/papers/fast-topic-model.pdf

Zhang, J., Song, Y., Zhang, C., & Liu, S. (2010). Evolutionary hierarchical Dirichlet processes for multiple correlated time-varying corpora. *KDD*. Retrieved from http://research.microsoft.com/en-us/um/people/shliu/p1079-zhang.pdf

Zhao, W. X., Jiang, J., Weng, J., He, J., Lim, E.-P., Yan, H., & Li, X. (2011). Comparing Twitter and traditional media using topic models. In *ECIR'11, Proceedings of the 33rd European Conference on Advances in Information Retrieval* (pp. 338–349). Berlin: Springer-Verlag. doi:10.1007/978-3-642-20161-5_34

Zhu, J., Ahmed, A., & Xing, E. P. (2009). *MedLDA: Maximum margin supervised topic models for regression and classification*. ICML. doi:10.1145/1553374.1553535

Zhu, J., & Xing, E. P. (2010). *Conditional topic random fields*. ICML.

KEY TERMS AND DEFINITIONS

Dynamic Topic Model: Dynamic topic models are generative models that can be used to analyze the evolution of (unobserved) topics of a collection of documents over time. This family of models was is an extension to Latent Dirichlet Allocation (LDA) that can handle sequential documents.

KDD: Knowledge Discovery in Databases (KDD) is an integration of multiple technologies for data management such as database management and data warehousing, statistic machine learning, decision support, and others such as visualization and parallel computing.

Latent Dirichlet Allocation: In natural language processing, latent Dirichlet allocation (LDA) is a generative model that allows sets of observations to be explained by unobserved groups that explain why some parts of the data are similar.

Microblogging: Microblogging is a broadcast medium that exists in the form of blogging. A microblog differs from a traditional blog in that its content is typically smaller in both actual and aggregated file size. Microblogs allow users to exchange small elements of content such as short sentences, individual images, or video links. These small messages are sometimes called microposts.

Tf-idf: Tf–idf, short for term frequency–inverse document frequency, is a numerical statistic that is intended to reflect how important a word is to a document in a collection or corpus.

Topic Model: In machine learning and natural language processing, a topic model is a type of statistical model for discovering the abstract "topics" that occur in a collection of documents.

Chapter 5
Design Consideration of Sociomaterial Multi–Agent CSCW Systems

Tagelsir Mohamed Gasmelseid
King Faisal University, Saudi Arabia

ABSTRACT

The recent technological advancements have significantly redefined the context in which organizations do business processes including the processes used to acquire, process, and share information. The transformations that emerged across the organizational and institutional landscapes have led to the emergence of new organizational forms of design and new business models. Within this context, the new business patterns, platforms, and architectures have been developed to enable for the maximization of benefits from data through the adoption of collaborative work practices. The main focus of such practices is oriented towards the improvement of responsiveness, building of alliances, and enhancing organizational reach. The use of global networks and Web-based systems for the implementation of collaborative work has been accompanied with a wide range of computer-supported collaborative systems. This chapter examines the context of collaboration, collaborative work, and the development of agent-supported collaborative work system. It also examines the implications of the ontological positions of sociomateriality on agent-supported collaborative work domains in terms of the multi-agent architecture and multi-agent evaluation.

1. INTRODUCTION

The growing organizational, institutional, economic and technological transformations exhibited during the last decade have been accompanied with a wide range of transformations and shifts that warrant the attention of policy makers. Such attention originates from the intensity of trans-

formations (in terms of magnitude and scale), the complexity of interactions among their variables and the growing difficulty in crystallizing their dysfunctional impacts on organizations and individuals. Organizationally, there has been more emphasis on making organizations flat, decentralized, highly concerned with stakeholders such as clients and suppliers, and widely involved in

DOI: 10.4018/978-1-4666-6639-9.ch005

transactions with suppliers through out-sourcing mechanisms. Institutionally, the migration towards decentralization has resulted into an increasingly growing focus on the delegation of authorities, the adoption of new styles of institutional reporting and the re-definition of managerial styles in use. On the other hand, the economic transformations associated with the new economic order are continuously re-shaping the context of production by moving emphasis from traditional labor-intensive production approaches to modern production tools and mechanisms. As a result, organizations are becoming more cost-sensitive, efficiency-focused and highly concerned with the use of organizational knowledge and its networks to produce knowledge-intensive products and services. On the technological side, the developments witnessed in the context of information systems, telecommunications infrastructure and IT configurations (hardware, software, databases, etc.) have also affected organizational performance and dictated new axioms for doing business. Coupled with their process-oriented "enabling" features, the use of global networks and web based systems has turned enterprises into an archipelago of "integrated" islands of performance interacting across global networks of "capital", "information" and "power" and driven by institutional concepts of "deregulation", "liberalization", and "re-engineering" (Gasmelseid, 2006). While the relationship between organizational and technological transformations tends to be debatable (i.e., whether technological developments lead to organizational and institutional transformations or technological developments have accompanied them), it goes without mentioning that technological developments have resulted into significant organizational impacts. They have significantly affected the organizational context of data acquisition, processing and sharing and led to the emergence of new forms of organizational design, the enactment of new business models and the redefinition of organizational and work boundaries (in terms of work relationships, relationship between work and place of work and key performance indicators).

Taken together, such transformations have increased the attention of business organizations on the merits of to be gained from using the concept of collaboration, collaborative work and the adoption of computer-supported collaborative work systems (CSCWs) and technologies. While new patterns, platforms and architectures are being developed for the maximization of benefits from data, the growing emphasis on "collaborative work", "responsiveness" and "building of alliances" is reshaping the way global enterprises do business (Gasmelseid, 2009). Within this context, the emphasis of organizations continued to be focused on the development of effective and efficient technology-enabled processes, the orchestration and mainstreaming of databases, model coupling, the mobilization of deployable resources and improving their capacity to manage knowledge-intensive processes.

2. COLLABORATION AND COLLABORATIVE WORK

At the abstract level, collaboration focuses mainly on making a joint effort towards the achievement of agreed-upon goals and objectives. According to Turban et al (2010), the motivations for collaboration include vision sharing, building trust and synergy, sharing work and information, making decisions and solving problems, reviewing and building consensus and socializing. Collaborative work denote situations in which different collaborating parties working across different time and space differences and sharing resources to achieve collaborative objective (s). Especially in today's competitive environment, organizations focus on collaborative work in pursuit of optimizing resources, improving responsiveness, enhancing communication and involvement of stakeholders, improving the consistency of tools and procedures and maintain a conducive sharing work environment (Steve & Mann, 2003; Siriwan & Haddawy 2006; David, Jenkins & Joseph, 2006). Depending on the type of organization, the work to be done and the context of collaboration, different degrees of collaboration can be established with varying domains of focus and multiplicity of processes and orientation. Low collaboration takes the form of collective work but un-coordinated work efforts and activities where the collaborating partners work independently towards the achievement of collaborative work. Medium collaboration takes the form of having coordinated work and coordinated efforts of individuals collectively aimed towards the realization of collective objectives. High collaboration, on the other hand, exists when both the tasks of the work to be done and efforts of teams (rather than individuals) are highly concerted and orchestrated in a wider organizational context. However, irrespective of the degree of collaboration thought, the success of collaborative work depends upon the availability of deployable resources, the existence of good perception and understanding of the responsibilities, activities and intentions of other members of a collaborating ensemble (Minh, Gitesh & Yun Yang, 2006).

Collaboration and collaborative work is being made possible by the technological developments (including the internet) and their contribution towards supporting the acquisition and sharing of collaboration resources (including information) necessary for collective task handling. The use of such technologies continued to have significant impacts on the methods, styles and environments in which collaborative work takes place. As a result, it has been increasingly possible for individuals, groups and organizations located in remote trajectories to engage in synchronous (collective online working on tasks) and asynchronous (when at least some of tasks are worked on separately offline) collaborative work processes.

However, realizing the potential of collaboration is challenged by a wide range of personal, institutional and technological issues. These issues include working with the wrong people, poorly defined problem domains, using inadequate resources, lack of planning and mechanisms for examining alternatives, dominance of different elements, conflicts and fear and lack of suitable information and collaboration systems and platforms. Despite its growing complexity, difficulty and high costs, collaboration remains a "must" rather than a choice for business organizations since none of them have all knowledge, expertise, resources insights and abilities to achieve objectives in such a highly competitive environment.

3. COMPUTER-SUPPORTED COLLABORATIVE WORK SYSTEMS AND TECHNOLOGIES

Computer Supported Collaborative work (CSCW) aims at understanding how collaborative activities, their coordination, productivity and effectiveness can be supported by means of computer systems (Kevin, 2003; Carstensen & Schmidt, 2002). It focuses on the adoption of technology-oriented and the emphasizing socially-organized practices of the collaborating members (Suchman, 1989; Bannon & Schmidt, 1989; Wilson, 1999) through the use of technological tools and mechanisms. This means that it is a design-oriented process that incorporates technological issues (i.e., ways to design computer technology to better support collaborative work) and work-related issues (understanding work processes and designing necessary support for collaborative interactions).

Collaboration processes are made possible through the use of CSCWs which influence the way of doing things and the methods to be used acquire, process and share collaborative work-related information. The use of group support systems, as widely adopted CSCW system, is providing powerful communication facilities that allow for inexpensive, fast, capable and reliable means of information sharing among groups and individuals. The basic functionality is to acquire and integrate relevant information to support distributed problem solving and processing and improve the capacity of collaborating parties to address relevant collaboration phenomenon. The list of group support systems technologies include web based group support systems, decision room based systems (cool, cooler, mobile, and on-demand) multimedia document presentation systems, document sharing systems, whiteboards, video and audio conferencing, videoconferencing playback and group workflow management systems. They also allow for the improvement of collaborative planning, forecasting and replenishment since they are centered on harnessing collective intelligence that originates from collaboration processes among the collaborating parties in an open, global and peer-oriented environment. Collective intelligence allow for the coordination of Ad-hoc communities of practice and their actions and provide the cooperation necessary for building networks of trust, peer-to-peer business interactions and the exploitation of open source software components. On the other hand, the cognition dimensions of collective intelligence facilitate the projection of future events and emerging trends. CSCWs are characterized by their functional base that include a wide range of tasks, processes and procedures, therefore organizations think of them as vehicles for maintaining transparency, trust and openness of communication (Henk, Paul & Jan van Doremalen, 2004). Their openness and parallelism facilitate the exchange and use of knowledge for the production of knowledge-intensive products and services without being challenged with individual limitations of the work force (Silvia, Saskia, Wim & Nick, 2007; Yan Xiao & Seagull, 2006). They focus on content rather than persons and merits rather than source and therefore, they promote equal participation and anonymity. Their triggering, synergies and structures also promote

the integration of ideas, systematic thinking and problem solving in an open environment in a way that improves the memory of organizations through record keeping.

Computer supported collaborative work groupware (software and related computer networks) constitute the backbone of CSCWs as it facilitates interaction among the collaborating parties, resource sharing and collective accomplishment of tasks. They play essential and integral roles in group collaboration by simplifying communication, supporting coordination and providing chances for process management and coupling in pursuit of group collaboration. The functionality of the CSCWs' groupware includes the management of interdependencies, the provision of sophisticated interfaces and the promotion of group awareness necessary for the enrichment of "mutual understanding" among the collaborating members. They enable the collaborating parties (and their concerned agents) to interact with databases, application servers, content management systems, data warehouses, workflow systems, search engines, message queues, web crawlers, mining and analysis packages, and other enterprise integration applications. The groupware includes the learning spaces of Lotus Notes domino server, Netscape Collabra server, Microsoft net-meeting, Novell Group-wise and WebEx. It also include software for tracking document changes, electronic mail software, application-sharing programs, videoconferencing software, instant and email messaging, groupware, wiki web, computer assisted design (CAD) and software that support collaborative viewing of web pages (Gasmelseid, 2008).

4. DESIGNING CSCWS

The expansion of collaborative work and internet-based collaborative business models, there has been a growing demand for systematically examining organization-wide collaborative determinants of information acquisition, processing and sharing.

It is also becoming highly important for organizations to understand and forecast patterns of group behavior, detect collaboration breakdowns and support group activity with adequate feedback (Thanasis, Alejandra, & Fatos, 2006). The design and development of CSCWs is a complex task that requires the mobilization of different resources, a thorough understanding of collaborative deliverables and the crystallization of functionalities that emerge from the utilization of such resources. Such complexity calls for the optimization of collaborative functionalities and model coupling at the level of the entire collaborative work system as well as at the level of the network. Such optimization is essential for maintaining the flexibility and efficiency of collaboration processes.

Different theories have been used to approach the development of CSCWs including the activity theory, conversation analysis, coordination theory, distributed cognition theory, ethno-methodology, grounded theory, situated action and social/symbolic interactionism (Gasmelseid, 2010; Shapiro, 1994; Engestrom, Miettinen & Punamaki, 1999; Ackerman & Halverson, 1999; Strauss & Corbin, 1998; Schiff, Van House & Butler, 1997; Fitzpatrick, Kaplan & Mansfield, 1996). The development of group support systems, for example, utilize traditional techniques of collaboration such as the Nominal Group Technique (where individuals work alone to generate ideas which are pooled under guidance of a trained facilitator) and Delphi techniques (where a structured process for collecting and distilling knowledge from a group of experts by means of questionnaires).

However, the development processes adopted in CSCW systems tend to focus on describing the "cooperative" task (s) of the work to be done and the type of computer support needed for the accomplishment of such task(s) in stable organizational settings of interaction. This means that emphasis tend to be made on understanding the type of technologies to be used to enable collaborative work, the configuration of infrastructure and the functional and dysfunctional consequences associated with the use of such systems. The basic assumption is that the collaborating members (human and agent actors) are interrelated as parts of specialized communities (in which the principles of division of labor applies) to contribute different kinds of "interactive expertise". Based on this understanding, the design of CSCW systems is regarded as a joint activity expanding across different communities of practice directly involved in interdependent and collaborative activities. Theories such as the corporate organizational memory regarded the development of CSCW systems as a vehicle for capturing accumulated knowledge and making it available and accessible to the collaborating members. The basic aim of such activity is to improve the efficiency and effectiveness of the collaborating parties. This approach is guided by the concepts of "active remembering" as a means for improving the potential of "organizational memory" by incorporating organizational, technical, and process-specific constraints. This means that the focus is made on "tasks" and "processes" rather than on "the way" to develop necessary collaborative work information systems.

Previous studies reveal that CSCW did not seem to be achieving the functionalities it promised. The problem with such technology-oriented approach of CSCWs design is that it didn't cover the majority of technologies and technological platforms and update its methodological base in accordance with the pace of technological change. As a result, the majority of these efforts are constrained by their linearity and limited focus on certain variables without accounting for the multiplicity of variables interacting in un-stable organizational settings. Because of the lack of integrated design dimensions that address the dynamics of individual and group interactions and the context of information exchanged, the majority of theories used to conceptualize CSCW did not display a sophisticated level of integration. There has been more emphasis on "multidisciplinary" working and less "interdisciplinary" working (Steve & Mann, 2003). The transformations experienced in the context of collaboration and collaborative work have shifted the orientation of system development from "system-centered views" of information systems to "user-centered" paradigms that focus on contextual enquiry, participatory design and end user development (Bayer & Holtzblatt 1998; Greenbaum & Kyng 1991). In practice few theories and approaches have explicitly and thoroughly approached such shift and incorporated them into the entire development processes. Little has been done to investigate the nature and magnitude of collaboration, the "socio-behavioral" styles of collaborating members, the sophistication of the entire collaborative work, and the "envisioned" support to be provided by computer technologies in a "shared" environment (Gasmelseid, 2008).

5. MULTI-AGENT SYSTEMS: DOMAIN AND DESIGN METHODOLOGIES

Software agents' technology and agent-based collaborative work support systems can be used for the implementation complex collaborative work processes. Software agents are program entities that carry out some of the tasks on behalf of their users, other agents or programs with some degree of autonomy using appropriate information and communication platforms (Hyacinth, 1996; Bradshaw, 1997). They assist in task delegation, users training, event monitoring, information search, matchmaking and filtering based on their widely cited attributes of autonomy, reactivity, collaboration, mobility, goal orientation rationality and social-ability (Gasmelseid, 2007a). Based on the complexity of the agent representation style (individual vs. multi agent) additional agent qualities can be crystallized. Because they perform different functions and tasks for different users or programs, agent classification includes collaborative, interface, information, task, mobile and reaction agents, among others. Especially in complex environments (such as electronic com-

merce, healthcare, stock exchanges etc), software agents are usually deployed in the form of multi-agent organizations or systems. A multi agent system consists of a set of heterogeneous agents that communicate and cooperate to carry out work using certain levels of intelligence, communication and cooperation paradigms, and employ massive parallel processing capabilities to allow for collaborative work. They share knowledge and resources to perform their tasks and deal with a multiplicity of interconnected processes whose solutions demand the allocation of fusion of information and expertise from demographically distributed sources (Sycara, 1998).

Multi-agent concepts incorporate technological, organizational and decision making issues that support the realization of the objectives of collaborative work in a wider socio-organizational context. In such a context, the objectives of the collaborating parties and their tasks are represented in terms of agents. Such representation goes hand-in-hand with the measures that govern the organizational structure, division of labor and hierarchy of responsibilities at different decision making and organizational levels. Therefore, the agent organization reflects the organization of task assignments together with their related hierarchy of command and goal congruence mechanisms. The diversity of organizational settings, therefore is reflected in the type and functionalities and privileges of the agents interacting within the entire multi-agent organization. The potential and applicability of multi-agent paradigm to support collaborative work is driven by the following considerations. Especially in complex situations, multi-agent configurations facilitate collaboration and manage tasks through the shift of some collaboration tasks to agents and allowing some space for wider interactions and the production of user-created content. Throughout the collaboration process, the collaborating parties can mainstream their tasks in a functional way by using functional and task-oriented agents such as the information and interface agents without breaking organizational chains of command. They also contribute to the negotiation of tasks and the use of cooperative distributed applications.

Different software engineering methodologies have been used for the design and development of multi-agent systems such as Gaia, TROPOS, MESSAGE and Multi-agent Systems Engineering methodology (MaSE), among others (Gasmelseid, 2014). While some of the available AOSE methodologies represent an extension to and/or application of existing "conventional" software engineering methodologies (especially object oriented) to agent oriented applications, others have focused on defining a number of models that use the basic guidelines of agent theory as a guide for analyzing and designing agent oriented applications and systems (Iglesias, et al, 1998; Wooldridge, et al, 2000; Odell et al, 2000; Kendall, 1999; Lind, 1999). Gaia methodology deals with both the societal (macro) and agent (micro) level aspects of information system design. The main concepts in Gaia are divided into two categories: "abstract" and "concrete". At the high level of conceptualization, "abstract" concepts involve the definition of roles including protocols, permissions, activities and responsibilities. On the other hand, "concrete" concepts put more emphasis on the articulation of agent types, services and acquaintances. The outcomes of the analysis phase are used as inputs for design phase which focuses on creating an agent-based model.

TROPOS methodology pays more attention to understanding the organizational context of the multi-agent information system by focusing on the very early phase of software development in which the system as well as it's context are studied as a larger social-technical system (Bresciani, et al, 2002; Perini, et al, 2001a; 2001b; Giunchiglia et al, 2001; Giorgini, et al, 2001a; 2001b; Giunchiglia et al, 2002). It includes five phases of software development: early requirements analysis, late requirements analysis, architectural design, detailed design and implementation (Paolo & Sannicolo,

2002). Being an organizationally-oriented methodology, TROPOS tries to improve the ability of designers to justify the entire multi-agent system as well as its "traceability" dimensions by enabling artifacts produced during later phases to be clearly referred back to artifacts or requirements produced earlier. MESSAGE methodology is more oriented towards knowledge representation. Most of the knowledge level entity concepts of the MESSAGE methodology fall into three main categories: "Concrete-Entity", "Activity", and "Mental-State-Entity" (Caire, et al, 2001). The main types of Concrete-Entity are: agents, organizations, roles, and resources. The main types of Activity are: tasks, interaction and interaction protocols. The basic type of Mental-State-Entity is the goal. A goal (whether intrinsic or transient) associates an agent with a situation in terms of a rule-based utility function. An analysis model in MESSAGE is contingent upon a number of views describing organization, goal-task, agent-role, interaction, and domain. The Prometheus methodology consists of three phases: system specification, architectural design and detailed design (Padgham & Winiko, 2002a; 2002b). The system specification phase, involves two activities: determining the system's internal and external environment (in terms of percepts denoting incoming information from the environment and actions by which an agent affects its environment), and determining the goals and functionality of the system. The architectural design phase involves three activities: defining agent types, designing the overall system structure, and defining the interactions between agents. The internals of each agent and how it will accomplish its tasks within the overall system are addressed in the detailed design phase which focuses on defining capabilities, internal events, plans and detailed data structure for each agent type identified in the previous step. Multi-agent Systems Engineering methodology (MaSE) is similar to Gaia with respect to generality and the application domain supported, but in addition MaSE goes further to support for automatic code creation through the MaSE tool (DeLoach, 1999; Wood & DeLoach, 2000). It is divided into seven phases: goal capture, application of use cases, goal refinement, agent classes' creation, conversations construction, agent class assembly and system design.

Some of these methodologies have been criticized for their limited deployment due to the lack of maturity and their failure to capture the autonomous and proactive behavior of agents, as well as the richness of the interactions (Zambonelli, 2001). Current agent-oriented methodologies focus mainly on multi-agent systems analysis and design, but without providing straightforward connections to the implementation of such systems (Mercedes et al, 2005; Wooldridge, et al 2000; DeLoach, et al 2001). Some of the existing software development techniques are characterized with a fundamental mismatch between the concepts used by object-oriented developers and the agent-oriented view (Wooldridge, 1997). In particular, extant approaches fail to adequately capture an agent's flexible, autonomous problem-solving behavior, the richness of an agent's interactions, and the complexity of an agent system's organizational structures. Most of these methods feature a technology-driven, model-oriented and sequential approach for the development of multi-agent applications that may not be always adequate for the development of agent-oriented systems. Most of them assume (in advance) the suitability of multi-agent technology for the entire problem domain. While the model orientations of methodologies are obvious, the process of model coupling and integration process does not explicitly reflect the links between models (Lind, 1999). Besides as the main issues to be addressed by agent oriented software engineering methodologies (such as autonomy, reactivity, proactive-ness and social ability), the concern for mobility have been growing over time (White, 1997). In spite of the growing diffusion of mobile agent technology, little research has been done to settle "design" directions to be followed in order to determine

when mobile agents are convenient to be used or not. However, the current agent oriented software engineering methodologies used for developing multi agent systems do not provide methods to determine in which cases mobile agents should be used. Many of the existing methodologies intentionally do not support intelligent agents; rather, they aim for generality and treat agents as black boxes.

Except for the case of TROPOS and to some extent Gaia, AOSE methodologies tend to focus on system design (basically definition of agents, capabilities and communication) without providing a thorough understanding of the "actual problems" facing decision makers, the causes and consequences of these problems and whether the use of multi agent systems can contribute to the solution space envisioned. Because these methodology are characterized by the limited communication between the "decision maker" and the "designer" and the fact that agent technology has already been decided in advance to be the appropriate paradigm for solving problems, the chance of developing systems on the basis of "imagined" potentials of designers is highly probable.

The use of MESSAGE methodology results into a large amount of data and demands additional processing resources (time, cost and skills) in a way that complicates the process of system design because it is necessary to undertake resource-consuming investigations of the interactions among different "views" and associating them with corporate objectives. Such a consideration may result into complexities with regards to information update and system maintenance. Because of the complex view-coupling process any mistake that exists at later stages of the system development process demands intensive rework that delays design. Although the methodology does not provide in depth emphasis on "problem analysis" and the early phases of decision making, the process of coupling problem dynamics with agent capabilities will be cumbersome. While the process of system analysis and design require extensive user involvement to enrich and enable the articulation of system linkages and agent functionalities, they validity of such methodology will be seriously threatened if such involvement is not maintained appropriately.

Prometheus methodology does not provide emphasis on the early phases of decision making (decision intelligence and problem-objective orchestration) therefore, the resulting system specifications are not directly related to the basic "information requirements" of the users who "delegate" some of their authorities to "agents. As it is the same limitation in conventional system development and engineering methodologies, the entire system dynamic will be based on the designer's perception of "what will be his information requirements if he were the decision maker for whom the entire agent module or organization provides support" rendering the entire agent-oriented applications to be "operationally" out right failures although "technically sound" and reduce their applicability with regards to the provision of appropriate decision support. Although Prometheus is regarded as supporting the development of intelligent agents in accordance with goals, beliefs, plans, and events (Padgham & Winikoff, 2002), many other methodologies treat agents as "simple software processes that interact with each other to meet an overall system goal" (DeLoach, 2001). Like other methodologies, Prometheus is envisioning implementation through the emphasis on the "automation" of the stages of the methodology rather than the "implementation" of the target system.

Although Gaia is viewed as being neutral with respect to both the target domain and the agent architecture, it does not present a procedure to guide roles and protocols identification (Pablo et al, 2003) when building agent-based systems when it is regarded as an organizational design process. While the analysis models used in Gaia methodology are based on well-defined concepts, they only represent a subset of the concepts re-

quired for agent oriented analysis with the design models remain not clearly explained (Giovanni et al, 2001). Although it has been proven as a good approach for developing closed domain agent-systems, the above mentioned restrictions delimit its applicability to open and unpredictable domain of internet applications. The methodology has been extended by adding some organizational concepts such as organizational rules, structures and patterns (Zambonelli et al, 2001a).

Because the MaSE methodology is similar to Gaia with respect to generality and application domains supported, it inherits the same limitations. The "process" of using the MaSE methodology tends to be oriented towards the "tool itself" by focusing on the use of diagrams rather than focusing on the orientation of the whole process directed towards the investigation and solution of decision-making problems. On the other hand, MaSE methodology has been characterized by a long system development process that complicates the process of integration in addition to the fact that it does not support the initial phases of decision making.

6. MULTI-AGENT SUPPORTED COLLABORATIVE WORK SYSTEMS (MASCWS)

Gasmelseid (2008) suggested the use of multi-agent methodologies and concepts of "agency" to capitalize on the development of CSCW systems and the articulation of relevant new design dimensions. As shown in figure (1) below, the multi-agent computer supported collaborative work model views interaction at two layers: (a) participants' layer (a.k.a interactions and understanding domain) and (b) agents' layer (a.k.a cooperation and collaboration domain) in the form of computer mediated communication. At each layer, computerized (processing and functional) artifacts are used to support coordination, cooperation and

Figure 1. MASCWS's interaction framework (Gasmelseid, 2008)

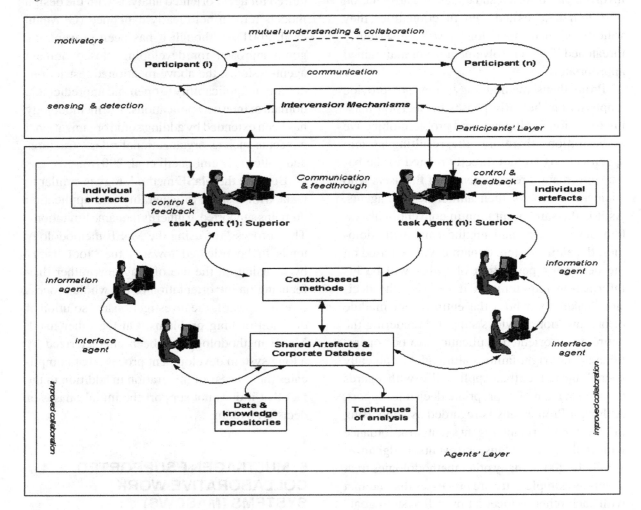

negotiation and the achievement of objectives. It also includes context-based models and methods, data repositories and analytical techniques.

Artifacts are controlled and acted upon by all agents capable of perceiving the state of artifacts in the entire multi-agent organization. They include agent-specific artifacts and shared artifacts created and incrementally transformed to enable the accomplishment of collaborative work. Agent-specific artifacts are agent-based, context-related and are usually incorporated and represented into the agent's knowledge base and interface engine in order to guide its agent-user interaction and

maintain conviviality across its specific and corporate domain of interaction. Shared artifacts reflect the dynamics and functionality of not only inter-agent interaction and cooperation but also the nature and magnitude of tasks, changes of agents' behavior, expectations and actions to be undertaken within a shared environment. The maintenance of functional and shared artifacts is based on the functionality orchestration mechanisms used in the entire organization such as standard operating procedures, coherent sets of shared rules, behaviors, expectations and authority relationships. The success of such artifacts is dependent upon the availability of appropriate feedback and feed through mechanisms that enable agents to directly interact, perceive, control artifacts and states of objects and observe the reactions of the collaborating users and agents. Based on the functions and levels of agents, access to artifacts follows a layered fashion in a way that significantly affects the achievement of collaborative work. Accordingly, agents can be able to collaboratively communicate through artifacts and indicate different objects or reactions by moving, sending information or doing any other action which may be accompanied with phrases.

The model's database includes different types of re-usable data required by the collaborating parties and their agents in order to achieve collaboration objectives. To improve the usability of such data special emphasis should be paid to the maintenance of data integration, the discovery of database dependencies and the necessary for the achievement of collaboration tasks corporate database that represents different types of re-usable data that can be used by the collaborating parties including agents. The basic consideration here is the mainstreaming of processes through integrated data and improved discovery and management of database dependencies and the management of privileges and access control. However, the congruence and consistency of the models used for the implementation of intelligent collaborative work requires high organizational capacity to mainstream process modeling at both individual and collective levels of functionality. On the other hand, the type and nature of work to be done in asynchronous and asynchronous modes significantly affects the model base of the multi-agent organization and the mechanisms to be used for implementation. However, models should reflect the practices, processes and expectations of the collaborating parties who interact within the context of the entire multi-agent computer supported collective work.

The set of analytical methods of the model constitute the tools used for analysis required for the achievement of collaborative work. The tools include data mining techniques, OLAP and multidimensional data analysis, task scheduling and prioritizing, information acquisition and sending, dialogue enablers, and user-agent interventions, among others. Such tools can be embedded into shared artifacts of the system as well as in the knowledge and interface engine of the collaborating agents. The model base of the entire multi-agent computer supported collaborative work system includes two types of models. Agent specific models (denoting the functionality of the entire agent in pursuit of achieving its individual or collaborative goals). On the other hand, system-oriented models denote the overall functionality of the collaboration process which dictate the axioms for task accomplishment and resource sharing.

7. SOCIOMATERIALITY IMPLICATIONS OF MASCWS

The development of CSCWS is generally regarded as a dynamic organizational change and a development process oriented towards maintaining the coherence of collaborative tasks, the distribution of control, and goal congruence. According to Martin (1992), organizational change (and its cultural dimensions) can be approached using three perspectives: integration, differentiation and fragmentation. Integration perspectives view organizational change as a neat, carefully planned, rational and non-political process that focuses mainly on outcomes. Differentiation perspectives focus on the difficulty to avoid conflicts, lack of consensus and the existence of different subcultures. Fragmentation perspectives include change related aspects such as the ambiguity and complexity of relationships among manifestations. This means that the construction and reconstruction of organizational reality is oriented towards the organization of tasks and processes. Because of the variety of transformations exhibited in the internal and external environments of business organizations, there has been a tendency towards rethinking the context of organizational change and the use of information systems by adopting sociomaterial ontologies. Agency-related theories such as Actor-Network Theory (Callon, 1986; Latour, 1987), socio-technical ensembles (Bijker, 1995), mangle of practice (Pickering, 1995) and relational materiality (Law, 2004) are used to enable such rethinking.

Sociomateriality regards people and technology (or any other non-human actors) as constitutively entangled inseparable sociomaterial assemblages (Latour, 2005; Orlikowski 2007; Zammuto et al. 2007; Leonardi and Barley 2008; Markus and Silver 2008; Orlikowski and Scott 2008), rather than viewing them as primarily self-contained independent entities mutually influencing each other (Slife 2004). While social actions are used for the co-configuration of technology and human, the constitutive entanglements and social relations generated between them are used as a means for understanding the way through which new forms of organizing tend to emerge and get negotiated and performed. Because material agency tend to be continuously mangled in practice, emergently transformed and delineated, it can be used as an infrastructural tool for enabling organizational activities and processes. The mangling of practice and practice of people with technology enables them to know themselves by configuring their identities, desire, capabilities, and vision for the future in (Pickering, 1995; Harraway, 1991). It also allows for the continuous review of social relations through such ongoing social interactions.

Sociomateriality pays considerable attention to learning and material knowing processes through which knowledge can be acquired, codified and shared. Together with their cultural and historical dimensions, such processes regard knowledge as being situated, emergent, pragmatic, and contested (Blackler, 1995; Tsoukas, 1996; Nicolini, et al. 2003. Material knowing and learning involve different timelines (objective and subjective) and different spaces in which different stakeholders interact and share different types of expertise. While objective time denotes the timeframe or timeline of collaborative processes, subjective time describes how the collaborating parties interpret such timeframes (Sawyer and Southwick, 2002; Halford and Leonard, 2005; Schatzki, 2006; Nicolini, 2007; Saunders and Kim, 2007). Both types of times are usually interpreted differently either because task related differentials and/or the ability of the collaborating members to know about such times through organizational practice. Especially when there is no agreement about the deadlines of collaborative work phases, each collaborating partner may interpret the timeframe in different ways.

Space refers to distributedness (Sahay, 1997; Halford and Leonard, 2005; Nicolini, 2007) of people, expertise, tasks and resources. Objective space represents the geographical aspect of distributedness as it can be shown in terms of physical proximity or distance and incorporates expertise differentials that shape collaboration across different departments and communities of practice. The way the collaborating parties view space and time depends on their perceptions about proximity and how it affects and reflects both organizational and personal cultures. According to Orlikowski (2006) material knowing can be scaffolded by the materiality of technology. The size of a meeting room chosen, for example, scaffolds the way meeting members may interact and the capabilities of a conference call machine may scaffold the kind of communications the collaborating members can make during meetings. The growing importance of enhancing material knowing in collaborative work and enabling the collaborating members to know each other and coordinate activities has led to the emergence of frequent face-to-face meetings and boundary documents such as meeting documents (Orlikowski, 2002). By interacting with these material forms and configuring relationships with them, the collaborating members will know their capabilities.

The implications of sociomateriality ontologies for MASCWS are conceptualized within the context of the adoption of such ontologies in information systems in general. Different perspectives have been used to conceptualize the mutual entanglement of technology and human actions in information systems (Monteiro and Hanseth 1995; Jones 1998; Orlikowski and Iacono 2001; Latham and Sassen 2005; Kallinikos 2006; Orlikowski 2007; Orlikowski and Scott 2008). The implications of the ontological and epistemological concepts of sociomateriality on the development and conceptualization of MASCWS can be discussed using two dimensions.

The Multi-Agent Architecture

Architecture specifies how the agent can be incorporated as a part of a multi-agent system and how these "parts" (hardware and/or software modules) should be made to interact using specific techniques and algorithms (Maes, 1995). According to Anumba et al, (2003), there are several common ways of structuring the entire agent organization:

1. *Organizational Structuring* in which all agents share the same explicit end goal. Due to the fact that only one agent posses a global view of the full task, it is very difficult for peer agents with different goals to resolve their difficulties.
2. *Contracting* where a manager agent breaks the entire problem into component problems and then announce each task for contracting agents to make their bids, the manager then reviews the bids and awards the contract. Because contract nets are best used when the problem can be broken down via a well-defined hierarchical nature into a set of tasks, planning has to be done centrally.
3. *Multi-agent planning* which involves a central arbiter who reviews all potential plans of individual agents and resolve conflict when they exist.

4. *Peer-to-peer negotiation* where agents communicate directly with each other in pursuit of achieving both individual and collective goals.

The type of architecture used significantly affects the type of agents to be incorporated into the collaboration process, their functionalities, the type of data repositories to be used and the models to work on. Because the context of collaboration incorporates a wide range of technological, organizational and institutional issues, it plays an integral role in shaping the multi-agent architecture. The ontological perspectives of sociomaterial assemblages lead to some architecture-based implications:

1. **The Emergence of Tasks and Processes:** The ontological positions of sociomateriality, the processes of material knowing and scaffolding issues are closely related to temporal emergence of new practices, work processes and forms and boundary documents. Such emergences originate from in response to the potential resistance of people to materiality and their efforts to development of new patterns of behaviour and tasks in their collaboration environment. Iinteractions that lead to such emergences can be internal or external (human-human, agent-agent and/or human-agent) interactions and therefore they result into different domains of emergence and different types of tasks and processes. An emerging process may have different implications that can be user-specific (such as change of tasks), group-related (such as changing the utility matrix of the collaborating members) and work-related (such as changing resource allocation and sharing plans and schedules). On the other hand, the artifacts to deal with such emerging processes may encounter agent-specific arrangements (including the type, number and functionality of agents to

be a part of the collaborating process) as well as other arrangements necessary to streamline the overall collaboration processes and activities.

The articulation and orchestration of such emerging tasks and the updating and management of artifacts significantly affect the way the entire multi-agent architecture is being developed. Generally speaking, some agent oriented software engineering methodologies are used for the design of multi-agent architectures such as TROPOS, Gaia methodology, MESSAGE methodology, Prometheus methodology and MaSE, among others. Such methodologies are based on the assumption that "any software life cycle, process or product model must be tailored towards the characteristic needs of the application domain of the target system (Basilsi, et al, 1994). Despite their contribution to the development of multi-agent systems in different domains and areas of application, their capacity to absorb such sociomaterial emergences remains questionable.

2.   **The Conceptualization of Agent Qualities:** The qualities of the agents involved into the collaboration process constitute the criterion to be used for the development of the matrix that related the capabilities of agents to the tasks to be implemented. Such matrix represent the coordination and control backbone of the entire multi-agent collaboration architecture. However, the material knowing positions associated with collaborative sociomaterial assemblages also affect the qualities to be maintained by the collaborating members both humans and agents such as learning, mobility, sociability and conviviality. The context of learning is also affected by the sociomaterial aspects of distributedness and space that dictate new axioms for collaborative learning. This is because material knowing in within the context of the entire MASCWS is not lim-

ited to the ability and capacity of members to know individual tasks and assignments but it also expands to cover knowing the impact of someone's (person and/or agent) on others (persons and/or agents). While it remains acceptable that the materiality of technology scaffolds sociomaterial communication and collaboration-oriented knowing, the existence of open source methods such as social media tools allows for a wider supplementary assistance that can be used to extend such knowing.

The emergence of tasks and processes is also related to the qualities of the collaborating agents and their ability to maintain "ethical and moral agency" and make a principle-based choice between competing alternatives. Agent based ethical decision making requires that the agent approaches problems "logically" and make decisions based on well-reasoned, defensible "ethical principles", value judgments, and (formal & informal) guidelines (Gasmelseid, 2009). Ethical and moral agency is directly related to learning and material knowing processes as it deals with the acquisition, organization, classification, recording, processing and distribution of collaborative knowledge and information. The question of ethical and moral agency is looming very big when agents possess mobility qualities and attributes that allow them to move across a wider landscape of locations, resources and processes. Such mobility increases the agent's exposure to commit an ethical dilemma either because of its movement to access information and/or perform transactions or because of the materiality of technology and its situation-specific ethic-oriented dimensions of technology such as amplification, routinization and sublimation. Practicing with technology the entire agent may be subject to many consequences including denying access, wrong-directing, and arresting. Such interactions with technology which may incorporate human interactions and lead to many processes and tasks that complicate the context of architectures. This brings to the attention the level of learning and autonomy an agent must have in order to "adjust its behavior" in response to the changes taking place in its environment.

The Evaluation of Multi-Agent Systems

The question of evaluating multi-agent collaborative work systems continues to be a complex task not only because of its dependence of software agents' technology but also because of the difficulty of developing an objective evaluation matrix. The ontological and epistemological positions that humans and non-humans are constitutively entangled advocated by some authors (Leonardi and Barley 2008 and Zammuto *et al*. 2007), seem to be static and linear and may not be able to account for the dynamic human and non-human constitutive entanglements and how they bring about new forms of organizing. "Organizational change" implies a concrete, emotionless development, generated in a cause and effect fashion, with clear boundaries between what was there before and after the 'intervention'. Such a conceptualization is at odds with the tenets of sociomateriality. Such a conceptualization means that it is not enough to consider the interactions between humans and technology as a base for understanding organizational change and evolution. The context of collaborative work and their supporting systems expressed in terms of "organizational change" should be studied in a wider and more open way. A way that facilitates an exploration of the continuous formations of constitutive entanglements between human and non-human actors, and that accounts for (intended and unintended) consequences of these entanglements. However, within the context of agent-supported collaborative work, the notion of "organizing" seems to be insufficient to facilitate such an exploration. The emphasis on "outcomes" of interactions of sociomaterial assemblages in terms of tasks or

processes complicates the process of evaluation since unique tasks and processes may emerge for which no evaluation criteria can be developed. As a result, evaluation of processes tend to focus on the movement of information and/or the collaborating members to perform tasks and excludes the qualitative aspects of such processes and the collaborating members such as their feelings, intentions and emotions, negotiations, successes and failures. On the other hand, because of the lack of separation between the actions of humans and agents (i.e., agency), the time and space dimensions of material knowing and scaffolding involve that decisions are already been taken by agents in a complex environment and it is difficult to specify responsibility for them.

8. CONCLUSION

The severity of interactions that characterize the external environments of organizations has led to significant organizational and institutional transformations and increased emphasis on collaboration and collaborative work. Together with the accompanying technological developments such transformations have also re-shaped the context of information acquisition, sharing and use. The motivations for collaboration and collaborative work processes range from simple needs for information sharing and socialization purposes to complicated competitiveness-oriented collaboration. However, the differences of collaboration domains dictate differences in terms of computer supported collaborative work systems and their infrastructures. The use of software agents' technology improves collaboration processes as it enhances communication, coordination, information sharing and negotiation. A part of the overall theme of information systems, the development of multi-agent supported collaborative work systems has been affected by the epistemological and ontological positions of sociomateriality. Sociomaterial assemblages are associated with the theorization of the relationships between human (people) and technology and using the resulting patterns of interaction as a vehicle for understanding organizational change. The implications of sociomateriality on the development of MASCWS include its impacts on the architecture of multi-agent systems and their evaluation processes. However, to account for such implications it is important for the epistemological and ontological positions of sociomateriality to follow a comprehensive approach for understanding the context of organizational change. The thought comprehensiveness aims at incorporating a wide range of factors (other than humans and technology) to avoid the potential linearity of results. It is also aimed at understanding the context of material agency and the balance of qualities to be maintained.

REFERENCES

Ackerman, M., & Halverson, C. (1999). Organizational memory: Processes, boundary objects, and trajectories. In *Proceedings of 32nd Hawaiian International Conference on Systems Science*. Maui, HI: IEEE. Retrieved February 2, 2012 from: www.eecs.umich.edu/~ackerm/pub/99b26/hicss99.pdf

Amor, M., Fuentes, L., & Vallecillo, A. (2005). Bridging the gap between agent-oriented design and implementation using MDA*. In *Agent-Oriented Software Engineering V* (LNCS), (vol. 3382, pp. 93-108). Springer-Verlag GmbH.

Anumba, C. J. Z., Ren, A., Thorpe, O., Ugwu, O., & Newnham, L. (2003). Negotiation within a multi-agent system for the collaborative design of light industrial buildings. *Advances in Engineering Software*, 34(7), 389–401. doi:10.1016/S0965-9978(03)00038-3

Bannon, L., & Schmidt, L. (1989). CSCW: Four characters in search of a context. In *Proceedings of the First European Conference on Computer Supported Cooperative Work*. Retrieved February 2, 2012 from: http://www.it-c.dk/~schmidt/papers/cscw4chart.pdf

Basilsi, V. R., Caldiera, G., & Rombach, H. D. (1994). Experience factory. In Encyclopedia of software engineering (vol. 1, pp. 469-476). John Wiley & Sons.

Beyer, H., & Holtzblatt, K. (1998). *Contextual design: Defining customer-centered systems*. San Francisco, CA: Morgan Kaufmann.

Bijker, W. (1995). *Of bicycles, bakelites, and bulbs: Toward a theory of sociotechnical change*. Cambridge, MA: MIT Press.

Blackler, F. (1995). Knowledge, knowledge work and organizations: An overview and interpretation. *Organization Studies*, *16*(6), 1021–1046. doi:10.1177/017084069501600605

Bradshaw, J. (1997). An introduction to software agents. In Software agents (pp. 3-46). Menlo Park, CA: AAAI Press.

Bresciani, P., Giorgini, P., Giunchiglia, F., Mylopoulos, J., & Perini, A. (2002). TROPOS: An agent-oriented software development methodology. *Journal of Autonomous Agents and Multi-Agent Systems*.

Caire, G., Chainho, P., Evans, R., Garijo, F., Gomez Sanz, J., Kearney, P., . . . Stark, J. (2001). *Agent Oriented Anlysis Using MESSAGE/UML*. Paper presented at the Second International Workshop on Agent-Oriented Software Engineering, Montreal, Canada.

Callon, M. (1986). Some elements of a sociology of translation: Domestication of the scallops and the fishermen of St Brieux Bay. In J. Law (Ed.), *Power, action and belief: A new sociology of knowledge?* (pp. 196–229). London: Routledge & Kegan Paul.

Carstensen, P., & Schmidt, K. (2002). Computer supported cooperative work: New challenges to systems design. In *Handbook of human factors*. Retrieved February 2, 2012 from: http://www.it-c.dk/people/schmidt/papers/cscw_intro.pdf

David, G., Jenkins, J., & Joseph, F. (2006). Collaborative bibliography. *Information Processing & Management*, *42*(3), 805–825. doi:10.1016/j.ipm.2005.05.007

DeLoach, S. A. (1999). Systems engineering: A methodology and language for designing agent systems. In Proceedings of Agent Oriented Information Systems (pp. 45-57). Academic Press.

DeLoach, S. A., Wood, M. F., & Sparkman, C. H. (2001). Multiagent system engineering. *International Journal of Software Engineering and Knowledge Engineering*, *11*(3), 231–258. doi:10.1142/S0218194001000542

Durfee, E. (1987). *A unified approach to dynamic coordination: Planning actions and interactions in a distributed problem solving network*. (Ph.D. dissertation). Department of Computer and Information Science, University of Massachusetts.

Efraim, T., Sharda, R., & Delen, D. (2010). Decision support and business intelligence systems. Pearson Publishing.

Engeström, Y., Miettinen, R., & Punamaki, R. (1999). *Perspectives on activity theory*. Cambridge University Press. doi:10.1017/CBO9780511812774

Fitzpatrick, G., Kaplan, S., & Mansfield, T. (1996). Physical spaces, virtual places and social worlds: A study of work in the virtual. In *Proceedings of the Conference on Computer Supported Cooperative Work*. ACM. doi:10.1145/240080.240322

Gasmelseid, T. (2006). Multi agent web based DSS for global enterprises: An architectural blueprint. *Engineering Letters*, *13*(2), 173-184. Available online at: http://www.engineeringletters.com/issues_v13/issue_2/EL_13_2_16.pdf

Gasmelseid, T. (2007, July-September). From operational dashboards to effective e-business: Multi-agent formulation and negotiation of electronic contracts. *International Journal of E-Business Research*, *3*(3), 77–97. doi:10.4018/jebr.2007070106

Gasmelseid, T. (2008). Modern design dimensions in multi agent computer supported collaborative work systems (CSCW). In *Handbook on modern system analysis and design Applications and technologies*. Academic Press.

Gasmelseid, T. (2009). Intelligent collaboration: The paradox of "ethical agency" and "corporate governance". *Journal of Electronic Commerce in Organizations*, *2009*(1), 50–58. doi:10.4018/jeco.2009010104

Gasmelseid, T. (2014). On the orchestration of stakeholder concerns in large scale information systems. In Agent oriented analysis using MESSAGE/UML. Konradin Verlag.

Giunchiglia, F., Perini, A., & Mylopoulus, J. (2002). The Tropos software development methodology: Processes, models and diagrams. In *Proceedings of the First International Joint Conference on Autonomous Agents and Multiagent Systems* (pp. 63-74). Bologna, Italy: ACM Press. doi:10.1145/544743.544748

Giunchiglia, F., Perini, A., & Sannicol, F. (2001). Knowledge level software engineering. In Intelligent Agents VIII (LNCS), (vol. 2333, pp. 6-20). Seattle, WA: Springer-Verlag.

Greenbaum, J., & Kyng, M. (1991). *Design at work: Cooperative design of computer systems.* Hillsdale, NJ: Lawrence Erlbaum.

Halford, S., & Leonard, P. (2005). Place, space and time: Contextualizing workplace subjectivities organization. *Studies, 27*(5), 657–676.

Harraway, D. (1991). *Simians, cyborgs and women: The reinvention of nature.* New York: Routledge.

Henk, A., & Paul, B. (2004). Travail, transparency and trust: A case study of computer-supported collaborative supply chain planning in high-tech electronics. *European Journal of Operational Research, 153*(2), 445–456. doi:10.1016/S0377-2217(03)00164-4

Hyacinth, S. (1996). Software agents: An over view. *The Knowledge Engineering Review, 11*(3), 1–40.

Iglesias, C., Garrijo, M., & Gonzalez, J. (1998). A survey of agent-oriented methodologies. In *Intelligent Agents V – Proceedings of the 1998 Workshop on Agent Theories, Architectures and Languages.* Academic Press.

Jones, M. R. (1998). Information systems and the double mangle: Steering a course between the scylla of embedded structure and the charybdis of strong symmetry. In *Proceedings of the IFIP WG 8.2 and 8.6 Joint Working Conference on Information Systems.* Academic Press. doi:10.1007/3-540-49057-4_21

Kallinikos, J. (2006). *The consequences of information: Institutional implications of technological change.* Cheltenham, UK: Edward Elgar Publishing. doi:10.4337/9781847204301

Kendall, E. (1999). Role modeling for agent system analysis, design, and implementation. In *Proceedings of Third International Symposium on Mobile Agents* (MA'99). Palm Springs, FL: Academic Press.

Kevin, L. M. (2003). Computer-supported cooperative work. In Encyclopedia of library and information science (pp. 666-677). Academic Press.

Latham, R., & Sassen, S. (2005). *Digital formations: It and new architectures in the global realm.* Princeton, NJ: Princeton University Press.

Latour, B. (1987). *Science in action.* Cambridge, MA: Harvard University Press.

Latour, B. (2005). *Reassembling the social: An introduction to actor-network theory.* Oxford, UK: Oxford University Press.

Law, J. (2004). *After method: Mess in social science research.* Routledge.

Leonardi, P. M., & Barley, S. R. (2008). Materiality and change: Challenges to building better theory about technology and organizing. *Information and Organization, 18*(3), 159–176. doi:10.1016/j.infoandorg.2008.03.001

Lind, J. (1999). *A review of multiagent systems development methods: Technical report.* Martlesham Heath, UK: British Telecom, Adastral Park Labs.

Maes, P. (1995). Artificial life meets entertainment: Life like autonomous agents. *Communications of the ACM, 38*(11), 108–114. doi:10.1145/219717.219808

Markus, M. L. & Silver, M. S. (2008). A foundation for the study of IT effects: A new look at DeSanctis and Poole's concepts of structural features and spirit. *Journal of the Association for Information Systems, 9*(10/11), 609-632.

Martin, J. (1992). *Cultures in organizations: Three perspectives.* New York: Oxford University Press.

Minh, H., Tran, G., Raikundalia, K., & Yun Yang, S. (2006). An experimental study to develop group awareness support for real-time distributed collaborative writing. *Information and Software Technology*, *48*(11), 1006–1024. doi:10.1016/j.infsof.2005.12.009

Monteiro, E., & Hanseth, O. (1995). Social shaping of information infrastructure: On being specific about the technology. In Information technology and changes in organizational work. Chapman & Hall.

Nicolini, D. (2007). Stretching out and expanding work practices in time and space: The case of telemedicine. *Human Relations*, *60*(6), 889–920. doi:10.1177/0018726707080080

Nicolini, D., & Gherardi, S. (2003). *Knowing in organizations: A practice-based approach*. Armonk, NY: M.E. Sharpe Inc.

Odell, J., Parunak, V. D., & Bauer, B. (2000). Extending UML for agents. In *Proc. of the Agent-Oriented Information Systems Workshop at the 17th National Conference on Artificial Intelligence*. Academic Press.

Orlikowski, W. (2002). Knowing in practice: Enacting a collective capability in distributed organizing. *Organization Science*, *13*(3), 249–273. doi:10.1287/orsc.13.3.249.2776

Orlikowski, W. (2006). Material knowing: The scaffolding of human knowledgeability. *European Journal of Information Systems*, *15*(5), 460–466. doi:10.1057/palgrave.ejis.3000639

Orlikowski, W. (2007). Sociomaterial practices: Exploring technology at work. *Organization Studies*, *28*(9), 1435.

Orlikowski, W., & Iacono, C. (2001). Research commentary: Desperately seeking the "it" in IT research-A call to theorizing the IT artifact. *Information Systems Research*, *12*(2), 2. doi:10.1287/isre.12.2.121.9700

Orlikowski, W., & Scott, S. V. (2008). Sociomateriality: Challenging the separation of technology, work and organization. The Academy of Management Annals, 2(1), 433-474.

Padgham, L., & Winiko, M. (2002a). Prometheus: A pragmatic methodology for engineering intelligent agents. In *Proceedings of the OOPSLA 2002 Workshop on Agent-Oriented Methodologies* (pp. 97-108). Seattle, WA: OOPSLA.

Padgham, L., & Winiko, M. (2002b). *Prometheus: Engineering intelligent agents*. Tutorial notes. Unpublished.

Perini, A., Bresciani, P., Giorgini, P., Giunchiglia, F., & Mylopoulos, J. (2001). Towards an agent oriented approach to software engineering. In A. Omicini & M. Viroli (Eds.), WOA 2001 Dagli oggetti agli agenti: tendenze evolutive dei sistemi software. Modena, Italy: Pitagora Editrice Bologna.

Perini, A., Bresciani, P., Giunchiglia, F., Giorgini, P., & Mylopoulos, J. (2001). A knowledge level software engineering methodology for agent oriented programming. In J. P. M®uller, E. Andre, S. Sen, & C. Frasson (Eds.), *Proceedings of the Fifth International Conference on Autonomous Agents* (pp. 648-655). Montreal, Canada: Academic Press.

Pickering. (1995). *The mangle of practice: Time, agency, and science*. The University of Chicago.

Sahay, S. (1997). Implementation of information technology: A time-space perspective. *Organization Studies, 18*(2), 229–260. doi:10.1177/017084069701800203

Saunders, C., & Kim, J. (2007). Perspectives on time. *Management Information Systems Quarterly, 31*(4), iii–xi.

Sawyer, S., & Southwick, R. (2002). Temporal issues in information and communication technology-enabled organizational change. *The Information Society, 18*(4), 263–280. doi:10.1080/01972240290075110

Schatzki, T. R. (2006). On organizations as they happen. *Organization Studies, 27*(12), 1863–1873. doi:10.1177/0170840606071942

Schiff, L., Van House, N., & Butler, M. (1997). Understanding complex information environments: A social analysis of watershed planning. In *Proceedings of the Conference on Digital Libraries* (pp. 161-168). Academic Press.

Shapiro, D. (1994). *The limits of ethnography: Combining social sciences for CSCW.* Chapel Hill, NC: ACM. doi:10.1145/192844.193064

Silvia, D., Saskia, B., Wim, J., & Nick, J. (2007). Students' experiences with collaborative learning in asynchronous computer-supported collaborative learning environments. *Computers in Human Behavior, 23*(1), 496–514. doi:10.1016/j.chb.2004.10.021

Siriwan, S., & Peter, H. (2006). A Bayesian approach to generating tutorial hints in a collaborative medical problem-based learning system. *Artificial Intelligence in Medicine, 38*(1), 5–24. doi:10.1016/j.artmed.2005.04.003 PMID:16183267

Slife, B. (2004). Taking practice seriously: Toward a relational ontology. *Journal of Theoretical and Philosophical Psy., 24*, 2.

Steve, G., & Phebe, M. (2003). Interdisciplinary: Perceptions of the value of computer-supported collaborative work in design for the built environment. *Automation in Construction, 12*(5), 495–499. doi:10.1016/S0926-5805(03)00035-9

Strauss, A. L., & Corbin, J. M. (1998). *Basics of qualitative research: Techniques and procedures for developing grounded theory.* Sage Publications.

Suchman, L. A. (1989). *Notes on computer support for cooperative work.* Department of Computer Science, University of Jyvaskyla.

Sycara, K. P. (1998). Multi-agent systems. *AI Magazine, 19*(2), 79–92.

Thanasis, D., Alejandra, M., & Fatos, X. (2006). A layered framework for evaluating on-line collaborative learning interactions. *International Journal of Human-Computer Studies, 64*(7), 622–635. doi:10.1016/j.ijhcs.2006.02.001

Tsoukas, H. (1996). The firm as a distributed knowledge system: A constructivist perspective. *Strategic Management Journal, 17*(S2), 11–25. doi:10.1002/smj.4250171104

Villarreal, P., Alesso, M., Rocco, S., Galli, M. R., & Chiotti, O. (2003). Approaches for the analysis and design of multi-agent systems. *Inteligencia Artificial, Revista Iberoamericana de Inteligencia Artificial, 21*, 73-81. Retrieved from http://www.aepia.org/revista

White, J. (1997). Mobile agents. In Software agents. AAAI Press.

Wilson, P. (1991). *Computer supported cooperative work: An introduction.* Kluwer Academic Publishers.

Wooldridge, M. (1997). Agent based software engineering. *IEEE Proceedings of Software Engineering, 144*(1), 26–37.

Wooldridge, M., Jennings, N. R., & Kinny, D. (2000). The gaia methodology for agent-oriented analysis and design. *Journal of Autonomous Agents and Multi-Agent Systems*, *3*(3), 285–312. doi:10.1023/A:1010071910869

Yan, X., & Jacob, F. S. (2007). Emergent CSCW systems: The resolution and bandwidth of workplaces. *International Journal of Medical Informatics*, *76*(1), S261–S266. PMID:16822715

Zambonelli, F., Jennings, N. R., & Wooldridge, M. (2001). Organizational rules as an abstraction for the analysis and design of multi agent systems. *International Journal of Software Engineering and Knowledge Engineering*, *11*(3), 303–308. doi:10.1142/S0218194001000505

Zammuto, R. F., Griffith, T. L., Majchrzak, A., Dougherty, D. J., & Faraj, S. (2007). Information technology and the changing fabric of organization. *Organization Science*, *18*(5), 749–762. doi:10.1287/orsc.1070.0307

KEY TERMS AND DEFINITIONS

Emergency Response Management: The integrated process of managing emergency situations including initial assessment, in-filed and operational orchestration and post emergency coordination and follow up.

Emergency Simulation: The process of investigating the operational and managerial relevance of alternative decision making scenarios using different simulation and optimization tools.

Emergency Stakeholders: All institutions (such as healthcare, regulatory and control institutions), organizations (such as hospitals) and individuals involved in or affected by the decisions taken to manage emergency using private or public perspectives.

Healthcare Business Units: All departments and sections that are specialized in the provision of healthcare service at the level of service provision such as specialized departments in hospitals. They constitute the base of emergency management and coordination and the identification of agent-based functionalities.

Multi-Agent Organization: The structure used to demonstrate the relationships between different agents (making up an agent-based organization), the roles to be played by each agent (individually and collectively) and the contribution of agents towards the realization of the objectives of the entire system.

Operational Databases: Used to represent and process all activity specific data that emerges on operational bases especially during emergency incidents.

Software Agents: Computational entities that interact and cooperate together and use resources collectively in order to achieve their own objectives or the objectives of their owners or other agents.

Chapter 6
Segmentation of Renal Calculi in Ultrasound Kidney Images Using Modified Watershed Method

P. R. Tamilselvi
Kongu Engineering College, India

ABSTRACT

US images are a commonly used tool for renal calculi diagnosis, although they are time consuming and tedious for radiologists to manually detect and calculate the size of the renal calculi. It is very difficult to properly segment the US image to detect interested area of objects with the correct position and shape due to speckle formation and other artifacts. In addition, boundary edges may be missing or weak and usually incomplete at some places. With that point of view, the proposed method is developed for renal calculi segmentation. A new segmentation method is proposed in this chapter. Here, new region indicators and new modified watershed transformation are utilized. The proposed method is comprised of four major processes, namely preprocessing, determination of outer and inner region indictors, and modified watershed segmentation with ANFIS performance. The results show the effectiveness of proposed segmentation methods in segmenting the kidney stones and the achieved improvement in sensitivity and specificity measures.

INTRODUCTION

The most widespread problem in the human urinary system is renal calculus which is also known as kidney stones or urinary stones (Manousakas, Lai, & Chang, 2010). Though considerable suffering and at times renal failure are caused by kidney stone diseases that occur in roughly 10%

of the U.S. population affected, the mechanism for this disease is not adequately known (He, Deng, & Ouyang, 2010). The principal organ in the urinary system namely, kidney not only produces urine but it is also useful in purifying the blood. Disposing poisonous substances from the blood and maintaining the useful components in proper balance are the two essential functions of kidney.

DOI: 10.4018/978-1-4666-6639-9.ch006

Among the diverse types of kidney stones that exist, calcium-containing stones, Uric acid stones, Struvite, or infected stones and Cystine stones are four fundamental types (Shah, Desai, & Panchal, 2010). Kidney diseases are commonly classified into hereditary, congenital or acquired (Bommanna, Madheswaran, & Thyagarajah, 2010). The identification of calcifications inside the body is a large field of study including many dynamic areas of research, which is especially useful for diagnosing the kidney stone diseases. Prominent effects that are utilized to detect fracture in real kidney stones that can have arbitrary non-spherical shape are related to the reverberation time across the length of the stone (Manousakas et al., 2006).

Strong speckle noise and attenuated artifacts present in the abdominal ultrasound images poses a unique challenge in using these images for stone segmentation (Gupta, Gosain, & Kaushal, 2010). Accordingly, this task entails the usage of as much beforehand knowledge as possible, like texture, shape, spatial location of organs and so on. The performance of the several automatic and semiautomatic methods that have been proposed deteriorates quickly when the structures are inadequately defined and have low contrast like the neuroanatomic structures, such as thalamus, globus pallidus, putamen, etc., though it has normally a good performance when the contrast-to-noise ratio is high (Maulik, 2009). Regular clinical practice Numerous extensively available medical imaging methods like X-ray, positron emission tomography (PET), computer tomography (CT), Ultrasound (US) and magnetic resonance imaging (MRI) are extensively used in regular clinical practice (Jouannot et al., 2004). As compared to other medical imaging modalities such as computed tomography (CT) and magnetic resonance imaging (MRI), the US is particularly difficult to segment because Ultra Sound is especially hard to segment because its image quality is somewhat low compared to other medical imaging modalities like computed tomography (CT) and magnetic resonance imaging (MRI) (Xie, Jiang, & Tsui, 2005). Quality of image data significantly affects the segmentation of Ultra Sound (US) images (Noble & Boukerroui, 2006). It is difficult to extract features that describe the kidney tissues by segmenting the kidney area (Bommanna, Madheswaran, & Thyagarajah, 2010). Despite this, ultrasound images are extensively used in the medical field (Jeyalakshmi & Kadarkarai, 2010). Tamilselvi (2013) proposed the segmentation method using Squared Euclidean Distance (SED) with ANFIS in supervised learning has made the technique more efficient than the previous techniques. Thus the obtained error is minimized when compared to the existing algorithm that leads to high efficiency.

As ultrasound imaging is a cost-effective and non-invasive as well as radiation-free imaging technique, it is popular in the field of medicine (Gupta, Gosain, & Kaushal, 2010). US imaging on account of its real time capabilities permits faster and more precise procedures. In addition, it is economical and user-friendly. In several applications, an important role is played by the precise identification of organs or objects that are present in US images (Xie, Jiang, & Tsui, 2005). Resolutions required by murine imaging could be achieved in ultrasonic imaging which already has a broad variety of clinical applications for human imaging, if higher frequencies (20 – 50 MHz) are used instead of the normally used frequencies (3 – 15 MHz) (Jouannot et al., 2004). The speckle noise which makes the signal or lesion difficult to detect is the main performance restricting aspect in visual perception of US imaging (Loizou et al., 2002, 2004). Diverse methodologies have been utilized in the diverse research papers that have been published on segmentation of kidney region in US images. Utilization of a-priori information may be used as an alternative in robust methods to compensate for the difficulty caused by noise and poor signal-to-noise ratio of US kidney images (Bommanna, Madheswaran, & Thyagarajah, 2006). The segmentation of renal calculi using renal images is a difficult task. Lots of researches have been performed for the successful segmentation of renal calculi using ultra sound images. However, there are no effective renal image based calculi segmentation approaches to date. Hence, the objective of this research is to develop a novel approach for the segmentation of renal calculi utilizing renal images and to demonstrate the effectiveness of the approach.

The remainder of the paper is organized as follows. A few recent works related to calculi segmentation from the literature are reviewed in Section 2. The proposed IORM segmentation process is briefly explained in Section 3. In Section 3.1 preprocessing process is performed and outer region indicator process is described in Section 3.2. The Section 3.3 and 3.4 explains the inner region indicator and modified watershed segmentation process. The experimental result and conclusion of this paper is given sections 4 and 5, respectively.

RELATED WORK

In order to detect the renal calculi, (Sridhar & Kumaravel, 2001) developed an automated system based on the physical characteristics of renal calculi. They implemented in the working platform of MATLAB/IDL, but failed to analyze the accuracy in segmenting the calculi regions. Further, they developed an algorithm (Sridhar, Kumaravel, & Easwarakumar, 2002) to build a framework for renal calculi segmentation. They analyzed the performance of a set of five known algorithms using the parameters such as success rate in calculi detection, border error metric and time. Their algorithm was tested by using the ultrasound images of 37 patients. In the test results, they achieved only 95% accuracy, which is not sufficient when working with medical relevance.

Benoit, Pierre, & Jerome (2011) proposed a region growing algorithm for segmenting the renal calculi on ureteroscopic images. They measured the statistics on different image metrics, such as Accuracy, Recall, and Yasnoff Measure, for cal-

culating the ground truth using real video images and for comparing their segmentation with reference segmentation. Practically, the invasive type of imaging is not preferable in detecting or taking decision about the treatment. So, segmentation of renal calculi in Ultrasound images is preferred in any situations. To accomplish this, Tamilselvi & Thangaraj(2011) proposed an enhanced seeded region growing based method that performed segmentation and classification of kidney images with stone sizes using ultrasound kidney image for the diagnosis of stone and its early identification. The images were classified as normal, stone and early stone stage by employing intensity threshold variation diagnosis. The intensity threshold variation obtained from the segmented portions of the image was used as the basis for performing the diagnosis process and the size of the portions was compared with the standard sizes of stones. The work lacks in analysis of performance in terms of standard performance measures.

Quanquan et al., (2013) developed a method which use level set to segment and extract calcifications. It is nice to segment and extract calcifications from uterus ultrasound images that are a group of database with typical characteristics from Ultrasound Diagnosis Department of Lanzhou local Hospital. It is helpful to make a correct scheme for patients.

Chen et al. (2010) have proposed a fuzzy neural approach for the study of yield forecasting. They have integrated a method, which is modified from chen and lin's approach by incorporating two collaboration mechanisms. From the results it is proved that *neuro fuzzy* approaches yields very good solution to the problem. Ali et al. (2007) have proposed an approach based on feature reduction, classification and retrieval for image databases using content-based image retrieval systems. This approach combines the image texture features with color features and classification is performed correctly. Azzam ul-Asar Sadeeq, Ahmed, and Riaz-ul-Hasnain (2009) proposed an approach uses an Artificial Neural Network (ANN) that uses optimized weights for learning process. The ANN generates minimum plains to address minimum real time traffic demands. They have concluded that neural network based approaches produces best results by using training process.

Qi, Song, Yoon, and Watrous-de Versterre (2011) evaluates the efficiency of various supervised learning techniques on biomedical analysis. They have used Sequential Minimal Optimization and K-Nearest Neighbor. The authors use these techniques to extract key phrases from PubMed and the results shows that supervised learning techniques produce best results in biomedical analysis. Rani and Deepa (2011) proposed a modified form of operator based on Particle Swarm Optimization (PSO) for designing Genetic Fuzzy Rule Based System (GFRBS). They have implemented and tested. Statistical analysis of the experimental results shows that the proposed fuzzy based system produces a classifier model with minimum number of rules and higher classification accuracy.

The usual procedure of velocity updating in PSO is modified by calculating the velocity using chromosome's individual best value and global best value based on an updating probability without considering the inertia weight, old velocity and constriction factors. This kind of calculation brings intelligent information sharing mechanism and memory capability to Genetic Algorithm (GA) and can be easily implemented along with other genetic operators.

Hence, Tamilselvi and Thangaraj, (2011) proposed an efficacious segmentation method for an exact segmentation of renal calculi. The experimental showed that their proposed segmentation method has been found the accurate renal calculi from US images. They have analyzed the performance of the proposed method as well as compared with the Neural Network (NN) and SVM classifier. In the method, the ANFIS system is used to segment the stones from the kidney stone images. When compared to other effective segmentation methods, this method achieves high accuracy in segmentation. However, this method has a drawback in sensitivity and specificity measures. To avoid this drawback, we propose new inner-outer regions based new modified-watershed (IORM) segmentation method, which is discussed in the next section.

THE IORM SEGMENTATION

The proposed IORM stone segmentation method enhances the performance of previous method in terms of *sensitivity* and *specificity* measures. The proposed method performs four major processes, namely, (i) Preprocessing, (ii) Determining outer *region indictors* (iii) Determining inner region indictors and (iv) modified watershed *segmentation*. The block diagram for IORM stone segmentation method is shown in Figure 1.

In Figure 1 (i), the noises in the *training images* are removed and the noise free image is given to the outer region indictors. The result of the outer region indictors is the pixel values, which is then given to the ANFIS system to perform the training process. In Figure 1 (ii), the noises in the testing images are removed by preprocessing and the kidney centroid coordinates values are found by inner region indictors. The modified watershed algorithm is used to segment the regions and the outer region pixel values are found through the outer region indictor's procedure. Then the indictor pixel values results are used to perform the testing process through ANFIS system.

Preprocessing

In this preprocessing stage, LPG-PCA based image *denoising algorithm* is used to remove the noise from the ultra-sound kidney stone images. The given ultrasound image pixel and its nearest pixels are molded as vector variable by LPG method, and the PCA perform denoising in the images (Zhang et al., 2010). The *preprocessing* process is performed in both training and testing images.

Figure 1. Proposed IORM renal calculi segmentation method (i) training stage and (ii) testing stage

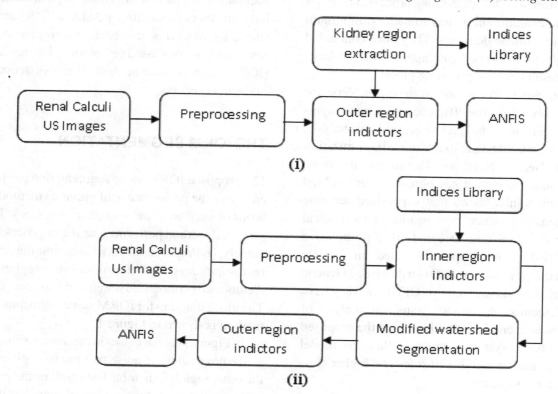

Outer Region Indicators

Let an ultra sound noise free renal calculi image U with size MxN contains regions

$$\{R_i\} : i = 1 \cdots n \in U$$

where, n is the number of regions in U. Next, we find the centroid $\{C_i(x, y)\} : i = 1 \cdots n \in \{R_i\}$:

$$0 \leq x \leq M - 1, 0 \leq y \leq N - 1.$$

The neighbor pixel values of every region, which can be represented as

$$\{p_{ij}\} : i = 1 \cdots n, j = 1 \cdots 8,$$

are found by using the *centroid* values of the corresponding region. The calculation steps for the eight *neighbor pixel* values are given below

$$\{A_j\} \subseteq \begin{cases} p_{ij} = (x + \beta_x k, y + \beta_y k); \\ if \ (x + \beta_x k, y + \beta_y k) \notin R_i \\ \varphi; \ otherwise. \end{cases} \tag{1}$$

In Equation (1) k value is increment by 1 such that, $p_{ij} \in R_i$ and β_x, β_y values are function of j, this values are given in Table 1.

Where, $\{A_1\}$ has the first neighbor pixel values of all the regions, $\{A_2\}$ has the second neighbor values of all the regions and so on. Now, every neighbor pixel values for a particular region

Table 1. Value is incremented by 1 such that, $p_{ij} \in R_i$ and β_x, β_y values are function of j

j	β_x	β_y
1	-1	0
2	-1	1
3	0	1
4	1	1
5	1	0
6	1	-1
7	0	-1
8	-1	1

is extracted from $\{A_j\}$ and $\{X_j^i\}$ is generated, where $\{X_j^i\}$ has the eight neighbor pixel values of ith region. Then, a distance measure is performed each neighbor pixel value and their centroid as follows

$$D_j^i = X_j^i - C_i \qquad (2)$$

Subsequently, the histogram equalization process is performed over the image U and the outer region indicators are also determined for the image that is obtained from histogram equalization. Thus obtained neighbor pixel values for all regions $\{Y_j^i\}$ $\{Y_j^i\}$ are determined and the difference values $\{D(h)_j^i\}$ are calculated. Then *K-Means clustering* algorithm is applied over the elements $\{D_j^i\}$ and $\{D(h)_j^i\}$. Hence obtained clustered elements are fed to ANFIS for learning.

Determining Inner Region Indicators

To perform the determination of *inner region indicators,* firstly, the kidney regions are manually marked in the known ultra sound images.

Then the whole image is divided into L number of blocks and for every block, an index value, which can be represented as $B = \{I_i\} : i = 1 \cdots L$, is allocated. Then, each block in B is checked to find the presence of *edge pixels* of the kidney. If any block contains edge pixels of the kidney, then the index value of the corresponding block is kept as $K = \{I_l\} : l \in L$. Hence, K which can also be called as *indices library*, contains the indices of blocks of all the known images. As the connectivity of the blocks form a region plane, a centroid can be calculated. The similar process is performed for all the known images to determine the centroids $\{C_c^h\}, h = 1, 2$, $c = 1 \cdots t_m$ where t_m is a number of *training images* and $\{C_c^h\}$ represents the hth centroid of cth image and it contains only the x and y co-ordinates of the centroid.

When a *test image* is given, initially, a mask with similar size is created. The mask and the subjected image are divided into blocks as done earlier. The blocks in K are marked in the subjected image and then the pixel values that are covered by the blocks are placed in the mask in the corresponding location. Subsequently, h centroids are determined by assuming all the connected blocks in the mask as *region plane*. Using the centroid portion, the kidney regions are marked in the subjected image.

New Modified Watershed Segmentation

Watershed segmentation is a morphological based method of image segmentation. The gradient magnitude of an image is considered as a topographic surface for the watershed transformation (Gupta, Gosain, & Kaushal 2010). The *watershed transformation* based segmentation approach function based on the morphological principle (Roshni & Raju, 2011). The watershed transformation technique is used for reducing the over-segmentation of the watershed algorithm (Salman, 2006). The objective of the watershed transform is to search for regions of high intensity gradients (watersheds), which separate the neighboring local minima (basins) (Mkwelo, Jager, & Nicolls, 2003). If we consider a grayscale image as a topographic relief, the gray value at a given location exhibits the altitude at that point. When this relief is flooded, first the water will fill up the lower elevation points, and then the water level will increase. A watershed is created, when the water coming from two different regions are met (Jungj & Scharcanski, 2005). The different regions that were flooded are known as *catchment basins*. If this process is applied on a gradient image (where each pixel corresponds to the modulus of the gradient at a certain point), the watersheds correspond exactly to the crest lines of the gradient, which are associated with the edges of the image. Hence, the catchment basins are the segmented objects in the image (Vincent & Dougherty, 1994).

In this paper, the traditional watershed segmentation algorithm is modified to obtain an enhanced segmentation results by performing K-means clustering-filtering-Morphological operation and a Centroid matching-*multidirectional traversal* operation before and after the conventional watershed segmentation.

The procedure of the enhanced watershed algorithm is discussed as below,

Step 1: Find clusters and filtered image result from $G(x,y)$ is represented as $G^r(x,y)$ and $S_f(G(x,y))$. Then calculate

$$Q' = G^r(x,y); \quad r = \max(w(p)) \qquad (3)$$

where $G^r(x,y)$ is the rth cluster, $w(p)$ is the white pixels in Equation (3) the cluster which have the highest white pixel value is found and it stored in Q'.

Step 2: In spatial plane, morphological operations are performed from $G^r(x,y)$ and the resultant image is denoted as $M_o'(x,y)$.

Step 3: Find the *minimum and maximum* pixel value of $p(x,y)$ as min and max, where $p(x,y)$ is the pixel value of coordinate (x,y). Assign the coordinate of min into m_i. The topography will be flooded in integer flood increments from $n = \min + 1$.

Step 4: Calculate

$$c_n(m_i) = c(m_i) \cap t[n] \quad (4)$$

If $(x,y) \in c(m_i)$ and $(x,y) \in t(n)$,

$$c_n(m_i) = \begin{cases} 1; & at\,(x,y) \\ 0; & otherwise \end{cases}$$

In Equation (4), $c_n(m_i)$ as the coordinates in the *catchment basin* associated with minimum m_i that is flooded at stage n. Let $t(n)$ be the set of coordinates (a,b) and $t(n)$ stated as

$$t(n) = \left\{ (a,b) \mid p(x,y) < n \right\} \qquad (5)$$

Step 5: Compute $c[n]$,

$$c[n] = \bigcup_{i=1}^{R} c_n(m_i); \; n = n+1 \qquad (6)$$

where, $c[n]$ denote the union of the *flooded* catchment basins at stage n.

Step 6: Find set of connected components in $t[n]$ denoted as G, for each connected component $g \in G[n]$, there are three conditions:

a. If $g \cap c[n-1]$ is empty, connected component g is incorporated into

$c[n-1]$ to form $c[n]$ because it represents a new minimum is encountered.

b. If $g \cap c[n-1]$ contains one connected of $c[n-1]$, connected component g is incorporated into $c[n-1]$ to form $c[n]$ because it means g lies within the catchment basin of some regional minimum.

c. If $g \cap c[n-1]$ contains more than one connected component of $c[n-1]$, it represents all or part of a ridge separating two or more *catchment basins* is encountered.

Step 7: Construct $c[n]$ according to (4.4) and (4.6). Set $n = n + 1$.

Step 8: Repeat step 3 and 4 until n reaches max+1.

The processes of clustering, filtering and morphological operations are briefly explained in the following subsections.

K-Means Clustering: K-means clustering is a method of cluster analysis which aims to partition observations into number of clusters in which each observation belongs to the cluster with the *nearest mean* (Singh, Malik, & Sharma, 2011). The steps involved in the K-means clustering used in our method is described as follows

Convert the subjected ultrasound *test image* from RGB *color space* to gray scale G.

Partition the gray scale data points to R arbitrary centroids, one for each cluster.

1. Establish new *cluster centroid* by calculating the mean values of all the cluster elements

2. Find out distance between the cluster centroid and the cluster elements and obtain new cluster

3. Repeat process from step (ii) till a defined number of iterations are performed.

The k-means algorithm aims at minimizing an *objective function*

$$H = \sum_{r=1}^{R} \sum_{g=1}^{G} \left\| d_g^r - C_r \right\|^2 \tag{3}$$

In Equation (3) d_g^r represents data points and C_r means *cluster center*. The resultant of the k-means clustering process has r number of clusters, which forms a cluster-enabled image Q_R. Here we select the cluster, which has the maximum white color pixel values, and is applied to the newly created mask Q'. Then the edges for the regions in mask Q' is determined and stored as Q''.

Filtering: In the image G, a sobel filtering method is applied and the filtered results is given as

$$S_f = I_x^{f'} + I_y^{f'} \tag{4}$$

In Equation (4), $I_x^{f'}$ and $I_y^{f'}$ are the squared matrices of I_x^f and I_y^f respectively, where I_x^f and I_y^f are obtained by sobel filtering over G using filtering matrix I_x and transpose filtering matrix I_y respectively.

Morphological Operations: A sequence of different *morphological operations* is performed in the resultant image Q_R. In Q_R, we initially perform morphological eroding operation to obtain Q_R^{erode1}. Then a morphological reconstruction process is performed over Q_R^{erode1} to obtain Q_R^{rec}. Two complementary images Q_{c1} and Q_{c2} are obtained by complementing Q_R^{rec} and by complementing the morphologically dilated image of Q_R^{dilate}, respectively. Then a second stage reconstruction process is performed using Q_{c1} and Q_{c2} and the resultant is morphologically complemented again to obtain Q_{c3}. Then *regional maxima* function is performed over Q_{c3} to replace the image pixel values, which have maximum frequency in the image, are replaced by 255s. A final morphological closing and erosion operation followed by a process of removing the connected components (objects), which have lesser number of pixels than a defined threshold, is performed over Q_{c3}, which was obtained after *regional maxima* function, to obtain M_o. Eventually, a *regional minima* function is applied over M_o so as to obtain M_o'. The resultant is applied to the conventional *watershed segmentation* algorithm (Gupta, Gosain, & Kaushal, 2010).

Pixels Matching: Here, firstly watershed segmented image W is divided into m number of blocks and the index values $w = \{I_{wL}\}$ are allocated as already performed in section 3.3. Then $w = \{I_{wL}\}$ is compared against K using the following conditions

Retain the pixel values in the block $w_L \in W$; if an index value $I_{wL} = I_L$, then.

Change the block $w_L \in W$ pixel values into *0*; or else.

And hence W' is generated. A logical *AND* operation is performed over W' and Q' followed by a morphological closing operation and hence the resultant image D is obtained.

Multidirectional Traversal: Here two major traversals called *bottom-up traversal* and *top-down traversal* are proposed. In each traversal, a left-right traversal is applied. The traversals are applied over D, which is in binary. At the time of two major traversals, once the pixel with '1' is obtained, then left-right traversal is enabled so that all the regions in the same axis and the region of the first obtained pixel are removed from the mask. The survival pixel values are marked in the original test image and it is subjected to the consequent process of *Thresholding*.

Thresholding: Here, a chain of *thresholding* process is performed in the original image based on different criterions. They are described as follows

Firstly, the pixel values that are marked using the previous process are compared against a defined *threshold* value t_1. The pixel values those are greater than t_1 are stored in a newly created mask D_s.

The pixel values of the center of the regions, which are formed by t_1-*thresholding*, in D_s and before in Q' are located. The distance between the coordinate values of those center pixels determined. The region is considered for the subsequent processes only if the distance is less than the threshold t_2.

Again, a distance is determined between the coordinates of center pixels of the selected regions in Q' and C_c'. As in the previous *thresholding*, the regions are selected only if the distance is lesser than the threshold t_3

Outer region indicators (as already described in Section 3.2) are determined from the obtained regions and given to ANFIS to get the ANFIS score. If the ANFIS score is greater than t_4, then the regions are selected.

As a final *thresholding* process, the neighbor pixels are determined for the selected regions and its intensity level is compared against the threshold t_5. If the intensity level is greater than t_5, then the regions are selected.

By performing all the above described processes in the subjected ultrasound test kidney image, the renal calculi are segmented.

EXPERIMENTAL RESULTS

The proposed IORM segmentation technique was implemented in MATLAB platform (version 7.12) and it was evaluated using 40 medical ultra sound kidney images, which are collected from various medical diagnosis centers. Among the 40 images, 20 are normal and 20 are with renal calculi. Around 75% of the image set is fed for training process and 25% of the image set is given to the testing process. The proposed segmentation method is applied over these images and the performance is evaluated. Figure 2, 3a, b shows the ultra sound input, preprocessing and *histogram equalization*

result images and Figure 4 and 5 gives the intermediate results of the whole IORM segmentation.

The final outcome of the proposed IORM segmentation method is shown in Figure 6, in which the renal calculi are marked in the image as red color.

Performance Analysis

The performance of the IORM segmentation method is analyzed by various statistical measures as well as by comparing segmented stone area against the conventional segmentation algorithms. The *statistical performance measures*, which are

Figure 2. Input image

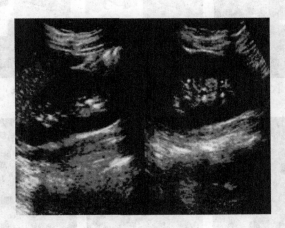

Figure 3. Output images from (a) Preprocessing (b) Histogram equalization

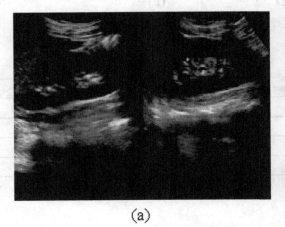
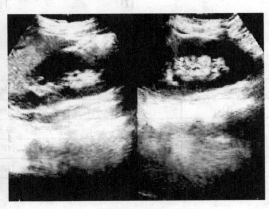

(a)   (b)

Figure 4. Images obtained from (a) K-means clustering (b) Filtering (c) Morphological operation (d) conventional watershed algorithm (e) Pixel Matching process (f) Top-Down traversal (g) Bottom-Up traversal (h) Thresholding

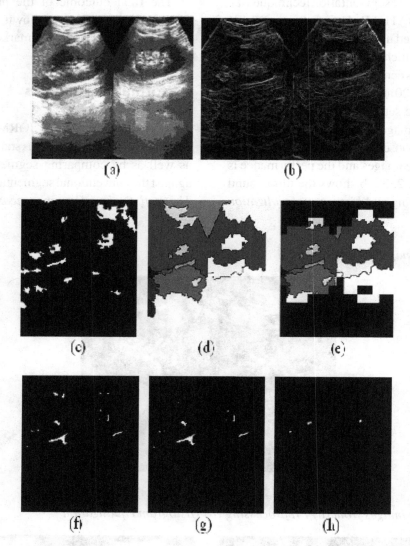

Table 2. TP, FP, TN and FN values

Images	True Positive (TP)	False Positive (FP)	True Negative (TN)	False Negative (FN)
Image ID1	316	0	65220	0
Image ID2	369	913	65167	0
Image ID3	204	0	65332	0
Image ID4	307	168	65229	0

Figure 5. Output Image from (a) morphological erosion (b) morphological reconstruction (c) Dilation (d) Regional Maxima (e) Closing (f) Erosion and (g) Regional Minima

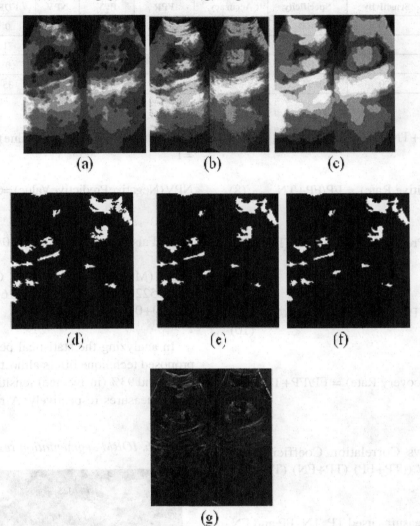

obtained for four different US images, of our proposed segmentation method are shown in Table 3.

They are calculated using the following parameters:

- **True Positive (TP):** Stone area correctly marked as stone.
- **False Positive (FP):** Normal area wrongly marked as stone.
- **True Negative (TN):** Normal area wrongly unmarked as stone.

- **False Negative (FN):** Stone area correctly unmarked as stone.

The statistical measures are detailed in http://en.wikipedia.org/wiki/Sensitivity_and_specificity, however they are given below

$$Sensitivity = TP/TP+FN \qquad (5)$$

$$Specificity = TN/FP+TN \qquad (6)$$

Table 3. Statistical performance measures for four different US images with renal calculi

Image ID	Sensitivity	Specificity	Accuracy	FPR	PPV	NPV	FDR	MCC
1	100	100	100	0	100	100	0	6.9
2	100	98	98	1.38	28	100	71	7.4
3	100	100	100	0	100	100	0	5.5
4	100	74	99	0.26	64	100	35	6.8

$$\text{Accuracy} = TP+TN/TP+FP+FN+TN \qquad (7)$$

$$\text{FPR (False Positive Rate)} = FP/FP+TN \qquad (8)$$

$$\text{PPV (Positive Predictive Value)} = TP/TP+FP \qquad (9)$$

$$\text{NPV (Negative Predictive Value)} = TN/TN+FN \qquad (10)$$

$$\text{FDR (False Discovery Rate)} = FP/FP+TP \qquad (11)$$

$$\text{MCC (Matthews Correlation Coefficient)} = TP*TN-FP*FN/ ((TP+FP) (TP+FN) (TN+FP) (TN+FN))^{1/2} \qquad (12)$$

Statistical measures used TP, TN, FP and FN values for four images are listed in the Table 2.

A Sample calculation for statistical measures over Image ID 1 statistical is given below.

$$\text{Sensitivity} = 316/316+0 = 1$$

$$\text{Specificity} = 65220/0+65220 = 1$$

$$\text{Accuracy} = 316+65220/316+0+0+65220 = 1$$

$$\text{FPR (False Positive Rate)} = 0/0+65220 = 0$$

$$\text{PPV (Positive Predictive Value)} = 316/316+0 = 1$$

$$\text{NPV (Negative Predictive Value)} = 65220/65220+0 = 1$$

$$\text{FDR (False Discovery Rate)} = 0/0+316 = 0$$

$$\text{MCC (Matthews Correlation Coefficient)} = 316*65220-0*0/ ((316+0) (316+0) 65220+0) (65220+0))^{1/2} = 6.9$$

In analyzing the statistical performance, the proposed technique offers almost 99% accuracy, 100% and 93% (in average) sensitivity and specificity measures respectively. A relative error is

Figure 6. IORM segmentation result image

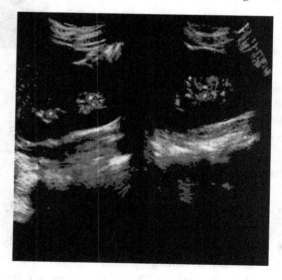

calculated between the stone area marked by the proposed method and the expert radiologist. The errors are compared against the relative errors that are obtained from the conventional renal calculi segmentation algorithms given in (Gupta, Gosain & Kaushal, 2010). The stone area, which is determined by the proposed algorithm and the expert radiologist, and its relative error are given in Table 4.

Table 4. IORM segmentation relative error performance

Expert Radiologist (mm2)	Stone Area (mm2)	Relative Error IORM Method
293	292	0.341
126	128	1.587
87	87	0
316	319	0.949
205	204	0.488
153	153	0
103	103	0
270	271	0.370

In Table 5 the relative error of stone area calculation is described below.

Relative Error =| stone area is computed by IORM method −stone are is marked by our expert radiologist/ stone area is marked by our expert radiologist| (13)

In Figure 7, a graphical representation is given that interprets the comparison with relative error between the proposed and existing renal calculi segmentation algorithms. The relative error of IORM segmentation is *25% and 17%* higher than the existing algorithm II for images 4 and 8, respectively. However, the IORM *segmentation* algorithm shows *80%* and *45%* more mean accurate stone area calculation rather than algorithm I and II

FUTURE RESEARCH DIRECTIONS

The performance of this method on other applications such as gall bladder and ureter calculi segmentation can be studied in future. Only two-dimensional images are dealt in this work.

Figure 7. Comparison graph of IORM, Algorithm I&II relative error performance

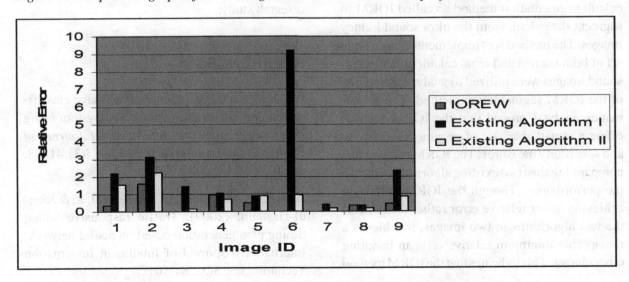

Table 5. Comparison result of IORM segmentation relative error and existing algorithm (I&II) performance

Image ID	Relative Error of IORM Method	Relative Error from Algorithm I SRAD (in Gupta, Gosain & Kaushal, 2010)	Relative Error from Algorithm II Log Decompression (in Gupta, Gosain & Kaushal, 2010)
1	0.341	2.180	1.557
2	1.587	3.142	2.243
3	0	1.441	0.153
4	0.949	1.038	0.692
5	0.488	0.908	0.893
6	0	9.207	0.929
7	0	0.381	0.198
8	0.370	0.370	0.192
Mean	0.467	2.333	0.857

However, this method can be easily expanded to a three–dimensional one by making changes in the existing work. From the results, it is observed that *Neuro Fuzzy* based approaches produces efficient results in segmentation. So this type of segmentation method can be used for other US images also.

CONCLUSION

In this paper, we proposed a new kidney renal calculi segmentation method so called IORM to segment the calculi from the ultra sound kidney images. The method was implemented and a huge set of both normal and renal calculi kidney ultrasound images were utilized to analyze the results of the IORM segmentation method. The performance analysis proved that the IORM method offers a remarkable rate of accuracy, sensitivity and specificity measures. The IORM method was compared against two existing algorithms to prove the performance. Though the IORM suffers in achieving lesser relative error rather than one of the two algorithms in two images, it achieves a remarkable minimum relative error in handling other images. This indicates that the IORM method more accurately segments over the other two algorithms. This asserts that the IORM is more effective in *segmentation* and it can be more suitable for the corresponding medical applications.

ACKNOWLEDGMENT

The Researchers are thankful to Adharsh Diagnostics Scan Centre, Erode, Tamilnadu, India for providing kidney ultrasound images for the research study.

REFERENCES

Ali, J. M. (2007). Content-based Image classification and retrieval: A rule-based system using rough sets framework. *International Journal of Intelligent Information Technologies*, *3*(3), 41–58. doi:10.4018/jiit.2007070103

Azzam, U. A., Sadeeq, U. M., Ahmed, J., & Riazul-Hasnain. (2009). Traffic responsive signal timing plan generation based on neural network. International Journal of Intelligent Information Technologies, 5(3), 84-101.

Benoit, R., Pierre, M., & Jerome, S. (2011). An algorithm for calculi segmentation on ureteroscopic images. *International Journal of Computer Assisted Radiology and Surgery, 6*(2), 237–246. doi:10.1007/s11548-010-0504-x PMID:20574798

Bommanna, R. K., Madheswaran, M., & Thyagarajah, K. (2006). A general segmentation scheme for contouring kidney region in ultrasound kidney images using improved higher order spline interpolation. *International Journal of Biological and Life Sciences, 2*(2), 81–88.

Bommanna, R. K., Madheswaran, M., & Thyagarajah, K. (2010). Texture pattern analysis of kidney tissues for disorder identification and classification using dominant gabor wavelet. *Journal Machine Vision and Applications, 21*(3), 287–300. doi:10.1007/s00138-008-0159-6

Chen, T. (2010). A fuzzy-neural approach with collaboration mechanisms for semiconductor yield forecasting. *International Journal of Intelligent Information Technologies, 6*(3), 17–33. doi:10.4018/jiit.2010070102

Gupta, A., Gosain, B., & Kaushal, S. (2010). A comparison of two algorithms for automated stone detection in clinical b-mode ultrasound images of the abdomen. *Journal of Clinical Monitoring and Computing, 24*(5), 341–362. doi:10.1007/s10877-010-9254-0 PMID:20714793

He, J.Y., Deng, S.P., & Ouyang, J.M. (2010). Morphology, particle size distribution, aggregation, and crystal phase of nanocrystallites in the urine of healthy persons and lithogenic patients. *IEEE Transactions on Nanobioscience, 9*(2), 156-163. doi:10.10.1109/TNB.2010.2045510

Jeyalakshmi, R., & Kadarkarai, R. (2010). Segmentation and feature extraction of fluid-filled uterine fibroid-A knowledge-based approach. *Maejo International Journal of Science and Technology, 4*(3), 405–416.

Jouannot, E., Huyen, J. P. D. V., Bourahla, K., Laugier, P., Pegorier, M. L., & Bridal, L. (2004). Comparison and validation of high frequency ultrasound detection techniques in a mouse model for renal tumors. In *Proceedings of IEEE International Ultrasonic Symposium* (Vol. 1, pp. 748-751). IEEE. doi:10.1109/ULTSYM.2004.1417832

Jungj, C. R., & Scharcanski, J. (2005). Robust watershed segmentation using the wavelet transform. *Image and Vision Computing, 23*(7), 661–669. doi:10.1016/j.imavis.2005.03.001

Loizou, C. P., Christodoulou, C., Pattischis, C. S., Istepanian, R. S. H., Pantziaris, M., & Nicolaides, A. (2002). Speckle reduction in ultrasound images of atherosclerotic carotid plaque. In *Proceedings of IEEE International Conference on Digital Signal Processing* (Vol. 2, pp. 525-528). IEEE. doi:10.1109/ICDSP.2002.1028143

Loizou, C. P., Pattischis, C. S., Istepanian, R. S. H., Pantziaris, M., Tyllis, T., & Nicolaides, A. (2004). Quality evaluation of ultrasound imaging in the carotid artery. In *Proceedings of IEEE Mediterranean Electro technical Conference* (Vol. 1, pp. 395 – 398). IEEE. doi:10.1109/MELCON.2004.1346891

Manousakas, I., Lai, C. C., & Chang, W. Y. (2010). A 3D ultrasound renal calculi fragmentation image analysis system for extracorporeal shock wave lithotripsy. In *Proceedings of the International Symposium on Computer, Communication, Control and Automation* (*Vol. 1*, pp. 303-306). Academic Press. doi:10.1109/3CA.2010.5533823

Manousakas, I., Pu, Y. R., Chang, C. C., & Liang, S. M. (2006). Ultrasound image analysis for renal stone tracking during extracorporeal shock wave lithotripsy. In *Proceedings of the IEEE EMBS Annual International Conference* (pp. 2746-2749). IEEE.

Maulik, U. (2009). Medical image segmentation using genetic algorithms. *IEEE Transactions on Information Technology in Biomedicine, 13*(2), 166–173. doi:10.1109/TITB.2008.2007301 PMID:19272859

Mkwelo, S., Jager, D. G., & Nicolls, F. (2003). Watershed-based segmentation of rock scenes and proximity-based classification of watershed regions under uncontrolled lighting conditions. In *Proceedings of the Fourteenth Annual Symposium of the Pattern Recognition Association* (pp. 107-112). Academic Press.

Noble, A., & Boukerroui, D. (2006). Ultrasound image segmentation: A survey. *IEEE Transactions on Medical Imaging, 25*(8), 987–1010. doi:10.1109/TMI.2006.877092 PMID:16894993

Qi, Y., Song, M., Yoon, S. C., & Watrous-deVersterre, L. (2011). Combining supervised learning techniques to key-phrase extraction for biomedical full-text. *International Journal of Intelligent Information Technologies, 7*(1), 33–44. doi:10.4018/jiit.2011010103

Quanquan, Z., Yingjie, L., & Weiliang, Z. (2013). Uterine calcifications segmentation and extraction from ultrasound images based on level set. In *Proceedings of International Conference on Information Management, Innovation Management and Industrial Engineering* (vol. 2, pp. 591–594). Academic Press. doi:10.1109/ICIII.2013.6703222

Rani, C., & Deepa, S. N. (2011). An intelligent operator for genetic fuzzy rule based system. *International Journal of Intelligent Information Technologies, 7*(3), 28–40. doi:10.4018/jiit.2011070103

Rezaee, M. R., Zwet, P. M. J., Lelieveldt, B. P. F., Geest, R. J., & Reiber, J. H. C. (2000). A multiresolution image segmentation technique based on pyramidal segmentation and fuzzy clustering. *IEEE Transactions on Image Processing, 9*(7), 1238–1248. doi:10.1109/83.847836 PMID:18262961

Roshni, V. S., & Raju, G. (2011). Image segmentation using multiresolution texture gradient and watershed algorithm. *International Journal of Computers and Applications, 22*(6), 21–28. doi:10.5120/2588-3579

Salman, N. (2006). Image segmentation based on watershed and edge detection techniques. *The International Arab Journal of Information Technology, 3*(2), 104–110.

Shah, S. R., Desai, M. D., & Panchal, L. (2010). Identification of content descriptive parameters for classification of renal calculi. *International Journal of Signal and Image Processing, 1*(4), 255–259.

Singh, K., Malik, D., & Sharma, N. (2011). Evolving limitations in k-means algorithm in data mining and their removal. *International Journal of Computational Engineering & Management, 12*, 105–109.

Sridhar, S., & Kumaravel, N. (2001). Automatic segmentation of medical images for renal calculi and analysis. *Medical Informatics and the Internet in Medicine, 37*, 405–409. PMID:11347425

Sridhar, S., Kumaravel, N., & Easwarakumar, K. S. (2002). Segmentation of renal calculi in ultrasound images. *Medical Informatics and the Internet in Medicine, 27*(4), 229–236. doi:10.1080/1463923021000054217 PMID:12745904

Tamilselvi & Thangaraj. (2011). An efficient segmentation of calculi from us renal calculi images using anfis system. *European Journal of Scientific Research, 55*(2), 323–333.

Tamilselvi & Thangaraj. (2011). Computer aided diagnosis system for stone detection and early detection of kidney stones. *Journal of Computer Science, 7*(2), 250-254. doi:10.3844/jcssp.2011.250.254

Tamiselvi, P. R. (2013). Segmentation of renal calculi using squared euclidean distance method. *International Journal of Scientific Engineering and Technology*, *2*(7), 651–655.

Vincent, L., & Dougherty, E. R. (1994). Morphological segmentation for textures and particles. In E. Dougherty (Ed.), *Digital image processing: Fundamentals and applications* (pp. 43–102). New York, NY: Marcel-Dekker.

Wikipedia. (n.d.). *Statistical measures*. Retrieved from http://en.wikipedia.org/wiki/Sensitivity_and_specificity

Xie, J., Jiang, Y., & Tsui, H. (2005). Segmentation of kidney from ultrasound images based on texture and shape priors. *IEEE Transactions on Medical Imaging*, *24*(1), 45–56. doi:10.1109/TMI.2004.837792 PMID:15638185

Zhang, L., Dong, W., Zhang, D., & Shi, G. (2010). Two-stage image denoising by principal component analysis with local pixel grouping. *Pattern Recognition*, *43*(4), 1531–1549. doi:10.1016/j.patcog.2009.09.023

KEY TERMS AND DEFINITIONS

Catchment Basins: The term watershed refers to a point that divides areas tired by diverse river systems. A catchment basin is the geographical area tiring into a river or reservoir.

Centroid: The spot at the centre of any contour, sometimes called centre of area or centre of volume.

Clustering: Clustering is a collection of similar type of objects. The dissimilar objects belong to other clusters.

Denoising: The original image is obtained by suppressing the noise from noise contaminated image.

Preprocessing: Used to remove noise from the image and also eliminates irrelevant information.

Region: Regions are areas broadly divided by physical characteristics.

Segmentation: Partitioning an image into set of regions that cover it. Image segmentation should be uniform with respect to some characteristics.

Thresholding: It is useful in discerning foreground from the background by selecting a sufficient threshold value T.

Section 2
Soft Computing and Decision Support

Chapter 7
Influencing Actions–Related Decisions Using Soft Computing Approaches

Frederick E. Petry
Naval Research Lab, Stennis Space Center, USA

Ronald R. Yager
Machine Intelligence Institute, Iona College, USA

ABSTRACT

This chapter describes soft computing approaches for human-agent communications in the context of influencing decision-making behavior for health-related actions. Several methods are illustrated including using a person's predispositions and generalization techniques that allow issues to be viewed in a more favorable light with social interaction persuasion tendencies modeled with soft computing. The context of a robotic assistant for the elderly is used to illustrate the various communication techniques. Hierarchical generalization is introduced as a technique for generating potential alternatives in choices that might be more broadly acceptable to an individual who is being motivated towards a better choice. Finally, the related topic of negotiations using some the developed techniques is presented.

INTRODUCTION

It has been widely recognized by medical and health experts that it is critical to recognize the problems of convincing the public to make appropriate and effective choices regarding their health. This paper will describe how soft computing approaches support the development of tools and formal mathematical concepts to enable the necessary communication to affect the health related decisions (Lin & Kraus, 2010).

An important issue that arises with specific decisions is the need to provide a common understanding of shared information, situation assessments and the goals and tasks of a specific environment. We will use as running example the use of types of possible automated and robotic assistance in eldercare situations (Fischer, 2010; Matsusaka, Tojo & Kobayashi, 2003; Yamazaki, Yamazaki, Burdelski, Kuno & Fukushima, 2010). The problem is particularly acute between the human and the non-human components as they

DOI: 10.4018/978-1-4666-6639-9.ch007

essentially employ differing communication modalities. We show how some approaches utilizing fuzzy sets and the related theory of approximate reasoning can play an important role in helping solve this problem by providing a bridge between the types of linguistic expression and cognition that human beings use with the types of formal mathematical representations needed for the digitally based autonomous agents. In particular some of the common linguistic aspects of social situational behavior (Kenrick, Goldstein & Braver, 2012) can be represented by soft computing techniques and utilized in persuasive communication.

BACKGROUND

Robotic Elder Care

Robotic aids for the disabled and elderly is a growing area of research (Goth, 2011; Jacobs & Graf, 2012). This is strongly motivated by the rapidly increasing population in this age group. Japan has several active research programs (Kanda, Nabe, Hiraki, Ishiguro & Hagita, 2008; Severinson-Eklundh, Green & Huutenrauch, 2003) as 22% of their population is 65 or older and quickly expanding in the coming decades. In the United States the National Science Foundation has established the Quality of Life Technology Center at Carnegie Mellon and University of Pittsburgh.

For this paper we will illustrate our approach using a scenario in which a robotic assistant (RA) in the future can provide various forms of assistance in rehabilitation and even daily living requirements of the elderly. Often elderly residents of a nursing home may be somewhat addled or recalcitrant. So it is very important that a robotic assistant be able to communicate to persons with whom they are trying to persuade about issues such as medications or rehab activities. In particular social aspects of the assistants' interaction have to

be considered (Bemelmans, Gelderblom, Jonker & de Witte, 2012; Klein, Gaedt & Cook, 2013). We will describe how this communication can be modeled with soft computing techniques and recognize the social aspects of such interactions.

Context of Social Situations and Persuasion

In describing approaches to persuasion that are used in everyday social interactions, Cialdini (Cialdini, 2001, 2008) describes basic tendencies of human behavior that come into play in generating a positive response: reciprocation, social validation, liking, authority and scarcity. By reciprocation he means that a norm exists that expects people to repay in kind what they have received including the concessions that people might make to one another. A basic way in which people decide what to do in a situation is to pay attention to what others are doing which is know as social validation. If many persons are seen as being in favor of a particular idea, others are more likely to follow, since they see this as being more correct or valid. The idea of liking can be captured in words such as "affinity," "rapport" and "affection" all of which describe a feeling of connection between people since they tend to agree with people they like. Another aspect of liking that can lend itself to agreement is some sort of similarity such as having gone to the same school or from the same city. Authority is very commonly used where an expert or authority figure that is respected such as a physician lends credibility to a statement or position. Finally scarcity often effects decisions. Statements such as "only a few remaining" or "limited time offer" influence actions and decisions.

In this paper we discuss soft computing approaches that can support these sorts of social persuasions in the framework of a problem of trying to influence a person's decisions by the manner in which relevant linguistic information is presented to them (Niculescu, van Dijk, Nijholt, Li & See, 2013) In section three of the paper, we show that linguistic information expressed in a statement such as $S = B$ may be useful in helping to persuade a person perform a certain action or infer a desired related statement $S = A$. Often, as we shall see, this is accomplished by using the person's predispositions. So consider trying to convince someone to make a purchase by using the idea of scarcity. A valid statement that might be made is $S =$ "only a few items are left", where the validity of S depends on the interpretation of the soft linguistic term "few." Here of course if a person is somewhat predisposed to want the item, they will interpret the term "few" in a way that will increase their anxiety about the possibility of not being able to get the item if they do not rapidly move toward the purchase.

As discussed, the idea of liking can arise from some perceived connection between individuals. A similarity of people's regional backgrounds lends itself to this sort of connection. In this paper approaches to linguistic generalization using concept hierarchies, discussed in section four, can be used to facilitate this type of connection. For example geographic generalizations might be used to provide this regional affinity. Let one person be from the Mid-West region of the United States. The other individual may be from one of the states that are considered as border-states to this region as these regional categories are not crisp but fuzzy concepts. So let a state such as Missouri be considered as belonging to the Mid-West category with a membership degree of 0.7 (the other category might be the Southern United States). Then this generalization might allow the other person to say with sufficient believability that they were from the Midwest, establishing the desired connection. Clearly other affinities with soft categories can be used in a similar manner.

Often the process of persuasion becomes one of negotiation involving some amount of mutual exchange, a topic which is discussed in section five of the paper. This is a social situation in which reciprocation could be applied. For example, if a health care professional finds an elderly resident at a senior home is reluctant to take their medication or participate in rehabilitation, the health professional might reciprocate by suggesting that tomorrow he will arrange for him to have a "much larger" portion of the rice pudding desert. This must be couched in linguistic expressions in which the terms such as "much larger" use fuzzy set representations

SOFT COMPUTING PERSUASION APPROACHES

A person's decision making process is generally affected by the information available to them about the state of the world. Often such information can be expressed in linguistic terms and we make use of the equivalence between fuzzy sets and linguistic expressions as developed by Zadeh (Zadeh, 1975, 1996). Our approach considers the problem of trying to influence an individual's decisions by the way in which this information is expressed. We examine possibilities such as using a person's predispositions and generalization techniques that allow issues to be viewed in a more favorable light. Let S be a linguistic statement drawn from a vocabulary universe X and B be a fuzzy subset of X representing some linguistic values, i.e. words or phrases, for S that will be used to persuade a person to agree with some desired outcome.

For example consider a situation in which the robotic assistant (RA) is attempting to persuade an elderly resident to do some therapy exercise such as walking. Using some of the previously described persuasion techniques the RA could employ authority by "doctor prescribed", social validation by "Sam walks", etc. Then the RA could make the statement B describing the reasons he should go for a walk such as B= {doctor prescribed, Sam walks, …fun}. The resident may be somewhat reluctant and really just wants to watch television so we want him to conclude or agree with the statement, **S** is A where A= {fun}, i.e. "Walking is fun" Note these are fuzzy sets as for example, the degree to which walking is perceived as fun might be less than watching television. We denote this problem of persuading someone to be agreement with the statement S=A given S=B as PS(B,A).

We want to consider some of the cases of PS(B,A) (Yager, 2004). If B = A then the statement **S** = B is clearly equivalent to **S** = A. Another case for assuring PS(B,A) is if **S** = B provides information allowing someone to logically deduce **S** = A. For example, by noting that the temperature outside is 20 degrees F., this certainly conveys the impression it is "chilly" outdoors.

It may not be possible to make a valid statement about the state of the world, **S** = B, that would support the conclusion that **S** = A is certain. In this case we must consider how to make another valid statement which makes it tractable for someone to be persuaded of the statement that **S** = A is true.

To persuade a person to agree with the desired conclusion, the robotic assistant must take advantage of the pragmatic cognitive component since a person's reasoning and inference is not purely deductive and objective but has a strong subjective component which uses induction and abduction (Burch, 2010; Josephson & Josephson,1995) among other mechanisms. It is also strongly influenced by the preferences, expectations and desires of the person (Ackert & Deaves, 2009).

Now consider the case where A is a subset such that A ⊂ B. We use the term reduction her for PS(B,A) While this process is not a sound logi-

cal process it is often used in human reasoning. The process of reduction plays a central role in non–monotonic and default reasoning (Ginsberg, 1987; Reiter, 1980; Yager, 1988) and provides a pragmatic aid to enable human beings to act in the face of uncertainty.

So we focus on this to represent the process of RA persuading a person to agree with the more specific statement **S** = A based on the broader statement **S** = B. We can observe that generally the greater the portion of B that A constitutes, the easier it will be for someone to become convinced of PS(B,A).

At a formal level reduction is based upon a valid reasoning process where in starting with the statement that **S** = B we can correctly conclude **S** = A <u>is possible</u> given **S** = B. Then reduction essentially involves going beyond this by changing what is only possible to making it certain. That is, by introducing artificial certainty we change **S** = A is possible to obtain **S** = A.

Reduction has the advantage of pragmatic uncertainty and complexity simplification, but allows the possibility of coming to invalid conclusions. A purely logical reasoner will only use deduction. However, in the name of pragmatism, humans have found it beneficial to use the non-logical operation of reduction. This sort of reasoning can be taken advantage of to lead people to come to a conclusion satisfying a certain perception we desire. Our purpose here is to be able to use language to influence people in their decisions. Central here is the entailment principle as found in approximate reasoning to express information.

Influence Measure

Next we want to develop a measure of the difficulty which a person may have with respect to PS(B,A). We call this the <u>Influence</u> of A from B, Inf(A | B), where basically the problem is that of ignoring the portion of B that is not contained in A. Thus the "difficulty" associated with the desired reduction is related to how hard it will be to convince someone to focus just on A. Some changes of focus or softening of linguistic terms can help in overcoming this.

For clarity we assume here all the sets are crisp. However this is not a limitation as we can use the common fuzzy set operations and definition of fuzzy set cardinality in this approach. A simple, but useful measure of ease (or naturalness) of the reduction process is

$$Inf\,(A\,|B) = |A \cap B| \,/\, |B|$$

This measure captures this difficulty relative to the portion of B, denoted C = B-A, to be ignored.

Utilizing an Individual's Preferences to Influence Decisions

People are typically not neutral in making decisions but have some predispositions, preferences and prejudices. These affect the inferences they draw from the information they are presented with. Overweight people, for example, may seize on any justification to allow them to believe their weight is not that bad for their health. We look at such inclinations to see how they can be used to persuade a person to draw a desired conclusion.

Again let $\mathbf{S} = A$ be a perception we want the participant to draw. Let us denote P as their predisposition about $\mathbf{S}$; this can be what they want S to be or what they believe a prior. If a statement $\mathbf{S}=B$ is made, a person will often filter this information through their predispositions P. So the person would be construing $\mathbf{S}$ as $(B \cap P)$ and now

$$Inf(A\,|\,B \cap P) = |A \cap B \cap P| \,/\, |B \cap P|$$

Let $P \subseteq B$ so that $B \cap P = P$ and denote $A \cap P = P1$. Then

$$Inf(A\,|\,B \cap P) = |P1| \,/\, |P|$$

Assume a default situation to start that $|P1| \approx |P|/2$ and so

$$Inf(A\,|\,B \cap P) = (|P|/2)\,/\,|P| = \tfrac{1}{2}$$

As more of P overlaps A, $|P1|$ is larger and $Inf(A\,|\,B \cap P)$ is respectively larger. In typical cases we observe that $Inf(A\,|\,B \cap P) \geq Inf(A\,|\,B)$ and so taking the dispositions P into account would be generally advantageous in trying to influence the person to concur. Often such predispositions, although evident to us, might be more implicit to a person. So it would be significant in such large overlapping cases to bring such predisposition to forefront of the person's attention in drawing a conclusion.

This shows that we can formulate effective strategies when we are informed about a person's preferences. To reiterate, what we desire here is for B to contain as much as possible of $A \cap P$, that is, the information that the person sees should agree with this belief as well as A. This will add things in A that support P. Thus we can use this to target people of who have this certain belief P. That is here we pad the truth with as many terms that support both A and P. We should note the connection here to the idea of participatory learning (Yager, 1990, 2009).

GENERALIZATION

Another approach that the robotic assistant might use in persuading a resident is to generalize some of the words or phrases used related to the outcomes that are desired. This puts the discussion into a generalized space in which the person may be more inclined to agree with the RA's statement. We want to assess how to make use of generalization for the problem of PS(B,A). If a person is not convinced to initially agree that $\mathbf{S} = A$, we consider the possibility of recasting this into a vocabulary space X' in which B and

A have been generalized to B' and A'. To begin with, we overview the background of generalization and hierarchies.

Generalization is a broad concept that has been used in several contexts. One is the idea of data summarization, a process of grouping of data, enabling transformation of similar item sets, stored originally in a database at the low (primitive) level, into more abstract conceptual representations. Summarization of data is typically performed with utilization of concept hierarchies (Han, 1995; Han, Cai & Cercone, 1992; Wu, Chen & Chang, 2011), which in ordinary databases are considered to be a part of background knowledge as seen in the geographical hierarchy example of Figure 1.

Hierarchies and Data Partitions

In this section we discuss concept hierarchies associated with a specific attribute. Let V be an attribute (variable) and let D (V) be the domain of possible data values of V. A concept hierarchy consists of a number of levels each of which is a partitioning of the space D (V). Furthermore this partitioning becomes coarser and coarser as we go up the hierarchy. The lowest possible level of a hierarchy consists of a partitioning by the individual elements of D (V) and the highest level possible is the whole domain D (V).

This implies that if $k > j$ then for any equivalence class E_{jlh} at level j there exists an equivalence class E_{kli} at level k such that $E_{jlh} \subseteq E_{kli}$

So at each level k, the concept hierarchy is a partition of the set of possible data values D(V) into n_k categories (equivalence classes) (Petry & Yager, 2008):

$$E_{k|1}, E_{k|2}, \ldots .E_{k|n_k}$$

If we have m levels then the concept hierarchy is a collection of m partitions of the space D(V). In particular the concept hierarchy consists of

Partition 1: E_{1li} for $i = 1$ to n_1
Partition 2: E_{2li} for $i = 1$ to n_2
Partition m: E_{mli} for $i = 1$ to n_m

Generalization with Fuzzy Hierarchies

Fuzzy hierarchies enable the expression of partial ISA relationships with membership values as fractional numbers between two incident concept nodes (Lee & Kim, 1997; Petry & Zhao, 2009). For fuzzy hierarchies, a concept is regarded as a partial specification of its upper concept with the corresponding membership degree μ in the

Figure 1. Typical concept hierarchy for the concept of U S location

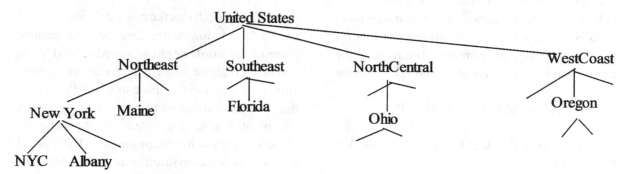

[0, 1] interval. If $\mu = 1$, there is a complete specification as in crisp concept hierarchies. For example if the RA is trying to persuade someone to take their medication promptly, it might need to adapt some of the words used about the importance of doing this. The fuzzy hierarchy in Figure 2 illustrates some possible words to be used and their relationships.

Next we describe a fuzzy hierarchy in terms of partitions where for a fuzzy hierarchy the appropriate defining relationship for an attribute is:

$$Z_k: D(V) \times D(V) \rightarrow [0,1]$$

As a consequence rather than a partitioning of D(V) we have a decomposition. This means that at each level there are particular G_{kl1}, G_{kl2}, .. where in general

$$G_{kli} \cap G_{klj} \neq \varphi$$

This implies that there may not be a unique concept at level k to which a value at level k-1 generalizes. Graphically we can illustrate this in Figure 3.

The G_{kli} corresponding to C_{kli} is the set { ...p,q,r,...} and G_{klj} representing C_{klj} is { ...r,s,t...}. An overlapping data value such as r has a degree of membership μ_{kli} (t) in G_{kli} and μ_{klj} (t) in G_{klj} as determined by Z_k.

Recall that we want to consider the use of generalization for persuasion problem of PS(B,A). In order to focus on the specific words involved in a generalization, we introduce the notation for the sets of words in B and A as WB and WA, WA $\subseteq$ WB, denoted as WB = {w_1, ...w_n} and WA = {w_i, ...w_k}, where. w_i, ...w_k $\in$ WB Assume we have some hierarchy H that generalizes B:

$$H: B \rightarrow B'$$

The domain for this hierarchy must include the set of words WB and thus produces a set of generalized terms for B:

$$WB' = \{w'_1, ...w'_n\}$$

This also means that the set A $\subseteq$ B has its terms generalized to obtain WA' where $w'_j \in$ WA' $\Rightarrow$ w'_j $\in$ WB', i.e. WA' $\subseteq$ WB'. Since several words in

Figure 2. Fuzzy Hierarchy Example

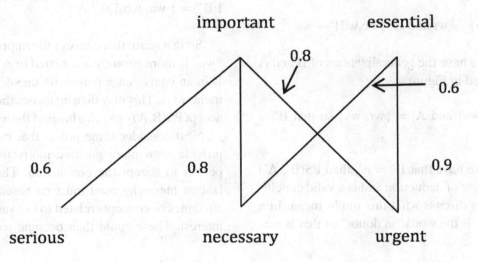

Figure 3. Fuzzy Hierarchical Structure

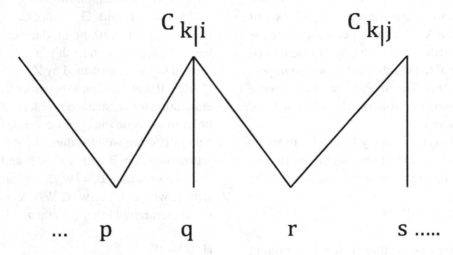

WB can generalize to the same words in WB', then | WB | > | WB' | and similarly for WA and WA'.

First let us discuss how this recasting of the desired conclusion can help to influence a person to accept the original conclusion. Consider conveying that S = B implies S = A as shown in Figure 4. For simplicity of discussion, let there be only one term in B, wa, not in A, which causes the individual to be disinclined to accept the desired conclusion.

Now assume we have a hierarchy H which generalizes the words in B such that

H: {wa,wb} → wr and H: {wc,wd} → ws

Then we have the generalizations of B and A as illustrated in Figure 4:

B' = {wr,ws} and A' = {wr, ws} so that B' = A'.

Since we have that B' = A', then PS(B', A') is a clear case of deduction and is a valid conclusion. Let us discuss what this might mean. In a sense "wa" is the word "in doubt" or that is act-ing as a hindrance to the person in drawing the desired conclusion in the initial reduction case. We might say the person cannot "get around" the term "wa" not belonging to A. But we can phrase the discussion as: "Well, let's take another more general look or viewpoint on this," and then generalize with H as described above. This will now "cover" the word by a generalization that puts it into an equivalence class induced by H with one or more of the terms of A. Specifically in terms of equivalence classes

$$EB'_1 = \{ wa, wb \} = EA'_1$$

So in a sense this conveys the impression that "wa" is more strongly associated to A because it is in an equivalence class with one or more elements of A. This may then influence the person to accept PS(B,A) on such a basis of the association.

Next consider some points that may help to provide even more positive motivation for the person to accept the conclusion. The generalization hierarchy used must be based on some attributes or concepts related to the variable S of interest. These could then become some of the

Figure 4. Example of B with overlap with $\overline{A}$

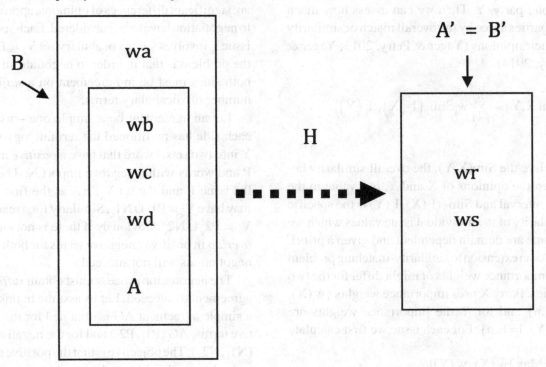

criteria for searching the space of hierarchies to find appropriate generalizations. Indeed if more than one generalization hierarchy covers "wa" then this lends more evidence or credibility to help the person reach the desired conclusion. That is, even from different viewpoints, "wa" is still seen to be associated with A. It might even be possible to elicit from the person which of the related attributes or concepts are most important to them, and if these predispositions can be used for generalization this could also strengthen their conviction.

If we have a case where we cannot find a hierarchy that subsumes all of the terms of $\overline{A}$ with A during generalization, then we still have only the situation of a reduction relative to B' and A'. However if a significant number (preponderance) of terms of $\overline{A}$ are covered by generalization with those in A, we may have convinced the person to

become less reluctant to accept the conclusion PS(B,A). We might consider that certain terms in $\overline{A}$ may have more or less semantic "difficulty" for the listener to ignore and this could also guide us to find hierarchies that could cover these terms and make the conclusion easier to accept.

NEGOTIATION

Often if the robotic assistant is trying to persuade a resident to participate in some optional activities, this can become a process of negotiation (Lin & Kraus, 2010). This might involve m issues $\{I_1,...,I_m\}$ over the domain D_v of the vocabulary involved with these issues

First we consider how to model a comparison of the two parties, (denoted X, Y), viewpoints of these issues. Let $I_i(X)$ be the opinion of the first party, X, about issue I_i and similarly $I_i(Y)$ for the second party, Y. Then we can assess how much the parties agree by the overall match or similarity of their opinions (Yager & Petry, 2013; Yager & Petry, 2014).

$$Sim(X,Y) = \sum_{i=1}^{n} w_i Sim_i \left(I_i(X), I_i(Y) \right).$$

Here the Sim(X,Y), the overall similarity between the opinions of X and Y, is a value in the unit interval and $Sim_i(I_i(X), I_i(Y))$ is the specific similarity of the individual issue values which we assume are domain dependent and given a priori.

As an extension to similarity-matching problem the importance weights of might differ for the two parties. Party X uses importance weights $\{w_i(X), i=1..n\}$ and for Y the importance weights are $\{w_i(Y), i=1..n\}$. For each issue we first calculate

$u_i = Max [w_i(X), w_i(Y)]$.

Using these values we obtain a new set of unified attributes weights denoted v_i where

$$v_i = \frac{u_i}{\sum_{i=1}^{n} u_i} = \frac{Max[w_i(X), w_i(Y)]}{\sum_{i=1}^{n} Max[w_i(X), w_i(Y)]}.$$

We now use these weights in the above similarity and obtain

$$Sim(X,Y) = \sum_{i=1}^{n} v_i \, Sim_i(A_i(X), A_i(Y)).$$

Essentially here in using $u_i = Max [w_i(X), w_i(Y)]$ we saying if an issue is important in one of the parties' view, it should be important in determining the similarity.

Now if the similarity measure shows that there are significant differences of opinions, approaches to negotiation have to be considered. Each specific issue I_k involves some vocabulary set $V_k \subseteq D_V$. So the problem is that in order to negotiate an issue both sides must be in agreement on a *sufficient* number of vocabulary terms.

Let an agreement be a simple one – assume each side has partitioned the terminology space Y into two sets – word that have a *positive* import P and words with a *negative* import N. Then for the issue I_k and the set V_k, RA as the first party may have $V_k = P1_k \cup N1_k$. Similarly for a resident, $V_k = P2_k \cup N2_k$. Obviously if there is not *enough overlap* in positive / negative terms for both sides negotiations will not succeed.

The negotiation process must obtain *sufficient* agreement to succeed. Let us assume in this case a simple agreement AG is obtained for the positive terms, AG $(P1_k, P2_k)$ and for the negative AG $(N1_k, N2_k)$. The objective is that the positive terms agreed upon should *mostly* cover the vocabulary set V_k under negotiation and the negative terms agreed upon should *mostly* be avoided in the negotiation issue I_k. This means AG $(N1_k, N2_k) \cap V_k$ should be *small*.

Now let there be two hierarchies over D_V: H_1 and H_2 respectively for the two parties in the negotiation. In order to achieve these agreements the sets of words in dispute can be generalized by the two sides' hierarchies H_1 and H_2. Then it might be possible that there are more general concepts that the two sides can accept as agreeable (Petry & Yager, 2010).

Clearly much of the inexact negotiation process involves subjective and soft criteria mentioned above such as "sufficient" agreement or "most" coverage. The representation of such linguistic terms used during the negotiation can be assisted by the concept of linguistic quantifiers. Zadeh (1975) noted that human dialogue makes considerable use of terms such as *most*, *about 50%*, *some*, *all* which he referred to as linguistic quantifiers. These terms are used to provide a linguistic explanation of some proportion and can be represented by fuzzy subsets over the unit interval such that the membership measures the satisfaction to the concept. In Figure 5 we illustrate a typical graphical representation of the concept "About Half".

Sometimes parties are unable to resolve differences by negotiation, in which case a third party may step in to lead them to a solution by compromise. This is termed mediation. A mediator may even play an active role in this process and be flexible or innovative enough to obtain some agreement. Such an individual should have psychological understanding to appreciate the way in which the two parties are visualizing the issues between them.

This leads us to consider the issues of partially generalizing hierarchies and a space of concept hierarchies. – a partially partitioned space. So we consider the process of trying to reach agreements to do negotiations as a search thru this space – an exploration of such a space. This fits into the aspect of creativity – exploration. So we can see that inherently the process of negotiation can be viewed as a creative process.

SUMMARY

In this paper we have presented a number of approaches using soft computing for human-agent communications in the context of influencing decision making behavior. We examined several methods of representing the process of engendering such influences. These included using a person's predispositions and generalization techniques that allow issues to be viewed in a more favorable light. The social interaction persuasion tendencies were considered with soft computing. The context of a robotic assistant for the elderly was used to illustrate the various communication techniques. Lastly we discussed approaches to the related topic of negotiations making use of some the developed techniques.

Additional research under consideration is the use of granular computing techniques (Bargiela & Pedrycz, 2003) and the use of rough set hierarchies in generalization (Beaubouef, Petry & Yager, 2011). Both of these extensions can provide closer approximations to the uncertainty found in human decision making behavior.

Figure 5. Example for criterion "About Half"

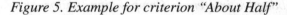
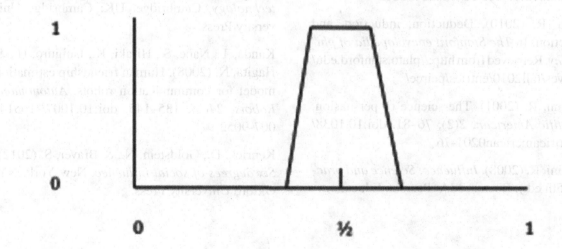

ACKNOWLEDGMENT

The authors would like to thank the Naval Research Laboratory's Base Program, Program Element No. 0602435N and ONR Grant Award No. N000141010121 for sponsoring this research.

REFERENCES

Ackert, L., & Deaves, R. (2009). *Behavioral finance psychology, decision-making, and markets*. Houston, TX: South-Western Educational Publishers.

Bargiela, A., & Pedrycz, W. (2003). *Granular computing: An introduction*. Amsterdam: Kluwer Academic Publishers. doi:10.1007/978-1-4615-1033-8

Beaubouef, T., Petry, F., & Yager, R. (2011). Attribute generalization with rough set hierarchies. In *Proceedings World Conference on Soft Computing* (pp. 222-227). New York: Springer.

Bemelmans, R., Gelderblom, G., Jonker, P., & de Witte, L. (2012). Socially assistive robots in elderly care: A systematic review into effects and effectiveness. *Journal of the American Medical Directors Association, 13*(2), 114–120. doi:10.1016/j.jamda.2010.10.002 PMID:21450215

Burch, R. (2010). Deduction, induction, and abduction. In *The Stanford encyclopedia of philosophy*. Retrieved from http://plato.stanford.edu/archives/fall2010/entries/peirce/

Cialdini, R. (2001). The science of persuasion. *Scientific American, 2*(2), 76–81. doi:10.1038/scientificamerican0201-76

Cialdini, R. (2008). *Influence: Science and practice* (5th ed.). Boston, MA: Pearson Education.

Fischer, K. (2010). Why it is interesting to investigate how people talk to computers and robots. *Journal of Pragmatics, 42*(9), 2349–2354. doi:10.1016/j.pragma.2009.12.014

Ginsberg, M. (1987). *Readings in nonmonotonic reasoning*. Los Altos, CA: Morgan Kaufmann.

Goth, G. (2011). I, domestic robot. *Communications of the ACM, 54*(5), 16–17. doi:10.1145/1941487.1941494

Han, J. (1995). Mining knowledge at multiple concept levels. In *Proceedings 4th International Conference on Information and Knowledge Management* (pp. 19-24). New York: ACM Press.

Han, J., Cai, Y., & Cercone, N. (1992). Knowledge discovery in databases: An attribute-oriented approach. In *Proceedings of 18th Very Large Database Conference* (pp. 547-559). Los Altos, CA: Morgan Kaufmann.

Jacobs, T., & Graf, B. (2012). Practical evaluation of service robots for support and routine tasks in an elderly care facility. In *Proceedings of IEEE Workshop on Advanced Robotics and its Social Impacts* (pp 46-49). Hoboken, NJ: Wiley-IEEE Press. doi:10.1109/ARSO.2012.6213397

Josephson, J., & Josephson, S. (Eds.). (1995). *Abductive inference: Computation, philosophy, technology*. Cambridge, UK: Cambridge University Press.

Kanda, T., Nabe, S., Hiraki, K., Ishiguro, H., & Hagita, N. (2008). Human friendship estimation model for communication robots. *Autonomous Robots, 24*(2), 135–145. doi:10.1007/s10514-007-9052-9

Kenrick, D., Goldstein, N., & Braver, S. (2012). *Six degrees of social influence*. New York, NY: Oxford University Press.

Klein, B., Gaedt, L., & Cook, G. (2013). Emotional robots: Principles and experiences with Paro in Denmark, Germany, and the UK. *GeroPsych: The Journal of Gerontopsychology and Geriatric Psychiatry*, 26(2), 89–99.

Lee, D., & Kim, M. (1997). Database summarization using fuzzy ISA hierarchies. *IEEE Transactions on Systems, Man, and Cybernetics. Part B, Cybernetics*, 27(1), 68–78. doi:10.1109/3477.552186 PMID:18255840

Lin, R., & Kraus, S. (2010). Can automated agents proficiently negotiate with humans? *Communications of the ACM*, 53(1), 78–88. doi:10.1145/1629175.1629199

Matsusaka, Y., Tojo, T., & Kobayashi, T. (2003). Conversation robot participating in group conversation. *IEICE Transactions on Information and Systems*, E86(1), 23–36.

Niculescu, A., van Dijk, B., Nijholt, A., Li, H., & See, S. (2013). Making social robots more attractive: The effects of voice pitch, humor and empathy. *International Journal of Social Robotics*, 5(2), 171–191. doi:10.1007/s12369-012-0171-x

Petry, F., & Yager, R. (2008). Evidence resolution using concept hierarchies. *IEEE Transactions on Fuzzy Systems*, 16(2), 299–308. doi:10.1109/TFUZZ.2007.895966

Petry, F., & Yager, R. (2010). Negotiation as creative social interaction using concept hierarchies. In *Proceedings of International Conference on Informaion Processing and Management of Uncertainty* (pp. 281-289). New York, NY: Springer. doi:10.1007/978-3-642-14049-5_29

Petry, F., & Zhao, L. (2009). Data mining by attribute generalization with fuzzy hierarchies in fuzzy databases. *Fuzzy Sets and Systems*, 160(15), 2206–2223. doi:10.1016/j.fss.2009.02.014

Reiter, R. (1980). A logic for default reasoning. *Artificial Intelligence*, 13(1-2), 81–132. doi:10.1016/0004-3702(80)90014-4

Severinson-Eklundh, K., Green, A., & Huutenrauch, H. (2003). Social / collaborative aspects of interaction with a service robot. *Robotics and Autonomous Systems*, 42(3-4), 223–234. doi:10.1016/S0921-8890(02)00377-9

Wu, Y., Chen, Y., & Chang, R. (2011). Mining negative generalized knowledge from relational databases. *Knowledge-Based Systems*, 24(1), 134–145. doi:10.1016/j.knosys.2010.07.013

Yager, R. (1988). A generalized view of non-monotonic knowledge: A set theoretic perspective. *International Journal of General Systems*, 14(3), 251–265. doi:10.1080/03081078808935007

Yager, R. (1990). A model of participatory learning. *IEEE Transactions on Systems, Man, and Cybernetics*, 20(5), 1229–1234. doi:10.1109/21.59986

Yager, R. (2004). On the retranslation process in Zadeh's paradigm of computing with words. *IEEE Transactions on Systems, Man and Cybernetics, A*, 34(2), 1184-95,

Yager, R. (2009). Participatory learning with granular observations. *IEEE Transactions on Fuzzy Systems*, 17(1), 1–13. doi:10.1109/TFUZZ.2008.2005690

Yager, R., & Petry, F. (2012). A linguistic approach to influencing decision behavior. *IEEE Transactions on Fuzzy Systems*, 20(2), 249–261.

Yager, R., & Petry, F. (2013). Intuitive decision-making using hyper similarity matching. In *Proceedings IFSA-NAFIPS'13* (pp. 386-389). Hoboken, NJ: Wiley-IEEE Press.

Yager, R., & Petry, F. (2014). Hyper matching: Similarity matching with extreme values. *IEEE Transactions on Fuzzy Systems*, 22(4), 949–957. doi:10.1109/TFUZZ.2013.2278988

Yamazaki, A., Yamazaki, K., Burdelski, M., Kuno, D., & Fukushima, M. (2010). Coordination of verbal and non-verbal actions in human-robot interaction at museums and exhibitions. *Journal of Pragmatics*, 42(9), 2398–2414. doi:10.1016/j.pragma.2009.12.023

Zadeh, L. (1975). The concept of a linguistic variable and its application to approximate reasoning. *Information Sciences*, 8(3), 199–249. doi:10.1016/0020-0255(75)90036-5

Zadeh, L. (1996). Fuzzy logic = computing with words. *IEEE Transactions on Fuzzy Systems*, 4(2), 103–111. doi:10.1109/91.493904

KEY TERMS AND DEFINITIONS

Authority Persuasion: Where an expert or authority figure that is respected such as a physician lends credibility to a statement or position.

Concept Hierarchy: A tree structure in which the concepts or terms are related successively to parents in the tree that represent broader concepts covering several lower level concepts.

Fuzzy Hierarchy: Concept hierarchy using partial ISA relationships with membership values as fractional numbers between two incident concept nodes.

Fuzzy Set: A set in which an element can have a degree of membership in set.

Generalization: The process of replacing more specific terms or concepts by more general or broader concepts.

Reciprocation: A norm exists that expects people to repay in kind.

Social Validation: Where people make decisions based on what others are doing.

Soft Computing: Techniques based on fuzzy set theory to represent and manipulate uncertainty with subjective linguistic aspects.

Chapter 8
A Smart and Dynamic Decision Support System for Nonlinear Environments

S. Uma
Hindusthan Institute of Technology, India

J. Suganthi
Hindusthan College of Engineering and Technology, India

ABSTRACT

The design of a dynamic and efficient decision-making system for real-world systems is an essential but challenging task since they are nonlinear, chaotic, and high dimensional in nature. Hence, a Support Vector Machine (SVM)-based model is proposed to predict the future event of nonlinear time series environments. This model is a non-parametric model that uses the inherent structure of the data for forecasting. The dimensionality of the data is reduced besides controlling noise as the first preprocessing step using the Hybrid Dimensionality Reduction (HDR) and Extended Hybrid Dimensionality Reduction (EHDR) nonlinear time series representation techniques. It is also used for subsequencing the nonlinear time series data. The proposed SVM-based model using EHDR is compared with the models using Symbolic Aggregate approXimation (SAX), HDR, SVM using Kernel Principal Component Analysis (KPCA), and SVM using varying tube size values for historical data on different financial instruments. A comparison of the experimental results of the proposed model with other models taken for the experimentation has proven that the prediction accuracy of the proposed model is outstanding.

INTRODUCTION

Decision making is imperative in all fields of science and engineering. With the advent of high and ultra high frequency observations of massive and complex data sets, the classical paradigms of linear time series is not applicable. Though

human beings have developed skills for sensing the context and identifying *patterns, modeling* and recognizing complex patterns for all contexts is a relatively tough task due to varying human intelligence, memory power, physical abilities and expertise in the field of application. Due to the *dynamic* and *chaotic* nature of the *nonlinear*

DOI: 10.4018/978-1-4666-6639-9.ch008

time series systems, the traditional decision support systems find more difficulty in extracting meaningful statistics. Hence a booming interest in developing a novel methodology for nonlinear time series *analysis* to use the retrieved information and assist the decision making process is realized (Fulcher & Jones, 2014).

The design of a *time series model* requires the modeling of the temporal data (Wu et al., 2005; Grando et al., 2010). The decrease in the cost of storage devices and increase in the performance of computational facilities has motivated the storage of large volumes of data to support the decision making process. Most of this data are *time series* data which is measured typically at successive times spaced at uniform intervals of time. Since, the time series datasets thus measured are *nonlinear,* high dimensional and noisy, a *dynamic* forecasting *model* that gives importance to the internal structure is required for efficient decision making and *analysis*. Hence, an intelligent approach towards knowledge extraction from historical database that enables sustainable competitive advantage is essential (Singh, 2007). In *nonlinear* systems, the changes in the environment are influenced by the previous history of actions or due to external events which is outside the control of the decision maker.

A smart and *dynamic* decision support system is proposed to overcome the limitations mentioned above for nonlinear environments. The proposed model leverages the advantages of integrating SVM and EHDR representation, thereby providing robust decision support. This research work is aimed at: a) reducing the high dimensionality of nonlinear time series datasets, b) controlling the noise that hinders the analysis and to c) design a smart and dynamic decision support system for nonlinear environments. In this context, the contributions of this chapter are, First the time series representations Hybrid Dimensionality Reduction (HDR) and Extended Hybrid Dimensionality Reduction (EHDR) techniques that reduces the high dimensionality and controls the noise and Second, the SVM based model that uses EHDR for providing a smart and dynamic decision support for nonlinear environments.

Financial Markets are the primary and secondary source of income for a large mass of population. But they are nonlinear, *chaotic,* noisy and dynamic in nature. The financial instruments like stocks, commodities, futures and options are subject to nonlinear price fluctuations due to the changes in the social, economic, political and climatic conditions. Hence, decision making is a challenging task under such circumstances. To solve the decision making process, historical data and *patterns* of the past are used. But, historical data are voluminous in nature and remembering the patterns of the past for identifying a solution is a difficult task even for an experienced person adept at technical analysis / reading charts. Hence, the experimentation of the proposed model was done in comparison with ε descending Support Vector Regression (SVR), SVR using KPCA, SVM using SAX and SVM using HDR for forecasting the financial markets, a real time application used in our daily life. The experimental results have proved that the performance of the proposed SVM based model using EHDR is outstanding compared with other models taken for experimentation.

The chapter is organized as follows. The literature review of related work and the motivation for using SVM for subsequence clustering are given under the sections titled, "Background" and "Support Vector Machines" respectively. Following these sections, the proposed dimensionality reduction methods and the proposed dynamic decision support model are explained. A discussion of the various models taken for the experimentation and a brief description of the metrics used for the evaluation of these models are given in the subsequent sections. Research findings are discussed under the experimental results section and a conclusion is given.

BACKGROUND

Decision support systems are extensively used in computational procedures to forecast the future events, to estimate the parameters of a model, to optimize resource utilization or to describe the random behavior. The *non-parametric* study of nonlinear time series analysis is done with the aim of scientific understanding and forecasting (Mukhopadhyay & Parzen, 2013). The interdisciplinary diversity of time series data makes it more difficult to determine how methods developed in different methods are related to each other and to select the most appropriate method for the time series data (Fulcher et al, 2013).Though a given time series could be fit in several different types of models, the challenge is in finding a model that will be a perfect fit.

Several methods like autoregressive filters, neural networks, genetic algorithms and fuzzy systems exist for solving time series *prediction* problems. Autoregressive filters can be computationally efficient for low order models but assumes linearity and computationally expensive for higher order models (Sapankevych et al., 2009).

Traditional time series analysis methods like Box-Jenkins or Auto Regressive Integrated Moving Average (ARIMA) method tries to characterize and predict all points in a time series. Hence, the design of the ARIMA model is limited by the requirement of stationarity of the time series, normality and independence of the residuals (Aydin et al., 2009). The traditional time series analysis methods are unable to identify complex, non periodic, nonlinear, irregular, and chaotic characteristics of time series data. ARIMA models assume that the system generating the time series is linear (Khashei & Bijari, 2011). But it is not necessarily linear or stationary. The traditional models used for decision making give less importance to the internal structure of the time series.

Though several methods are used for solving pattern recognition problems, due to the universal approximation capabilities, adaptation of the *prediction* quickly to changed conditions and robust performance, neural networks are widely used for pattern prediction problems (Raj & Raj, 2011). Neural networks are suitable for nonlinear approximations but require more training data and are hard to interpret. The pattern recognition of neural networks is also limited by the presence of noise and complexity of the nonlinear data (Slim, 2006).

Fuzzy system incorporates human expert knowledge and could be interpreted easily (Rani & Deepa, 2011). But, the adaptability is relatively low (Chen & Han, 2007). Genetic algorithm provides good optimization but takes more time. Due to the complexity and dynamic nature of nonlinear data, data supporting tools do not provide the required information to support a decision (Hillbrand, 2007). Hence, the need for an intelligent and dynamic decision support system for nonlinear environments is realized.

SVM is a supervised machine learning technique that analyses and recognizes patterns. *Non-parametric* methods have been very popular both for prediction and characterizing nonlinear dependence (Saart et al, 2014). Support vector machines are non-parametric, meaning that the number of parameters and their values are data driven and depends on data complexity (Cherkassky, 2002). Training SVM with more samples produces good forecasting results (Carbonneau et al., 2007). Using kernels, absence of local minima, sparseness of the solution and the capacity control obtained by optimizing the margin are the key features of SVMs. The SVM based on the Structural Risk Minimization principle minimizes the training error and maximizes the confidence interval leading to good performance (Nagi et al 2011 ; Qi et al., 2011). Hence, the computational intelligence of SVM is used in the proposed SVM based model.

The performance of SVM is limited, when the input dimension is large (Gharipour et al., 2011). High dimensionality of the time series data is a limitation for modeling any decision support system for nonlinear systems. Since, the design of a time series model for effective decision support requires dimensionality reduction, it is adapted as the first preprocessing step to enhance the computational speed, efficiency and accuracy of time series analysis. Besides reducing the risk of over-fitting, the low dimensional representation of the data improves the generalization capability of the classification / clustering algorithms (Garg & Murty, 2009). Espinoza et al., (2006) suggests the usage of a sparse representation of the data to achieve computational benefits out of SVM. The SVM using Kernel Principal Component Analysis (KPCA), a technique based on Principal Component Analysis (PCA) (Keogh et al., 2000) was used for feature extraction by Chen and Han (2007). Genetic algorithms, PSO (Particle Swarm Optimization) and wavelet decomposition techniques are used in literature for reducing the dimensionality to improve the accuracy of SVM.

The main challenge of time series analysis is in representing the time series data (Ben and Nick, 2014). Discrete Fourier Transformation (DFT), Symbolic Aggregate approXimation (SAX) (Keogh et al., 2005), Discrete Wavelet Transformation (DWT), Piecewise Aggregate Approximation (PAA), Adaptive Piecewise Constant Approximation (APCA) and Singular Value Decomposition (SVD) are the time series representations (TSR) used to reduce the dimensionality of the time series data. Though feature selection as a preprocessing step towards data mining eliminates redundant and irrelevant data and increases the classification accuracy, it is not given due importance especially for financial time series data sets (Xue-shen et al., 2007). Also the existing TSRs have certain limitations. For example, the Fourier decomposition method does not provide a better approximation for bursty signals and for signals with flat and busy sections. In PAA and APCA, the time series is represented as a sequence of fixed and variable length segments respectively (Lin et al., 2003; Keogh et al., 2000). SAX represents the time series data

as symbolic codes using PAA and the properties of normal probability distribution. A limitation of these methods is that since the average of a certain length of input data is taken to represent the time series data, certain important features of the time series data may get masked. Due to the window size and alphabet size, a tradeoff between efficiency and the approximation accuracy arises in SAX (Agrawal et al., 1995).

The internal structure of the data recorded over a period of time has potential information for accurate analysis of time series. Hence, the dimensionality reduction of time series data should not mask its important features. It should be rather meaningful and optimal. Thus, the need for an optimal dimensionality reduction technique that will meaningfully represent the internal structure of the data while preserving its originality is realized. Hence, in this chapter, the nonlinear time series representations HDR and EHDR representations are introduced. Besides reducing the dimensionality, HDR and EHDR representations are used to build decision support systems, which is used to analyze the past and current behaviors, identify the date of occurrence of a pattern in history and predict the future event of the nonlinear system under study.

The proposed SVM based model using EHDR provides an optimum solution for dynamic decision making and increases the prediction accuracy. It is applicable to dynamic nonlinear time series applications like stock predictions, commodity trading, forex trading, etc.

SUPPORT VECTOR MACHINES

Support Vector Machine is a powerful machine introduced by Vapnik in the early 60's in which the learning method is based on the ideas of the statistical learning theory (Harland, 2002). It is used for solving pattern recognition and prediction problems (Xu et al., 2011). Conventional regression analysis methods like linear regression and ordinary least squares are parametric, meaning that the regression function is expressed in terms of a finite number of unknown parameters estimated from the data. nonlinear time series datasets are high dimensional, complex and chaotic in nature and hence it is difficult to use conventional regression methods. Support vector machines are non-parametric that allows the regression function to lie in a specified set of functions.

The goal of SVM is in minimizing an upper bound on the generalization error. That is, it works by the Structural Risk Minimization (SRM) principle (Dubois & Adbellatif, 2005). Conventional regression methods are based on the Empirical Risk Minimization (ERM) principle, to minimize the training error. Since, the performance of SVM is better than conventional regression methods, support vectors are used for regression and classification / prediction of the future event of nonlinear time series models in the proposed model.

DIMENSIONALITY REDUCTION METHODS

A time series representation that best suits a particular model is essential to provide an efficient and accurate solution. Piecewise Constant Approximation (PCA) also known as Piecewise Aggregate Approximation (PAA), SAX, HDR, EHDR are the nonlinear time series representations used in this chapter. Given a time series, X=x1,x2,...xn, in PCA, the n dimensional time series data is transformed into an N dimensional series of the form $\overline{X} = \overline{x}_1, ..., \overline{x}_N$. The ith element of $\overline{X}$ is calculated as follows:

$$\overline{X}_i = \frac{N}{n} \sum_{j=\frac{n}{N}(i-1)+1}^{\frac{n}{N}i} X_j \tag{1}$$

The transformed series consists of N equal sized frames and each frame is represented by the average value of the elements in the frame (Keogh et al., 2000). SAX is an extension of PCA that symbolizes the PCA representation into a discrete string (Lin et al., 2003). Since the average of a set of features represents the frame, important features may get masked while using PCA and SAX. Hence, HDR and EHDR TSRs are proposed in this chapter.

The following observations motivated the proposal of HDR and EHDR.

Financial practitioners, traders and investors make their investment / trading decisions based on the previous high and low values made by the financial instruments.

As financial time series datasets are continuous, large and unbound, considering the entire dataset for analysis, may lead to over fitting or under fitting problem (Cao, 2003).

Hybrid Dimensionality Reduction (HDR) Representation

The HDR technique is an extension of SAX that gives importance to feature points of the time series data. The limitations of using SAX are overcome in HDR as given below:

By considering only the low and high feature values of the time series datasets.

The data length being equal to the size of the feature set ensures that no important features are masked.

Similarity search functions leads to different results by varying the number of symbols and segment length in SAX. This ambiguity is overcome by using only four symbols and a segment length of one.

HDR Algorithm

The HDR algorithm consists of the following steps:

Select the successive high and low feature values of the given time series dataset.

Filter noise by removing a feature value, if the percentage deviation from the previous feature value is less than the set threshold.

Select the successive high and low feature values from the filtered time series dataset.

Use the SAX representation on the dimensionally reduced data set obtained in step 3 with segment length =1 and alphabet size = 4 to transform the data into PAA and to symbolize the transformed PAA into a sequence of discretized strings.

The alternate symbols of HDR represent the high/low values of the selected features. As the range of occurrence of the symbols is also indicated by the HDR code, it is easy to determine the oversold / overbought zone of the financial time series dataset. The oversold zone is the zone to buy and the overbought zone is the zone to sell. In HDR, if the range of occurrence of the low and high values is the same, it is difficult to differentiate the feature points as low or high. Hence, an extension of HDR, the EHDR time series representation is proposed.

Figure 1. Closing price of ICICI shares traded in NSE, India

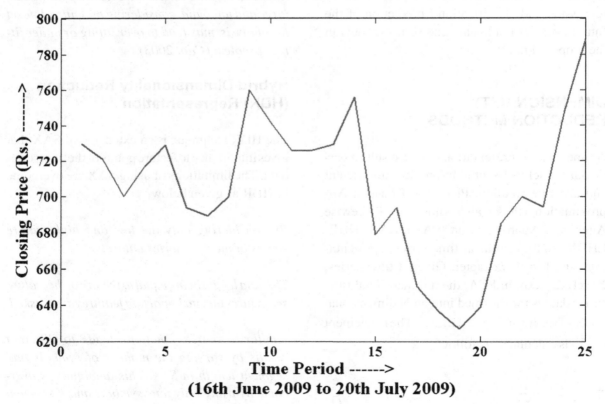

Figure 2. HDR representation

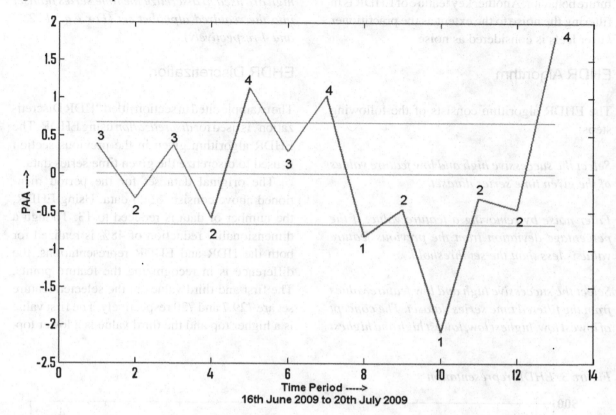

HDR Discretization

The closing price of ICICI Bank shares traded in the National Stock Exchange (NSE) of India for the period from 16th June 2009 to 20th July 2009 (Data Source: http://in.finance.yahoo.com) and its HDR representation are given in the figures 1 and 2 respectively. The HDR algorithm given in the previous section is used to discretize the time series data.

Extended Hybrid Dimensionality Reduction (EHDR) Representation

In EHDR, the low and high values of the time series data are considered as important feature points. It accounts for optimal dimensionality reduction and improves the efficiency and accuracy of similarity search functions significantly. EHDR provides

a more meaningful representation for many different datasets, especially for the high frequency datasets such as financial datasets, since the trend in a series exists for at least a short duration of time. In financial models, a comparison of the current value with the previous low/high value is essential to determine the direction of the trend. In EHDR, the successive low and high values of the feature set alone is selected and four symbols 1, 2, 3 and 4 are used to meaningfully represent the low and high values as lowest low, highest low, lowest high and highest high with respect to the adjacent low/high feature points. In the EHDR code, 4 means that the current feature point is a high value which is higher than the adjacent high values. EHDR coding is done with respect to the most recent historic values. This kind of relative coding mechanism aids efficient representation of the time series data and accurate prediction of future behavior. Another key feature of EHDR is in filtering the noise to the extent as the practitioner / user feels is considered as noise.

EHDR Algorithm

The EHDR algorithm consists of the following steps:

Select the successive high and low feature values of the given time series dataset.

Filter noise by removing a feature value, if the percentage deviation from the previous feature value is less than the set threshold.

Select the successive high and low feature values from the filtered time series dataset. The concept of lowest low, highest low, lowest high and highest

high are used to discretize the time series dataset into the required alphabet set (For e.g., 1, 2, 3 and 4 respectively).

EHDR Discretization

The example cited in section titled "HDR Discretization" is used for *discretization* using EHDR. The EHDR algorithm given in the previous section is used to discretize the given time series data.

The original data set for the period mentioned above consists of 25 data. Using EHDR, the number of data is reduced to 13. Though a dimensionality reduction of 48% is realized for both the HDR and EHDR representations, the difference is in recognizing the feature points. The first and third values in the selected feature set are 729.7 and 729 respectively. The first value is a higher top and the third value is a lower top.

Figure 3. EHDR representation

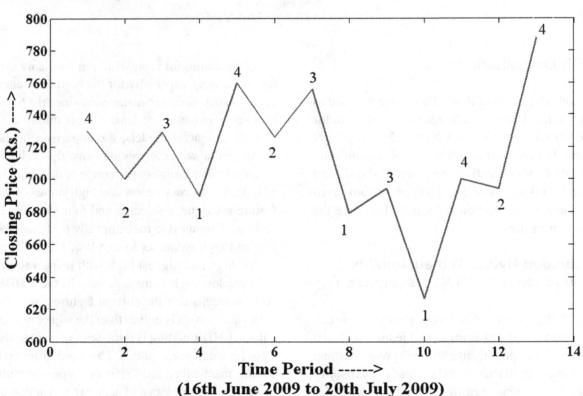

In EHDR, these values are represented by 4 an 3 which means that the first value is the highest high and the second value is the lowest high. But such a differentiation could not be realized with the HDR technique. Both are coded as 3 (figure 2). HDR is useful in applications where the area of occurrence of the feature values is important.

In EHDR, the analysis is refined progressively by accumulating more robust knowledge of the time series (Guyet et al., 2007). The user can fix the percentage of variation between the high and low values to determine a profitable trade of required percentage by changing the noise level.

PROPOSED MODEL FOR DYNAMIC DECISION MAKING

Decision making in dynamic, nonlinear and noisy environments is a tough task. Hence a reference to the historical behavior of the environment is usually made for an efficient decision making process. Time series data has different dynamics at different regions of the time series. The presence of noise in the time series misleads the analysis. Hence, it makes it difficult for a forecasting model to exactly identify the relation between the past and the future and may lead to over fitting or under fitting problem. The success of designing a time series analysis model lies in effectively selecting an appropriate technique for solving its nonlinearity and a suitable time series representation for its computations. Considering the advantages and unique features of the EHDR representation explained in detail in this section and the section titled, "Dimensionality Reduction Methods", the need for a model using EHDR to predict the future event of a nonlinear time series system is realized.

SVM needs relatively low numbers of parameters to be fitted compared with other techniques. It is based on the convex optimization problem and hence it does not suffer from local minima, unlike other methods such as neural networks. SVM is used in building highly nonlinear classifiers by using kernel methods. Hence, to take advantage of the computational intelligence of SVM, an SVM based model using EHDR is proposed.

Though SVM has more advantages, there are certain limitations in using SVM when applied to real world problems. Pattern prediction using Support Vector Regression (SVR) is not probabilistic (Tipping, 2000). The best way to provide solution for a complex problem is to use the divide and conquer method, which divides the complex problem into several sub problems, solves them separately and uses the sub problem solutions to provide solution for the complex problem. Clustering related data provides more useful information (Sridevi & Nagaveni, 2011). Hence, the pattern prediction of nonlinear time series data is achieved by clustering and classifying the subsequences to improve the prediction accuracy.

The subsequences that exhibit similar characteristics are not equally sized. They are of varying lengths. In literature, subsequencing of time series data is done using a time series representation and a similarity measure for identifying time series discords, motifs, longest common subsequence matching, sequence averaging, segmentation, indexing etc.,. Using the sliding window concept on the entire length of the time series data will lead to a number of comparisons, increasing the computational time and reducing the computational efficiency. EHDR accounts for optimum dimensionality reduction and controls noise, besides giving importance to the internal structure of the time series model. Hence, EHDR is used for time series representation in the proposed model.

EHDR coding gives a knowledge of differentiation of the feature values as lowest low, highest low, lowest high and highest high. This information is used in the financial domain to aid the decision making process. The unique and important feature of EHDR is that, the time series representation is done with respect to the most recent historical values.

The entire set of subsequences is clustered into two groups based on the next low / high value realized in history. One group of subsequences leads to a down trend and other leads to an up trend. The set of subsequences that lead to down trend / uptrend are trained using SVM to classify the subsequences into two groups each, one that leads to lowest low / lowest high and the other that leads to a highest low / highest high respectively. The last subsequence of the time series data is used to predict the next event of the nonlinear time series data. A prediction of the lowest low means that the next low value realized will be below the current low level. Similarly, the next events, highest low, lowest high and highest high are interpreted. Changing the percentage deviation of the high value from the low value is used to select significant low and high values. Thus, using EHDR, it is possible to have control over the detection of lowest low, highest low, lowest high and highest high as per user requirements. Repeating the experimentation with different percentage deviations to select the significant low and high values is used to confirm the prediction of the next event. Similarly, the prediction of the

next event is also confirmed by using EHDR subsequences of different lengths. The steps involved in the proposed SVM based model using EHDR is given in figure 4.

For example, consider the closing price of ICICI Bank shares cited in the section titled, "HDR Discretization". The EHDR code for this time series data is 4231423131424. As mentioned in this section, the dimensionality is reduced to 48% using EHDR.

The various possible subsequences of length four for this EHDR code are 4231, 2314, 3142, 1423, 4231, 2313, 3131, 1314, 3142 and 1424. Though certain subsequences are repeated, since the data corresponding to these subsequences are different, all the subsequences of the EHDR code are taken. For example, the data corresponding to the first and second occurrence of the EHDR code '4231' are 729.7, 721, 700, 717.15, 729, 694, 689.15 and 760, 741.7, 725.6, 726, 729.25, 755.9, 679 respectively.

The next event for each of these subsequences is one of the values between 1 and 4. The subsequences are grouped into two categories as given in table 1, based on the next event. The subsequences for which the next event is lowest low (1) or highest low (2) are grouped into one class. Similarly, the subsequences for which the

Figure 4. The proposed SVM based model using EHDR

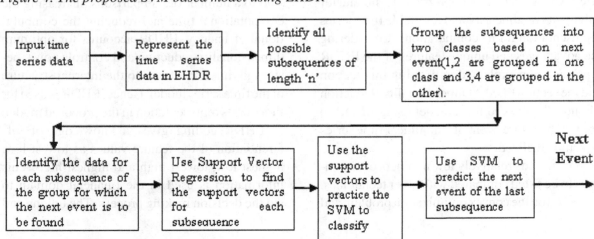

Table 1. Clustering of subsequences based on next event

Group 1		Group 2	
Subsequence	Next Event for This Subsequence	Subsequence	Next Event for This Subsequence
4231	4	2314	2
3142	3	1423	1
4231	3	2313	1
3131	4	1314	2
3142	4	1424	To be Predicted

next event is lowest high (3) or highest high (4) are grouped into one class. The first group of subsequences leads to a downtrend and the second group leads to an uptrend (Table 2 and Table 3).

The last subsequence of the EHDR code 4231423131*1424* in this example is 1424 which ends with 4, the highest high event. Sometimes, the last subsequence may end with 2 or 3. The event of highest low (2) may lead to lowest low (1) and the event of lowest high (3) may lead to highest high (4). In such cases, the previous subsequence is used to determine the next event of the nonlinear time series model otherwise the last subsequence is used to predict the next event.

The time series data corresponding to each of these EHDR subsequences are selected and the support vectors for the same are determined using the SVM. The support vectors for all the subsequences pertaining to a group are found and trained for classification by the support vector classifier. The data in one group is also in another group. The inclusion of certain data to a dataset determines whether the next event will be a low or high. The SVM is trained with different sets of data. This kind of cross validation of data for training improves the prediction accuracy of the model. As the support vectors are varying in length, RBF kernel function using dynamic time warping distance measure is used. RBF kernel is used since it gives better pattern recognition results (Keerthi & Lin, 2003).

For the given example, the proposed model has predicted the next event as the highest low which means that the next low will be a value

Table 2. Group1 of subsequences based on next event

EHDR Sub Sequence	Next Event	Period of Occurrence	Subsequence Graph	Subsequence Data (Rs.)
4231	4	16th June 2009 to 24th June 2009		729.70 721.00 700.00 717.15 729.00 694.00 689.15

continued on following page

Table 2. Continued

EHDR Sub Sequence	Next Event	Period of Occurrence	Subsequence Graph	Subsequence Data (Rs.)
3142	3	22nd June 2009 to 30th June 2009	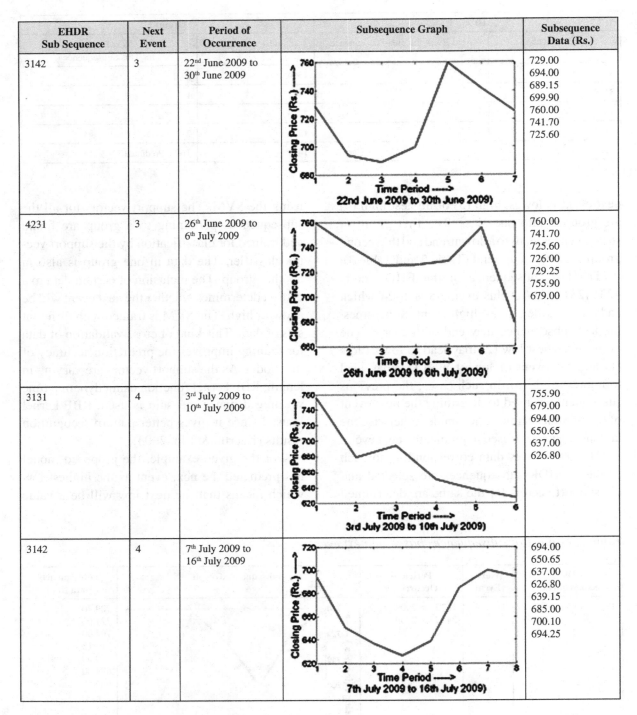	729.00 694.00 689.15 699.90 760.00 741.70 725.60
4231	3	26th June 2009 to 6th July 2009		760.00 741.70 725.60 726.00 729.25 755.90 679.00
3131	4	3rd July 2009 to 10th July 2009		755.90 679.00 694.00 650.65 637.00 626.80
3142	4	7th July 2009 to 16th July 2009		694.00 650.65 637.00 626.80 639.15 685.00 700.10 694.25

Table 3. Group 2 of subsequences based on next event

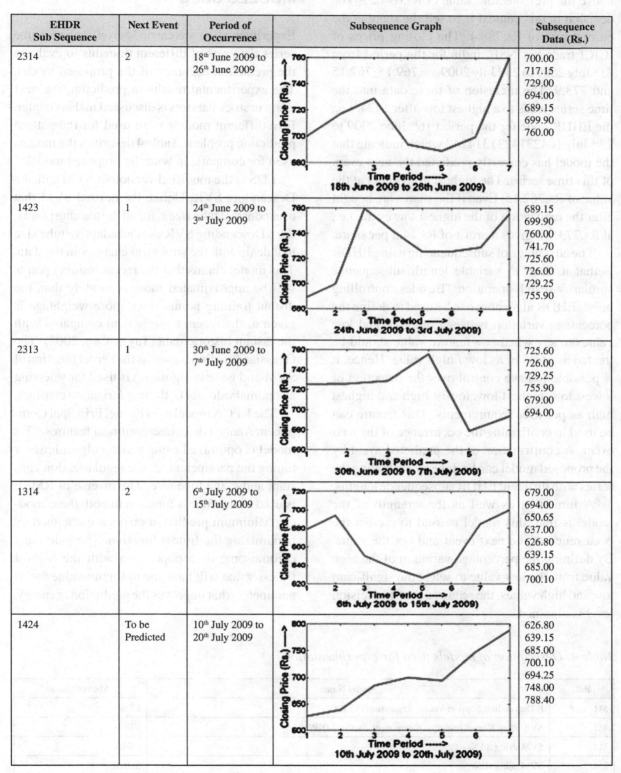

EHDR Sub Sequence	Next Event	Period of Occurrence	Subsequence Graph	Subsequence Data (Rs.)
2314	2	18th June 2009 to 26th June 2009		700.00 717.15 729.00 694.00 689.15 699.90 760.00
1423	1	24th June 2009 to 3rd July 2009		689.15 699.90 760.00 741.70 725.60 726.00 729.25 755.90
2313	1	30th June 2009 to 7th July 2009		725.60 726.00 729.25 755.90 679.00 694.00
1314	2	6th July 2009 to 15th July 2009		679.00 694.00 650.65 637.00 626.80 639.15 685.00 700.10
1424	To be Predicted	10th July 2009 to 20th July 2009		626.80 639.15 685.00 700.10 694.25 748.00 788.40

above the previous low value of Rs.694.25. The decision in this context is to sell the share at the current rate of Rs.788.4. The closing prices of ICICI traded in NSE, India for the period from 21st July 2009 to 23rd July 2009 are 769.15, 762.15 and 773.9. The inclusion of these data into the time series leads to a highest low after 1424. i.e., the EHDR code for the period 16th June 2009 to 23rd July is 42314231314242 which indicate that the model has correctly predicted the next event of this time series. The highest low occurs at the value of Rs.762.15. Even if the shares are bought after the realization of the highest low event, i.e., at Rs.773.9 it gives a profit of Rs.14.5 per share.

The advantage of subsequencing using EHDR is that it leads to variable length subsequence similarity search operations. Besides controlling noise, EHDR algorithm can be used to define the percentage variation between the high and low values to say whether a feature value should be treated as noise or as low / high value. Hence, it is possible to have control over the detection of lowest low, highest low, lowest high and highest high as per user requirements. This feature can be used in confirming the occurrence of the next event. A confirmation of the predicted event by the proposed model can be done by evaluating the series with different EHDR subsequence lengths.

A limitation as well as the strength of the model is that, this model is used to predict the occurrence of the next event and not the value. By defining the percentage variation of the high value from the low value to select the significant low and high values, the required profit / decision level is obtained.

MODELS USED

Experimentation was carried out on nonlinear time series data sets of different domains to evaluate the prediction accuracy of the proposed model. The experimental results in predicting the next event in stock datasets is discussed in this chapter. Five different models were used for the pattern prediction problem. Table 4 describes the models used for comparison with the proposed model.

EDS is the modified version of SVM called ε Descending SVR. Unlike the normal SVM that uses constant tube size ε, for all the training points, the ε Descending SVR uses an adaptive tube size that deals with the structural changes in the data. This model claims that the recent training points will be approximated more accurately than the distant training points since more weightage is given to the recent historic data compared with the distant historic data (Tay & Cao, 2002). The Gaussian function is used as the kernel function of SVM and genetic algorithm is used for selecting an optimal value for C, the regularization constant.

The KPCA model uses Kernel Principal Component Analysis to extract nonlinear features. This model is optimized using genetic algorithms for tuning the parameters, C, the regularization constant and ε, the tube size. The inverse of RMSE is used as the fitness function in both these models. Minimum prediction errors are obtained by maximizing the fitness function. The individual chromosome of a population with the highest fitness value will have the optimum value for its parameters that improves the prediction accuracy.

Table 4. Description of models used for experimentation

Ref.	Model Name	Abbreviation
M1	E Descending Support Vector Regression (SVR)	EDS
M2	SVR using Kernel Principal Component Analysis (KPCA)	KPCA
M3	SVM using SAX	SSAX
M4	SVM using HDR	SHDR
M5	SVM based Dynamic Decision making Model	Proposed Model

In the SSAX model, subsequencing of the time series data is done using SAX TSR and the prediction problem is solved as a classification task using the same procedure as explained for the proposed model. For this model, the input feature set consists of the data corresponding to the SAX code for the subsequence. A similar procedure is used for the SHDR model, but the subsequencing of the time series data is done using HDR TSR.

A detailed explanation of the proposed model is given in the section titled, "Proposed Model for Dynamic Decision making". In the proposed model, EHDŘ code of length five is used for subsequencing the input dataset. For each subsequence, support vectors are obtained using SVM for regression. Since the Gaussian kernel function provides good generalization capabilities in machine learning theories, it is used as the kernel function for selecting the support vectors (Zhou et al., 2008). The support vectors of the subsequences are variable in length for different inputs.

Compared with other models, the prediction accuracy of the proposed model is outstanding due to SVM and EHDR. Representing the relation among feature points is very much useful in predicting the future behavior in nonlinear time series datasets. A relation of the current feature point to the most recent historic value could be achieved using EHDR which is a difficult task with the other TSRs. EHDR gives a recognition of the low and high values as lowest low or highest low and lowest high or highest high respectively. Though HDR can also represent such a relation, it becomes difficult if the low and high values occur in the same range. HDR performs better when the range of occurrence of the low and high values is important. SAX does not provide any information about the relation of a particular feature point with the neighboring features. It uses symbolic code that represents only the range of occurrence of the average of several values of the feature points due to which important feature points may get masked. Hence, EHDR is more suitable for financial time series analysis and improves the accuracy of financial decision making. The reasons behind the robustness and the higher prediction accuracy of the proposed model are given in the section titled, "Proposed Model for Dynamic Decision making".

METRICS USED

The model for dynamic decision control of nonlinear time series model involves two important operations besides subsequencing. They are clustering of the subsequences and prediction of the next event. As the class labels are known, Rand Index is used to measure the clustering accuracy of SSAX, SHDR and the proposed model. For the EDS and KPCA models, the prediction is done using SVR and hence clustering accuracy is not calculated. The performance of the models taken for experimentation is measured using Rand Index, Mean Square Error (MSE), Root Mean Square Error (RMSE) and Mean Absolute Percentage Error (MAPE). The strategy behind the evaluation of the prediction errors of these models is different. Hence, three different metrics are used. The prediction accuracy is used to measure the performance of the models taken for experimentation.

Rand Index

In the experimentation, as the true class labels for the subsequences are known already, the external validity index like Rand Index is used to determine the clustering validity. External validity indices are so called since the evaluation of the clustering results is based on a pre-specified structure which is imposed on a dataset (Rendon et al., 2011). This method of clustering evaluation is based on external information that is not contained in the dataset. For supervised learning, the class labels are known already; hence we use Rand Index for measuring the clustering validity.

Rand Index is a measure of similarity between two data clustering. Given a set of 'n' elements, $S = \{O1, O2, \ldots On\}$ and two partitions of S to compare, X={x1, x2, ...xr} and Y={y1, y2, ... ys}, the Rand index, R, is defined as follows:

$$R = \frac{a+b}{a+b+c+d} = \frac{a+b}{\binom{n}{2}} \quad (2)$$

where 'a' is the number of pairs of elements in S that are in the same set in X and in the same set in Y, 'b' is the number of pairs of elements in S that are in different sets in X and in different sets in Y, 'c' is the number of pairs of elements in S that are in the same set in X and in different sets in Y and 'd' is the number of pairs of elements in S that are in different sets in X and in the same set in Y. Hence, a + b can be considered as the number of agreements between X and Y and c + d as the number of disagreements between X and Y. Rand Index takes a value between 0 and 1. A high value of Rand Index indicates good clustering performance.

Mean Square Error

MSE is the average of the square of the differences between the actual observation and the predicted observation of an estimator. It is measured using the formula given below:

$$MSE = \frac{1}{n} \sum_{j=1}^{n} (y_j - \hat{y}_j)^2 \quad (3)$$

Root Mean Square Error

RMSE is the square root of MSE. It is also known as the quadratic loss function. When the cost of the forecast errors is proportional to the absolute size of the forecast errors, it is highly appropriate to use this metric. It gives a measure of the differences between the values predicted by a model or an estimator and the actual values observed. The individual differences are also called residuals. The formula used in the calculation of RMSE is given below.

$$RMSE = \sqrt{\frac{1}{n} \sum_{j=1}^{n} (y_j - \hat{y}_j)^2} \quad (4)$$

Mean Absolute Percentage Error

MAPE is a relative error statistic and is measured as an average percent error of the historical data points. It is more appropriate to measure MAPE when the cost of the forecast is more closely related to the percentage error than the numerical size of the error. MAPE is calculated as given in the following equation:

$$MAPE = \frac{1}{n} \sum_{t=1}^{n} \left| \frac{A_t - F_t}{A_t} \right| \quad (5)$$

where A_t is the actual value and F_t is the forecast value and n, the number of observations.

Prediction Accuracy

The prediction accuracy (PA) is measured using the following formula:

$$PA = 1 - \frac{|E|}{P} \quad (6)$$

where E is the difference between the actual and predicted forecasts and P is the total number of predictions.

EXPERIMENTAL RESULTS

A comparison of the models used for experimentation is done on time series datasets of different domains to show that the performance of the proposed model is better than the models taken for experimentation. The performance of the models is measured in terms of the errors incurred during prediction, the accuracy of prediction and the time taken for experimentation. The errors are measured in terms of MSE, RMSE and MAPE. The experimental results in forecasting the future price of stock datasets is presented in this chapter. The closing price of Axis Bank Ltd., Bharat Heavy Electricals Ltd. (BHEL), Oil & Natural Gas Corporation Ltd. (ONGC), Tata Power Co. Ltd., and Tata Consultancy Services Ltd. (TCS), traded in the National Stock Exchange of India for the period from 07th March 2007 to 29th April

2011 are taken for experimentation. The data is available as a free download from http://in.finance.yahoo.com/.

The prediction accuracy of the models using SAX, HDR and EHDR depends on the clustering accuracy of these models. Hence, a comparison of the Rand Index metric for these models is given in figure 5. The performance comparison of all the models used in the experimentation is done in terms of the metrics MSE, RMSE, MAPE, time taken and prediction accuracy. The graphs depicting the comparison of the models taken for experimentation in terms of these metrics is given in Figures 6, Figure 7, Figure 8, Figure 9 and Figure 10.

Figure 5. Comparison of Rand Index for different models for uptrend (subsequences of Group 2) and downtrend (subsequences of Group1)

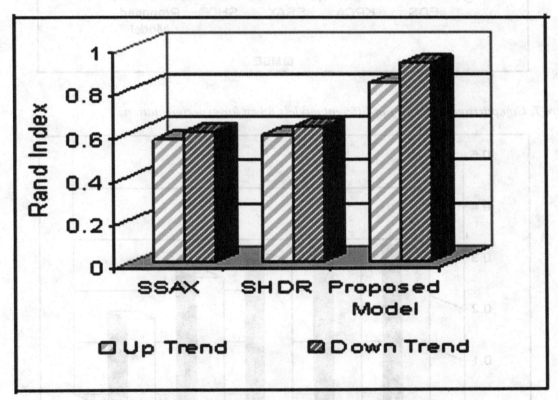

Figure 6. Comparison of MSE for different models taken for experimentation

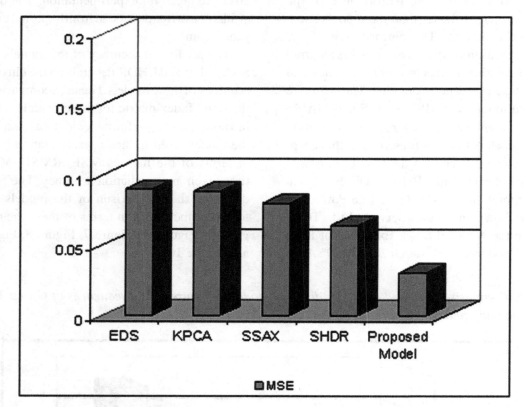

Figure 7. Comparison of RMSE for different models taken for experimentation

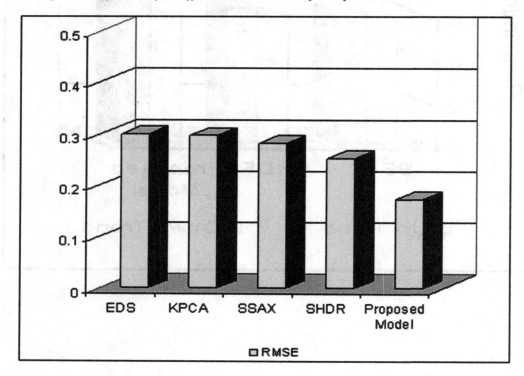

Figure 8. Comparison of MAPE for different models taken for experimentation

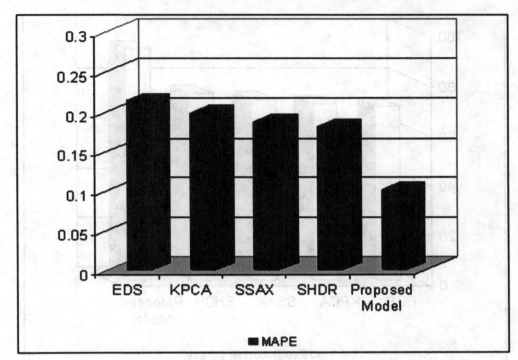

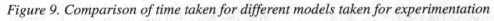

Figure 9. Comparison of time taken for different models taken for experimentation

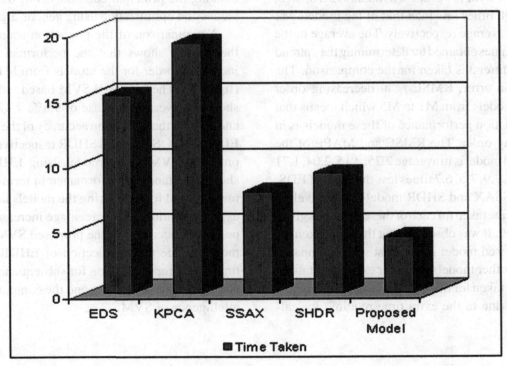

Figure 10. Comparison of Prediction Accuracy of different models taken for experimentation

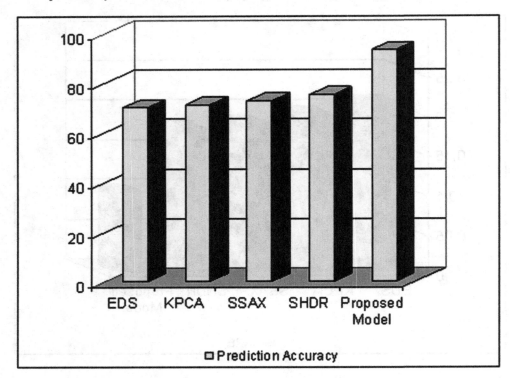

The MSE of the proposed model is 5.16, 4.73, 4.28, 2.98 times less than that of the models M1 to M4 in average respectively. The average of the RMSE values obtained for determining the uptrend and downtrend is taken for the comparison. The prediction error, RMSE is in decreasing order for the models from M1 to M5 which means that the prediction performance of these models is in increasing order. The RMSE and MAPE of the proposed model is in average 2.25, 2.15, 2.04, 1.71 and 8.31, 7.9, 7.5, 6.7 times less than that of EDS, KPCA, SSAX and SHDR models respectively.

The time taken for each of these models is given in figure 9. It was observed that the time taken for the proposed model is the least when compared with the other models taken for experimentation. The time taken for the KPCA model is the highest which is due to the extra time required for cal-

culating the principal components of the kernel values and optimization using genetic algorithm.

A comparison of the prediction accuracy of the models shows that the performance is in increasing order for the models from M1 to M5 (figure 9). The proposed SVM based model has shown an average increase of 9.8%, 7.3%, 4.6% and 2.7% of the prediction accuracy of the models EDS, KPCA, SSAX and SHDR respectively. The proposed SVM based model using EHDR has shown outstanding performance in terms of the metrics used for comparing the models taken for experimentation. The percentage increase in the prediction accuracy of the proposed SVM based model is due to the selection of EHDR as the time series representation for subsequencing the nonlinear time series data and the computational intelligence of SVM.

CONCLUSION

A computational intelligence model based on SVM and EHDR that predicts the next event of a nonlinear time series system is proposed in this chapter. HDR and EHDR TSRs that give importance to the internal structure of the data is proposed in this work. The sliding window concept of subsequencing the time series data using Euclidean distance measure and k-means clustering has the limitations of masking important features of the time series data. The proposed SVM using EHDR overcomes these limitations. Experimental results have proved that the prediction accuracy of the model is 9.8%, 7.3%, 4.6% and 2.7% higher than that of the models EDS, KPCA, SSAX and SHDR respectively. The prediction is done by subsequence clustering of the nonlinear time series data. The advantages of this model are due to the proposed nonlinear time series representation, EHDR and computational intelligence of SVM. The problems that normally arise when nonlinear computations are done, namely high dimensionality, noise and nonlinearity of data are handled more effectively by using EHDR. Besides optimally reducing the dimensionality of the nonlinear data set and controlling noise, the success behind the usage of EHDR is in selecting the percentage deviation which is used to define the low / high value as a feature. This factor can be suitably altered to determine a trade of required percentage of profit or above. The subsequences of the nonlinear data are clustered with cent percentage accuracy, since simple string comparison is used for determining the class. The strength of the proposed model is due to the computational intelligence of SVM and the accurate selection of subsequences for training the SVM which is achieved using EHDR.

The proposed model can be used successfully for all kinds of nonlinear time series applications where effective, dynamic real time decision making is essential. An extension of this work is to use the proposed model and EHDR for predicting the future event of a time series data based on technical analysis.

REFERENCES

Agrawal, R., Lin, K. I., Sawhney, H. S., & Shim, K. (1995). Fast similarity search in the presence of noise, scaling, and translation in times-series databases. In *Proceedings of the Twenty First International Conference on Very Large Data Bases* (pp. 490-510). Academic Press.

Aydin, I., Karakose, M., & Akin, E. (2009). The prediction algorithm based on fuzzy logic using time series data mining method. *World Academy of Science, Engineering, and Technology, 51*(27), 91–98.

Cao, L. (2003). Support vector machines experts for time series forecasting. *Neurocomputing, 51*, 321–339. doi:10.1016/S0925-2312(02)00577-5

Carbonneau, R., Vahidov, R., & Laframboise, K. (2007). Machine learning-based demand forecasting in supply chains. *International Journal of Intelligent Information Technologies, 3*(4), 40–57. doi:10.4018/jiit.2007100103

Chen, F., & Han, C. (2007). Time series forecasting based on wavelet KPCA and support vector machine. In *Proceedings of the IEEE International Conference on Automation and Logistics* (pp. 1487-1491). IEEE. doi:10.1109/ICAL.2007.4338806

Cherkassky, V. (2002). Model complexity control and statistical learning theory. *Natural Computing*, *1*(1), 109–133. doi:10.1023/A:1015007927558

Dubois, J. P., & Adbellatif, O. (2005). Improved m-ary signal detection using support vector machine classifiers. In *Proceedings of the International Conference on Signal Processing*. Academic Press.

Elayeb, B., Bounhas, I., Khiroun, O. B., Evrard, F., & Bellamine-BenSaoud, N. (2011). Towards a possibilistic information retrieval system using semantic query expansion. *International Journal of Intelligent Information Technologies*, *7*(4), 1–25. doi:10.4018/jiit.2011100101

Espinoza, M., Suykens, J. A. K., & Moor, B. D. (2006). Fixed-size least square support vector machines: A large scale application in electrical load forecasting. *Computational Management Science*, *3*(2), 113–129. doi:10.1007/s10287-005-0003-7

Fulcher, B.D., & Jones, N.S. (2014). *Highly comparative, feature-based time-series classification*. CoRR abs/1401.3531.

Fulcher, B. D., Little, M. A., & Jones, N. S. (2013). Highly comparative time-series analysis: The empirical structure of time series and their methods. *Journal of the Royal Society, Interface*, *10*(83), 20130048. doi:10.1098/rsif.2013.0048 PMID:23554344

Garg, V. K., & Murty, M. N. (2009). Feature subspace SVMs (FS-SVMs) for high dimensional handwritten digit recognition. *International Journal of Data Mining, Modelling, and Management*, *1*(4), 411–436.

Gharipour, A., Jazi, A. Y., & Sameti, M. (2011). Forecast combination with optimized SVM based on quantum-inspired hybrid evolutionary method for complex systems prediction. In *Proceedings of the IEEE Symposium on Computational Intelligence for Financial Engineering and Economics* (pp. 15-20). IEEE. doi:10.1109/CIFER.2011.5953562

Grando, N., Centeno, T. M., Botelho, S. S. C., & Fontoura, F. M. (2010). Forecasting electric energy demand using a predictor model based on liquid state machine. *International Journal of Artificial Intelligence and Expert Systems*, *1*(2), 40–53.

Guyet, T., Garbay, C., & Dojat, M. (2007). Knowledge construction from time series data using a collaborative exploration system. *Journal of Biomedical Informatics*, *40*(6), 672–687. doi:10.1016/j.jbi.2007.09.006 PMID:17988953

Harland, Z. (2002). Using support vector machines to trade aluminum on the LME. *Market Technician*, *44*, 9–12.

Hillbrand, C. (2007). Towards stable model bases for causal strategic decision support systems. *International Journal of Intelligent Information Technologies*, *3*(4), 1–24. doi:10.4018/jiit.2007100101

Kantz, H., & Schreiber, T. (2003). *Nonlinear time series analysis*. Cambridge University Press. doi:10.1017/CBO9780511755798

Keerthi, S. S., & Lin, C. J. (2003). Asymptotic behaviors of support vector machines with Gaussian kernel. *Neural Computation*, *15*(7), 1667–1689. doi:10.1162/089976603321891855 PMID:12816571

Keogh, E., Chakrabarti, K., Pazzani, M., & Mehrotra, S. (2000). Dimensionality reduction for fast similarity search in large time series databases. *Knowledge and Information Systems*, *3*(3), 263–286. doi:10.1007/PL00011669

Keogh, E., Lin, K., & Fu, A. (2005). HOT SAX: Finding the most unusual time series subsequence: Algorithms and applications. In *Proceedings of the Fifth IEEE International Conference on Data Mining* (pp. 226-233). IEEE. doi:10.1109/ICDM.2005.79

Khashei, M., & Bijari, M. (2011). Which methodology is better for combining linear and nonlinear models for time series forecasting? *Journal of Industrial and Systems Engineering, 4*(4), 265–285.

Lin, J., Keogh, E., Lonardi, S., & Chiu, B. (2003). A symbolic representation of time series, with implications for streaming algorithms. In *Proceedings of the Eighth ACM SIGMOD Workshop on Research Issues in Data Mining and Knowledge Discovery*. San Diego, CA: ACM. doi:10.1145/882082.882086

Mukhopadhyay, S., & Parzen, E. (2013). *Nonlinear time series modeling by LPTime, non-parametric empirical learning*. arXiv:1308.0642.

Nagi, J., Yap, K. S., Nagi, F., Tiong, S. K., & Ahmed, S. K. (2011). A computational intelligence scheme for the prediction of the daily peak load. *Applied Soft Computing, 11*(8), 4773–4788. doi:10.1016/j.asoc.2011.07.005

Qi, Y., Song, M., Yoon, S., & Watrous-deVersterre, L. (2011). Combining supervised learning techniques to key-phrase extraction for biomedical full-text. *International Journal of Intelligent Information Technologies, 7*(1), 33–44. doi:10.4018/jiit.2011010103

Raj, P., & Raj, K. (2011). Comparison of stock using different neural network types. *International Journal of Advanced Engineering & Application, 2*(1), 158–160.

Rani, C., & Deepa, S. N. (2011). An intelligent operator for genetic fuzzy rule based system. *International Journal of Intelligent Information Technologies, 7*(3), 28–40. doi:10.4018/jiit.2011070103

Rendon, E., Abundez, I. M., Gutierrez, C., Díaz, S., Zagal, Arizmendi, A., ... Arzate, H. E. (2011). A comparison of internal and external cluster validation indexes. In *Proceedings of the Fifth WSEAS International Conference on Computer Engineering and Applications* (pp. 158-163). WSEAS.

Saart, P., Gao, J., & Kim, N. H. (2014). Semiparametric methods in nonlinear time series analysis: A selective review. *Journal of Nonparametric Statistics, 26*(1), 141–169. doi:10.1080/10485252.2013.840724

Sapankevych, N. I., & Sankar, R. (2009). Time series prediction using support vector machines a survey. *IEEE Computational Intelligence Magazine, 4*(2), 25–38. doi:10.1109/MCI.2009.932254

Singh, R. (2007). A multi-agent decision support architecture for knowledge representation and exchange. *International Journal of Intelligent Information Technologies, 3*(1), 37–59. doi:10.4018/jiit.2007010103

Slim, C. (2006). Neuro-fuzzy network based on extended Kalman filtering for financial time series. *World Academy of Science. Engineering and Technology, 22*, 134–139.

Sridevi, U. K., & Nagaveni, N. (2011). An ontology based model for document clustering. *International Journal of Intelligent Information Technologies, 7*(3), 54–69. doi:10.4018/jiit.2011070105

Tay, F. E. H., & Cao, L. J. (2002). E-descending support vector machines for financial time series forecasting. *Neural Processing Letters, 15*(1-4), 179–195. doi:10.1023/A:1015249103876

Tipping, M. E. (2000). The relevance vector machine. *Advances in Neural Information Processing Systems, 12,* 652–658.

Wikipedia. (n.d.a). *Decision support system.* Retrieved from http://en.wikipedia.org/wiki/Decision_support_system

Wikipedia. (n.d.b). *Pattern recognition.* Retrieved from http://en.wikipedia.org/wiki/Pattern_recognition

Wikipedia. (n.d.c). *Statistical learning theory.* Retrieved from http://en.wikipedia.org/wiki/Statistical_learning_theory

Wikipedia. (n.d.d). *Structural risk minimization.* Retrieved from http://en.wikipedia.org/wiki/Structural_risk_minimization

Wikipedia. (n.d.e). *Support vector machine.* Retrieved from http://en.wikipedia.org/wiki/Support_vector_machine

Wu, H., Salzberg, B., & Sharp, G. C. (2005). Subsequence matching on structured time series data. In *Proceedings of the ACM International Conference on Management of Data* (pp. 682-693). ACM. doi:10.1145/1066157.1066235

XAP. (n.d.). *Time series with real time analytics.* Retrieved from http://docs.gigaspaces.com/sbp/time-series.html

Xu, K., Wang, W., Ren, J. S. J., Xu, J., Liu, L., & Liao, S. S. Y. (2011). Classifying consumer comparison opinions to uncover product strengths and weaknesses. *International Journal of Intelligent Information Technologies, 7*(1), 1–14. doi:10.4018/jiit.2011010101

Xue-shen, S., Zhong-ying, Q., Da-ren, Y., Qing-hua, H., & Hui, Z. (2007). A novel feature selection approach using classification complexity for SVM of stock market trend prediction. In *Proceedings of the Fourteenth International Conference on Management Science & Engineering* (pp. 1655-1659). Academic Press.

Zhou, J., Bai, T., Zhang, A., & Tian, J. (2008). The integrated methodology of wavelet transform and GA based-SVM for forecasting share price. In *Proceedings of the International Conference on Information and Automation* (pp. 729-733). Academic Press.

KEY TERMS AND DEFINITIONS

Decision Support System: "A Decision Support System (DSS) is a computer-based information system that supports business or organizational decision-making activities" (Wikipedia, n.d.).

Nonlinear Time Series Analysis: "Nonlinear time series analysis uses chaos theory and nonlinear dynamics to understand seemingly unpredictable behavior" (Kantz & Schreiber, 2003).

Pattern Recognition: "The assignment of a label to a given input value. In statistics, discriminant analysis was introduced for this same purpose in 1936. An example of pattern recognition is classification, which attempts to assign each input value to one of a given set of *classes* (for example, determine whether a given email is "spam" or "non-spam")" (Wikipedia, n.d.).

Statistical Learning Theory: "Statistical learning theory is a framework for machine learning drawing from the fields of statistics and functional analysis. Statistical learning theory deals with the problem of finding a predictive function based on data. Statistical learning theory has led to successful applications in fields such as computer vision, speech recognition, bioinformatics, and baseball" (Wikipedia, n.d.).

Structural Risk Minimization: "Structural risk minimization (SRM) is an inductive principle of use in machine learning. Commonly in machine learning, a generalized model must be selected from a finite data set, with the consequent problem of overfitting – the model becoming too strongly tailored to the particularities of the training set and generalizing poorly to new data. The SRM principle addresses this problem by balancing the model's complexity against its success at fitting the training data" (Wikipedia, n.d.).

Support Vector Machines: "Supervised learning models with associated learning algorithms that analyze data and recognize patterns,

used for classification and regression analysis" (Wikipedia, n.d.).

Time Series: "A time series is a sequence of data points, measured typically at successive points in time spaced at uniform time intervals" (XAP, n.d.).

Chapter 9
Determinants for the Goodness of Performance Measurement Systems:
The Visibility of Performance

Tim Pidun
Technische Universität Dresden, Germany

ABSTRACT

The supply of adequate information is one of the main functions of Performance Measurement Systems (PMS), but also one of its drawbacks and reason for failure. Not only the collection of indicators is crucial, but also the stakeholders' understanding of their meaning, purpose, and contextual embedding. Today, companies seek a PMS without a way to express the goodness of a solution, indicating its ability to deliver appropriate information and to address these demands. The goal of this chapter is to explore the mechanisms that drive information and knowledge supply in PMS in order to model a way to express this goodness. Using a grounded theory approach, a theory of visibility of performance is developed, featuring a catalog of determinants for the goodness of PMS. Companies can conveniently use them to assess their PMS and to improve the visibility of their performance.

INTRODUCTION

In a BARC study on BPM (BARC, 2009), 80% of the enterprises claim the persistent need to improve their overall performance management related *processes*. Deloitte stated that 53% of all companies still complain that their measures are inappropriate to anticipate future developments (Deloitte, 2007). 21% of them are even unable to determine the actual state and health of their company, and in particular 59% of all companies (Deloitte, 2004) miss an appropriate tool support for analysis. To address this issue, various types of *Performance Measurement Systems* (PMS) are used. PMS are business information systems that are collecting, compiling, analyzing, and disseminating data and valuable information (Neely et al., 1997) on organizational performance. Individual requirements and preferences force companies to choose an appropriate solution from many

DOI: 10.4018/978-1-4666-6639-9.ch009

different conceptual performance measurement approaches; from the customized visualization of some financial figures to highly adjustable and mature methodologies like the Balanced Scorecard (BSC).

The *theory of administrative behavior* by Simon (1959) explains this multitude of possibilities by the assumption that individuals are faced with multiple constraints when striving for the *best* information (the problem of bounded rationality) and therefor are using *satisfying* and sufficient information instead. This implies the impossibility of *one* optimum PMS solution that fits the needs of each stakeholder. Hence, it is of interest what drivers and determinants make a PMS beneficial and successful in order to deliver individual, appropriate, and sufficient performance information.

Hence, the goal of this investigation is to explore and expose the *mechanisms* that drive information and knowledge supply in PMS in order to assess their appropriateness for the organization.

There are quite a lot of PMS concepts, featuring their own mix of principal viewpoints, perspectives and measures. PMS originate from the domains of accounting and finance, the most prominent representatives being the Balanced Scorecard by Kaplan and Norton (1996) with four initial perspectives *financial, customer, internal* and *learning and development*, combined with the link to strategy and execution. Neely et al. (2002) propose the Performance Prism, adding *regulatory* requirements, *partnering* conditions, the competitive *environment* and the consideration of measuring *intangible* assets. Lynch and Cross introduce their Performance Pyramid (Lynch and Cross, 1992) incorporating views of the *customer*, the *employee* and the *shareholder*. Additional to these market leading systems, there are at least sixteen other systems available in the literature (Pidun and Felden, 2011), so in principle, there should be a dedicated concept or customizable system for every company.

Though, empirical research shows that many applications of PMS still *fail*. De Waal and Counet

(2009) claim that 56% of all PMS projects are not successful at all. Horvarth et al. (2008) note that 80% of all companies missed a certain tangible benefit while using a BSC. Even 54% of all of these companies do it just with very guarded enthusiasm and not to its full extent.

Explicitly accepting that there cannot be a *one size fits all* solution, it seems to be very hard to find the appropriate PMS for an adequate information supply. So there is a need for a way to express the *goodness* of a PMS by aspects of *appropriateness* of performance information, thus delineating a certain *visibility* of performance that is driven by specific determinants.

Thus, the contributions of this paper are the proposition of a *theory* of visibility of performance, reference models on the informational supply of a PMS based on organizational learning as well as a collection of *determinants* for the *goodness* and appropriateness of a PMS. They can be used to investigate the usefulness of information transported by the *current* PMS as well as the goodness of fit of a *prospective* PMS in order to support the enterprise's choice.

The remainder of this paper is as follows: The following *Background* Section contains the description of the status quo and the relevance of the problem. The next Section on the *Main focus of the chapter* discusses the chosen *Research framework* and the research approach. The latter is subdivided into the *Development of the theory* including hypotheses, two *Validation* approaches as well as a *Summary* and *Solutions and recommendations. Future research directions* as well as *Conclusions* complete the chapter.

BACKGROUND

Improving performance and competitiveness of business activities requires the right information at the right time for the right stakeholder in the right quality (see e.g. Kaplan and Norton, 1996; Bitici *et al.*, 2004; Bosilj-Vuksic *et al.*, 2008; Myles,

2008 or Nudurupati *et al.*, 2011) in order to reduce uncertainty and take appropriate decisions (Power, 1999; Bose, 2006). PMS are systems that support decision-making in general (cf. Simon, 1959) and in particular by delivering organizational data and valuable information (Neely *et al.*, 1997). Franco-Santos *et al.* (2007) name measures and a supporting infrastructure as minimal elements of a PMS. They also count *seventeen* definitions of PMS and expose many various emphases, e.g. on roles, processes and functions dependent on the viewpoint of the users. So PMS can be either designed from the financial point of view (Budgeting, ROI), aligned to the strategic viewpoint (BSC, Performance Prism) or to highlight the operational perspective (Six Sigma, The EFQM Excellence Model) with an optional connection to individual performance rewards (see e.g. Grüning, 2002; Buytendijk, 2009; Gleich, 2011). Different companies may use different systems, according to their primary needs, preferences or policy; they are used in and for a specific context. Dependent on the complexity and size of the enterprise, PMS already in operation are more or less *appropriate* (Marr, 2005; Horvarth & Partners, 2008). Hence, the usefulness and success of a certain PMS also relies on the *users* who are likely to change or adapt their PMS over time in order to reduce their effort or increase their benefits (Schäffer and Matlachowsky, 2008).

Users of PMS tend to highlight certain functions and areas of interest and benefit. Franco-Santos et al. (2007) distinct five principal functions of PMS: *measuring performance*, *strategy management*, *communication*, *influencing behavior*, and *learning* and *development*, with a significant amount of contributions on PMS explicitly addressing the necessity to enable appropriate *communication* and *information delivery*, e.g. Kaplan and Norton (1996) - already in the presentation of the BSC, Ittner and Larcker (2003), Franco-Santos *et al.* (2007) or Nudurupati *et al.* (2011). Moreover, there is a perception of bad *visibility* of performance in specific qualitative areas (Ed-

vinsson, 1997; Deloitte, 2004; Deloitte, 2007; Broadbent, 2007; Braz *et al.*, 2011; Pidun and Felden, 2013) in the sense of *quality of information* (Deloitte, 2004; Deloitte, 2007). Visibility in this sense means the degree of *comprehension* of performance by using appropriate indicators and refers to a certain *overview* on performance information. Recent studies reveal that the key motivations of roughly 100 contributions on PMS are the examination of the functions of *influencing behavior* and *learning and development* (Pidun and Felden, 2013). The paper also highlights that problems with PMS applications are not primarily caused by imperfect systems, but by a lack of *understanding* about their *contextual* embedding, purpose and results. It concludes that a PMS usage should be aiming at improvement of information supply and information quality in order to foster *personal understanding*, *organizational adaption* and finally the *usability* of the information. Another contribution emphasizes a deficit in information quality transported by PMS through comprised measures and the lack of *descriptive* features (Pidun *et al.*, 2011).

Hence, there's a need to investigate the success of PMS by means of their contribution to information supply and learning and development through their contextual embedding.

There are many investigations on expressing the success of Information systems in general. They identify e.g. system use as success factors (Lucas, 1978), user behavior (Gatian, 1994), productivity (Bailey and Pearson, 1983), individual performance (Goodhue and Thompson, 1995), support to business objectives (Rainer and Watson, 1995), lower cost (Byrd *et al.*, 2006) or most prominently the individual and organizational impact (DeLone and McLean, 1992) and in an updated form, net benefit (DeLone and McLean, 2003). These contributions on IS success do not address PMS in particular and do neither investigate the aspect of learning and development nor consider organizational information supply as a success factor. One of the reasons might be the technical emphasis of the investigations, best expressed by the Technology Acceptance Model (TAM), which puts down the IS success to user acceptance (Davis, 1989). Some concepts try to express data and information quality on a more general level (e.g. Hildebrand *et al.*, 2011), but do not offer a direct linking possibility to the domain of PMS as supplier of information. On the other hand, there are already some specific approaches to a goodness of PMS (e.g. Grüning, 2002; Kellen, 2003), but these concepts mainly rely on the quality of the *measurement* construct and subordinate the role of information supply to some extent. This might be one of the reasons that there is still no generally accepted way to determine the goodness of a PMS (Gleich, 2011).

Finally, it is imaginable to state a certain useful-ness and success of a given PMS by the fact that performance *itself* is increasing. This approach must not be considered for two reasons that are grounded in the domain of metrology (the science of measurement): First, there is the problem of *validity*. Of course, one primary expectation when putting PMS in place is to actually enhance performance to some extent (e.g. by communicat-ing goals and measures or influencing behaviour through incentives, cf. Hilgers, 2008). This means that the sheer existence of such a measurement instrument (the PMS) in the measurement chain (the company) already *influences* and falsifies the measurement itself (also known as the "Hawthorne Effect" (cf. Larcker, 2004; Steele-Johnson et al., 2000 for an example). So it would be impos-sible to tell performance changes caused by the producing unit (the company) from those caused by the measurement system (the PMS). Second, there is the problem of *calibration*. A calibration is performed by comparing an actual unit with a standard unit of the same dimension. If a PMS would be measuring the success of PMS, two different dimensions would be used, because the *precision* of the measurement (PMS goodness) would be measured with the *meaning* of the result (Performance change). Hence, the measurement

quality would focus on the producing unit of the result (the company) and not the measurement unit (the PMS).

Summing up, today the success of PMS by means of its contribution to a better *information supply* can only be expressed in terms of somehow *yes* or *no*. In highly competitive times and markets, this distinction might no longer be satisfactory and many companies might want so switch to a different system that *improves* their view on performance information. All in all, there's a necessity for an alternative approach that describes the success of a PMS by means of its contribution to information quality and knowledge supply.

MAIN FOCUS OF THE CHAPTER

The problem of lacking *visibility* of performance of has already been discussed in a preceding pub-lication (Pidun and Felden, 2012). It examined the interplay of knowledge creation via *subjective* information in PMS, but without the consideration of contextual aspects or feedback mechanisms that are necessary to enable organizational *learning* and development.

Using this preliminary model as an explanatory support, the *theory* of *visibility of performance* will be subsequently developed in this article. It explains the principle *ability* of any PMS to ad-equately foster information supply for individuals and the organization. In this theory, the success of a PMS is based on the increase of *domain knowledge*.

The theory presented in this paper distinguishes from the above mentioned 2012 version (visibility increases with 'a plus of subjective Information', explained in a structural composition of different domain knowledge elements, combined with their working mechanisms) in particular by

- The advanced understanding of indicators being not only subjective or objective, but possibly 'rich.'

- The consideration of *contextual* information as another contributing element to PMS.
- A feedback loop via the *annotation* of knowledge, which basically means 'learning.'
- The explication of *classes* and *dimensions* of domain knowledge – the determinants of the goodness of a PMS.
- The derivation of an additional *causal* reference model.
- Finally, the construction of a formal *theory*.

This section is divided into four subsections. First, an *overview* of the basic principles used and relevant for this contribution is given. Second, the *development* of the theory based on the Grounded Theory approach is presented, subsuming the findings under five rationales, a causal and a structural reference model, the theory itself and the derived ten hypotheses. In the third part Section, expert interviews as well as a case study are used for the *Validation* of the hypotheses. A *Summary* rounds up the investigation. This Section ends with the listing of appropriate *Solutions and recommendations*.

Research Framework

This investigation follows the principles of *Design Science* according to Hevner et al. (2004) to produce design artifacts that have to be validated separately. Gregor et al. (2007) define artifacts as *design theories* and distinct between material artifacts (products, methods) and abstract artifacts (theories). The discussion about the acceptance of *theories* as valid artifacts in design science is vivid. There is still a prevailing opinion that design (-science oriented) theories are not equivalent or comparable to probabilistic theories in behaviorism because of their specific entanglement of relations both to the design *process* and the design *product* (cf. Gregor et al., 2007). The historic design science oriented view actually was that

theories are not to be considered in *design* science *at all* because of their prevalence in *natural* sciences (March and Smith, 1995). Recent research on design science tries to address this dilemma and proposes the distinction between a *design practice theory,* which describes *how* to construct an artifact, and *explanatory design theory* which aims in describing *why* the components are constructed within an artifact (Baskerville and Pries-Heje, 2010). The latter can be seen as functional explanation with the goal to solve a problem or to satisfy *needs* and not to produce a theory that explains the phenomenon *best*. Hence, Baskerville et al. (2010) claim to consider a theory as appropriate and valid in the meaning of a design science artifact under the condition that there is awareness about its *specification* and subsequent *implications*; in this case, the developed theory in this contribution can considered to be an *explanatory* design theory.

Mohr (1982) introduced *variance* and *process* theories. Variance theories consider both necessary and sufficient conditions as well as variables and efficient causes, thus delineating a *deterministic* cause-effect view on theories that explains the phenomenon *best*. Process theories consider only with necessary conditions, discrete states and events, but also with the consideration of external forces and a probabilistic view on the final cause; thus outlining the rather *explanatory* side of a theory that addresses the *need* to explain a phenomenon. He subsumed it by describing process theories as consisting of "the *ingredients* plus the *recipe* that strings them together (...) to tell the *story*". This goes in line with the need to consider both *specification* and subsequent *implications* according to Baskerville et al. (2010). Hence, the developed theory can also be considered to be a *process* theory in Mohr's (1982) sense.

The theory in this contribution was developed using the *Grounded Theory* approach (Glaser and Strauss, 1967, recompiled in Glaser *et al.*, 2010), a heuristic-pragmatic research method originating in social science, and widely accepted as tool to develop *new* theories which are able to explain phenomena that were not previously understood or explained by *existing* theories. This is being done by observation and abduction (Peirce, 1991). The core methods of the Grounded Theory are constant and iterative collection and comparative analysis of the embodiments and surroundings of the phenomenon as well as the coding of the findings in order to find and to saturate *categories*. They in turn contain suitable elements or aspects of the theory. The goal of the method is to generate a theory that can both be generalized and used in practice (Strübing, 2008). Grounded Theory is a noticeably emerging method in the field of Information Science (see e.g. Urquhart et al., 2009 or Müller and Olbrich, 2012), but its application in design science to generate theories still is accompanied by a certain justification effort due to the somewhat prejudging view on theories as valid *artifacts* in design science *in general*. The method also includes the inherent obligation to constantly and incrementally validate the meaningfulness and plausibility of the obtained results (Strübing, 2008). This assessment has of course to be done by the researcher while performing the research activities, but can also be realized through discussion and peer review after publication. All in all, the Grounded Theory approach can be considered as helpful for predominantly iterative and *explorative* research activities.

Development of the Theory

According to the results of the *Background* Section, it can be stated state that there is currently no appropriate way to assess the success of PMS and that the search for the expression of PMS' appropriateness should focus on the *information supply* and *quality* in order to foster *personal understanding* and *adaption* by the *organization*. For calibration reasons, the success of a PMS must be assessed in the same dimensions. Combined with the focus on the *contextual relations* of a PMS and the demand to improve *communication*

and enable *learning* and development, following categories and contents for theory retrieval and derivation can be stated:

From December 2011 to July 2012, a thorough literature evaluation according to Denyer and Tranfield (2009) was performed to gather information on those categories, contents and on their combinations. The results can be distinguished into underlying *theories*, description of corresponding *aspects* and then merged in respect of their *relations*. The subsequent observations on theories and relevant aspects in the context of PMS are briefly discussed in the following parts. The reason to start with the basic theories of data, information, and knowledge creation is due to the fact that they are the *baseline* for the development of connections between the categories. The results and individual reflections then lead to concluding *rationales*.

There are already a noticeable amount of contributions on PMS in the context of knowledge creation and organizational learning. Among them, it could be found that implementing a PMS stimulates managerial changes and promotes organizational learning by acquiring, storing, analyzing, interpreting, and distributing data and knowledge about performance (Garengo *et al.*, 2007) with performance measurement being demanded to be a *learning* process rather than a static control instrument (Kotter *et al.*, 1986; Meekings, 1995; Davenport *et al.*, 2010) and to apply a feedback learning process, to trigger reflection and to enact a culture of accountability (Fried, 2010).

Table 1. Categories and content of the phenomenon

Category	Content
Focus	Individuals in an organization
Mechanism	Learning, comprehension, knowledge, visibility
Object	PMS
Framing conditions	Information supply and quality, contextual environment

These findings confirm the demands from the Background Section so far; hence it is eligible to consider the advancement of *knowledge* as an appropriate *success factor* of PMS.

The Knowledge-based View of the Firm by Grant (1996) backs this consideration as it sees knowledge as the most valuable, worth to be explored and to be exploited resource of an organization. He stated that the generation of organizational knowledge goes far beyond organizational learning, because previous approaches only considered learning to be a knowledge internalization process. In addition, the Dynamic Theory of Organizational Knowledge Creation by Nonaka (1994) explains the generation of organizational knowledge with a cyclical conversion process of knowledge embodiments. He names four conversions: from (internal, concealed) tacit to tacit knowledge (referred to as *socialization*), tacit to explicit *(externalization)*, explicit to explicit *(combination)*, and finally explicit to tacit *(internalization)*. Spender (1998) postulates four types of organizational knowledge: Explicit and social knowledge is called *objectified*, explicit and individual knowledge as *conscious*, implicit and social knowledge as *automatic* and finally, implicit and individual knowledge is being referred to as *collective* knowledge.

Fourth, North (2011) distincts between data, information, and knowledge: *Data* (also known as knowledge without purpose, processable by machines) are signs that are embedded in syntax, *information* is data enriched by context and semantics (synonymous to knowledge with purpose and (not) processable by machines (see also Müller-Merbach, 2004) and *knowledge* is generated through interpretation of information through an individual and cognitive process. Müller-Merbach (2004) also amends *opinion* as a fourth embodiment. This is a specific flavor of (objective) knowledge, which is generated through purely subjective judgment of information and is proposed to be a supportive sanity check for objective knowledge. Hence these two concepts can be

merged, because in this contribution, subjective interpretation is explicitly considered to be a *part* of knowledge generation. North's model is known as the *knowledge staircase*. In his model, data with a *meaning* becomes information, interconnected and individually *interpreted* information becomes knowledge and, further on, but outside of the focus of this examination, *applied* knowledge becomes *ability* and actually *conducted* ability becomes *action*. Derived from these investigations, it can be provided that

Rationale 1: The success of a PMS can actually be expressed via knowledge generation. Knowledge can be made accessible via externalization of internal knowledge, provided for the stakeholders via objectification and developed via the addition of context to data and the interpretation of information.

PMS as object of the investigation is displayed in three levels: Indicators, the PMS themselves, and the contextual environment. PMS basically consist of indicators and the framework in which they are put in purposeful relation to each other (Franco-Santos *et al.*, 2007; Pidun and Felden, 2011), hence delivering information. The addition of the *contextual environment* level results from the fact that the consideration of context of this Information System is a fundamental requirement out of the problem description.

Basically, an indicator is a tool which operationalizes the concept of representation-target for a specific context (Franceschini *et al.*, 2006). Three common approaches to integrate measures in this context exist: Direct *adopting* of a measure, based on the belief in the relationship of that measure to performance, comparative *analysis* of different variables and *aggregating*, assuming convergent validity based on the correlation between the measures (Richard *et al.*, 2009). Additionally, Cecconi *et al.* (2007) describe four ways by which properties of an object or an event can also be judged and described, including a subjective component. They introduce four indicator classes spanned along the two dimensions empiricity and objectivity. In this context, empiricity means that relations are observable, objectivity means independence from individuals (subjects). The four indicator classes are called *measurement,* which means being objective and reliable in the sense of observable as described above, *evaluation* as subjective, but reproducible descriptions of individual judgments, *preference as an* is intuitive choice based on internal values and *dictation,* which means the use of predefined results, independent of the judging subject. The need to use subjective indicators in performance measurement has actually been described in the aforementioned concept of *visibility* of performance (Pidun and Felden, 2012). In this contribution, the authors claim to mention subjective performance information (i.e. indicators and such that need interpretation) to deliver embedded and *rich* knowledge (Thomas *et al.,* 2001), which is significant and valuable to gain an understanding about performance that previously was described only in an objective way. Derived from these insights, it can be provided that

Rationale 2: Performance data is collected through adoption, analysis and aggregation; PMS combine them to purposeful performance information. Subjective Indicators are helpful to lever performance data to information via additional interpretation possibilities in the framework of a PMS. Summing up, rich indicators can be defined by considering the indicator classes of measurements, evaluations, preferences and dictation.

Information in performance measurement can be distinguished between factual, prognostic, and explanatory statements about real situations (Küpper, 2005). Explanatory information delivers *explanations* for states of measurement objects (Grüning, 2002). Hence, such contextual information helps to explain states of performance to better understand them.

Present approaches to the design of performance measurement systems omit the consideration of the organizational context (Strecker *et al.,* 2012). To clarify the term of context, first the definitions and characteristics of contextual

information have to be compiled. Mattern and Naghshineh (2002) postulated four principal characteristics of context information: It has *temporal* characteristics; it is *imperfect*, has many *alternative* representations and is highly *interrelated.* Therefore, a context model should support *multiple* representations of the same context in different forms, at different levels of abstraction, and capture the relationships between alternative representations. This demand is supported by the theory of Rosemann *et al.* (2008) who classify contextual information into four categories that are graded by the distance to the business process itself: The *immediate* context that captures essential elements to the understanding and execution of a business process, the *internal* context which is related to the direct environment of an organization, the *external* context which includes elements that are beyond the control sphere of an organization and the *environmental* context which includes macro-economic conditions. These findings can be put down to

Rationale 3: Contextual information is relevant for the interpretation of performance, and should cover more than one perspective, form or abstraction level to serve a certain triangulation approach. This can be done by considering the classes of immediate, internal, external and environmental context information.

This previously identified subjective information in performance measurement *(data)*, contextual *information* and *internal knowledge* embodies *domain knowledge* that must become *explicit* to the PMS users (hence objectified) and transferred to organizational knowledge for four reasons: To fulfill the demand for better *information supply* (though better access) for the involved people in the organization, to foster an enhanced *comprehension* of performance through additional insights, hence to lever information quality, to be able to cause *action* from this previously unknown knowledge and to use the knowledge to be *fed back* to the originators and stakeholders in order to enable learning via internalization. This explication is being supported by *annotation*. Annotation in this context means the explication and feeding back of knowledge in such a way that the codification level (the formalization of the knowledge documentation) as well as the diffusion level of knowledge (dissemination to others) increases in the three-dimensional model of Boisot (1998). The third dimension within this model, the abstraction level (by means of preparing and processing of knowledge) is in this case connected with a certain possible oversupply of information for the stakeholders at this stage. The information amount and quality has to match the demand of both stakeholders and organization. The annotator has to decide whether she/he is about to supply useful information or insights or to omit unnecessary information. Useful information has to be annotated based on the consideration of the *objective* information demand (driven by the decision, e.g. by the agreement to annotate relations between performance data) as well as the *subjective* information demand (driven by the decider and his subjective evaluation of the relevance of the information, e.g. additional marketing positions; cf. Boersch and Elschen, 2007).

The explication of domain knowledge is often connected to the use of semantic techniques. Current studies find that semantics in the use of PMS are rather uncommon (Pidun and Felden, 2011), present approaches to the *design* of performance measurement systems include only limited consideration of semantics and are mostly used in diagrammatic representations (Strecker *et al.*, 2012). Instead, the notation of information and knowledge on Performance is rather represented by *textual* explanations (notes or wikis) and free-form *drawings* attached as annotations to the PMS *documentation*. These findings lead to

Rationale 4: The explication of domain knowledge can be done through a structured way of annotating useful textual or graphical context knowledge to the elements of as well as documents processed in connection with the PMS; thus forming four classes of annotation. The ex-

plicated domain knowledge fosters organizational learning through the possibility of internalization. The annotation itself becomes part of the domain knowledge.

The concept of visibility of performance is designed on the basis of Caridi et al.'s three-step-procedural model of *visibility*, namely the classification of the main *types* of information which can be exchanged, the definition of the most important features of the information *flows*, and the development of a set of metrics and a *measurement* model to assess the level of visibility (Caridi *et al.*, 2010). Pidun and Felden (2012) applied this model to PMS and defined *visibility of performance* is the principal *ability* to deliver knowledge. Basically, the concept claims that the more (PMS domain) information stakeholders are able to interpret and to transform into knowledge, the more *visible* performance will be. In their case, delivered data from PMS's indicators can be aggregated, analyzed, and adopted to appropriate contexts in order to form objective performance information which in turn is interpreted individually by the stakeholders in order to gain knowledge on performance.

This approach is developed further by applying it to the present and contemporary universe of discourse. This means that the consideration of additional previously unused but useful domain knowledge (in the basic forming subjective indicators, in this form the dimensions *rich indicators*, *contextual information, internal knowledge* and *annotations*) can be used to increase the overall organizational knowledge. Moreover, it fosters organizational learning by using an annotation *feedback* loop to the originating PMS, which enables internalization. The connections between these first four rationales are depicted in Figure 1 and explain the causal reference model of *visibility of performance* and its synthesis.

Next, the three-step procedural model to explicate visibility, according to Caridi *et al.* (2010) is applied to the found rationales. In this model, the authors propose the steps *classification* of

Figure 1. Causal reference model for visibility of performance

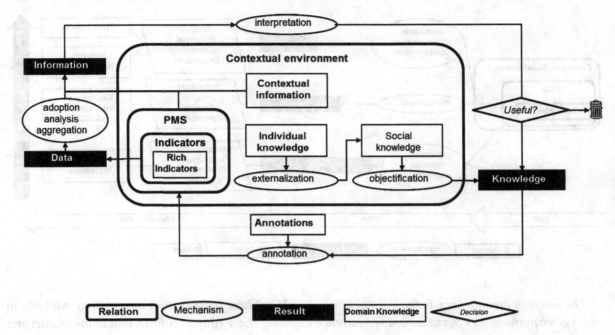

the main *types* of information to be exchanged, *definition* of the most important *features* of the information *flow* and finally the development of a set of metrics and a *measurement* model to assess the level quantitatively. The steps are represented as arrows in the horizontal axis of Figure 2, depicting a structural reference model of an Operationalization approach to the visibility of performance.

In this reference model, the different PMS levels (relations) deliver knowledge results through the flow of underlying mechanisms. The change in organizational knowledge can be measured by assessing the presence and usage of domain knowledge in different dimensions with specific classes. This declaration leads to

Rationale 5: The success of a PMS can be measured by the increase of the usage of domain knowledge (measured as visibility of performance) that has become explicit and which is assessable in various dimensions. Dimensions and the contained classes so far are presented in Table 2.

Table 2. Dimensions and classes of PMS domain knowledge

Dimension	Class
Indicator class (Cecconi *et al.*, 2007)	Measurement
	Evaluation
	Preference
	Dictation
Context class (Rosemann *et al.*, 2008)	Immediate
	Internal
	External
	Environmental
Annotation class (Strecker *et al.*, 2012)	Textual system element
	Textual system document
	Graphical system element
	Graphical system document

Summing up the five rationales and two models, following theory of *visibility of performance* (displayed as graphical model in Figure 3) can be stated:

Figure 2. Structural reference model for visibility of performance

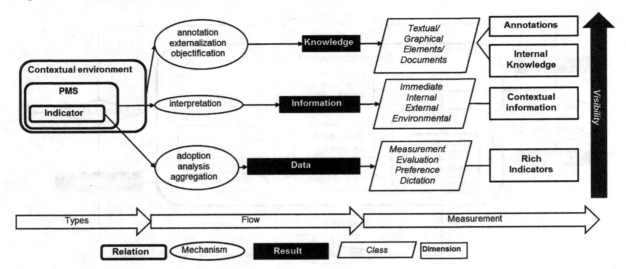

The usage of domain knowledge is associated with a given performance management system and generates organizational knowledge. This can be indicated by the visibility of performance.

As organizational knowledge generation expresses the success of a performance management system, visibility of performance is an indicator for the success of performance management systems.

To test the theory, the following ten hypotheses can be formulated. The relation between the theory model and the hypotheses is illustrated in Figure 4.

H1: There are rich Indicators in PMS that help to interpret and enrich objective data and information.

H2: There is contextual information available in the setting of a PMS that helps to interpret the information contained in a PMS.

H3: There is individual knowledge accessible from PMS stakeholders which contributes to the organizational knowledge.

H4: There are annotations associated to the PMS that help to explicate knowledge for subsequent use.

H5: Assessing this domain knowledge does not increase the efforts of PMS operation.

H6: Assessing this domain knowledge increases the benefits of a PMS usage.

H7: Assessing this domain knowledge increases the visibility of performance.

Figure 3. Theory model for visibility of performance

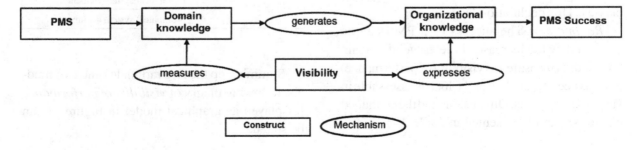

Figure 4. Hypotheses about the visibility of performance

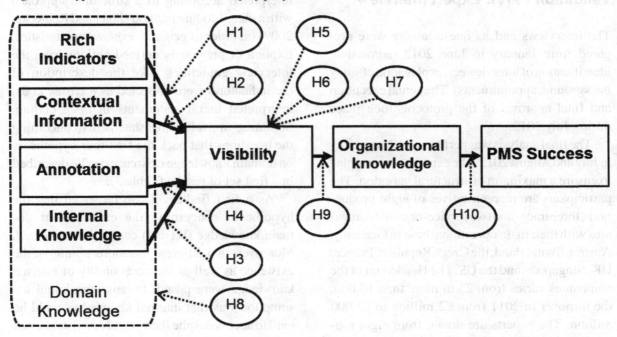

Hypotheses 1-7 focus on the *composition* of the visibility construct *as such* (H1-H4) and the test of its usability as an indicator for *domain knowledge* (H5-H7). The validation of these hypotheses was conducted with the use of *expert interviews* and is described in the first of the following validation subsections. It has to be noted that the primary goal of the expert interviews was to *establish* a concept for the goodness of PMS, not to additionally examine the relations between domain and organizational knowledge. So despite the fact that the complete theory model was presented to the interviewees, only the "left branch" of the theory model was actually tested. As this examination did not validate visibility as an indicator for *organizational knowledge* or *PMS success* (quasi the "right branch" of the theory model), some more relevant assumptions in this direction were put down to the three following hypotheses:

H8: Visibility of performance consists of the combination of domain knowledge dimensions, namely rich indicators, contextual information, internal knowledge and annotations.

H9: This domain knowledge on PMS generates organizational knowledge

H10: The increase of organizational knowledge indicates the success of the PMS.

H8 closes the gap in the chain of reasoning between H4 and H7 in such a way that the mentioned *concept* of domain knowledge actually *consists* of the previously acknowledged dimensions of domain knowledge, which was just *assumed* before *implicitly*. H9 and H10 focus on the usability of the visibility construct as an *indicator* for domain and organizational knowledge. H9 states that organizational knowledge is actually being generated out of domain knowledge on PMS and H10 aims on linking the increase of organizational knowledge with the representation of PMS success. These three hypotheses were validated in a separate case study that followed the expert interviews.

Validation Part I: Expert Interview

The interviews and its questionnaire were prepared from January to June 2012 (admission, identification of interviewees, explanation of study background, appointments). The actual execution and final approval of the protocols took place during July 2012.

The final analysis was performed subsequently in July and August 2012. The experts were sampled to ensure a maximum of structural variation. The participants are representatives of eight production-, three trade- and two service-oriented companies with their main operational base in Germany, Austria, Switzerland, the Czech Republic, France, UK, Singapore, and the US. The Headcount of the companies varies from 25 to more than 10,000, the turnover in 2011 from €2 million to €3,000 million. The experts are drawn from eight top-level- (e.g. CEOs), three second-tier- (e.g. VPs) and two staff management executives.

Only two of the companies were using a designated Balanced Scorecard, the rest used own approaches with both operational and financial indicators in various compositions. In seven cases the PMS that were investigated were used actively on a day-to-day basis. Two companies claimed to have a fully developed but less constantly used, and four a partly developed PMS, mainly due to the rearranging of the system or the current attachment of new viewpoints.

The content of the answers to the questions that were developed from the hypotheses were interpreted according to a structured approach with a mixed coding method (Jäger and Reinecke, 2009) on order to generate *explorative* statistics. Explicit or previously defined options from the interview guidelines (like the description of the indicators) were collected as a *closed* code, interpreted literal statements in *open* coding. Summing up, following statements concerning the questions that back the first four hypotheses on domain knowledge existence can be described in a first set of results (Table 3):

As a first finding, it can be stated that the hypotheses concerning the existence of domain knowledge (H1-H4) can all be *supported*. Moreover, two different questions aiming at the existence as well as the accessibility of internal knowledge were posed, because the initial assumption was that internal knowledge could be hard to access despite their possible existence and usefulness for PMS. The results impressively back these assumptions. Hence, the second finding is that internal knowledge *exists* and is accessed only to a small degree, but predominantly remains concealed and inaccessible. As a reason for this split, the interviewees named a delineation between internal knowledge as an *element of control*, hence knowledge is held back because the knowledge carrier feels to do so (*subjective* reason), or such knowledge that rather *must not be disclosed* by the management (*objective* reason). The existence and usability of these distinct specifications of Internal Knowledge have surely to be taken into consideration when trying to explain the suc-

Table 3. Results of the hypothesis concerning domain knowledge existence

Objective	Subjective Indicators	Contextual Information	Individual Knowledge Existing?	Individual Knowledge Accessible?	Annotations
Hypothesis No.	1	2	3	3	4
Description	Slightly more agreement	Mainly agreement	Mainly agreement	Mainly disagreement	Mainly agreement
Result	Weakly supported	Strongly supported	Strongly supported	Strongly rejected	Strongly supported

cess of a PMS; hence they must be added to the catalog of dimensions and classes. This leads to the *completion* of the catalog of determinants for PMS success in Table 4.

The second set of results describes the economic *value* of a consideration of domain knowledge. The primary condition for the introduction of an additional system in an organization is that the benefit of the system is greater than the effort to implement, to use and to maintain it. Hence, two questions on the benefit and effort of PMS conduction were posed, one assessing the PMS currently in place and one after the suggestion of collecting additional domain knowledge. To additionally back the visibility theory by factual interviewee impressions, the respective assessment of visibility of the company's performance before and after the consideration of additional domain knowledge was requested. The notions in the answers were compared and the trend in the answers was interpreted as an impression of visibility that is neutral, greater or less than

Table 4. Catalog of determinants for PMS success

Dimension	Class
Indicator class (Cecconi *et al.*, 2007)	Measurement
	Evaluation
	Preference
	Dictation
Context class (Rosemann *et al.*, 2008)	Immediate
	Internal
	External
	Environmental
Annotation class (Strecker *et al.*, 2012)	Textual system element
	Textual system document
	Graphical system element
	Graphical system document
Internal knowledge (Interview result)	Subjective element of control
	Objective management disclosure

before, hence forming a positive, negative, or neutral change. The results of the answers are listed in Table 5.

Summing up, it can be stated that most experts do *not* have the impression that using additional domain knowledge causes a greater effort. Hence, H5 is weakly supported. But in contrast, they do not see a significantly greater benefit by using domain knowledge, either. In this case, the answers reveal more ambivalent perceptions of a possible benefit, causing a more contrasted but finally slightly positive change in this case, thus also weakly supporting H6. The change in visibility of performance however is seen as mainly positive, thus strongly supporting H7. In conclusion, it can be stated that the visibility of performance actually changes by using the various dimensions of domain knowledge - without additional effort, but also only with an alleviated perception of benefit.

Validation Part 2: Case Study

The case study highlights the view of a specific company. It has been chosen because it represents the participants of the expert interviews well for several reasons. The responsible program manager in this large, multi-national high-tech company was already participating in the expert interview sessions and could be won over again for an in-depth one-day workshop in October 2012, which was also an excellent way for the management to catch up on the subject of visibility of performance again.

In the case company, business operations are run on a large extent on the basis of performance indicators. A Balanced Scorecard is used as PMS, which was under review at that point of time. The company's comprehension of a PMS was "a common code and a communication base" as well as "a tool for focusing, discussion, delivery of objectivity, synchronization as well as goal and countermeasure formulation". In contrast, links to strategic alignment and target achievement were

Table 5. Results of the hypothesis concerning economic value and visibility

Objective	Effort Change	Benefit Change	Visibility Change
Hypothesis No.	5	6	7
Description	Mainly neutral with strong positive emphasis	Mainly positive with strong negative counterbalance, polarizing	Mainly positive
Result	Weakly supported	Weakly supported	Strongly supported

not fully implemented. Hence, the PMS as such was given and not subject to change, but actually two versions of the PMS (pre and post optimization) could be assessed and compared, thus using different data sources for case triangulation (Yin, 2003). Besides that, additional findings from the full protocol material of the July 2012 expert interview could be used to interpret the answers and to better understand the company's view. In the first round part back then, only the findings directly related to the validation of H1-H7 had been used.

Basically, the aim of the workshop was to collect statements focusing on the validity of H8-H10. This was done directly by posing questions literally connected to the three hypotheses, but also by interpretation of the expert's statements during the workshop. One of the findings of the expert interview already in June was that the management demanded to improve the ability of the PMS to assess rather *subjective* domains; hence

the focus of the PMS review was on the design and implementation of adequate indicators and the addition of contextual information. In this connection, both PMS versions were analyzed along the proposed dimensions and classes of the theory in order to gain insights to their specific visibility of performance. These investigations mainly can be used for the validation to H8, but in combination with statements and core messages that came about during the workshop, H9 and H10 could be assessed from this side as well. The results of the validation are collected in Table 6 (explanations to quotes are added in brackets).

Summing up, Hypotheses 8-10 were supported in this case. This confirms the previously assumed link between domain knowledge, organizational knowledge and the usability of the construct of visibility as an indicator for the success of the PMS. Moreover, as a result of this workshop, the expert stated that actually the perceived *goodness* of his system after the optimization changed in a

Table 6. Results of the hypothesis concerning knowledge generation and success indication

Objective	Domain Knowledge Composition	Generation of Organizational Knowledge	Indication of PMS Success
Hypothesis No.	8	9	10
Description	Agreement	Agreement	Agreement
Core Message	"The KPIs alone were like a horizon line that we were gazing at to navigate. Now it seems that we have something more like a compass. We better know where we are, but still this is not a GPS."	"Now more people [in the company] know what we're [the performance team] talking about."	"The System is now really working a treat."
Result	Supported	Supported	Supported

positive way because of the intensified use of rich indicators and contextual information. Hence the alignment of the system along the dimensions of visibility was *beneficial* and *useful*; the PMS *as such* is successful because of the increased *visibility* of the company's performance; thus being an additional proof of the indicator concept.

Summary

During the literature review and using the Grounded Theory approach, five rationales could be identified. These rationales could be translated into two reference models and a theory. Ten hypotheses that could be derived from the theory were connected to questions pointing to the several components of the model and initially validated through the methodology of expert interviews and a case study. In detail, it can be subsumed that:

H1 to H4 are supported, which means the structural model of visibility is *confirmed*. This in turn indicates that domain knowledge on PMS, consisting of the dimensions *rich indicators*, *contextual information*, *internal knowledge* and *annotations* actually are existing phenomena that influence the availability of domain knowledge. In this context, the observation of the interviewees' rather cautious use of internal knowledge is especially worth mentioning. This means that internal knowledge is used deliberately as instrument of *control* and power in an organizational context. It is used to rule and manage and hence must not be shared with the employees. Though, it contains valuable information that at least *peers* should be able to access in order to interpret them in the context of PMS. Hence, its externalization should be encouraged, but the results should not be accessible to all stakeholders. This finally leads to the demand of a balanced *security* concept for the disclosure of internal knowledge.

The set of tests for H5 to H7 revealed that there actually is a perceived positive change in *visibility*

of performance through the consideration of additional domain knowledge. The second finding is that considering domain knowledge is *neutral* by means of effort. As the impact on benefit is considered to be neutral as well, the coinciding neutrality of both hypotheses at the same time can also be interpreted as either

- There is neither additional effort nor benefit for the company using additional domain knowledge, hence the perceived overall helpfulness of doing so is *low*.
- There is an increase of knowledge, but no additional benefit for the company in terms of increase of *value*, which usually is the perception of benefit for the company.
- There is a perception of additional benefit, but there are still *reservations* to the use of additional material in their PMS.

As H8 to H10 were also supported, the full theory could initially be *confirmed*. Hence the usage of domain knowledge generates organizational knowledge, and this generation expresses the success of a performance management system. Summing up, domain knowledge and with it the visibility of performance can be assessed with this kind of indicator. It can either be used to display of a status quo or as change before and after a PMS implementation or review.

SOLUTIONS AND RECOMMENDATIONS

This contribution consists of the development, construction and initial validation of artifacts that are able to indicate the *success* of a given PMS. Starting with the presentation of a universe of discourse about the success of PMS according to the Grounded Theory approach, followed by the derivation of appropriate dimensions and the formulation of structural and causal reference models, a theory and hypotheses, an approach to assess how well PMS are working was explicated, in this case through the generation of domain and organizational *knowledge*. Dimensions and classes of domain knowledge can be put down to a catalog of determinants of *goodness* of a PMS, the *visibility of performance*.

The applicability and suitability of the domain knowledge classes might be subject to further discussion. A company should e.g. critically assess their PMS' indicators in order to avoid *tendencies* in the 'dictation' direction. Second, the evaluation of contextual information close to the core of the business might be sufficient to gather information in most cases. But if more explanatory power for a good overview is needed, companies might want to *expand* their observations to domains further away from their business scope, like external of environmental information, as it is common in strategic analysis.

The lack of graphical annotations might result in the design and usage of the PMS itself. From a technical viewpoint, it is understandable that these systems primarily are supposed to deliver figures and strategic connections, not images by means of explanations. This might be a point for enhancement for software vendors.

From the view of *knowledge management*, this theory can be seen as an opportunity for a company to generate *value* out of its PMS domain knowledge. Through *process-orientation*, *interpretation*, the usage of *context* and *narration* additional to pure content, this approach it goes in line with the definition of the *third generation* of knowledge management (*value creation*) according to Vorakulpipat and Regzui (2008), leaving behind the first generation of a purely objectivistic view of knowledge as a manageable asset (*knowledge sharing*) and the second, subject-oriented generation which focuses on the conversion of implicit and explicit knowledge of people (*knowledge creation*).

FUTURE RESEARCH DIRECTIONS

In general, good scientific practice demands to use large empirical studies. Hence, it is understandable to question the use of these rather qualitative validation methods in this contribution. Usually, only *reflexive* Operationalization models of hypotheses can be tested for statistical significance, because in that case, the latent variables determine the manifest variables of the measurement construct. The proposed theory however features a *formative* measurement model, in which the manifest domain knowledge variables determine the latent variable *visibility*. Such constructs can better be validated by critical review and discussion by experts and the scientists themselves (e.g. Eberl, 2004). Secondly, Design Science practice rather emphasizes the explication and proof of *rigor* und *relevance* (e.g. Hevner et al., 2004) and the evaluation of *usefulness* (e.g. Kalb, 2009) instead of statistical significance. Moreover, the proposed theory is an *Explanatory Design Theory* according to Baskerville & Pries-Heje (2010) which can be considered as valid if it is *appropriate*, fully explicated and hence testable, because it is *not* designed to explain issues *best* like in natural science.

Summing up, the used qualitative validations methods can be considered as *suitable* in this specific setting, but additional empirical research on the validity and universality of the theory are *recommended*. Future research should then focus on application, usefulness, refinement, and discussion, especially because of the discovery of an ambivalent perceived *usefulness* of the approach during the course of the validation.

Moreover, a final Operationalization of the visibility of performance should be delivered. This would result in a questionnaire that retrieves the state of presence and usage of domain knowledge in their appropriate dimensions and classes, finally indicating e.g. a certain visibility *value* which is suitable for computation and comparison.

Finally, in automated PMS, the collection and processing of data, information and knowledge have to be taken into consideration, as the aim of information science is to *reasonably automate* the processing of business tasks. Today, only *data* collection and *indicator* computation are automated in PMS to some extent, and the processing of organizational knowledge is separately represented by concepts like wikis or expert systems. The additional challenge will be to investigate how the interpretation of information in PMS can be automated, e.g. via reasoning, mapping to concepts and the generation of suggestions for use and decisions.

CONCLUSION

The sheer usage of *any* PMS already helps to structure performance information in a company. As performance in the classical sense mainly stands for *financial* performance, historical PMS tried to display financial data exclusively. Since the evolution of "balanced" Systems, most prominently the Balanced Scorecard (BSC), the use of multi-perspective systems became state of the art. In the comprehension of the theory and the models presented in this contribution, they can be understood as suppliers of non-financial, *additional information* out of various *contexts* in order to broaden the view on the company's condition; the BSC featured four examples for *perspectives*, but explicitly left room for expansion.

Extrapolating this idea of adding information and knowledge to PMS in order to increase the visibility of the company's performance, a formal catalog of determinants, featuring four dimensions of domain knowledge on PMS could be presented. It can be easily used to assess the goodness of the current PMS in respect of its ability to deliver performance information. Companies are enabled to choose and review existing data, information

and knowledge in their PMS; 14 classes can be used to check their presence and usage. The more tailored the view on performance of the company according to these parameters, the more *appropriate* the performance information and the better their *visibility* on performance will be.

REFERENCES

Bailey, J., & Pearson, S. (1983). Development of a tool for measuring and analyzing computer user satisfaction. *Management Science*, *29*(5), 530–545. doi:10.1287/mnsc.29.5.530

BARC. (2009). *Performance management – Aktuelle Herausforderungen und Perspektiven*. Retrieved from www.barc.de/marktforschung/.../performance-management.html

Baskerville, R., & Pries-Heje, J. (2010). Erklärende Designtheorie. *Wirtschaftsinformatik*, *5/2010*(5), 259–271. doi:10.1007/s11576-010-0237-z

Bitici, U., Mendibil, K., Nudurupati, S., Turner, T., & Garengo, P. (2004). The interplay between performance measurement, organizational culture and management style. *Measuring Business Excellence*, *8*(3), 28–41. doi:10.1108/13683040410555591

Boersch, C., & Elschen, R. (2007). *Die grenzenlose Unternehmung: Information, Organisation und Management*. Wiesbaden: Gabler.

Boisot, M. (1998). *Knowledge assets: Securing competitive advantage in the information economy*. New York: Oxford University Press.

Bose, R. (2006). Understanding management data systems for enterprise performance management. *Industrial Management & Data Systems*, *106*(1), 43–59. doi:10.1108/02635570610640988

Bosilj-Vuksic, V., Milanovic, L., Skrinjar, R., & Indihar-Stemberger, M. (2008). Organizational performance measures for business process management: A performance measurement guideline. In *Proceedings of Tenth International Conference on Computer Modeling and Simulation (uksim 2008)*. IEEE. doi:10.1109/UKSIM.2008.114

Braz, R., Scavarda, L., & Martins, R. (2011). Reviewing and improving performance measurement systems: An action research. *International Journal of Production Economics*, *133*(2), 751–760. doi:10.1016/j.ijpe.2011.06.003

Broadbent, J. (2007). *If you can't measure it how can you manage it*. Research Paper, School of Business and Social Sciences, Roehampton University.

Buytendijk, F. (2009). *Performance leadership: The next practices to motivate your people, align stakeholders, and lead your industry*. New York: McGraw-Hill.

Byrd, T., Thrasher, E., Lang, T., & Davidson, N. (2006). A process-oriented perspective of IS success: Examining the impact of IS on operational cost. *Omega*, *34*(5), 448–460. doi:10.1016/j.omega.2005.01.012

Caridi, M., Crippa, L., Perego, A., Sianesi, A., & Tumino, A. (2010). Measuring visibility to improve supply chain performance: A quantitative approach. *Benchmarking: An International Journal*, *17*(4), 593–615. doi:10.1108/14635771011060602

Cecconi, P., Franceschini, F., & Galetto, M. (2007). The conceptual link between measurements, evaluations, preferences and indicators, according to the representational theory. *European Journal of Operational Research*, *179*(1), 174–185. doi:10.1016/j.ejor.2006.03.018

Davenport, T., Morison, R., & Harris, J. (2010). *Analytics at work: Smarter decisions, better results*. New York: Harvard Business Press.

Davis, F. (1989). Perceived usefulness, perceived ease of use, and user acceptance of information technology. *Management Information Systems Quarterly*, *13*(3), 319–340. doi:10.2307/249008

Deloitte. (2004). *In the dark: What boards and executives don't know about the health of their businesses*. New York: Deloitte.

Deloitte. (2007). *In the dark II: What many boards and executives still don't know about the health of their businesses*. New York: Deloitte.

DeLone, W., & McLean, E. (1992). Information systems success: The quest for the dependent variable. *Information Systems Research*, *3*(1), 60–95. doi:10.1287/isre.3.1.60

DeLone, W., & McLean, E. (2003). The DeLone and McLean model of information systems success: A ten-year update. *Journal of Management Information Systems*, *19*(4), 9–30.

Denyer, D., & Tranfield, D. (2009). Producing a systematic review. In *The Sage handbook of organizational research methods* (pp. 671–689). Los Angeles, CA: Sage.

Eberl, M. (2004). *Formative und reflektive Indikatoren im Forschungsprozess: Entscheidungsregeln und die Dominanz des reflektiven Modells*. Ludwig-Maximilians-Universität München, München. Retrieved from http://www.imm.bwl.uni-muenchen.de/forschung/schriftenefo/ap_efoplan_19.pdf

Edvinsson, L. (1997). Developing intellectual capital at Skandia. *Long Range Planning*, *30*(3), 366–373. doi:10.1016/S0024-6301(97)90248-X

Franceschini, F., Galetto, M., Maisano, D., & Viticchiè, L. (2006). The condition of uniqueness in manufacturing process representation by performance/quality indicators. *Quality and Reliability Engineering International*, *22*(5), 567–580. doi:10.1002/qre.762

Franco-Santos, M., Kennerley, M., Micheli, P., Martinez, V., Mason, S., Marr, B., & Neely, A. et al. (2007). Towards a definition of a business performance measurement system. *International Journal of Operations & Production Management, 27*(8), 784–801. doi:10.1108/01443570710763778

Fried, A. (2010). Performance measurement systems and their relation to strategic learning: A case study in a software-developing organization. *Critical Perspectives on Accounting, 21*(2), 118–133. doi:10.1016/j.cpa.2009.08.007

Garengo, P., Nudurupati, S., & Bititci, U. (2007). Understanding the relationship between PMS and MIS in SMEs: An organizational life cycle perspective. *Computers in Industry, 58*(7), 677–686. doi:10.1016/j.compind.2007.05.006

Gatian, A. (1994). Is user satisfaction a valid measure of system effectiveness? *Information & Management, 26*(3), 119–131. doi:10.1016/0378-7206(94)90036-1

Glaser, B., & Strauss, A. (1967). *The discovery of grounded theory: Strategies for qualitative research*. Chicago: Aldine Publishing Company.

Glaser, B., Strauss, A., & Paul, A. (2010). *Grounded theory: Strategien qualitativer Forschung*. Bern: Huber.

Gleich, R. (2011). *Performance measurement: Konzepte, Fallstudien und Grundschema für die Praxis*. Munich: Vahlen. doi:10.15358/9783800639151

Goodhue, D., & Thompson, R. (1995). Task-technology fit and individual performance. *Management Information Systems Quarterly, 19*(2), 213. doi:10.2307/249689

Grant, R. (1996). Toward a knowledge-based theory of the firm. *Strategic Management Journal, 17*(S2), 109–122. doi:10.1002/smj.4250171110

Gregor, S., & Jones, D. (2007). The anatomy of a design theory. *Journal of the Association for Information Systems, 8*(5), 312–335.

Grüning, M. (2002). *Performance-Measurement-Systeme: Messung und Steuerung von Unternehmensleistung*. Wiesbaden: Deutscher Universitätsverlag. doi:10.1007/978-3-663-08089-3

Hevner, A., March, S., Park, J., & Ram, S. (2004). Design science in information systems research. *Management Information Systems Quarterly, 28*(1), 75–105.

Hildebrand, K., Gebauer, M., Hinrichs, H., & Mielke, M. (2011). Informationsqualität – Definitionen, Dimensionen und Begriffe. Wiesbaden: Vieweg+Teubner.

Hilgers, D. (2008). *Performance Management. Leistungserfassung und Leistungssteuerung in Unternehmen und öffentlichen Verwaltungen*. Wiesbaden: Gabler.

Horvarth & Partners. (2008). *Balanced Scorecard Studie 2008: Ergebnisbericht*. Stuttgart: Horvarth&Partners.

Ittner, C., & Larcker, D. (2003, November). Coming up short on nonfinancial performance measurement. *Harvard Business Review*, 1–9.

Jäger, U., & Reinecke, S. (2009). Expertengespräch. In C. Baumgarth (Ed.), *Empirische Mastertechniken: Eine anwendungsorientierte Einführung für die Marketing- und Managementforschung* (pp. 29–66). Wiesbaden: Gabler.

Kalb, H. (2009). *Design Science bei der Schwester der Wirtschaftsinformatik – Teil 1*. Retrieved from http://lswiim.wordpress.com/2009/02/13/design-science-bei-der-schwester-der-wirtschaftsinformatik-teil-1/

Kaplan, R., & Norton, D. (1996). Using the balanced scorecard as a strategic management system. *Harvard Business Review*, (January-February), 150–161.

Kotter, J. P., Schlesinger, L. A., & Sathe, V. (1986). *Organization: Text, cases, and readings on the management of organizational design and change*. Homewood: Irwin.

Küpper, H. (2005). *Controlling: Konzeption, Aufgaben, Instrumente*. Stuttgart: Schäffer-Poeschel.

Larcker, D. (2004). *Performance measures: Insights and challenges, management accounting research group*. Retrieved from www.cimaglobal.com

Lucas, H. (1978). Empirical evidence for a descriptive model of implementation. *Management Information Systems Quarterly*, *2*(2), 27–42. doi:10.2307/248939

Lynch, R., & Cross, K. (1992). *Measure up!: The essential guide to measuring business performance*. London: Mandarin.

March, S., & Smith, G. (1995). Design and natural science research on information technology. *Decision Support Systems*, *15*(4), 251–266. doi:10.1016/0167-9236(94)00041-2

Marr, B. (2005). Corporate performance measurement - State of the art. *Controlling*, *11*(11), 645–652. doi:10.15358/0935-0381-2005-11-645

Mattern, F., & Naghshineh, M. (2002). *Modeling context information in pervasive computing systems*. Berlin: Springer.

Meekings, A. (1995). Unlocking the potential of performance measurement: A practical implementation guide. *Public Money & Management*, *15*(4), 5–12. doi:10.1080/09540969509387888

Mohr, L. (1982). *Explaining organizational behavior*. San Francisco: Jossey-Bass.

Müller, B., & Olbrich, S. (2012). Developing theories in information systems research: The Grounded theory method applied. In *Information systems theory: Explaining and predicting our digital society* (vol. 2, pp. 323-347). Berlin: Springer. doi:10.1007/978-1-4419-9707-4_16

Müller-Merbach, H. (2004). Organisationelle Intelligenz - ein historischer Überblick von 1967 bis heute. In P. Chamoni (Ed.), *Multikonferenz Wirtschaftsinformatik (MKWI) 2004* (pp. 287–300). Berlin: AKA.

Myles, J. (2008). *Discovering critical success factors for implementing an automated performance measurement system: A case study approach*. (Doctoral Dissertation). School of Management, Edith Cowan University.

Neely, A., Adams, C., & Kennerley, M. (2002). *The performance prism: The scorecard for measuring and managing business success*. London: Prentice Hall Financial Times.

Neely, A., Richards, H., Mills, J., Platts, K., & Bourne, M. (1997). Designing performance measures: A structured approach. *International Journal of Operations & Production Management*, *17*(11), 1131–1152. doi:10.1108/01443579710177888

Nonaka, I. (1994). A dynamic theory of organizational knowledge creation. *Organization Science*, *5*(1), 14–37. doi:10.1287/orsc.5.1.14

North, K. (2011). Wissensmanagement implementieren. In *Wissensorientierte Unternehmensführung* (pp. 265–339). Wiesbaden: Gabler. doi:10.1007/978-3-8349-6427-4_8

Nudurupati, S., Bititci, U., Kumar, V., & Chan, F. (2011). State of the art literature review on performance measurement. *Computers & Industrial Engineering*, *60*(2), 279–290. doi:10.1016/j.cie.2010.11.010

Peirce, C. (1991). Deduktion, Induktion und Hypothese. In C. Peirce & K. Apel (Eds.), *Schriften zum Pragmatismus und Pragmatizismus* (pp. 229–250). Frankfurt: Suhrkamp.

Pidun, T., Buder, J., & Felden, C. (2011). Optimizing process performance visibility through additional descriptive features in performance measurement. In *Proceedings of the 2011 IEEE 15th International Enterprise Distributed Object Computing Conference Workshops*. IEEE. doi:10.1109/EDOCW.2011.17

Pidun, T., & Felden, C. (2011). On the restriction to numeric indicators in performance measurement systems. In *Proceedings of the 2011 IEEE 15th International Enterprise Distributed Object Computing Conference Workshops*. IEEE. doi:10.1109/EDOCW.2011.16

Pidun, T., & Felden, C. (2012). On improving the visibility of hard-measurable process performance. *International Journal of Intelligent Information Technologies*, *8*(2), 59–74. doi:10.4018/jiit.2012040104

Pidun, T., & Felden, C. (2013). The role of performance measurement systems between assessment tool and knowledge repository. In *Proceedings of the 46th Hawaii International Conference on System Science (HICSS)*. IEEE. doi:10.1109/HICSS.2013.539

Power, M. (1999). *The audit society: rituals of verification*. Oxford, UK: Oxford University Press. doi:10.1093/acprof:oso/9780198296034.001.0001

Rainer, R., & Watson, H. (1995). The keys to executive information system success. *Journal of Management Information Systems*, *12*(2), 83.

Richard, P., Devinney, T., Yip, G., & Johnson, G. (2009). Measuring organizational performance: Towards methodological best practice. *Journal of Management*, *35*(3), 718–804. doi:10.1177/0149206308330560

Rosemann, M., Recker, J., & Flender, C. (2008). Contextualisation of business processes. *International Journal of Business Process Integration and Management*, *3*(1), 47. doi:10.1504/IJBPIM.2008.019347

Schäffer, U., & Matlachowsky, P. (2008). Warum die Balanced Scorecard nur selten als strategisches Managementsystem genutzt wird. *Zeitschrift für Planung & Unternehmenssteuerung*, *19*(2), 207–232. doi:10.1007/s00187-008-0055-2

Simon, H. (1959). Theories of decision-making in economics and behavioral science. *The American Economic Review*, *49*(3), 253–283.

Spender, J.-C. (1998). Pluralist epistemology and the knowledge-based theory of the firm. *Organization*, *5*(2), 233–256. doi:10.1177/135050849852005

Steele-Johnson, D., Beauregard, R., Hoover, P., & Schmidt, A. (2000). Goal orientation and task demand effects on motivation, affect, and performance. *The Journal of Applied Psychology*, *85*(5), 724–738. doi:10.1037/0021-9010.85.5.724 PMID:11055145

Strecker, S., Frank, U., Heise, D. and Kattenstroth, H. (2012). MetricM: A modeling method in support of the reflective design and use of performance measurement systems. *Information Systems and e-Business Management*, *10*(2), 241–276.

Strübing, J. (2008). *Grounded Theory: Zur sozialtheoretischen und epistemologischen Fundierung des Verfahrens der empirisch begründeten Theoriebildung*. Wiesbaden: Verlag für Sozialwissenschaften. doi:10.1007/978-3-531-91968-3

Thomas, J., Sussman, S., & Henderson, J. (2001). Understanding "strategic learning": Linking organizational learning, knowledge management, and sensemaking. *Organization Science*, *12*(3), 331–345. doi:10.1287/orsc.12.3.331.10105

Urquhart, C., Lehmann, H., & Myers, M. (2009). Putting the 'theory' back into grounded theory: Guidelines for grounded theory studies in information systems. *Information Systems Journal, 20*(4), 357–381. doi:10.1111/j.1365-2575.2009.00328.x

Vorakulpipat, C., & Rezgui, Y. (2008). An evolutionary and interpretive perspective to knowledge management. *Journal of Knowledge Management, 12*(3), 17–34. doi:10.1108/13673270810875831

Yin, R. (2003). Applied social research methods series: *Case study research: Design and methods* (3rd ed.; vol. 5). Thousand Oaks, CA: Sage Publications.

ADDITIONAL READING

Broadbent, J., & Laughlin, R. (2009). Performance management systems: A conceptual model. *Management Accounting Research, 20*(4), 283–295. doi:10.1016/j.mar.2009.07.004

Brudan, A. (2010). Rediscovering performance management: Systems, learning and integration. *Measuring Business Excellence, 14*(1), 109–123. doi:10.1108/13683041011027490

Lehmann, H. (2012). Grounded Theory and Information Systems: Are We Missing the Point? In Y. Dwivedi, M. Wade and S. Schneberger (Eds.): Integrated series in information systems 28-29/ Information systems theory. Explaining and predicting our digital society, New York: Springer, pp. 305–322. doi:10.1007/978-1-4419-9707-4_15

Marchand, M., & Raymond, L. (2008). Researching performance measurement systems: An information systems perspective. *International Journal of Operations & Production Management, 28*(7), 663–686. doi:10.1108/01443570810881802

Neely, A. (Ed.). (2007). *Business performance measurement: Unifying theories and integrating practice* (2nd ed.). Cambridge: Cambridge University Press. doi:10.1017/CBO9780511488481

Österle, H., Becker, J., Frank, U., Hess, T., Karagiannis, D., Krcmar, H., & Sinz, E. et al. (2011). Memorandum on design-oriented information systems research. *European Journal of Information Systems, 20*(1), 7–10. doi:10.1057/ejis.2010.55

Popova, V., & Sharpanskykh, A. (2010). Modeling organizational performance indicators. *Information Systems, 35*(4), 505–527. doi:10.1016/j.is.2009.12.001

Rausch, P. (2011). Performance Management. *Informatik-Spektrum, 34*(3), 304–308. doi:10.1007/s00287-011-0537-8

Taticchi, P., Tonelli, F., & Cagnazzo, L. (2010). Performance measurement and management: A literature review and a research agenda. *Measuring Business Excellence, 14*(1), 4–18. doi:10.1108/13683041011027418

KEY TERMS AND DEFINITIONS

Annotations: Annotations as expressions of performance are explications of domain knowledge and can be textual or graphical elements of the PMS as well as documents processed in connection with the PMS. The annotation itself becomes part of the domain knowledge.

Contextual Information: Contextual information as expressions of performance comprises the classes of immediate, internal, external and environmental context information.

Indicator: An indicator as an expression of performance can be used to assess performance by two different means: either success (indicating efficiency) or outcome (indicating effectiveness). An indicator does neither have to be *measurable* nor *numeric* by default. It can be either a *numeric* parameter that *evaluates* (puts a certain value to the performance) or a *verbal* description (factor) that rates (describes and judges the performance).

Performance: Performance is defined as class of expressions that are multi-dimensional, specific to the stakeholder and capable to express the actual or future condition or degree of goal achievement of an enterprise.

Performance Measurement System (PMS): A PMS stands for an Information System that is designed to specify, to collect, to convert, to analyze and to display performance.

Rich Indicator: Rich indicators as expressions of performance are a set of indicators that consider and use the classes of measurements, evaluations, preferences and dictation.

Visibility of Performance: Visibility of performance is the principal ability of a PMS to deliver knowledge. The usage of *domain* knowledge is associated with a given PMS and generates *organizational* knowledge. As the generation of organizational knowledge expresses the success of a PMS, visibility of performance is an indicator for the success of PMS.

Chapter 10
The Backbone of Key Successful Branding Strategies in the 21ˢᵗ Century:
Innovation in Design Technology, Decision Making on Product Quality, and Collaborative Communications

Ho Cheong Lee
University Malaysia Pahang, Malaysia

Ahmad Noraziah
University Malaysia Pahang, Malaysia

Tutut Herawan
University of Malaya, Malaysia

ABSTRACT

In the 21st century, the awareness of applying recent advanced intelligent technologies to promote a firm's brand image is the key to the success of expanding its business. Such implication demands efforts in strategic planning and massive investment from the top management team. However, most researches on branding strategies are narrowed to advertisement or classical marketing. Insufficient research on the backbone of making key successful branding strategies to effectively apply the intelligent technologies hinders the development of branding strategies. This chapter identifies three aspects: innovation in design technology, decision making on product quality, and collaborative communications to be the critical elements of the backbone. The methodology utilizes the power of the advanced computational technologies to generate innovative designs in a collaborative communication framework. Decision making on the quality of designs is monitored with EG-Kano reference models. Four case studies demonstrate that the backbone has potentials leading to ever-greater economic benefits.

DOI: 10.4018/978-1-4666-6639-9.ch010

INTRODUCTION

In the 21st century, one of the key successful criteria of a company to expand its business relies on promoting its brand. The awareness of applying recent advanced intelligent technologies to promote a firm's brand image is therefore becoming significant. Such implication demands efforts in strategic planning from the top management. Massive investment is sought to support all necessary activities related to determining and implementing branding strategies. However, most researches on branding strategies narrowed to advertisement or classical marketing. Insufficient research on the backbone of making key successful branding strategies to effectively apply the intelligent technologies hinders the development of branding strategies.

In this research, the important aspects affecting the brand strategies are treated as the backbone. Three aspects: 1) Innovative capabilities in design technology, 2) Decision making capabilities on quality of products, and 3) Collaborative communications among clients, top management team of the product developers, designers and engineers are identified to be the critical elements of the backbone. The methodology utilizes the power of the advanced computational technologies to generate innovative designs in a collaborative communication framework. Decision making on the quality of designs is monitored with EG-Kano reference models.

For the first aspect, creativity is the key successful factor and a global priority in engineering industries. Creating innovative designs involves research on new algorithms in addressing the design issues. Shape formulation is a critical issue in product and engineering design. Over thirty years of research on design computational algorithms like shape grammars has established a solid theoretic foundation in shape formulation for various domains like architecture, structural and engineering design. A comprehensive survey which compared the development processes, application areas and interaction features of different shape grammar approaches are given by Chase (2002). Recently, research in exploring shape grammar approaches to product and engineering design has received more attention by many researchers. For instance, Cagan et al. developed the coffeemaker grammar, motorcycle grammar, hood panel grammar and vehicle grammar (Agarwal et al., 1998, McCormack et al., 2002, Pugliese et al., 2002 and Orsborn et al., 2006). However, most of these approaches do not address the flexibility in modifying the grammar rules within the system. As a result, the generative capability of shape grammars is hindered to generate innovative product designs.

For the second aspect, a critical issue in creating innovative designs is affected by product design strategies on the quality of product. The ability for a product developer to successfully launch useful products to a market is tied to the company's product design strategies, thus making profitability. Due to the complexity of the perception and expectations on new product design from the various customers and the diverse perspectives of the product developer, any approaches without systematically analyzing these complex criteria to assess decision making on product design strategies are therefore deemed as inappropriate. A systematic approach to determine appropriate product design strategies based on the attributes of product design and customer expectations should therefore be considered by the product developer.

For the third aspect, communications play an important issue in decision making on a firm's strategy in running business. Without effective and accurate communications, wrong decisions of a firm's strategy may eventually be made and result in over budget, loss of revenue, penalties and delay in delivery.

The objectives of this research are to merge these three aspects into a collaborative communication framework: 1) Design a new evolutionary algorithm to dynamically evolve the grammar rules to explore innovative product designs, 2) Design a new approach to strategically integrate the proposed evolutionary grammar algorithm with Kano model to refine product design strategies on the quality of product, and 3) Develop a collaborative communication framework.

To merge the first two objectives into one paradigm, this research realizes the implications on the analysis results by comparing them against the attribute curves of Kano model. The Kano model is developed in the 80s by Professor Noriaki Kano to define product development strategies in relation to customer satisfaction which classifies customer preferences into five categories: Attractive, One-Dimensional, Must-Be, Indifferent and Reverse (Kano et al., 1984). The reasons for mapping Kano attribute curves to the product design analysis results are to: 1) Redevelop or modify the control strategies of the framework by the shape grammar developer, and 2) Refine or adjust the product design strategies on the quality of product by the product developer.

Evolutionary grammar algorithm can dynamically evolve new grammar rules to generate innovative designs. However, the evaluation criteria could be so complex with many multi-dimensional variables. This may lead the product developer to have difficulties in making decisions by interpreting the analysis results. In this research, the Artificial Selection Fitness parameters of the performance graph is selected to be modified in the new algorithm and integrated with Kano model so as to understand the complex relationships among product design attributes and customer satisfaction.

In order to consider how the most appropriate strategies might be chosen, and understand their effects on different design attributes, this research focuses on the investigation of shape formulation process using evolutionary grammars (EG) and non-linear product design analysis with Kano model to refine product design strategies. Through the strategic integration of evolutionary grammars and Kano model, the complex effects on the evolutionary design process and product design strategies are revealed to the product developer.

Experiments are described in detail and a comparison analysis on three different EG-Kano reference models is performed to demonstrate the viability of the approach. Upon determining the appropriate EG-Kano reference model after the comparison analysis, the product developer can refine the product design strategies to suit the targeted market. A total of four case studies are presented and evaluated in terms of their effectiveness in the context of supporting the development of branding strategies. The results demonstrate that the backbone has potentials leading to the ever-greater economic benefits. In particular, case 4 illustrates the collaborative communication framework in detail for the third objective.

The contributions of this research are: 1) Enhancing the generative capability of traditional shape grammar approaches to generate innovative designs, 2) Analyzing the complex effects on product design attributes and customer satisfaction through strategic integration of evolutionary grammars with Kano model to refine product design strategies on the quality of product, and 3) Developing a collaborative communication framework for project monitoring with effective and accurate communications among all the shareholders of the project.

BACKGROUND

In order to provide broad discussions on the topic, the following literature reviews are grouped into specific topics: Branding Strategies and Decision Making Strategies. Comments on each topic are subject to the standpoint on this research.

Branding Strategies

Forming a brand alliance between a supplier and an original equipment manufacturer (OEM) will have significant economic benefits on both partners. Zhang et al. (2013) developed an ingredient branding strategy to build up the supplier's goodwill. The strategy introduces a cooperative advertising program through which the supplier shares a portion of the OEM's advertising cost. The backbone of the strategy is a differential game framework which determines the equilibrium advertising efforts of the supplier and OEM. Within the framework, effects on the different interactions between suppliers against the channel members' advertising efforts, goodwill levels and their profits can be discovered.

To be globally competitive, a new trend in branding advertising campaign is emerging to personify the brand image through the association with certain human characteristics. The intention of this campaign leads the brand personifications to shape consumers' brand images. One of the critical issues in brand personification strategy is that consumers' appeals are varied from diverse cultural contexts. Aguirre-Rodriguez (2014) has summarized the cultural factors that impact on brand personification strategy effectiveness. It revealed that many research propositions were proposed and worth considering. For instance, one proposition may address the study of presenting brand personifications with cues in facilitating bicultural consumer interpretation of culturally relevant brand personality characteristics.

Branding plays an important role in marketing for small and medium enterprises (SMEs). Understanding good branding strategies will lead to the success of business. Cant et al. (2013) surveyed on the awareness of the importance of branding to South African SMEs. The survey acquired information from SMEs to determine their perceived brand distinctiveness and their facing barriers. It revealed that the skills and capabilities of SMEs have to be improved to ensure effective branding.

Social media networking has a great impact on the communication and social life as social media consumes large amounts of leisure time. The implications of the importance on the appropriate ways to use the social media in marketing are being aware by the industries. Arockiaraj (2013) researched on the ways to use this new channel effectively in promoting the brand image. Fast moving consumer goods (FMCG) brands have been chosen as the focused sector. The research revealed that the best use social media can be used to engage with the core customers. The firms should have a clear strategy to reach the different stages of brand awareness.

Decision Making Strategies

Decision making strategy on a complex project is difficult to be determined by the top management team. The difficulties are come from that the numbers of financial, technological and managerial issues are increasing, and the issues themselves are becoming more and more complex. In general, the problem of decision making strategy is solved by multi-criteria decision making techniques. State of the art of research in multi-criteria decision making techniques include Simple Additive Weighting (SAW) method, Weighted Product Method (WPM), Analytical Hierarchy Process (AHP), TOPSIS, VIKOR and preference ranking organization method for enrichment evaluation (PROMETHEE) (Vyas Gayatri et al., 2013).

For the financial issue, using the selection of a location for a new organization or expansion of an existing facility as an instance, the investment decision becomes long-term as the cost is associated with acquiring the land and facility construction. Appropriate decision made by the company may result in higher economic benefits. This is achieved through increased productivity and good distribution network. The problem is complex due to the consideration of many potential qualitative and quantitative criteria. This kind of problems has also appeared in the manufacturing environment. It can be solved by effective multi-criteria decision-making (MCDM) tools such as PROMETHEE II method. Athawale et al. (2010) have applied PROMETHEE II method to solve a real time facility location selection problem.

For the technological issue, using the selection of technologies as an instance, selecting the best alternative among other alternatives is a difficult task (Safari et al., 2013). The advanced theory of graphs can be applied to solve this complex problem in the selection of technologies. The representations of graph or digraph are powerful tools for modeling and analyzing various kinds of systems and problems in numerous fields of science and technology. Rao et al. (2013) have formulated a matrix approach to analyze the graph or digraph models. This approach expeditiously derives the system function and index to meet the objectives. Safari et al. (2013) have also applied interval graph theory and matrix approach (GTMA) method for selecting technology in the presence of both cardinal and ordinal data.

Performance measurement is a critical issue in determining the decision making strategy. Uncertainty is usually induced during the process of performance measurement. The uncertainty can be quantified by the graph theory to increase data quality of performance measurement (Lopes et al., 2013). In this approach, all the sources of uncertainty present in this process and their interdependences are analyzed. A graph is developed from these sources with association of the permanent function of the matrix. The function is used as the basis for determining the value of the uncertainty index of any performance measure.

Selection of process equipments is a typical complex multi criteria problem in a lean manufacturing environment. Similar to performance measurement, the uncertainty issue has to be addressed in the selection problem. It is difficult to express the decision maker's rating precisely in numerical values. Besides, the linguistic terms are often used for the evaluations. Ramachandran et al. (2013) have applied the VIKOR method to deal with this kind of problems. The VIKOR method is a MCDM method and can be applied to select the suitable equipment effectively (Ramachandran et al., 2013).

Selection of a most appropriate material is another important decision making issue in design process of every product. The problem is complex to consider a number of selection attributes and their interrelations, and in making right decisions. Rao et al. (2011) have developed a multiple attribute decision making (MADM) method for solving the material selection problem. The method employs a weighting strategy to determine the objective weights of importance of the attributes as well as the subjective preferences of the decision maker. After justification, the strategy decides the integrated weights of importance of the attributes.

For the managerial issue, using the selection of the best manufacturing system as an instance, uncertainty appears in the decision making process. This phenomenon is caused by the varying needs of the customers. This problem of uncertainty can be solved by complex proportional assessment (COPRAS) method. Mandal et al. (2012) have applied the COPRAS method with the help of case indexing and analytic hierarchy process (AHP) to select the best manufacturing system. The relationships among lead-time, cost, quality, and service level are studied for the measuring of the weight factor of the problem.

THE BACKBONE OF KEY SUCCESSFUL BRANDING STRATEGIES IN THE 21ST CENTURY

Innovation in Design Technology

Product design and decision making are complicated tasks which involve different professionals like engineers, designers and the product developer to cooperate in achieving the goal of creating innovative products. The new products must be manufactured to fulfill a diversity of requirements such as functional, stylistic and aesthetic requirements, and under constraints of time and cost. The decision making on product design strategies would direct the engineers and designers to modify product designs accordingly. One minor mistake in decision making would possibly lead to a great loss in cost of over one billion dollars. How to effectively determine the correct decision has been a key element for a product developer to survive and compete in today's marketplace.

Automation of all these important tasks within an evolutionary grammar system sounds perfect. However, this is not an easy task, because product design generation and decision making involve very complex activities. The recent related research and short comings on applying evolutionary grammars to product and engineering design are reviewed and divided into four phases: 1) Planning, 2) Evolution, 3) Control, and 4) Evaluation. This research is then positioned accordingly and clearly illustrates how it addresses the limitations.

Planning is the starting design activity in which theoretical design concepts by means of research are derived and practical skills of experts are quantified for computation. The quantified objects in terms of parameters, variables and transformation rules should be defined in order to build up the language of shape grammars for design applications. The language of shape grammars consists of a vocabulary of shape elements, a set of production (or transition) rules and an initial shape. For instance, Hohmann et al. (2010) formulated shape grammars using the Generative Modeling Language (GML) from Havemann (2005) to build semantically enriched 3D building models for facility surveillance application (Havemann, 2005 and Hohmann et al., 2010). However, technical and cultural issues are not balanced in most approaches while preparing the grammar rules in the planning phase.

Evolution is the design activity in which a blueprint of exploration is established and implemented in a well-controlled environment. Recent research on evolutionary design is focused on adding generative capability to existing Computer-Aided Design (CAD) systems. For instance, Krish (2011) demonstrated the Generative Design Method (GDM) based on parametric search and evolutionary algorithms to create unanticipated solutions in history based parametric CAD systems. However, most of the approaches address only specific problem in product design. The fact is that the design should fulfill a diversity of requirements such as functional, stylistic and aesthetic requirements, and under constraints of time and cost. Taking into account of a variety of product types, the evolutionary system should be capable of solving the real design problem with the high complexity.

Control is the design activity in which the rate of exploration determines the contraction or expansion of the design space. The design space can be contracted to avoid a radical change in generating the designs, or expanded for generating new designs without any constraints. Apart from the emergent property of shape grammars described in Stiny's recent book (Stiny, 2006), another advantage of applying shape grammars is to control the design process. As design problems are "ill-defined" as determined by Simon (1984 and 1990), control of design process is a critical issue in engineering design. Dorst (2006) further emphasized the issues of specifying appropriate design problems with right kind of abstractions and correctness. As most of the grammar based design approaches address only either in optimization or exploration, the flexibility of the system is limited and therefore it does not guarantee optimal performance.

Recent research on shape grammars in CAD, Computer-Aided Process Planning (CAPP) and Computer-Aided Manufacturing (CAM) are focused on the integration of shape grammars and cognitive approaches in automation, and utilization of emergent properties of shape grammars. For instance, Shea et al. (2010) have developed new fabrication systems with flexible and cognitive capabilities for autonomous design-to-fabrication automation. Fox (2009) has proposed the development of Unified Shape Production Languages with the power of emergent properties of shape grammars for sustainable product creation. However, these approaches do not much address the controllability issue in shape formulation. Lee et al. (2008) and Lee (2011) have developed control strategies to tackle this issue by interactively determining the exploration rate to modify the shape grammar rules.

Evaluation is the design activity in which the results are evaluated by a set of evaluation criteria. The new products must be manufactured to fulfill a diversity of requirements such as functional, stylistic and aesthetic requirements, and under constraints of time and cost. However, the evaluation criteria could be so complex with many multi-dimensional variables. This may lead the product developer to have difficulties in making decisions when interpreting the analysis results.

Decision Making on Product Quality

This research addresses the above issues and limitations by strategic integration of evolutionary grammars with Kano model. The Kano model is adopted in this research to enhance the analytical ability of evolutionary grammars. This approach would also enhance the generative capability of traditional shape grammar approaches to generate innovative designs. Besides, the complex effects on product design attributes and customer satisfaction can be analyzed through strategic integration of evolutionary grammars with Kano model to refine product design strategies.

The Kano model defines product development strategies in relation to customer satisfaction and expectations on product requirements. The expectations could include categorizations of requirements that relate to technical management

(Defense Acquisition University Press, 2001). For instance, the common categorizations of requirements include Customer, Architectural, Structural, Behavioral, Functional, Non-functional, Performance, Design, Derived and Allocated requirements.

Recent research on the Kano model covers a vast variety of applications. For instance, Arbore et al. (2009) have identified a non-linear and asymmetric relationship between attribute performances and overall customer satisfaction using a case study of retail banking. Chang et al. (2009) have applied the Kano model to extract the implicit needs from users in different clusters which were grouped by the artificial neural networks. This approach was applied to content recommendation in web personalization. The results indicated that the problem of information overloading was improved.

SOLUTIONS AND RECOMMENDATIONS

Case Study1: Engineering and Product Design

The development of the framework is first introduced with illustration by a case study using digital camera form design. Then it follows with the methodologies in mapping the Kano attribute curves to the performance graph to form three different EG-Kano reference models. The reference models could then be used to refine product design strategies.

Interactive Evolutionary Grammars

Parametric 3D shape grammars with labels are developed which follow the generative specification of the class of compact digital camera forms as illustrated in Figure 1.

Figure 2 shows the framework in which genetic programming is selected to explore and optimize

Figure 1. Generative specification of the class of compact digital camera forms (Lee et al., 2008) © [2008], [AIEDAM]. Used with permission.

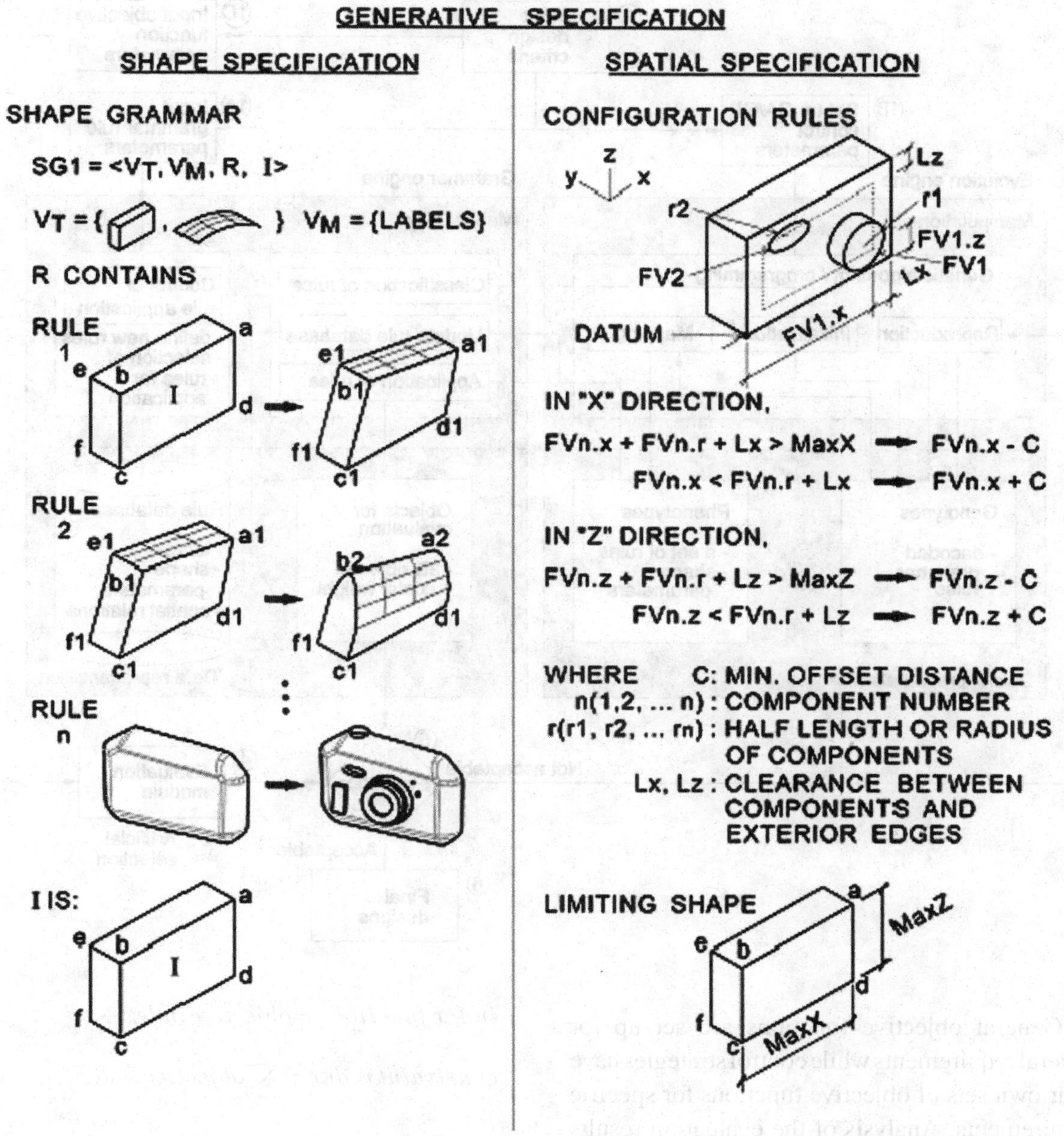

product form designs. Control strategies are also developed in manipulating the genetic representation and systematically evaluating the evolving designs during the evolutionary process.

Exterior form generation of compact digital cameras and the configuration of the components are designed to fulfill a set of requirements such as artificial selection, spatial geometric constraints and desired exterior shell volume. The design requirements can be formulated into objective functions. Objective functions are set up for the evaluation of the generated designs.

Figure 2. Evolutionary grammar based design framework (Lee et al., 2008) © [2008], [AIEDAM]. Used with permission.

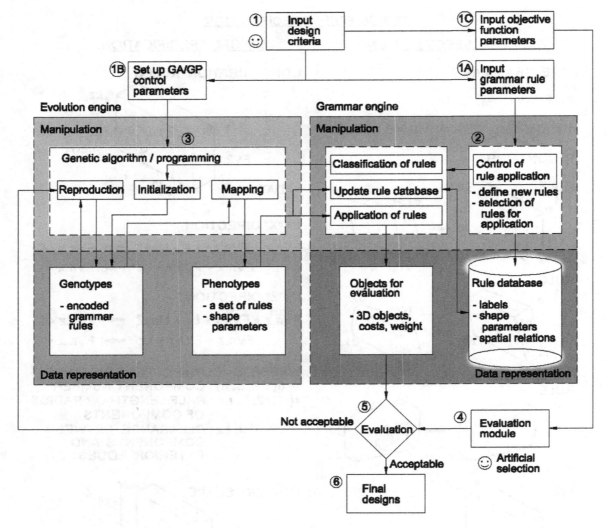

General objective functions are set up for general requirements while control strategies have their own sets of objective functions for specific requirements. Analysis of the evaluation results will help in the investigation of and understanding of combinatorial effects on the generated designs based on the control strategies. To effectively evaluate the design performance, a metric is formulated as the summation of design objectives and weighted constraint violations.

$$index\,function = objective\,index +$$

$$constraint\,index = \sum_{i=1}^{l} objective\,index_i \quad (1)$$

$$+ \sum_{j=1}^{m} constriant\,index_j$$

where: l=number of objectives,
m=number of constraints.

Objective and penalty functions are defined to assign positive and negative fitness scores respectively. Penalty functions are activated if the generated designs violate the constraints. Both design objectives and constraints have weighting factors to determine the relative trade-off among design objectives. The designers can assign different weighting factors on each variable.

$$objective\ index$$
$$= \sum_{i=1}^{l} (objective\ weight_i \cdot objective\ value_i)$$
$$(2)$$

$$where: l = number\ of\ objectives.$$

$$constraint\ index =$$
$$\sum_{j=1}^{m} (constraint\ weight_j \cdot constraint\ violation_j)$$
$$(3)$$

$$where: m = number\ of\ constraints.$$

For the artificial selection requirements, *objective index₁* is used as the measurement of accumulated effect on selected designs. The selected designs will be assigned with higher fitness scores if they are frequently selected by the designers.

$$objective\ index_1$$
$$= \sum_{i=1}^{n} (selection\ weight_i \cdot selection\ value_i)$$

$$\{selection\ value_i = 0\ or\ 1\} \qquad (4)$$

where n = number of generations; *objective index₁* is the accumulated score for each design; *selection weight₁* is the weighting factor for each

design; *selection value₁* is assigned with 1 when the designs are selected, otherwise 0. Since the selection cost of each design is the accumulated score from each generation, selection on one or more designs in a particular generation will not significantly impact the whole population. As a result, the population is determined by the accumulated effect on the selected designs.

Under the spatial geometric constraints, the components have to be configured without collision among each other and within the boundary of the exterior of camera body. Geometric variables of the component positions and the boundary positions of the exterior of the camera body are assumed to be configuration design variables, subject to a set of constraints. The objective functions of configuration of components can be determined by the designers with selective options. For example, the selective options of configuration are: to maximize or minimize the total distance (TD_1) among components.

For maximize option selected :

$$objective\ index_2 = configuration\ weight \cdot TD_1$$
$$(5)$$

For minimize option selected :

$$objective\ index_2 =$$
$$configuration\ weight \cdot \frac{1}{TD_1 + C} \qquad (6)$$

$$TD_1 = \sum_{i=1}^{n} \sum_{j=1}^{n} d_{ij}, \{i \neq j\} \qquad (7)$$

$$subject\ to\left(a\ set\ of\ constraints\right):$$

$$d_{ij} \geq l_i + l_j + l_c, \{i = 1 \, or \, 2 \, or \,, ..., \, or \, n\},$$

$$\{j = 1 \, or \, 2 \, or \,, ..., \, or \, n\}, and \{i \neq j\},$$

$$constraint \, index_1$$
$$= \sum_{i=1}^{n} \sum_{j=1}^{n} \begin{pmatrix} configuration \, constraint \\ weight \cdot constraint \, violation_{ij} \end{pmatrix},$$

(8)

$$\begin{bmatrix} constraint \, violation_{ij} \\ = -\left(l_i + l_j + l_c - d_{ij}\right), \\ if \, the \, constraints \, are \, violated \end{bmatrix},$$

$$\begin{bmatrix} constraint \, violation_{ij} = 0, \\ if \, the \, constraints \, are \, not \, violated \end{bmatrix}.$$

where C is a constant; n is the number of components; l_i, l_j are the half-length or radius of components; l_c is the clearance between components; coefficient d_{ij} is the distance between components i and j. The distance between two components is defined as the distance between the centres of both components. The summation of all the distances between any two components (TD_1) reflects the dispersion among components.

For exterior shell volume calculation, the objective is to minimize the difference between the shell volume and a desired target shell volume of the exterior of camera body.

$$objective \, index_3 = volume \, weight \cdot f\left(v\right)$$

(9)

$$minimise \, f\left(v\right) = \frac{1}{\left|\left(v - v_{target}\right)\right| + C}$$

(10)

where : $C = constant.$

The value of an exterior shell (v) refers to the approximate volume estimation of the exterior of the camera body. A constant C is added to *objective index_2* and *f(v)* to ensure that the objective indices take only positive values in their domains (Michalewicz, 1996). The addition of constant C to the objective indices also avoids the error arising from dividing zero.

Non-Linear EG-Kano Reference Models

The Kano model provides the determination of importance on the product attributes from the customer's point of view. This is achieved by quantifying the relationship between the quality performance of a product or service (X-axis in Figure 3) and customer satisfaction (Y-axis in Figure 3). The Kano model allows the product development team to better understand and discuss the issues in defining the specifications of the design problems. Figure 3 depicts three kinds of time independent attribute curves which represent conceptual relationships including Basic, Performance and Exciting relationships.

On the other hand, the product designs are generated and analyzed in non-linear time dependent manner by the evolutionary framework (Figure. 4). The analyzed results are time dependent and are plotted in the performance graph. This induces a technical problem that the Kano attribute curves could not directly map to the performance graph. Therefore, assumptions are made on the Kano attribute curves to suit the purpose in this application.

Refer to Figure 3; the Basic attribute curve refers to an essential performance of the product (X-axis) which is sufficient to satisfy the customers' need (Y-axis). It is assumed that the performance of the product (X-axis) is gradually improved along time using the same scale of generation. For instance, the performance of the product (X-axis) is started with zero at the beginning of

Figure 3. Kano model

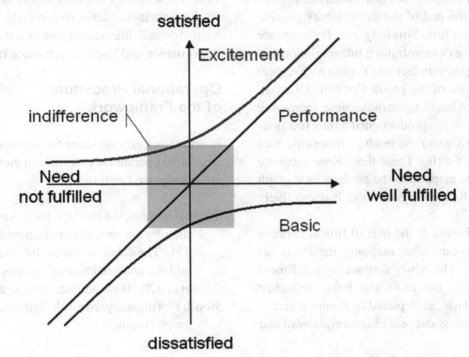

Figure 4. Original analyzed result (Lee et al., 2008) © [2008], [AIEDAM]. Used with permission.

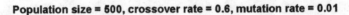

Population size = 500, crossover rate = 0.6, mutation rate = 0.01

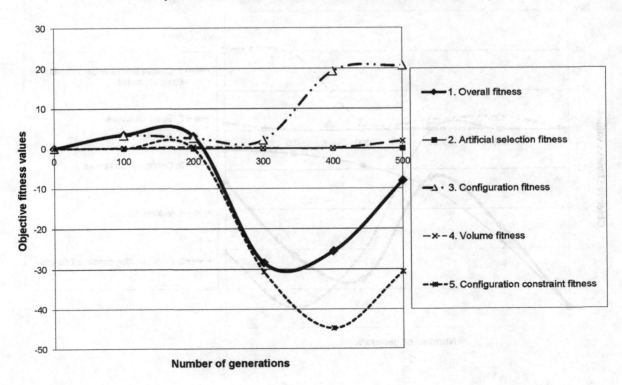

evolutionary process (0th generation) and ended with 500 at the end of the evolutionary process (500th generation). Similarly, the Performance attribute curve demonstrates a linear relationship in improving the satisfaction (Y-axis) with respect to performance of the product or time (X-axis). For the case of Exciting attribute curve, increasing performance of the product during the evolutionary process (X-axis) can produce more customer satisfaction (Y-axis). These three Kano attribute curves can be mapped to the performance graph to form EG-Kano reference models respectively (Figure 5 to 7).

Refer to Figure 5; the overall fitness curve is shifted downward after mapping the Basic attribute curve. The newly formed overall fitness curve becomes the EG-Kano Basic reference model. Similarly, as depicted in Figure 6 and 7, the overall fitness curve is twisted rightward and shifted upward after mapping the Performance and Exciting attribute curves respectively. The newly formed overall fitness curves become the EG-Kano Performance and Exciting reference models.

Operational Procedure of the Framework

In order to clearly illustrate the approach, the key steps in the operational procedure of the framework are summarized as follows:

Step 1: Generate the product designs and analyze them by the evolutionary framework (Figure 15). (The details of the evolutionary process and the analyzed results reported from Lee et al. (2008) are adopted in this case study.);

Step 2: Plot the analyzed results in the performance graph (Figure 4);

Figure 5. EG-Kano Basic reference model (Overall fitness under influence of Basic attributes)

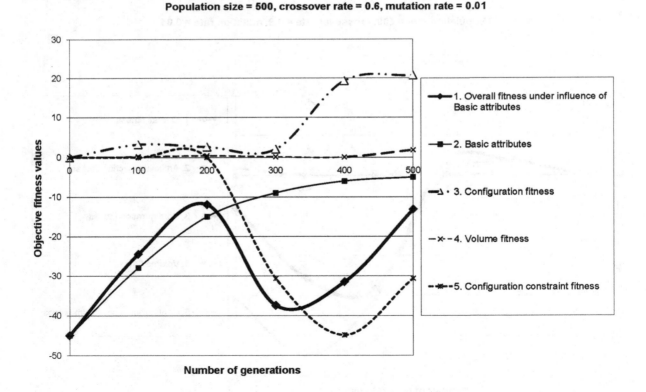

Population size = 500, crossover rate = 0.6, mutation rate = 0.01

Figure 6. EG-Kano Performance reference model (Overall fitness under influence of Performance attributes)

Population size = 500, crossover rate = 0.6, mutation rate = 0.01

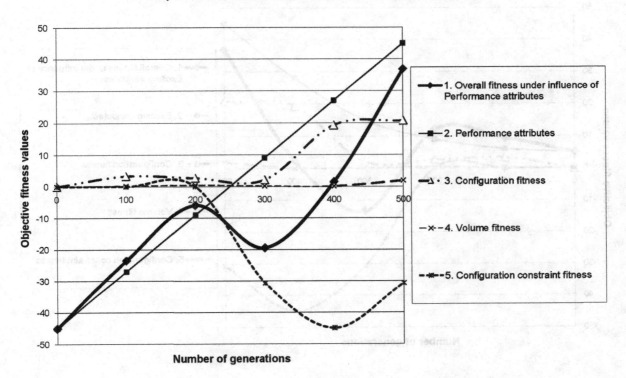

Step 3: Map the three Kano attribute curves: Basic, Performance and Exciting attribute curves to the performance graph to form the corresponding EG-Kano reference models (Figure 5 to 7);

Step 4: Modify the Artificial Selection Fitness parameters of the performance graph to simulate four overall fitness curves under the influence of four user groups (Figure 8 to 11);

Step 5: Compare the User overall fitness curves (User-1, 2, 3 and 4 preferences) against the three EG-Kano reference models respectively (Figure 12 to 14); and

Step 6: Decision making upon the comparison analysis of the EG-Kano reference models (see Table 1).

Comparison Analysis on the EG-Kano Reference Models

After forming the EG-Kano reference models, four typical cases of user preferences are proposed and simulated for testing the reference models. The user preference curves are simulated by modifying the Artificial Selection Fitness parameters of the performance graph (Figure 8 to 11).

Figure 7. EG-Kano Exciting reference model (Overall fitness under influence of Exciting attributes)

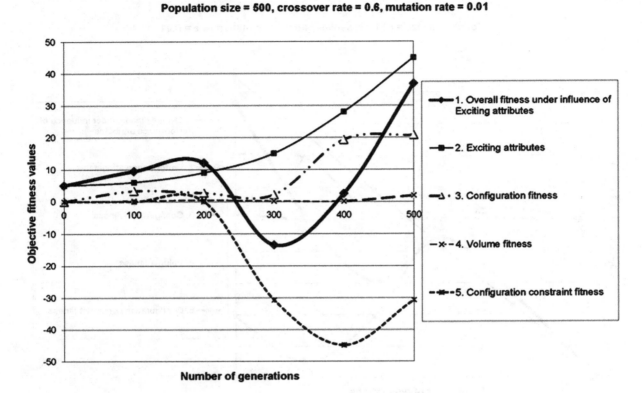

Population size = 500, crossover rate = 0.6, mutation rate = 0.01

Refer to Figure 8, the Artificial selection fitness parameters are formulated like a Sine function with 250 generations for one cycle. Same formulation is applied to Figure 9 but the difference is the shifting of the Sine function. These two user preference curves simulate the user behavior with frequent exploration habits.

On the other hand, Figure 10 and 11 depict two user groups who are favored in particular design characteristics. A better simulation performance could be obtained by further study on the user behavior. This would reflect closely the user intention in real life for modeling and simulation. Finally, a comparison analysis on the User overall fitness curves (User-1, User-2, User-3 and User-4) against the three EG-Kano reference models could be made respectively (Figure 12 to 14).

Implementation

The software implementation is illustrated with the operational procedure with respect to Genetic Programming. More details about the software prototype and how the system is used by the users are provided. It follows with the evaluation of the generated designs.

Genetic Programming

In the evolutionary shape grammar based design system, the genetic programming performs three main functions: 1) Modifying alleles within chromosomes using genetic operators, 2) Decoding the genotype to produce the phenotype in accordance to the control strategies, and 3) Evaluating the phenotype to identify the fittest solutions.

Figure 8. User-1 Overall Fitness Curve (Overall fitness under influence of User Preference 1)

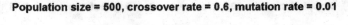

Population size = 500, crossover rate = 0.6, mutation rate = 0.01

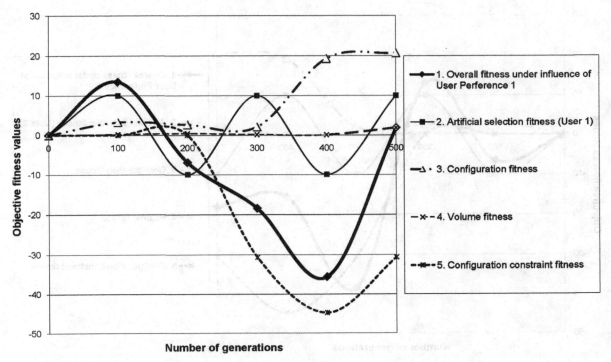

Number of generations

At the beginning of running the system, the genetic programming generates an initial population of 500 individuals with random values. Due to the complexity of displaying the virtual models in the limited display area of computer screen, a maximum of twelve individuals are extracted from the population for visualization. However, the designers can choose, to keep the displayed selected designs during evolution to trace the modification effects on the selected designs, or to replace the selected designs with the fittest ones during evolution while searching the best designs.

The main loop begins at this stage. Each individual is then evaluated and assigned a fitness value by fitness functions and artificial selection. Based on the scores obtained from each solution,

the solutions with higher scores will be selectively copied to a temporary area termed 'mating pool'.

Entering the second loop, two of the solutions are randomly selected as parents from this 'mating pool'. These two parents generate two offspring by random crossover and mutation operators and replace the parents of the population. The crossover and mutation processes repeat to generate offspring until every parent of the old population is replaced. A new population with fitter solutions is then established.

For each generation, the genotype is converted into the phenotype which represents the solutions. The solutions are a number of individuals, each of which consists of a set of parametric three dimensional shape grammar rules with labels and

Figure 9. User-2 Overall Fitness Curve (Overall fitness under influence of User Preference 2)

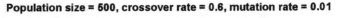

Population size = 500, crossover rate = 0.6, mutation rate = 0.01

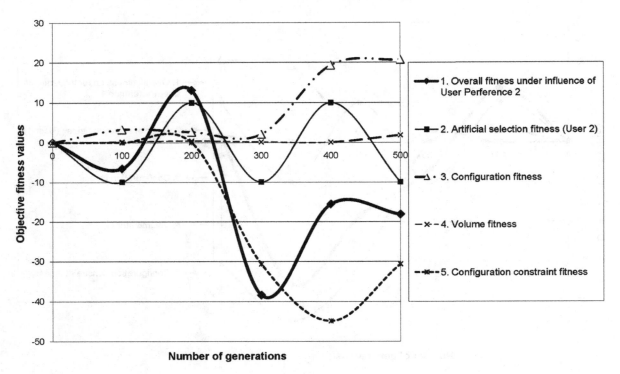

parameters. After execution of the shape grammar rules by the shape grammar implementation module in accordance to the generated rule sequences, both the exterior main bodies and components are generated. The genetic programming repeats the main loop of evaluation and reproduction processes for a specified number of generations, or the genetic programming will stop if satisfactory solutions emerge.

Software Prototype

A software prototype evolutionary grammar based design system has been developed using Visual C++ and ACIS 3D modeling kernel, and tested. At the beginning of running the evolutionary grammar based design system, the designers first input a set of design criteria such as selecting design control plan types, specifying types of components and their corresponding shape parameters, and initial setting of objective functions, e.g. weighting factors. Entering the evolutionary cycle, at the first generation, the system applies the construction and configuration rules to randomly generate a population of designs.

In order to clearly demonstrate the operations of the system, the first control strategy for designing regular or symmetric type designs is first applied and illustrated with examples. This experiment emphasizes and illustrates the interactions between the designer and the system. Continuing with the operations after the initial running of

Figure 10. User-3 Overall Fitness Curve (Overall fitness under influence of User Preference 3)

Population size = 500, crossover rate = 0.6, mutation rate = 0.01

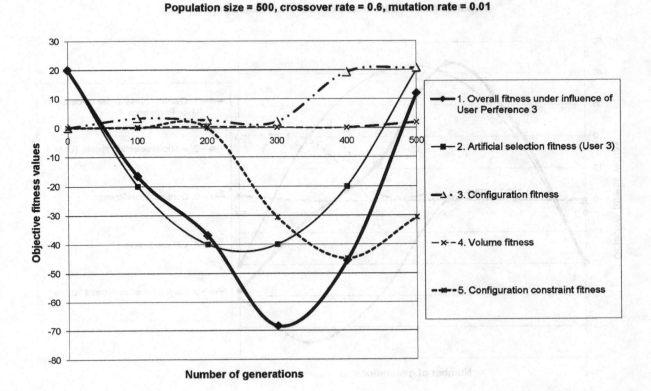

the system, the designer can select the favorable design intuitively from a set of generated designs. The designer can also choose to keep all displayed designs during evolution for tracing the modification effects on the designs.

By adjusting the parameters of the objective functions and selecting the appropriate control strategies, the designer can flexibly study the effects on the generated designs and then determine which strategy is most suitable for a particular application. Other control strategies such as slim, asymmetric and mixed can also be defined to test the flexibility and effectiveness of the evolutionary grammar based design approach in product form design generation. Finally, another evolutionary cycle starts and repeats until satisfactory results emerge or maximum generations are reached.

Evaluation

The setting of the evolutionary grammar based design system is initialized by the designer prior to the system runs. By setting the population size to be 500, crossover rate 0.6, and mutation rate 0.01, the system generates the designs in accordance to different requirements. Each individual design is assigned with a design number from 1 to 500. Implementation examples are carefully planned to demonstrate how the designers can interact with the system and what the results would be in respect to the requirements. By setting the control parameters of the evolutionary grammar based design system in each periodically observed generation in a tabular format and by evaluating the corresponding results visually and numerically,

Figure 11. User-4 Overall Fitness Curve (Overall fitness under influence of User Preference 4)

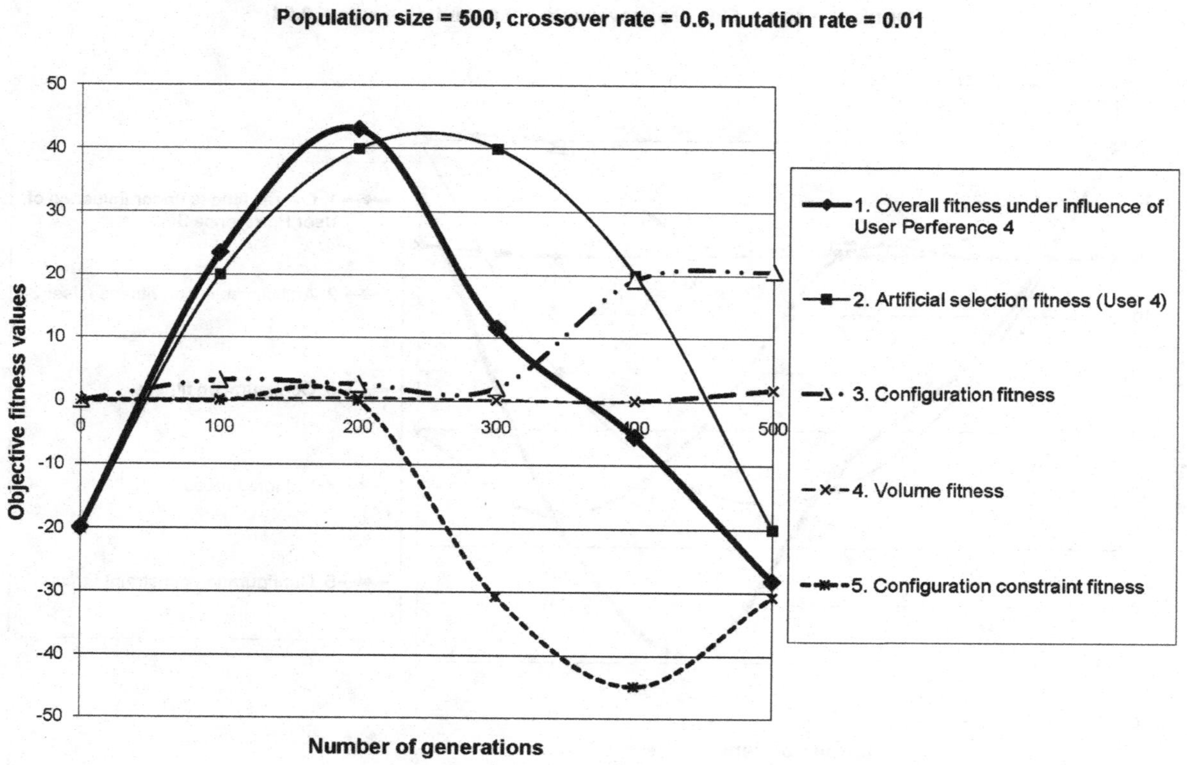

Population size = 500, crossover rate = 0.6, mutation rate = 0.01

a clear picture of the complex effects produced by the objective functions is depicted. Based on the analysis of the results, the designer can select appropriate control parameters and control strategies to explore designs during the evolutionary design process.

Figure 15 shows the implementation results obtained from the system, starting at the first generation and ending at five hundred generations. The generated models can be post-processed by other commercial software for rendering with surface contour patterns. The surface contour patterns allow the designers to evaluate the surface quality of the generated models more effectively. The designers can visually inspect the continuity between surfaces of the generated models.

Comparison Analysis

Decisions on refinement of the product design strategies could be made by the product developer upon the completion of comparison analysis of the EG-Kano reference models (Table 1). Which EG-Kano reference model is selected for comparison is depended on the product developer's strategies. For instance, targeting to sell products to the general public in underdeveloped countries, the expected product cost must be comparatively lower than to developed countries. As a result, the EG-Kano Basic reference model could probably be adopted by the product developer.

Figure 12. Comparison of EG-Kano Basic reference model

Population size = 500, crossover rate = 0.6, mutation rate = 0.01

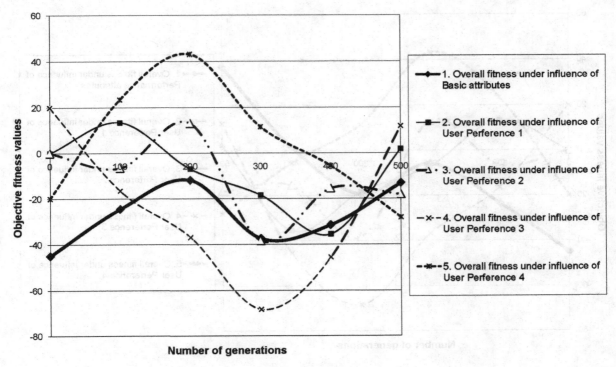

Comparison Analysis on the EG-Kano Basic Reference Model

As depicted in Figure 12, the User-1, User-2 and User-4 overall fitness curves are over the EG-Kano Basic reference model. This means that the generated designs outperform the essential performance of the product (X-axis) which leads to more customer satisfaction (Y-axis) than the expectation. Profitability would deteriorate somewhat when launching these new products in future, largely due to an increase in production expense percentage. The reasons are that the excess resources, services or functions are provided to the generated designs which cause higher production costs. Solutions may then be proposed by the product developer to

refine the product design strategies. For instance, reducing the excess functions on the generated designs would decrease the essential performance of the product (X-axis). The expenses on production would then be reduced and the profitability could be improved.

Figure 12 also reveals that the User-3 overall fitness curve is under the EG-Kano Basic reference model from generation 100 to generation 400. This indicates that the generated designs underperform the essential performance of the product (X-axis) which leads to less customer satisfaction (Y-axis) than expected. Profitability would depreciate somewhat when launching these new products to the market, largely caused by a decline in sales volume. The causes behind that need to be

Figure 13. Comparison of EG-Kano Performance reference model

Population size = 500, crossover rate = 0.6, mutation rate = 0.01

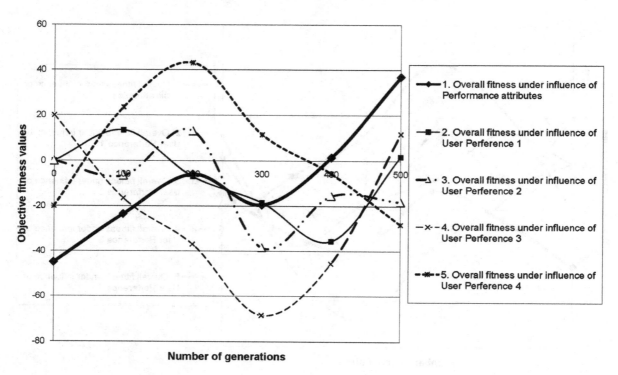

identified from the User-3 preference curve. For instance, the customer satisfaction (Y-axis) of the User-3 preference curve is lower at generation 200 to generation 300. This implies that lack of resources, services or functions are provided for the generated designs at this generation period which would cause a decline in sales volume. The product developer may request the shape grammar developer to make minor modification on the control strategies of the framework. For instance, major improvements on the customer satisfaction (Y-axis) could then be obtained at generation 200 to generation 300 by raising the functions on the generated designs at that generation period. The expenses on production could be higher but it would be compensated by the enhancement of the profitability.

Comparison Analysis on the EG-Kano Performance Reference Model

There are no obvious relationships to be found among the User-2, User-3 and User-4 overall fitness curves and the EG-Kano Performance reference model as depicted in Figure 13. The product developer may need to refine the product design strategies for each of these User overall fitness curves. Except the User-1 overall fitness curve, the closest match to the reference model appears at generation 200 to generation 300. The features and functions produced as well as the User-1 categories at this generation period may be focused by the product developer. A linear relationship between the reasonable production expenses and the profitability could then be obtained.

Figure 14. Comparison of EG-Kano Exciting reference model

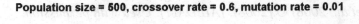

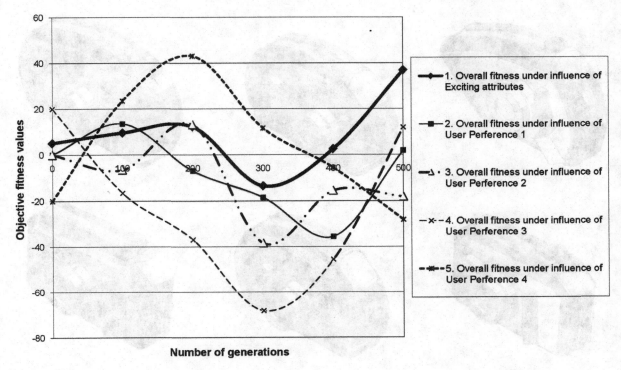

Number of generations

Comparison Analysis on the EG-Kano Exciting Reference Model

As depicted in Figure 14, the User-4 overall fitness curve is over the EG-Kano Exciting reference model from generation 100 to generation 400, whereas the User-1, User-2 and User-3 overall fitness curves are under the EG-Kano Exciting reference model. Again, identification of the causes behind that is necessary for refinement of product strategies. For instance, the customer satisfaction (Y-axis) of the User-4 preference curve is higher at generation 200 to generation 300. This implies that excess resources, services or functions are provided to the generated designs at this generation period which would cause an increase in produc-

tion expense percentage. The product developer may propose to reduce the excess functions on the generated designs at that generation period for the User-4 overall fitness curve. This would decrease the essential performance of the product (X-axis). The expenses on production would then be reduced and the profitability could be improved.

For the cases of User-1, User-2 and User-3 overall fitness curves, major improvements on the customer satisfaction (Y-axis) could then be obtained by raising the functions on the generated designs. The expenses on production could be higher but it would be compensated by the enhancement of the profitability. A summary of product development strategies in this case study is shown in Table 1.

Figure 15. Results obtained from the first generation (top left), 100 generations (top middle), 200 generations (top right), 300 generations (bottom left), 400 generations (bottom middle) and 500 generations (bottom right) (Lee et al., 2008) © [2008], [AIEDAM]. Used with permission.

Table 1. Decisions on refinement of the product design strategies

	Product Design Strategies	Kano Reference Model					
		Case 1 - Basic		Case 2 - Performance		Case 3 - Exciting	
		User 1, 2 & 4	User 3	User 2, 3 & 4	User 1	User 4	User 1, 2 & 3
1	Fostering innovation and creativity			✓			✓
2	Controlling production expense	✓	✓	✓	✓	✓	✓
3	Searching the targeted users			✓	✓		
4	Functionalities		■	■			■
	A) Enhancing		✓	✓			✓
	B) Lowering	✓		✓		✓	
5	Resources, features and services.			■			■
	A) Increasing		✓	✓			✓
	B) Decreasing	✓		✓		✓	

Elaboration on Comparison Analysis

For the EG-Kano Basic reference model, excess features are not necessarily provided to the products in order to maintain reasonable production expense. For instance, features adopted with high technology are usually not preferred to provide to the product. Instead, providing a variety of innovative stylistic designs with acceptable quality would be chosen.

For the EG-Kano Performance reference model, providing excess features and better functions to the products would result in customer satisfaction. Conversely, providing lack of features and poor functions to the products reduces customer satisfaction. Risk management on an increase of production expense in providing excess features and better functions to the product should be considered. For instance, would an increase of the price for the excess features and better functions deter the customers from purchasing the product?

For the EG-Kano Exciting reference model, excess features may be necessarily added to the products in order to provide the demanding customers an unexpected delight. For instance, features adopted with high technology are generally preferred to be provided to the products. In addition, supplying alternative innovative stylistic designs with excellent quality would also be chosen. Examples of this category of products are iPad, iPhone, Tablet PC and Portable game console with an autostereoscopic three-dimensional effect (one without 3D glasses). Somehow, risk management techniques should also be considered in using the EG-Kano Exciting reference model. For instance, in case most users do not accept the product with the features adopted with new technology, promotion of such features should be carried out. It is a difficult task to advertise new features to the customers without any clear explanations on the advantages of those features. As a result, costs of manpower in promotional activities should be taken into account in applying the EG-Kano Exciting reference model.

Case Study 2: Innovation in Design Technology

This case study focuses on the development of innovative evolutionary grammars to generate educational building designs (Figure 16). Shape grammars are one of the existing computational design technologies used in production systems that can generate three dimensional geometric shapes for different design applications. However, the capability of traditional shape grammars to generate educational building designs is not fully explored due to lack of research in merging and analyzing the cultural, functional, environmental and aesthetic requirements. This research extends their capability to generate educational building designs under a variety of these requirements.

In this research, basic building blocks with Western, Chinese, European and Malaysian culture were established as the vocabularies of the design language. The blocks were manipulated by the grammars of the language. The grammars consisted of various sets of rules which are evolved by the system. New rules and designs were generated to adopt new requirements. In order to achieve the goal in extending the capability of shape grammars, the system should not be limited by its well defined theoretical foundation of shape grammars. The system consisted of more than one type of computational design technologies. Any forms of knowledge representation that could be complied into grammar rules like shape and graph grammars as well as mathematical formulation, were investigated to be used in the system.

Formulation of building blocks should be considered their flexibility in transformation process and evolvability. For instance, L-shaped building

Figure 16. An example of educational building design generated within the environment of Kuala Lumpur

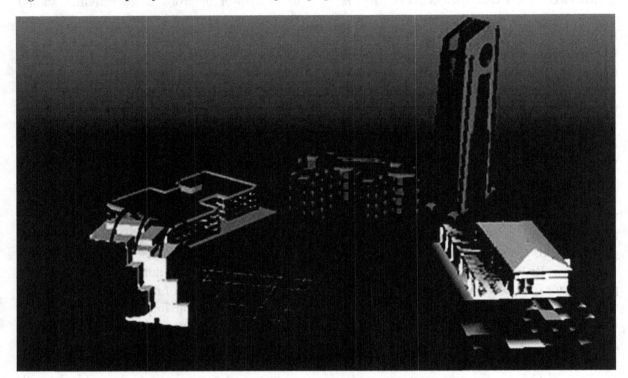

blocks oriented with specific angles could be combined with other elements in accordance to the grammar rules (Figure 17).

The rules themselves were evolved to generate more complex forms (Figure 18). The new generated forms with their elements, configuration and functions could be defined as new rules. As a result, the rule database was enriched to be adopted in new situation.

Conceptual educational building designs could also be generated using mathematical formulation. For example, an educational building design was

Figure 17. Formulation of L-shaped building blocks with the consideration of their flexibility in transformation process and evolvability

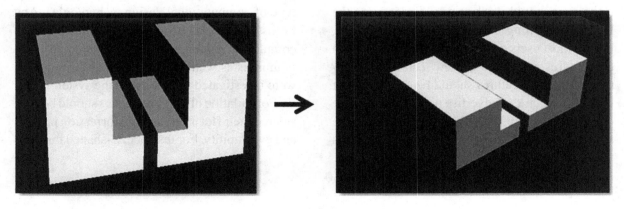

Figure 18. Complex form generated by the artificial simulated evolutionary grammars

based on the mathematical description of a helix (Figure 19). In mathematics, a helix is defined in the following parametrisation in Cartesian coordinates.

$$x(t) = \cos(t),$$

$$y(t) = \sin(t),$$

$$z(t) = t.$$

where t is a parameter.

During the generation of the conceptual helix form of building, the increase of parameter t would change the coordinate of the point $(x(t),y(t),z(t))$.

This would trace a right-handed helix of pitch 2π and radius 1 about the z-axis, in a right-handed coordinate system. This mathematical description can be represented as grammar rules provided that such representation can be applied to generate new educational building designs in three-dimensional space.

Case Study 3: Decision Making on Product Quality

This case study focuses on the development of decision making strategies on product quality (Figure 20). Traditional practice in measurement on product quality is to evaluate the desirability of the group of features and characteristics of a saleable good. Manufacturers or product developers put their efforts to control the product quality to

Figure 19. Conceptual educational building design generated using mathematical description of a helix

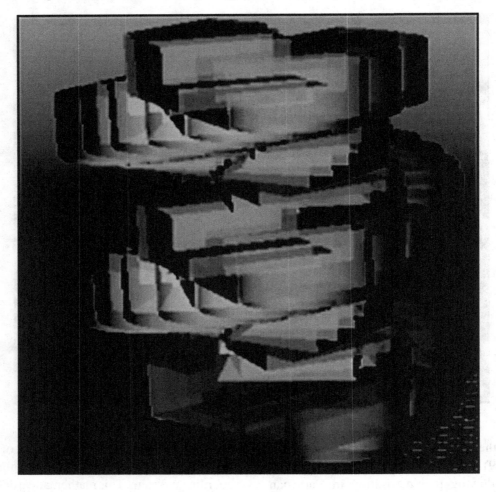

meet certain basic requirements. However, such requirements are generally limited in the scope of functional performance, the quality of material and workmanship. In the 21st century, consumer acceptability has a wider sense in the monitoring of outgoing products apart from these basic requirements. For instance, the measurement of suitability of a product used in different environments and situations may affect the customers' satisfaction. This gives another sense of the measurement of product quality. Do we need to purchase an expensive product with high quality? Is that product suited for our working environment or situation? In case one may not find such product suitable for whatever reasons, does this mean that product quality drops unreasonably?

Users' behaviors have significant impact on the decision making strategies in selecting the type of products against their quality, their applications in what kind of environment and situation. Since understanding users' behaviors in selecting products for different applications are complex, the scope of this research covers only one type of product. Among a variety of types of products, furniture

Figure 20. An example of Western style table design under specific decision making strategy on product quality

is an important type of product as it reflects our life style. In particular, table design is selected such that the research focuses on product quality of one particular product.

In addition to the manufacturing standards for controlling quality including statistical quality control and statistical process control of the production process, this research brought out another measurement of quality which was styling perception. The decision making strategy on product quality was based on styling perception from various cultural designs, environment and situations, together with manufacturing standards. A software prototype had been built to simulate the table design in a virtual interior environment (Figure 20). The corresponding interface is shown in Figure 21. The consumers became more conscious of the styling perception from various cultural designs, environment and situations, in addition

to the cost and quality of products and services. The firms began to focus on styling perception for attracting customers and achieving quality at minimum cost.

In order to scientifically measure the styling perceptions, the Total Styling Perception Index (TSPI) is defined for measuring the importance on the choice of appropriate cultural table design under different environments and situations (Figure 22). TSPI is formulated based on the weighting of importance on a particular group of attributes for each cultural table design under different environments and situations. In figure 22, "Case" represents the weighting assignment on environmental factor and table design factor. Whereas "Group" represents a particular group of attributes for each cultural table design. For instance, "Group 1" attributes include color of table, texture of wall and floor. As shown in fig-

Figure 21. Interface of table design in a virtual interior environment

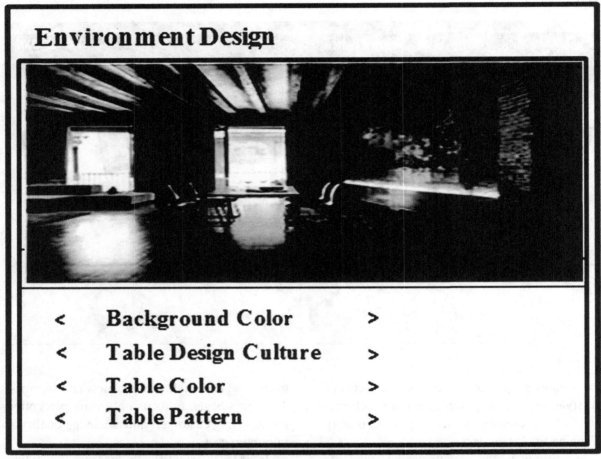

ure 7, "Group 3" and "Group 6" has the highest value in "Case 1". This means that under "Case 1" situation, "Group 3" and "Group 6" should be aware of since they are significant in styling perception analysis. Other measures, T-test and one-way ANOVA are also used to determine the effects of the groups of attributes.

Case Study 4: Collaborative Communication

The case study focuses on the development of collaborative communication framework (Figure 23). Communication is an important issue in decision making on a firm's strategy in running business. Without effective and accurate communications, wrong decision of a firm's strategy may eventually be made. For instance, the great danger of failing a large scale project in the history of aircraft industries, the development of the A380, is caused by poor communication and management. This results in over budget, loss of revenue, penalties of several billion euros, and delay in delivery (Robertson, 2006).

A complex project involving many companies around the world should be monitored with effective and accurate communication by the management team. For instance, a large interior design

Figure 22. Total styling perception index (TSPI) for Western style table design

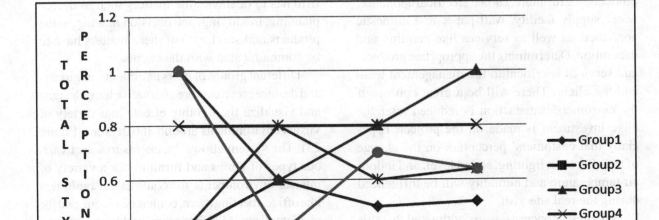

Figure 23. An example of living room design developed through the collaborative communication framework

firm has many vendors to provide a variety of products like furniture, carpet, electrical appliance, water supply facility, wall paper and domestic appliance, as well as services like painting and decoration. Determining the appropriate products and services is critical to the management team and the client. There will be a great concern if the customers' satisfaction is reduced after the huge investment is made on the project. Especially that customers' perception on the change of the effects on lighting, sound level, and indoor air temperature and humidity will be influenced during the real site visit.

All these concerns were addressed by this research and the lighting effects on different environments were focused. A collaborative communication framework was established to address the focused issue with a computational system called Lamp Planner. Lamp Planner is a three dimensional (3D) design system which can explore 3D lamp designs through effective and accurate communications among all the shareholders of the project. Not only do the management team,

engineers and designers within the interior design firm has to deal with the matters such as design planning, modifying, and decision making on the products and services, but these matters have to be communicated with the clients.

Different groups of users like clients, engineers and designers can explore alternative lamp designs and visualize the lighting effects in a variety of virtual environments around 360 degrees (Figure 23). The system allows the clients to select various types of lamps and furniture for a variety of interior environments for commercial buildings like office, meeting room, conference room, and for residential areas like bedroom, bathroom, kitchen and living room. It is flexible for the vendors to import their 3D models including lighting fixtures and furniture to the system. These models can be retrieved easily by the users from the built-in environment templates. A user friendly graphical user interface has been developed for the users to choose the built-in environment templates (Figure 24). After the selection of the appropriate template, the users could input and modify the values

Figure 24. The interface of Lamp Planner for simulation of a variety of lighting effects in a virtual residential environment

of the design variables and their corresponding parameters effectively. As a result, lighting effects could be simulated so realistically within the virtual environment.

Upon finishing the design, a survey could be carried out on-line for the evaluation of the results (Figure 25). The survey can be used for users' perception, behavior and preferences analysis. This is achieved by data mining and forecasting using statistical analysis techniques. Data mining on the users' perceptions, behavior and preferences can be performed on the types of products used with parameters on their corresponding valuables, and in a specific environment with various lighting effects. Similar to data mining, forecasting the latest fashion trend of lamp design can be achieved using the same set of data. Furthermore, decision making strategy can be determined by statistical analysis on the parameters of various variables for a specific product using T-test and one-way ANOVA. For instance, the variables of a lamp fixture include form whereas the variables of lighting effect include color, and lighting on or off. Common variables of wall, floor and lamp fixture include color and texture.

Users' perception, behavior and preferences are important issues when determining decision making strategy by the top management. They subjectively influence the customers' satisfaction from the beginning of the design process till the completion of the project. They have significant impact on every step in the project development, especially during the design process. They should not be overlooked and under estimated. These critical issues are addressed in this research by developing a collaborative communication framework. The framework supports the individual and academic users, manufacturers, and companies to enhance the efficiency in determining decision making strategy.

Figure 25. The interface of Lamp Planner for on-line survey on a variety of lighting effects in a virtual residential environment

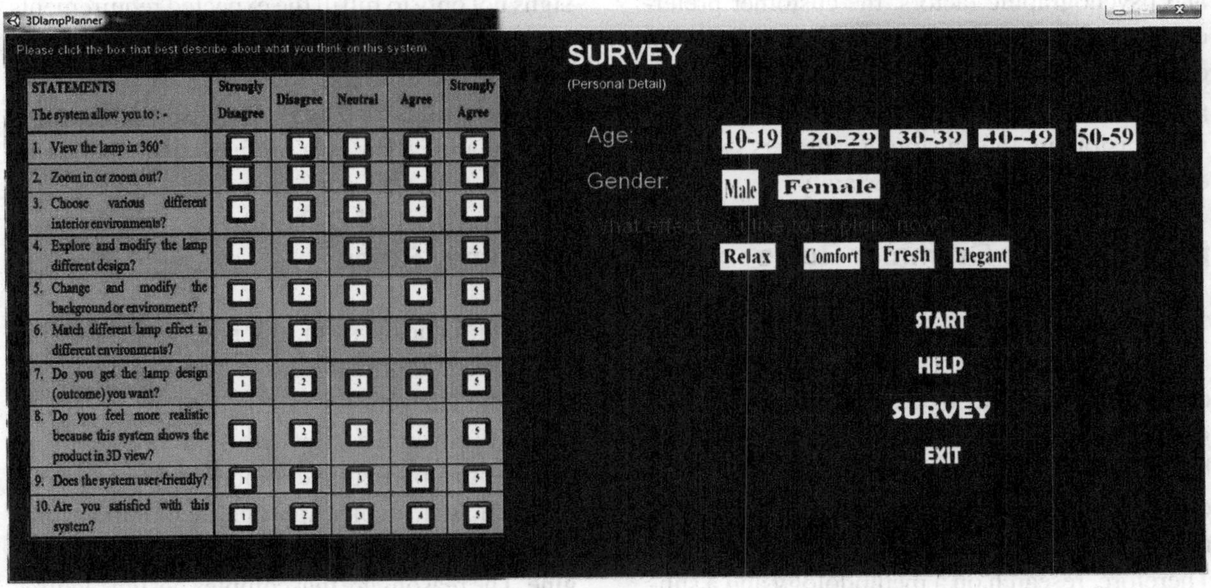

FUTURE RESEARCH DIRECTIONS

Several critical issues and the implications related to this research work are discussed and classified into seven areas: 1) Defining Product Attribute, 2) Defining User Grammar Rules, 3) Automation of Deriving Grammar Rules, 4) Classifying Consumer Preferences, 5) Creating User Preference Model, 6) Importance–Performance Analysis (IPA), and 7) Hybrid Genetic Programming and Genetic Algorithms. These issues should be considered for the practical and real world applications of the proposed approach.

Defining Product Attribute

Product attribute must be determined in accordance with specific requirements of the targeted product. A given product attribute is classified according to its corresponding type (Must-be, Attractive, One-dimensional, Indifferent, or Reverse attribute) in Kano model by customer preferences. In general practice, a prescribed form is used to obtain such preferences. Due to the demographic and psychographic factors, the customer preferences vary indefinitely which causes uncertainty in customer answers (Ullah et. al., 2011). However, general quantitative methods mainly address the imprecision in the customer answers without concerning the issue of uncertainty.

Defining User Grammar Rules

The creation of grammar rules for complex product design is hindered by the fact that they are very complex and can only be created by trained shape grammar developers. Without knowledge and a background in shape grammars, users will find difficult in design and creating their own set of rules using the evolutionary grammar system. Therefore, research on a methodology and a sup-

porting tool to facilitate the creation of grammar rules by a wider audience is necessary. It is good to have a tool-supported methodology for the user-friendly design and creation of grammar rules. The criteria of the methodology should cover aspects of grammar rules construction procedures and the underlying grammar concepts with adequate terminologies. The procedures should be well structured, self descriptive in the form of shape grammars, transparent and supported as a key input tool within the evolutionary grammar system.

The methodology should help users to identify logical errors in defining grammar rules. The rules defined should be robust and consistent. As a result, they should support conceptualization flexibility for the evolutionary grammar system to generate creative designs. An example of this methodology can be referenced from Dahlem et al., 2011 who have designed a methodology which enables domain experts and users without a background in logically to design ontologies. Such a methodology could facilitate the users to effectively construct their own set of grammar rules. As a result, the system could generate designs not only to fulfill the expected requirements but also include the users' preference of their own interest. For example, the users can create their own set of rules for their own stylistic products, or to simulating their own professional experience.

Automation of Deriving Grammar Rules

In evolutionary system, the process of deriving appropriate grammar rules to generate designs is difficult. The process can be automated only in part of the overall design with high complexity, or specific to a particular component. For example, it is difficult to evolve appropriate grammar rules from scratch to generate creative design of an engine. The reasons are that complex design requires many different experts from different fields to apply sophisticated theories and their experience to articulate and solve the problems. With the support of Web service, a collaborative environment can facilitate these design tasks by integrating existing technology within a process-centric framework. An example of this collaborative environment can be referenced from Dollmann et al., 2011 who have developed process automation in virtual organizations using a hybrid web service, grid or cloud resources. Such an environment can breed up effective enterprise collaboration and efficient utilization of appropriate information technology. As a result, the successful cooperation among companies would lead to an enhancement of the automation in deriving appropriate grammar rules to generate creative product designs.

To increase the flexibility of automation in an evolutionary grammar system, the system must be capable of extending the grammar rule database, and evolving new rules with adjustable factors. An example of this system can be referenced from Chen et al., 2011 who have developed a dynamically optimized fluctuation smoothing rule to improve the performance of scheduling jobs in a wafer fabrication factory.

Such a system can introduce new rules to overcome the drawbacks of the static adjustable factors in existing rules. In other words, the whole set of rules will be modified and updated over time. However, future research in obtaining the following objectives has to be performed: 1) The rules can be dynamically evolved to adapt new situations, and 2) The rules can be applied either for exploration or optimization.

Classifying Consumer Preferences

The development and application of Web 2.0 have a great impact on the communication and social life. The ways of communication and social life are evolving with a huge volume of Web content generated by users at online forums, wikis, blogs, and social networks, among others. Potential opportunities in business intelligence can be obtained by mining customer preferences from these user-contributed contents. By analyzing the preferences on relative product strengths or weaknesses on existing products, the product developer can refine the product design strategies accordingly to develop better products to meet consumer requirements. From consumers' view, they can compare the various features of similar products from the analysis before making purchasing decisions. Xu et al. (2011) have developed a novel Support Vector Machine-based method to analyze the customer preferences by mining the volume of consumer opinions posted on the Web. The preferences are reflected from that certain comparison opinions exist among the numerous user opinions regarding products, services, or political issues.

Future work on enhancing product design process might investigate various aspects of the quality criteria for satisfaction in the EG-Kano reference model analysis. This may be achieved by using a combination of on-line questionnaires and interactive modeling and simulation of the evolutionary designs running on a Web 3.0 site.

Creating User Preference Model

A semi-cooperative learning negotiation agent, where the agent can make an offer until it reaches an agreement, was introduced by Crawford (2009). A user preference model is developed by the agent while it is observing the negotiation process. The methodology employed in the agent requires a set of the historical data (system log). However, it is a time consuming learning process to understand a users' preference by the agent. Another drawback is that the agent does not have any facilities regarding the history of negotiation for the case of null information.

Rigi et al. (2011) have circumvented this problem by using Analytical Hierarchy Process (AHP) in order to make a prior model of the users' preference. In their approach, pair wise preferences of choices are acquired from a user at the beginning with the learning ability. Relevant information will be updated automatically in the model when the user negotiates with other participants. The learning ability emerged from this exercise. As a result, the model is capable to deal properly with situations dependent on experience (learning data). This approach is originally targeted on Meeting Scheduling Problem (MSP) which provides some insights and implications to the user preference modeling for product design domain.

Implications on this approach (Rigi et al., 2011) in analogous with the user preference modeling for product design domain include the reaching consensus among customers is difficult and time-consuming. The complexity of the problem increases further when the number of customers is large and the huge diversity of cultures and ages of customers exist. In order to apply multi-agents in eliciting user preferences in an effective way, the design requirements like utility, usability, accessibility, desirability, affordability, viability, compatibility, and the design parameters like feature, material, function, costing and aesthetic requirements, must be analyzed systematically against different types of customers like the differences in culture, age and gender.

Importance-Performance Analysis

Improvement on decision strategies in product design allows the product developer to define appropriate features on new products, adding value on products and enhancing customer satisfaction. One of the effective customer satisfaction evaluation methods is Importance-Performance Analysis (IPA). In IPA, statistic method and Artificial Neural Network (ANN) are used to obtain attribute importance implicitly. The effectiveness of both methods relies on sufficient and confident data to be provided and the attribute original importance about attribute's contributing level to customer value realization to be considered.

To address these drawbacks, Geng et al. (2012) have applied decision making trial and evaluation laboratory (DEMATEL) to study the mutual influence relationships among attributes. In their approach, Kano model is integrated into a modified IPA to identify Product-Service System (PSS) improvement strategies. As a result, the dependence of the attribute performance and importance, and the non-linear relationship between the attribute performance and the overall satisfaction could be realized.

Hybrid Genetic Programming and Genetic Algorithms

Hybrid genetic programming and genetic algorithms have been applied to wireless sensor node placement (Tripathi et al., 2011). The flexibility of applying these evolutionary computing techniques to this problem domain is higher than product design domain due to the ease of use and re-configuration in a wireless network.

However, most of the existing product designs are not easy to be modified under the functional constraints. This paper reports the development of a hybrid representation and manipulation algorithm for integrating genetic programming, genetic algorithm and shape grammars to control the generation of innovative designs under a diversity of design requirements. The layer concepts adopted in this approach facilitate both exploration and optimization of the product structure, configuration and component features in a hierarchical implementation. Future work includes that the deployment of the hierarchical implementation can be refined and modified to network architecture for handling complex product designs. This is one of the challenges in developing a genetic evolutionary grammar system.

CONCLUSION

Innovation and creativity are the key successful factors and a global priority in engineering industries. The emergence of a new computational design technology utilizing the power of evolutionary grammars has a significant impact on the business area, especially in making key successful branding strategies. One of the issues in generating innovative and creative designs is to define appropriate evaluation criteria. The evaluation criteria could be so complex with many multidimensional variables. This leads the product developer to have difficulties in making decisions when interpreting the analysis results. This paper addresses this issue with a new framework which incorporates the non-linear product design analysis and the EG-Kano reference models for engineering design applications.

In theory, the contributions of this research are: 1) Enhancing the generative capability of traditional shape grammar approaches to generate innovative designs, 2) Analyzing the complex effects on product design attributes and customer satisfaction through strategic integration of evolutionary grammars with Kano model to refine product design strategies on the quality of product, and 3) Developing a collaborative communication framework for project monitoring with effective and accurate communication among all the shareholders of the project.

First, most of the grammar based design approaches do not address the flexibility in modifying the grammar rules within the system. As a result, the generative capability of shape grammars is hindered to generate innovative product designs. In order to tackle this issue, this research work extends the previous research paradigm (Lee et al., 2008) to dynamically evolve grammar rules to generate innovative designs. The Artificial Selection Fitness parameters of the performance graph is selected to be modified in the algorithm and integrated with Kano model so as to understand the complex relationships among product design attributes and customer satisfaction.

Second, one minor mistake in decision making may lead to a great loss in cost of over one billion dollars. How to effectively determine the correct decision has been a key element for a product developer to survive and compete in today's marketplace. This research work allows the product developer to make decisions on product designs strategies effectively. The complex relationships among product design attributes and customer satisfaction are revealed. In addition, through the strategic integration of evolutionary grammars and Kano model, the complex effects on the evolutionary design process and product design strategies can be revealed to the product developer.

In practice, the contributions of this evolutionary grammar system include the generation of new product designs which fulfill a diversity of functional, aesthetic and costing requirements. The generated designs are analyzed against the EG-Kano reference models to reflect the customer perception and expectation of the quality of a new product or service, and to assess decision making strategies. The relative importance of attributes or functions of the generated designs are focused and subject to change in accordance with the decisions.

In future, a new focus on the impact on the control of design process which goes beyond the performance requirement, the creative aspect of exploration in product design by evolutionary grammars (an excitement or attractive quality), should also be investigated. The introduction of evolving grammars for generating new features or replacing the use of existing component material, or reconfiguration of components could add significant value and help to differentiate a new product design concept, and give it a unique character and identity in the market. It is important that any new designs generated by the evolved grammars do not lead to many similar features, material or configuration for specific components, with the loss of excitement for the more demanding customers with high expectations. This is similar to the digital camera case study as shown in the implementation example, where as well as a diversity of features and configurations generated are suitable for a particular set of requirements. For instance, the generated designs are under volume and size constraints and fulfill functional requirements, aesthetic requirements with artificial selection subject to the users' preference on the perception on different styles like sports or luxury types, configuration requirements with collision detection checking against the component or feature settings, financial requirements with costing control, and innovative or creative design requirements with new features generated. The product developer would discover this invaluable technology to generate new designs and refine decision making on product design strategies in order to differentiate their brand from competitors.

Product design strategies have been provided in this research upon decision making based on the interpretation of the EG-Kano reference models. At this stage, the results are analyzed artificially based on visual interpretation by comparing the significant differences among the User overall fitness curves against the three EG-Kano reference models respectively. Further research will be considered in enhancing the performance of the framework by implicitly embedding the Kano model within the framework rather than explicitly map the Kano functions onto the performance graph. This allows the analysis of the generated products more precisely to reflect the dynamic change on customer satisfaction. As well as the on-going research of this emerging technology, there are other means by which the EG-Kano reference models could be encouraged to be more widely and implicitly embraced within the framework.

Finally, a total of four case studies have been presented and evaluated in terms of their effectiveness in the context of supporting the development of branding strategies. The results demonstrated that the backbone has potentials leading to the ever-greater economic benefits. In particular, case 4 illustrated the collaborative communication framework in detail for the third contribution.

ACKNOWLEDGMENT

Appreciation conveyed to Universiti Malaysia Pahang (UMP) for project financing under UMP Short Term grant RDU120386. The authors wish to thank the following research assistants from UMP: Mr. Sebastian Heng Junjie who focused on the development of innovative evolutionary grammars to generate educational building designs; Ms. Lau Siew King who focused on the development of decision making strategies on product quality; and Ms. Tan Shu Ying who focused on the development of collaborative communication framework, for their valuable literature supports in making this research successfully.

REFERENCES

Agarwal, M., & Cagan, J. (1998). A blend of different tastes: The language of coffeemakers. *Environment and Planning. B, Planning & Design, 25*(2), 205–226. doi:10.1068/b250205

Aguirre-Rodriguez, A. (2014). Cultural factors that impact brand personification strategy effectiveness. *Psychology and Marketing, 31*(1), 70–83. doi:10.1002/mar.20676

Arbore, A., & Busacca, B. (2009). Customer satisfaction and dissatisfaction in retail banking: Exploring the asymmetric impact of attribute performances. *Journal of Retailing and Consumer Services, 16*(4), 271–280. doi:10.1016/j.jretconser.2009.02.002

Arockiaraj, G., & Baranidharan, K. (2013). Impact of social media on brand awareness for fast moving consumer goods. *International Journal of Logistics & Supply Chain Management Perspectives., 2*(4), 472–477.

Athawale, V. M., & Chakraborty, S. (2010). Facility location selection using PROMETHEE II method. In *Proceedings of the 2010 International Conference on Industrial Engineering and Operations Management (IEOM 2010)* (pp. 59-64). Bangladesh Society of Mechanical Engineers Press.

Cant, M. C., Wiid, J. A., & Hung, Y. T. (2013). The importance of branding for south african SMES: An exploratory study. *Corporate Ownership & Control, 8*, 735–744.

Chang, C. C., Chen, P. L., Chiu, F. R., & Chen, Y.K. (2009). Application of neural networks and Kano's method to content recommendation in web personalization. Expert Systems with Applications, 36(3), 5310-5316.

Chase, S. C. (2002). A model for user interaction in grammar-based design systems. *Automation in Construction, 11*(2), 161–172. doi:10.1016/S0926-5805(00)00101-1

Chen, T. (2011). A dynamically optimized fluctuation smoothing rule for scheduling jobs in a wafer fabrication factory. *International Journal of Intelligent Information Technologies, 7*(4), 47–64. doi:10.4018/jiit.2011100103

Crawford, E. (2009). *Learning to improve negotiation in semi-cooperative agreement problem.* (PhD Thesis). School of Computer Science, Carnegie Melon University, Pittsburgh, PA.

Dahlem, N. (2011). OntoClippy: A user-friendly ontology design and creation methodology. *International Journal of Intelligent Information Technologies, 7*(1), 15–32. doi:10.4018/jiit.2011010102

Dollmann, T., Loos, P., Fellmann, M., Thomas, O., Hoheisel, A., Katranuschkov, P., & Scherer, R. J. (2011). Design and usage of a process-centric collaboration methodology for virtual organizations in hybrid environments. *International Journal of Intelligent Information Technologies, 7*(1), 45–64. doi:10.4018/jiit.2011010104

Dorst, K. (2006). Design problems and design paradoxes. *Design Issues, 22*(3), 4–17. doi:10.1162/desi.2006.22.3.4

Fox, S. (2009). *Generative production systems for sustainable product creation.* VTT.

Geng, X., & Chu, X. (2012). A new importance–Performance analysis approach for customer satisfaction evaluation supporting PSS design. *Expert Systems with Applications, 39*(1), 1492–1502. doi:10.1016/j.eswa.2011.08.038

Havemann, S. (2005). *Generative mesh modeling.* (PhD Thesis). Technical University Braunschweig.

Hohmann, B., Havemann, S., Krispel, U., & Fellner, D. (2010). A GML shape grammar for semantically enriched 3D building models. *Computers & Graphics, 34*(4), 322–334. doi:10.1016/j.cag.2010.05.007

Kano, N., Seraku, N., Takahaashi, F., & Tsuji, S. (1984). Attractive quality and must-be quality. *Hinshitsu: The Journal of the Japanese Society for Quality Control, 14*(2), 39–48.

Krish, S. (2011). A practical generative design method. *Computer Aided Design, 43*(1), 88–100. doi:10.1016/j.cad.2010.09.009

Lee, H. C. (2011). Engineering design analysis using evolutionary grammars with Kano's model to refine product design strategies. *Communications in Computer and Information Science, 180*(6), 627–641. doi:10.1007/978-3-642-22191-0_54

Lee, H. C., & Tang, M. X. (2008). Evolving product form designs using parametric shape grammars integrated with genetic programming. *Artificial Intelligence for Engineering Design, Analysis and Manufacturing, 23*(02), 131–158. doi:10.1017/S0890060409000031

Lopes, I. S., Sousa, S. D., & Nunes, E. (2013). Quantification of uncertainty of performance measures using graph theory. In *Proceedings of the XI Congreso Galego de Estatística e Investigación de Operacións*, (pp. 264-269). Universidade da Coruña Press.

Mandal, U. K., & Sarkar, B. (2012). An exploratory analysis of intelligent manufacturing system (Ims) under fuzzy utopian environment. *IOSR Journal of Engineering, 2*(8), 129–140. doi:10.9790/3021-0281129140

McCormack, J. P., & Cagan, J. (2002). Designing inner hood panels through a shape grammar based framework. *AI EDAM, 16*(4), 273–290.

Michalewicz, Z. (1996). *Genetic algorithms + data structures = evolution programs*. London: Springer-Verlag. doi:10.1007/978-3-662-03315-9

Orsborn, S., Cagan, J., Pawlicki, R., & Smith, R. C. (2006). Creating cross-over vehicles: Defining and combining vehicle cases using shape grammars. *AIEDAM, 20*(03), 217–246. doi:10.1017/S0890060406060185

Pugliese, M. J., & Cagan, J. (2002). Capturing a rebel: Modelling the Harley-Davidson brand through a motorcycle shape grammar. *Research in Engineering Design: Theory Applications and Concurrent Engineering, 13*(3), 139–156.

Ramachandran, L., & Alagumurthi, N. (2013). Appraisal of equipments for lean manufacturing environment - A MCDA approach. *International Journal of Recent Technology and Engineering, 2*(1), 44–47.

Rao, R. V. (2013). *Decision making in the manufacturing environment using graph theory and fuzzy multiple attribute decision making methods* (Vol. 2). London: Springer Verlag. doi:10.1007/978-1-4471-4375-8

Rao, R. V., & Patel, B. K. (2011). Material selection using a novel multiple attribute decision making method. *International Journal of Manufacturing, Materials, and Mechanical Engineering, 1*(1), 43–56. doi:10.4018/ijmmme.2011010104

Rigi, M. A., & Khoshalhan, F. (2011). Eliciting user preferences in multi-agent meeting scheduling problem. *International Journal of Intelligent Information Technologies, 7*(2), 45–62. doi:10.4018/jiit.2011040103

Robertson, D. (2006). Airbus will lose €4.8bn because of A380 delays. *The Times (UK)*. Retrieved December 30, 2011, from http://www.thetimes.co.uk/tto/business/industries/engineering/article2170403.ece

Safari, H., & Jafarzadeh, A. H., Khanmoham-madi, E., & Fathi, M. R. (2013). Applying interval GTMA method for technology selection in the presence of both cardinal and ordinal data. *World Applied Programming*, *3*(4), 142–149.

Sharif Ullah, A. M. M., & Tamaki, J. (2011). Analysis of Kano-model-based customer needs for product development. *Systems Engineering*, *14*(2), 154–172. doi:10.1002/sys.20168

Shea, K., Ertelt, C., Gmeiner, T., & Ameri, F. (2010). Design-to-fabrication automation for the cognitive machine shop. *Advanced Engineering Informatics*, *24*(3), 251–268. doi:10.1016/j.aei.2010.05.017

Simon, H. A. (1984). The structure of ill-structured problems. In C. Nigel (Ed.), *Developments in design methodology*. New York: John Wiley & Sons.

Simon, H. A. (1990). *The sciences of the artificial* (2nd ed.). Cambridge, MA: The MIT Press.

Stiny, G. (2006). *Shape, talking about seeing and doing*. Cambridge, MA: The MIT Press.

Systems Engineering Fundamentals. (2001). Defense Acquisition University Press.

Tripathi, A., Gupta, P., Trivedi, A., & Kala, R. (2011). Wireless sensor node placement using hybrid genetic programming and genetic algorithms. *International Journal of Intelligent Information Technologies*, *7*(2), 63–83. doi:10.4018/jiit.2011040104

Vyas Gayatri, S., & Misal Chetan, S. (2013). Comparative study of different multi-criteria decision-making methods. *International Journal on Advanced Computer Theory and Engineering*, *2*(4), 2319–2526.

Xu, K., Wang, W., Ren, J. S. J., Xu, J., Liu, L., & Liao, S. S. Y. (2011). Classifying consumer comparison opinions to uncover product strengths and weaknesses. *International Journal of Intelligent Information Technologies*, *7*(1), 1–14. doi:10.4018/jiit.2011010101

Zhang, J., Gou, Q., Liang, L., & He, X. (2013). Ingredient branding strategies in an assembly supply chain: Models and analysis. *International Journal of Production Research*, *51*(23–24), 6923–6949. doi:10.1080/00207543.2013.825747

ADDITIONAL READING

Caterino, N., Iervolino, I., Manfredi, G., & Cosenza, E. (2009). Comparative analysis of multi-criteria decision-making methods for seismic structural retrofitting. *Computer-Aided Civil and Infrastructure Engineering*, *24*(6), 432–445. doi:10.1111/j.1467-8667.2009.00599.x

Chandna, R., & Ansari, S. R. (2012). Comparison of fuzzy and multi-criteria decision making approach to measure manufacturing flexibility. *International Journal of Scientific & Engineering Research*, *3*(5), 522–530.

Darvish, M., Yasaei, M., & Saeedi, A. (2008). Application of the graph theory and matrix methods to contractor ranking. *International Journal of Project Management*, *27*(6), 610–619. doi:10.1016/j.ijproman.2008.10.004

De Chernatony, L. (2010). From brand vision to brand evaluation (Third edition). The strategic process of growing and strengthening brands. Elsevier Ltd.

Fifield, P. (2007). Marketing strategy (Third edition). The difference between marketing and markets. Elsevier Ltd.

Gadakh, V. S. (2011). Application of MOORA method for parametric optimization of milling Process. *International Journal of Applied Engineering Research. Dindigul, 1*(4), 743–758.

Gangurde, S. R., & Akarte, M. M. (2011). Ranking of product design alternatives using multi-criteria decision making methods. *Proceedings of the Tenth International Conference on Operations and Quantitative Management (ICOQM-10),* (pp101-111). International Forum of Management Scholars Press.

Ghaemi Nasab, F., & Rostamy-Malkhalifeh, M. (2010). Extension of TOPSIS for group decision-making based on the Type-2 fuzzy positive and negative ideal solutions. *International Journal of Industrial Mathematics, 2*(3), 199–213.

Guenther, M. (2012). *Intersection. How enterprise design bridges the gap between business, technology, and people.* Elsevier Inc.

Hazarika, M., Deb, S., Dixit, U. S., & Davim, J. P. (2011). Fuzzy set-based set-up planning system with the ability for online learning. *Proceedings of the Institution of Mechanical Engineers, Part B: Journal of Engineering Manufacture.* (pp.225: 247-263). Institution of Mechanical Engineers Press.

Jamil, N., Besar, R., & Sim, H. K. (2013). A study of multicriteria decision making for supplier selection in automotive industry. *Journal of Industrial Engineering. Article ID, 841584,* 1–22.

Leibtag, A. (2013). *The digital crown. Winning at content on the web.* Elsevier Ltd.

Lin, Y. H., Lee, P. C., Chang, T. P., & Ting, H. I. (2008a). Multi-attribute group decision making model under the condition of uncertain information. *Automation in Construction, 17*(6), 792–797. doi:10.1016/j.autcon.2008.02.011

Lin, Y. H., Lee, P. C., & Ting, H. I. (2008b). Dynamic multi-attribute decision making model with grey number evaluations. *Expert Systems with Applications, 35*(4), 1638–1644. doi:10.1016/j. eswa.2007.08.064

Mandal, U. K., & Sarkar, B. (2012). Selection of best intelligent manufacturing system (IMS) under fuzzy Moora conflicting MCDM environment. *International Journal of Emerging Technology and Advanced Engineering, 2*(9), 301–310.

Manokaran, E., Subhashini, S., Senthilvel, S., Muruganandham, R., & Ravichandran, K. (2011). Application of multi criteria decision making tools and validation with optimization technique-case study using TOPSIS, ANN & SAW. *International Journal of Management & Business Studies IJMBS, 1*(3), 112–115.

Martin, G., & Hetrick, S. (2006). *Corporate reputations, branding and people management. A strategic approach to HR.* Elsevier Ltd.

Misra, S. K., & Ray, A. (2012). Comparative study on different multi-criteria decision making tools in software project selection scenario. *International Journal of Advanced Research in Computer Science, 3*(4), 172–178.

Morgan, N., Pritchard, A., & Pride, R. (2011). Destination brands (Third edition). Managing place reputation. Elsevier Ltd.

Rai, D., Jha, G. K., Chatterjee, P., & Chakraborty, S. (2013). Material selection in manufacturing environment using compromise ranking and regret theory-based compromise ranking methods: A comparative study. *Universal Journal of Materials Science*, *1*(2), 69–77.

Ramachandrana, L., & Alagumurthib, N. (2013). Lean manufacturing facilitator selection with VIKOR under fuzzy environment. *International Journal of Current Engineering and Technology*, *3*(2), 356–359.

Rao, R. V., Bleicher, F., Singh, D., Kalyankar, V., & Dorn, C. (2011). Selecting environmentally conscious manufacturing program using combinatorial mathematics approach. *Proceedings of the International Conference on Engineering Project and Production management (EPPM 2011)* (pp. 97-107). National University of Singapore Press.

Rao, R. V., & Rajesh, T. S. (2009). Software selection in manufacturing industries using a fuzzy multiple criteria decision making method, PROMETHEE. *Intelligent Information Management*, *1*(03), 159–165. doi:10.4236/iim.2009.13023

Rossiter, N. (2008). *Marketing the best deal in town. Your library*. Woodhead Publishing Limited. doi:10.1533/9781780631271

Singh, D., & Rao, R. V. (2011). A hybrid multiple attribute decision making method for solving problems of industrial Environment. *International Journal of Industrial Engineering Computations*, *2*, 631–644. doi:10.5267/j.ijiec.2011.02.001

Sloan, P., Legrand, W., & Chen, J. (2009). *Sustainability in the hospitality industry. Principles of sustainable operations*. Elsevier Ltd. Ansari, S. R., Mittal, P. K., & Chandna, R. (2010). Multi-criteria decision making using fuzzy logic approach for evaluating the manufacturing flexibility. [JETR]. *Journal of Engineering and Technology Research*, *2*(12), 237–244.

Yousefi Nejad Attari, M., Bagheri, M. R., & Neishabouri Jami, E. (2012). A decision making model for outsourcing of manufacturing activities by ANP and DEMATEL under fuzzy environment. *International Journal of Industrial Engineering & Production Research*, *23*(3), 163–174.

KEY TERMS AND DEFINITIONS

Branding Strategies: Long-term marketing support for a brand, based on the definition of the characteristics of the target consumers. It includes understanding of their preferences, and expectations for the brand.

Collaborative Communications: Connote working together to accomplish goals through effective communications with people from diverse cultural backgrounds, in different space and time.

Design Strategies: Design strategy is a discipline which helps firms to determine what to do, why do it and how to innovate contextually, both immediately and over the long term.

EG-Kano Reference Model: A reference model generated by the integration of evolutionary grammars and Kano model.

Evolutionary Grammars: Evolving sets of grammar rules to generate product or engineering designs.

Genetic Programming: Genetic Programming (GP) is an evolutionary algorithm-based methodology inspired by biological evolution to find computer programs that perform a user-defined task.

Intelligent Technologies: Enable users to accomplish complex tasks in web-centric environments with relative ease, utilizing such technologies as intelligent agents, distributed computing in heterogeneous environments, and computer supported collaborative work.

Chapter 11
Hybrid Privacy Preservation Technique Using Neural Networks

R. VidyaBanu
Sri Krishna College of Engineering and Technology, India

N. Nagaveni
Coimbatore Institute of Technology, India

ABSTRACT

A novel Artificial Neural Network (ANN) dimension expansion-based framework that addresses the demand for privacy preservation of low dimensional data in clustering analysis is discussed. A hybrid approach that combines ANN with Linear Discriminant Analysis (LDA) is proposed to preserve the privacy of data in mining. This chapter describes a feasible technique for privacy preserving clustering with the objective of providing superior level of privacy protection without compromising the data utility and mining outcome. The suitability of these techniques for mining has been evaluated by performing clustering on transformed data and the performance of the proposed method is measured in terms of misclassification and privacy level percentage. The methods are further validated by comparing the results with traditional Geometrical Data Transformation Methods (GDTMs). The results arrived at are significant and promising.

1. INTRODUCTION

Data mining is one of the main steps in Knowledge discovery in databases. Data mining is a technique of extrapolating useful information and valid knowledge from a collection of data that can be used to predict future behavior. There are several data mining techniques that have been developed for fulfilling these objectives. Some of the common techniques include associations, classifications, sequential patterns and clustering. Data mining brings a lot of advantages when used in a specific industry. Data mining can aid direct marketers by providing them with useful and accurate trends about the purchasing behavior of their customers, assist financial institutions in areas such as credit

DOI: 10.4018/978-1-4666-6639-9.ch011

reporting and loan information, aid law enforcers in identifying criminal suspects as well as apprehending these criminals by examining trends in location, crime type, habit, and other patterns of behaviors and assist researchers by speeding up their data analyzing process.

Data mining has been used extensively in the banking, health care, business and financial sectors to model and predict credit fraud, evaluate risk, perform trend analysis, profitability analysis, in stock-price forecasting, disease prediction, option trading, bond rating, portfolio management, commodity price prediction, key phrase extraction from digital libraries (Qi et al., 2011), intelligent information retrieval (Veeramalai & Kannan, 2011), software effort estimation (Deng, 2011), comparison opinion, stock prediction in mergers and acquisitions, forecasting financial disasters etc.

Data mining, with its promise to efficiently discover valuable, non obvious information from large datasets, is particularly vulnerable to misuse (Agarwal and Srikant 2000). Although mining is expected to produce remarkable knowledge and uncover interesting patterns, there are growing concerns about the privacy of personal and sensitive information. This creates a great threat to privacy. The sensitive data used in the process of data mining often get exposed to several parties including data collectors, owners, users and miners. Trends obtained through data mining intended to be used for marketing purpose or for some other ethical purposes, may be misused. People hesitate to share their personal data. This can result in skewing the outcome of the data mining because the data collected may then contain incorrect or incomplete information.

Privacy refers to the ability of an individual or group to protect themselves or information about themselves from unwanted exposure. Flaherty (1989) forwards an idea of privacy as "information control", where the individuals want to be left alone and to exercise some control over how information about them is used. The right to privacy is our right to keep a domain around us, which includes all those things that are part of us, such as our body, home, thoughts, feelings, secrets and identity. Onn (2005) define the right to privacy as, "the ability to choose which parts in this domain can be accessed by others and to control the extent, manner and timing of the use of those parts we choose to disclose".

1.1 Privacy Issues in Data Mining

Due to explosion of data, demands for privacy issue are increasing at an alarming rate. Privacy of individuals can be violated in different ways and with different intentions. Privacy may be voluntarily sacrificed, in exchange for perceived benefits and very often with specific dangers and losses. We are witnessing many threats to data through our day to day activities such as, using credit cards, swapping security cards, using emails etc. Ideally, the data should be collected with the consent of the individual or the organization, with some assurance that the individual privacy will be protected. With the advent of technology and internet, people voluntarily provide personal information to banks, hospitals, surveys, super markets, government, commercial organizations and social networking web sites for different purposes without realizing that this information may cause serious threats to their privacy.

There are multiple factors that contribute to a violation of privacy in data mining, and data can be misused in a number of ways. One source of data privacy violation is the use of "data magnets" which are tools used for collecting private data. They include techniques such as collecting information through on-line registration, identifying users through IP addresses and indirectly collecting information for secondary usage. In most of the cases, the users will be totally or partially unaware of the fact that their personal information is being collected. Secondary use of collected data for a purpose other than the purpose for which it was collected has become very common. Organizations also sell the collected data to third parties, which use these data for their marketing and analysis purposes. In some cases, beyond the voluntary exchange of personal data, people are sometimes forced in some circumstances to surrender their personal data in order to gain something (Wright et al 2009). They do not even have the right to opt out from the sharing their personal data and the burden of data privacy protection falls on the shoulder of the data holder.

Recent advances in data collection, data dissemination and related technologies have inaugurated a new era of research where existing data mining algorithms should be reconsidered from a different point of view, that of privacy preservation. Privacy issues are constantly under the limelight and the public dissatisfaction may well threaten the exercise of data mining and all its benefits. The difficulty arises of how mining can be done effectively while still preserving the privacy of data. In the current scenario that witnesses enormous production of data, the need of the hour is to develop algorithms to protect the privacy of the data in such a way that the outcome of mining is not affected.

It is thus of paramount importance to develop sufficient techniques for protecting privacy and confidentiality of individual's personal data used for data mining. As a result, a prospective research area has emerged for developing data mining techniques under a framework called Privacy Preserving Data Mining (PPDM). The main intention behind PPDM is to develop algorithms that transform the original data in some way, so that the private data and private knowledge remain private even after the mining process.

Cluster analysis is a technique for assigning data objects into related groups such that the objects within each group exhibit similar characteristics. Cluster analysis addresses the problem of arranging a set of vectors into a number of clusters. Clustering has a wide range of applications in various fields, such as marketing, insurance, finance, medicine and bioinformatics

In the current scenario that witnesses enormous production of data, the need of the hour is to develop algorithms to protect the privacy of the data in such a way that the outcome of mining is not affected. There is a need to bridge the gap between these two parameters – privacy preservation and data utilization, and this is the basic goal of PPDM. Therefore, it is necessary to develop techniques for protecting individual privacy while allowing data mining. Clustering is a common technique in data mining and in many cases the problems of privacy disclosure is associated with the process of clustering. Data transformation methods which are suitable for statistical databases often do not perform well when combined with data clustering.

1.2 Contributions

Privacy is an issue that is vehemently debated today, and it is likely that it will continue to be debated in the future. In this work, the threats to privacy in data mining have been investigated. The shortcomings of the existing PPC techniques, in terms of their applicability to real life applications have been systematically studied, and alternate solutions for some of those have been provided. Privacy comes at a price and higher privacy usually means reduced data utility. In this framework, it is attempted to strike a balance between these two parameters.

1. Maximizing the data privacy,
2. Maximizing the data utility.

The major objective of this work is to address the demand for privacy preservation in clustering analysis using ANN and LDA based dimensionality transformation techniques with the goal of providing superior level of privacy protection without compromising the data utility and mining outcome.

The contributions of this work are the following.

- Investigation of the dimension expansion property of multi layer feed forward neural networks for developing a technique for mapping low dimensional data to high dimensional space.
- Design of a novel technique using Artificial Neural Network to address the problem of privacy preservation of low dimensional data.
- Preparation of an LDA based transformation matrix from some of the randomly selected records of ANN transformed data sets.
- Design of a hybrid ANN-LDA based privacy preservation technique using an LDA based transformation matrix.
- Analysis of the performance of ANN and ANN-LDA based techniques in terms of misclassification and privacy level percentage and comparison of the proposed techniques with existing GDTMs.

2. REVIEW OF LITERATURE

Data mining research community has shown a keen interest in PPDM and as a result, PPDM has been widely discussed in literature since 2000. Agarwal and Srikanth (2000) have proposed many methods in literature for PPDM. Most of the algorithms for PPDM that are proposed in the literature are based on perturbation, anonymization and secure multi-party computation techniques. Many generalization and suppression based methods have been studied.

Data perturbation technique represents one of the common approaches in PPDM, where the original dataset is perturbed and the result is released for data analysis. These methods usually require that a dedicated transformed database is created for secondary use, and they have evolved from a simple method for a single attribute to multi-attribute methods (Oliveria and Zaiane 2010). Secure Multiparty Computation (SMC) Technique is a very popular technique for privacy preserving distributed data mining, where two or more parties owning confidential databases wish to run a data mining algorithm on the union of their databases without revealing any unnecessary information. The cryptographic approaches (Sharma and Ojha 2010) to PPDM assumes that the data are stored at several private parties who agree to disclose the result of a certain data mining computation performed jointly over their data. The parties engage in a cryptographic protocol; that is, they exchange messages encrypted to make some operations efficient while others computationally intractable (Evfimievski and Grandison 2009). In effect, they blindly run their data mining algorithm.

Anonymization techniques for KDD were studied by Klosgen (1995). Machanavajjhala et al (2006) introduced the l-diversity method to protect sensitive values with high confidence when the sensitive data is lack of diversity. Very recently, Matatov et al (2010) suggested an approach for achieving k-anonymity by partitioning the original dataset into several projections such that each adheres to k-anonymity. Tian and Zhang (2011) have proposed an extended l-diversity model called the functional diversity measure, to constrain the frequencies of base sensitive attribute values that are induced by general sensitive attribute values.). Yeh and Hsu (2010) have proposed algorithms that focus on privacy preserving utility mining for hiding sensitive item sets from adversaries. Yang and Qiao (2010) have proposed a method that anonymises data by randomly breaking links among attribute values in records.

Over the last few years, several algorithms have been developed for privacy preserving clustering. Liu, Kargupta & Ryan (2006) used a random projection technique to transform the data. Indumathi & Uma (2009) proposed novel three tier architecture for optimized privacy preserving data mining using an innovative desultory technique. Bertino et al. (2008) classified the existing privacy preserving data mining techniques according to the following five different dimensions (i) data distribution (centralized or distributed); (ii) the modification applied to the data (encryption, perturbation, generalization, and so on) in order to sanitize them; (iii) the data mining algorithm which the privacy preservation technique is designed for; (iv) the data type (single data items or complex data correlations) that needs to be protected from disclosure; and (v) the approach adopted for preserving privacy (heuristic or cryptography-based approaches). Anbumani & Nedunchezhian (2006) have proposed a rapid privacy preserving algorithm to access the generating transactions with minimum effort from the transactional database while reducing the time complexity of any hiding algorithm. RajaLakshmi et al. (2010) proposed a solution for collusion free privacy preserving mining of global frequent item sets in a distributed environment with minimal communication among sites. They used the technique of splitting and sanitizing the item sets and communicating to random sites in two different phases, thus making it difficult for the colluders to retrieve sensitive information. Ashrafi et al. (2005) presented a methodology for privacy preserving distributed association rule mining that generates association rules without revealing confidential inputs such as statistical properties of individual sites, and yet retains a high level of accuracy in the resultant rules. Sang et al. (2009) addressed the problem of privacy preserving duplicate tuple matching (PPDTM) and Privacy-Preserving Threshold Attributes Matching (PPTAM) in the scenario of a horizontally partitioned database among N parties, where each party holds a private share of the database's tuples and all tuples have the same set of attributes. VidyaBanu & Nagaveni (2009, 2013) used Principal Component Analysis based transformation technique to preserve the privacy of data in clustering analysis. VidyaBanu & Nagaveni (2012) proposed soft computing based technique for preserving the privacy of low dimensional data sets. Oliveira & Zaiane (2010) introduced a family of geometric data transformation methods which ensures that the mining process will not violate privacy up to a certain degree of security.

However the drawback with the existing methods is that there is no proper balance between preservation of privacy and utility of data. Though the existing methods ensure privacy to a certain degree, not all methods make the data suitable for mining. For example the geometrical transformation based methods, which have been traditionally used to preserve privacy provide a comparatively low level of privacy and are highly vulnerable because a geometric transformation function is invertible so that one may estimate the real values of the data under clustering. Most of the existing algorithms that are proposed in literature do not preserve the utility of data in real sense. Because of this the outcome of mining may vary and the utility of data is lost. This will produce misleading results and serious consequences, particularly in domains like health care, finance etc. where accuracy is an important consideration.

3. PRELIMINARIES

3.1 Geometrical Data Transformation Methods (GDTMs)

Geometric transformation methods describe methods for transforming data in such a way that similarities between data objects are maintained.

Geometric Data Transformation Methods are designed to be simple, mathematically sound and to preserve the general features of the clusters generated, independent of the chosen clustering algorithm. They generally tie the concepts of translation, scaling and rotation, from the domain of image processing, to the ideas behind data distortion, from existing work with statistical databases. Oliveira & Zaiane (2010) look at privacy preservation in the context of clustered data mining. They define a family of GDTMs for privacy preserving transformation as follows:

Translation Data Perturbation (TDP) involves perturbing the confidential attributes by adding a constant noise term. Scaling Data Perturbation (SDP) involves perturbing the confidential attributes by multiplication with a constant noise term. In both TDP and SDP, each attribute is perturbed independently of the others, and the noise term can be either negative or positive. Rotation Data Perturbation (RDP) involves perturbing the confidential attributes two at a time. To ensure that all confidential attributes are perturbed, some may need to be perturbed more than once. The attributes are perturbed by rotation through a noise angle, measured clockwise. Values can be rounded after perturbation, for consistency with real-world values. Hybrid Data Perturbation (HDP) involves perturbing the confidential attributes, one at a time, using a perturbation method randomly chosen from TDP, SDP and RDP. These methods ensure that the mining process will not violate privacy up to a certain degree of security.

3.2 Decision Boundaries of Neural Network

ANNs have been successfully used in various pattern recognition problems including data mining. Neural networks are capable of defining arbitrary decision boundaries without assuming any under-

lying distribution. In a classification problem with only two classes, a decision boundary is defined as a hyper surface that partitions the underlying vector space into two sets, one for each class. The classifier will classify all the points on one side of the decision boundary as belonging to one class and all those on the other side as belonging to the other class. If the decision surface is a hyper plane, then the classification problem is linear, and the classes are linearly separable.

Decision boundaries are not always clearly defined. The transition from one class in the feature space to another is not discontinuous, but gradual. In the case of back propagation based multi layer ANNs, the type of decision boundary that the network can learn is determined by the number of hidden layers the network has. If it has no hidden layers, then it can only learn linear problems. If it has one hidden layer, then it can learn problems with convex decision boundaries and some concave decision boundaries. The network can learn more complex problems if it has two or more hidden layers.

The working principle of neural networks has been extensively discussed in literature. However, the mechanism of how the neural network defines decision boundaries and the relationship between the number of hidden neurons and the decision boundaries is not clearly understood. Jung & Lee (2000) systematically analyzed the decision boundary of feed forward neural networks from a different perspective and provide a helpful insight into the working mechanism of neural networks. They consider the outputs of the hidden neurons as a non-linear-mapping of inputs, since a typical activation function is a non-linear function such as the sigmoid function. They further observe that adding a hidden neuron is equivalent to expanding the dimension of the hidden neuron space. Thus, if the number of hidden neurons is larger than the number of inputs, the input data will be warped into a higher dimensional space. However, the intrinsic dimension of the data distribution in the hidden neuron space cannot exceed the dimension of the original input space.

Jung & Lee (2000) also showed that decision boundaries in the hidden neuron space will be always linear boundaries. From this point of view, it can be seen that, when neural networks are used as a classifier, the input data is first mapped non-linearly into a higher dimensional space and then divided by linear decision boundaries. Finally, the linear decision boundaries in the hidden neuron space will be warped into complex decision boundaries in the original input space. They investigated the decision boundaries of neural networks that use the sigmoid function. The classification mechanism of neural networks consists of two parts: expanding the dimension by hidden neurons and drawing linear boundaries by output neurons. They analyzed the decision boundaries in the hidden neuron space and showed how the linear boundaries in the hidden neuron space can define complex decision boundaries in the input space with some interesting properties.

The aggregation and selective use of these decision boundaries is what makes ANNs interesting. ANNs can be created to permit machines to form these decision boundaries with their associated class regions as derived from the data. Neural networks can be used to combine these decision regions together to form higher levels of abstraction, which can result in neural networks with some amazing properties. In this work, the capabilities of decision boundary of feed forward neural networks are used to model a privacy preservation technique for preserving privacy in low dimensional data sets.

3.3 Linear Discriminant Analysis (LDA)

A vital task in machine learning is dimensionality reduction and a large number of techniques for dimensionality reduction like Discriminant analysis, Logistic regression, principal components, and factor analysis have been proposed in literature over the last few decades. Linear discriminant analysis (LDA) is a statistical approach for dimensionality reduction and classification. LDA computes an optimal transformation by minimizing the within-class distance and maximizing the between-class distance simultaneously, thus achieving maximum class discrimination. The optimal transformation in LDA can be readily computed by applying an eigen decomposition on the so-called scatter matrices (Ye & Ji, 2010). Linear discriminant analysis finds a linear combination of features that characterizes two or more classes of objects. The resulting combination may be used as a linear classifier, or for dimensionality reduction before later classification. LDA is a supervised technique that attempts to maximize the linear separability between data points belonging to different classes in the low-dimensional representation of the data. The Matlab Toolbox for Dimensionality Reduction comprises of implementations for 27 techniques including the classical techniques like Linear discriminant Analysis, Principal Component Analysis, Factor etc. for dimensionality reduction.

4. PRIVACY PRESERVING METHODOLOGY

4.1 ANN Transformation

The different methods for privacy preservation that exist in literature focus on transforming the data in some way that the privacy of confidential data is preserved. However in some of the methods the utility suffers as a result of privacy. A novel technique for PPC of low dimensional data using the dimension expansion capabilities of multilayer feed forward ANN is proposed. Low dimensional data refers to data with k number of dimensions such that k is small enough to guess the identity of the owner. Since this work deals with the problem of privacy preservation, the goal is to mine the outcome accurately without sacrificing the input privacy by increasing the dimension of data.

The basic idea is to transform the original low dimensional data set to a high dimensional one by feeding the original data as input to multilayer feed forward neural network with a hidden layer, and computing the output of hidden layer to get the transformed data set that corresponds to the original input.

There exist many potential computer applications that are difficult to implement. Some applications may be required to perform complex data translation, yet they may have no pre defined mapping function that describes the mapping process. Some application may be required to provide a best guess of the correct output when presented with noisy input data. A feed forward neural network (Beale et al 2011) trained using back propagation algorithm has been successfully used in addressing such problems. Feed forward networks often have one or more hidden layers of sigmoid neurons followed by an output layer of linear neurons. Multiple layers of neurons with nonlinear transfer functions allow the network to learn nonlinear relationships between input and output vectors. The linear output layer is most often used for function fitting or nonlinear regression problems. On the other hand, to constrain the outputs of a network, the output layer should use a sigmoid transfer function. This is the case when the network is used for pattern recognition problems in which a decision is being made by the network.

4.2 Calculation of Hidden Layer Output

In practical neural network implementations, the network only provides the final output, final weights and bias values. So it is not possible to access the hidden layer output of all corresponding inputs directly with the network object.

A feed forward neural network is generally denoted by "net" in matlab and the notations used are described in Table 1.

The sequence of steps used to calculate the output to the hidden layer is depicted using the following steps.

Step 1: Initialize values for $net.IW$, $net.LW$, $b1$, $b2$ and X

Step 2: Compute the input of the Hidden layer using the equation

$$Z = f\left(net.IW * X + b1\right) \qquad (1)$$

Step 3: Compute the output of the Hidden layer using equation

$$Y = net.LW * Z + b2 \qquad (2)$$

Another simple way of calculating the output of hidden layer is to construct the network with input, hidden and output layers and train the network with sample data. Now store the input weights of all the layer net.IW and bias of all the layers net.b. Again construct a single layer neural network of neurons equal to that of hidden layer and initialize it with the previously stored weight and bias. If we test this single layer neural network with the input X, then it will directly give the hidden layer output.

Table 1. Notations used in net

Notation	Description
$net.IW$	input weights
$net.LW$	layer weights
$b1$ and $b2$	bias of two layers under consideration
X	vector representing the input of the network

Thus, if the number of hidden neurons is larger than the dimension of the inputs X, then the input data will be warped into a higher dimensional space with respect to the number of neurons in the hidden layer. Here the size of the input layer will be equal to the dimension of the data d. The size of the output layer will depend upon the number of classes. It may be any number depending on the application. The size of the hidden layer will be decided based on the size to which we want to transform the input data.

The process of implementing the ANN based privacy preservation framework is described in the following steps.

Step 1: Prepare a multi-attribute synthetic data set $\mathbb{S}$ with dimension d using the Gaussian distribution function.

Step 2: Let $N = |\mathbb{S}|$ and $C = \left\{ C_1, C_2, \ldots, C_k \right\}$ be the known classes of $\mathbb{S}$.

Step 3: Choose sample $S \subseteq \mathbb{S}$ such that $S \cap C_i \neq \varnothing$,

$\forall i = 1, 2, \ldots, k$ and $n = |S|$.

Step 4: Create a three layer feed-forward back propagation network NN with one input layer I, one hidden layer H and one output layer O such that

$|I| = d, |O| = k \, and \, |H| = D \, where \, D > d$.

Step 5: Train NN with S.

Step 6: Measure the weight $w(H)$ and bias $b(H)$ of the hidden layer H.

Step 7: Using $w(H)$, $b(H)$ computed in step 6, calculate the D dimensional output of the hidden layer $out(H)$, corresponding to each d dimensional input $in(I)$.

Step 8: The D dimensional transformed data set $\mathbb{S}'$ corresponding to original data set $\mathbb{S}$ is given by $\mathbb{S}' = out(H)$.

4.3 Hybrid ANN – LDA Transformation

A Hybrid ANN – LDA based Transformation technique is proposed for increased level of privacy protection. In the proposed methodology the LDA based transformation matrix is prepared from some of the randomly selected records of the ANN transformed dataset. We assume that the random samples will contain all kinds of data from the original data set. The transformation matrix can be shifted by multiplying it with an arbitrarily selected shifting factor. This will further increase the security against any reverse mechanism which can be used to guess the original data by doing some reverse transformation. This is used to transform the original data to a lower dimension.

The dimension of the transformed data will be always less than that of original number of dimension and will be increasing with respect to dimensions of the data under consideration. K-means based clustering is applied to the transformed data and the perfrmance of the proposed techniques are measured using two metrics – *Privacy level* and *Misclassification Error*.

The process of implementing and evaluating the Hybrid ANN-LDA Transformation is described in the following steps.

Step 1: Let $\mathbb{S}'$ be The D dimensional ANN transformed data set corresponding to original data set $\mathbb{S}$ of dimension d.

Step 2: Let $N = |\mathbb{S}'|$ and $C = \left\{ C_1, C_2, \ldots, C_k \right\}$ be the known classes of $\mathbb{S}'$.

Step 3: Choose sample $S \subseteq \mathbb{S}'$ such that $\mathbb{S} \cap C_i \neq \varnothing$, $\forall i = 1, 2, \ldots, k$

Step 4: Prepare a transformation Matrix T_s corresponding to $\mathbb{S}'$ using a LDA-based transformation such that $\dim(T_s) = d' < D$

Step 5: Project $\mathbb{S}'$ on T_s to obtain the final ANN-LDA transformed data set $\mathbb{S}'_T$.

Step 6: Cluster the ANN transformed data set $\mathbb{S}$ and Hybrid ANN-LDA transformed data set $\mathbb{S}'_T$ by using K-means algorithm.

Step 7: Evaluate the performance of the proposed techniques in terms of Misclassification error and privacy level percentage and compare with the traditional GDTMs

5. RESULTS AND DISCUSSION

5.1 Experimental Setup

To implement the proposed privacy preserving transformation a large multidimensional data set is needed. Since the number of dimension is varied during evaluation, it has been proposed to use a synthetic data set of in a very controlled manner for the creation of very fine well defined data clusters using Gaussian distribution function.

A snapshot of the sample record set of a 3 attributes Synthetic original data set of Student exam result dataset prepared using the Gaussian distribution function is given in Table 2.

5.2 ANN Transformed Dataset

A three layer feed forward back propagation network is created with one input layer, one hidden layer and one output layer using the neural network took kit of Matlab. The *pureln* transfer function in the neural network tool kit is used to calculate the layer's output from its net input. The neural network is trained using *traingdx*. The *traingdx* is a network training function that updates weight and bias values according to gradient descent momentum and an adaptive learning rate. After training the network, the weight and bias of the hidden layer is measured and used to compute the output of the hidden layers using Equation (2).

Table 3 gives a snapshot of the sample of the transformed data set that was obtained after applying ANN based transformation to the original three- dimensional data set. In the transformed data set, the dimensionality is increased. In this case, the number of dimension is 6.

5.3 Results with Different Number of Records

Table 4 shows the time taken for transforming the original data set of varying dimension and different numbers of records using the proposed ANN transformation technique.

Table 2. Original low dimensional dataset

54.00	28.00	53.00
47.00	26.00	61.00
50.00	30.00	56.00
57.00	30.00	60.00
58.00	26.00	57.00
48.00	32.00	54.00
50.00	29.00	55.00
54.00	31.00	60.00
52.00	28.00	61.00
49.00	27.00	60.00

Table 3. ANN transformed dataset

0.03	1.46	0.21	0.91	0.80	0.26
0.15	1.71	0.16	0.38	0.90	0.54
0.02	1.60	0.33	0.39	0.70	0.15
0.25	1.64	0.27	0.82	0.44	0.48
0.15	1.51	0.08	1.29	0.74	0.65
0.05	1.59	0.44	0.12	0.66	0.11
0.05	1.56	0.28	0.49	0.78	0.18
0.18	1.68	0.34	0.52	0.44	0.34
0.05	1.69	0.21	0.59	0.66	0.53
0.07	1.68	0.19	0.47	0.81	0.48

Table 4. ANN transformation time

Sl. No	Total Number of Records	Time Taken For Transformation (sec)		
		Dim = 7	Dim = 5	Dim = 3
1	300	0.90	0.95	0.99
2	600	1.65	1.73	1.76
3	900	2.42	2.51	2.63
4	1200	3.19	3.26	3.32
5	1500	4.02	4.10	4.17
6	1800	4.70	4.78	5.06

The transformation technique is tested by performing clustering on data sets with different dimensions and variable number of records.

Some of the Parameters Used for Testing

- **Dimension/Attributes of Data:** 3, 5, 7.
- **Total Student Records:** 300, 600, 900, 1200, 1500 and 1800 Records.
- **No. of dimension to be expanded:** 10.
- No. of hidden layers.

Table 4 shows a linear increase in CPU time with respect to the increase in number of records used for transformation. Further the transformation time is indirectly proportional to the dimension of data. This is because in this example all the records have been transformed to the same dimension (in this case 10). So it takes more time for records with lesser dimensions. But in practical applications, the number of hidden layers may be varied. So there is no need to consider the performance lag with respect to number of dimensions.

5.4 Hybrid ANN-LDA Transformed Datasets

LDA based transformation matrix is prepared from some of the randomly selected records of the ANN transformed dataset. During this evaluation, only 10% of the original records were used as a model to prepare the transformation matrix.

A snapshot of ANN transformed data set after applying the LDA Transformation is shown in Table 5.

After the LDA transformation dimension is reduced to 4.

5.5 Validation

To validate our approach we performed clustering using K-Means algorithm on the transformed data and evaluated the performance of the proposed techniques in terms of misclassification error and privacy level percentage. Our method was further validated by comparing our results with the traditional GDTM's.

The purpose of validation is:

- To prove that our method does not compromise the accuracy in the process of transforming the data set to provide privacy.
- To show that the ANN based privacy preservation methods are very much suitable, especially when the data is of lower dimension. Privacy preservation of low dimensional data is generally not efficient using existing methods like suppression, generalization or traditional perturbation

Table 5. Hybrid ANN-LDA transformed dataset

4.33	2.89	1.31	1.98
5.67	2.28	2.41	0.78
3.83	2.27	1.50	0.05
5.14	2.11	1.82	2.61
4.23	1.31	2.48	0.06
4.62	1.89	1.10	0.69
5.32	1.85	1.41	1.85
3.28	1.47	0.11	2.04
4.23	2.18	0.78	0.44
4.35	0.61	1.11	0.76

The Time Taken for LDA Transformation: 7.035645 sec

based methods because it is easy to predict the identity of the owner using quasi identifiers.

• To show that our methods provide a better level of privacy when compared to the classical GDTMs when using the same metrics for similar data measured sets.

For this validation, we used some of the results of (Oliveira & Zaiane, 2010) namely Table 1 and Table 2. We did not use the results from the other tables because they intentionally added noise with input data to enhance privacy by sacrificing accuracy and achieved those results.

5.5.1 Measuring Effectiveness

After privacy preserving transformation, clustering is performed on the transformed data and the effectiveness can be measured by comparing the clustering results. That is, the clusters in the original dataset should be equal to those in the transformed data sets. However, we may have some potential problems after data transformation: a noise data point end up clustered, a point from a cluster becomes a noise point, or a point from a cluster migrates to a different cluster and hence the clustering results may not be the same. Misclassification Error is measured in terms of the percentage of legitimate data points that are not well classified in the distorted database. Ide-

ally, the misclassification error should be 0%. The misclassification error, denoted by ME, is measured as follows (Oliveira & Zaiane, 2010):

$$M_E = \frac{1}{N} \times \sum_{i=1}^{k} (| \text{Cluster}_i (D)| - |\text{Cluster}_i (D')|)$$

(3)

where N represents the number of points in the original dataset, k is the number of clusters under analysis, and $\left|\text{Cluster}_i (X)\right|$ represents the number of legitimate data points of the ith cluster in the database X. Even though this metric will not be so accurate, we decided to use it here because, we compare our results with the results in (Oliveira & Zaiane, 2010) in which the authors have used this metric to measure the performance of their algorithm.

Table 6 shows the classification error of GDTM based Methods (Oliveira & Zaiane, 2010).

In Table 6, the last column was derived by taking average values of all the previous columns which were presented in table 1 of Oliveira & Zaiane (2010).

Table 7 shows the classification error in the Proposed ANN based methods.

Figure 1 compares the percentage of misclassification using GDTMs and the proposed ANN based methods.

Table 6. Misclassification in GDTMs

Sl. No	Method	% of Misclassification (Clustering by k-Means)					
		K=2	K=3	K=4	K=5	K=6	Avg
1	TDP	0.00	0.00	0.07	0.07	0.07	0.04
2	SDP	0.00	0.03	0.06	0.08	0.08	0.05
3	RDP	0.02	0.15	0.15	0.17	0.13	0.12
4	HDP	0.02	0.08	0.10	0.08	0.08	0.07

Table 7. Misclassification in ANN based methods

Sl. No	Method	% of Misclassification (Clustering by k-Means)					
		K=2	K=3	K=4	K=5	K=6	Avg
1	ANN	0.00	0.01	0.04	0.05	0.07	0.03
2	*ANN-LDA*	0.00	0.01	0.03	0.05	0.06	0.04

Figure 1. Percentage of misclassification

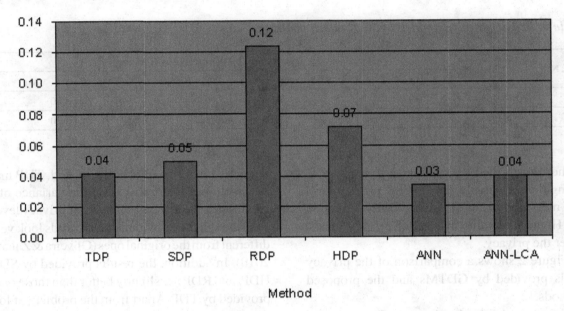

In Figure 1, the Misclassification Error is measured using the metric of the Eq (3). The ANN Transformation technique performs better than the Hybrid ANN-LDA method in terms of classification error.

5.5.2 Measuring Performance

Oliveira & Zaiane (2010) measure the privacy provided by a perturbation technique as the variance between the actual and the perturbed values given by $\mathbf{Variance}(\mathbf{X} - \mathbf{Y})$ where $\mathbf{X}$ represents a single original attribute and $\mathbf{Y}$ the distorted attribute. This measure can be made scale invariant with respect to the variance of $\mathbf{X}$ by expressing security as

$$Security = Variance(X - Y) / Variance(X)$$

(4)

and this measure to quantify privacy is based on how closely the original values of a modified attribute can be estimated (Oliveira & Zaiane, 2010).

Table 8 shows the results of privacy provided by GDTM based Methods (Oliveira & Zaiane, 2010).

In Table 8, the rows 1, 2, 3 and 4 were derived from the average values of security measure of the two attributes presented in table 2 of the paper (Oliveira & Zaiane, 2010).

Table 9 shows the privacy levels provided by the Proposed ANN based Methods.

In Table 9 we used the average of n dimensions of the input data as well as the first n dimensions

Table 8. Privacy levels provided by the GDTMs

Sl. No	Method	Privacy Level % (Clustering by K Means)					
		K=2	K=3	K=4	K=5	K=6	Avg
1	TDP	0.00	0.00	0.00	0.00	0.00	0.00
2	SDP	0.85	0.85	0.85	0.85	0.85	0.85
3	RDP	0.48	0.74	0.48	0.45	0.36	0.50
4	HDP	0.32	0.32	0.32	0.32	0.32	0.32

Table 9. Privacy levels provided by ANN based methods

Sl. No	Method	Privacy Level % (Clustering by K Means)					
		K=2	K=3	K=4	K=5	K=6	Avg
1	ANN	0.97	1.01	1.03	0.98	0.99	1.00
2	ANN-LDA	1.27	1.31	1.09	1.21	1.13	1.20

of the transformed data for quantifying / measuring the security. In Table 9, the privacy level was measured using the metric of the Equation (4). Higher the value of level of privacy means better the privacy.

Figure 2 shows a comparison of the privacy levels provided by GDTMs and the proposed methods.

Based on the results shown in Figure 2, one may claim that GDTMs (the first four 4) could be restrictive in terms of privacy. Indeed, TDP may be sometimes restrictive since the variance of a single attribute always yields 0% of privacy level, even though the individual data records look very different from the original ones (Oliveira & Zaiane, 2010). In addition, the results provided by SDP, HDP, and RDP are slightly better than those ones provided by TDP. Apart from the problem of low privacy, a geometric transformation function is invertible so that one may estimate the real values

Figure 2. Comparison of Privacy levels

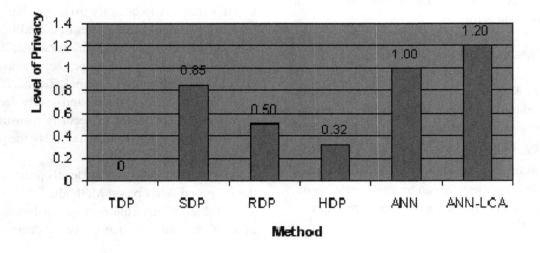

of the data under clustering. But, the proposed ANN based methods provided superior privacy level compared with the traditional GDTMs. The ANN method is well suited for low dimensional data in terms of misclassification Error. However when both Misclassification error as well as Privacy percentage is taken into consideration the Hybrid ANN-LDA transformation technique outperforms all other methods.

6. CONCLUSION

The proposed method has been successfully implemented using Matlab under windows xp. In this work, a novel idea of preserving the privacy of the low dimensional data set using the dimension expansion property of multilayer feed forward neural network is introduced. Since the dimensionality of the data can be increased to any higher degree, predicting the original values from the transformed values will be highly impossible. For further level of security a LDA based transformation technique is applied on the ANN transformed dataset. The ANN-LDA method is well suited for clustering data in a situation where the data holders have to give their confidential data to a third party for mining.

The suitability of this transformed data for mining has been evaluated by performing clustering on transformed data and the performance of the proposed method is measured in terms of Miscalssification and Privacy level percentage. The proposed ANN based dimension transformation methods are evaluated further by comparing the results with four Geometric data transformation methods. The proposed methods are found to perform well, if classification error, as well as

the privacy level is considered as the metric. In GDTMs, accuracy sometimes suffers as a result of security. But in the proposed methods, the accuracy has been preserved even without sacrificing privacy level. Further, the proposed model can be used to protect privacy in a multi party collaborative clustering scenario. Randomly generated, low-dimensional data have been experimented on in this work for the sake of comparison with similar data in GDTMs.

When presenting data as important as medical information that could potentially be used in the future to help save people's lives, it would seem logical that data should be mined as accurately as possible. These are issues that need to be worked out in the future. Privacy preserving data mining is by every means, a work in progress, and it will be interesting to see where new research on it leads in the following years. This work addresses the Privacy preserving clustering of low dimensional data. Future works may address the possibilities of using other kind of neural networks for more enhanced levels of privacy protection in multivariate datasets.

REFERENCES

Agarwal, R., & Srikant, R. (2000). Privacy-preserving data mining. In *Proc of the 2000 ACM SIGMOD International Conference on Management of Data* (pp. 439–450). ACM. doi:10.1145/342009.335438

Anbumani, K., & Nedunchezhian, R. (2006). Rapid privacy preserving algorithm for large databases. *International Journal of Intelligent Information Technologies*, 2(1), 68–81. doi:10.4018/jiit.2006010104

Ashrafi, M. Z., Taniar, D., & Smith, K. (2005). PP-DAM: Privacy-preserving distributed association-rule-mining algorithm. *International Journal of Intelligent Information Technologies*, *1*(1), 49–69. doi:10.4018/jiit.2005010104

Beale, M. H., Hagan, M. T., & Demuth, H. B. (2011). *R2011b documentation -Matlab help pages of neural network toolbox*. Retrieved October 2011 from http://www.mathworks.com/help/pdf_doc/nnet/nnet_ug.pdf

Bertino, E., Lin, D., & Jiang, W. (2008). A survey of quantification of privacy preserving data mining algorithms. In Privacy-preserving data mining. Springer. doi:10.1007/978-0-387-70992-5_8

Deng, J. D., Purvis, M. K., & Purvis, M. A. (2011). Software effort estimation: Harmonizing algorithms and domain knowledge in an integrated data mining approach. *International Journal of Intelligent Information Technologies*, *7*(3), 41–53.

Evfimievski, A., & Grandison, T. (2009). Privacy preserving data mining. In *Handbook of research on innovations in database technologies and applications: Current and future trends*. IGI Global.

Flaherty, D. (1989). *Protecting privacy in surveillance societies*. The University of North Carolina Press.

Indumathi, J., & Uma, G.V. (2009). A novel framework for optimised privacy preserving data mining using the innovative desultory technique. *International Journal of Computer Applications in Technology, 35*(2/3/4), 194 - 203.

Jung, K., & Lee, C. (2000). Dimension expansion of neural networks. In *Proc of the Geoscience and Remote Sensing Symposium* (*Vol. 2*, pp. 678-680). Academic Press.

Klosgen, W. (1995). Anonymization techniques for knowledge discovery in databases. In *Proc of the First International Conference on Knowledge Discovery and Data Mining Montreal* (pp. 186-191). Academic Press.

Liu, K., Kargupta, H., & Ryan, J. (2006). Random projection-based multiplicative data perturbation for privacy preserving distributed data mining. *IEEE Transactions on Knowledge and Data Engineering, 18*(1), 92–106. doi:10.1109/TKDE.2006.14

Machanavajjhala, A., Gehrke, J., Kifer, D., & Venkitasubramaniam, M. (2006). l-Diversity: Privacy beyond k-anonymity. In *Proceedings of the 22th International Conference on Data Engineering*. Academic Press.

Matatov, N., Rokach, L., & Maimon, O. (2010). Privacy-preserving data mining: A feature set partitioning approach. *Information Sciences, 80*(14), 2696–2720. doi:10.1016/j.ins.2010.03.011

Oliveira, S. R. M., & Zaiane, O. R. (2010). Privacy preserving clustering by data transformation. *Journal of Information and Data Management, 1*(1), 37–51.

Onn, Y. (2005). Privacy in the digital environment. Haifa Center of Law and Technology, 1-12.

Qi, Y., Song, M., Yoon, S. J., & Watrous-de-Versterre, L. (2011). Combining supervised learning techniques to key-phrase extraction for biomedical full-text. *International Journal of Intelligent Information Technologies*, 7(1), 33–44. doi:10.4018/jiit.2011010103

Rajalakshmi, M., Purusothaman, T., & Pratheeba, S. (2010). Collusion-free privacy preserving data mining. *International Journal of Intelligent Information Technologies*, 6(4), 30–45. doi:10.4018/jiit.2010100103

Sang, Y., Shen, H., & Tian, H. (2009). Privacy-preserving tuple matching in distributed databases. *IEEE Transactions on Knowledge and Data Engineering*, 21(12), 1767–1782. doi:10.1109/TKDE.2009.39

Sharma, A., & Ojha, V. (2010). Implementation of cryptography for privacy preserving data mining. *International Journal of Database Management Systems*, 2(3), 57–65. doi:10.5121/ijdms.2010.2306

Tian, H., & Zhang, W. (2011). Extending l-diversity to generalize sensitive data. *Data & Knowledge Engineering*, 70(1), 101–126. doi:10.1016/j.datak.2010.09.001

Veeramalai, S., & Kannan, A. (2011). Intelligent information retrieval using fuzzy association rule classifier. *International Journal of Intelligent Information Technologies*, 7(3), 14–27. doi:10.4018/jiit.2011070102

Vidya Banu, R., & Nagaveni, N. (2013). Evaluation of a perturbation-based technique for privacy preservation in a multi-party clustering scenario. *Information Sciences*, 232, 437–448. doi:10.1016/j.ins.2012.02.045

VidyaBanu, R., & Nagaveni, N. (2009). Preservation of data privacy using PCA based transformation. In *Proc of the IEEE International Conference on Advances in Recent Technologies in Communication and Computing* (pp. 439-443). IEEE.

VidyaBanu, R., & Nagaveni, N. (2012). Low dimensional data privacy preservation using multi layer artificial neural network. *International Journal of Intelligent Information Technologies*, 8(3), 17–31. doi:10.4018/jiit.2012070102

Wright, D., Gutwirth, S., Friedewald, M., Hert, P. D., Langheinrich, M., & Moscibroda, A. (2009). Privacy, trust and policy-making: Challenges and responses. *Computer Law & Security Report*, 25(1), 69–83. doi:10.1016/j.clsr.2008.11.004

Yang, W., & Qiao, S. (2010). A novel anonymization algorithm: Privacy protection and knowledge preservation. *Expert Systems with Applications*, 37(1), 756–766. doi:10.1016/j.eswa.2009.05.097

Ye, J., & Ji, S. (2010). Discriminant analysis for dimensionality reduction: An overview of recent developments. In *Biometrics: Theory, methods, and applications*. New York: Wiley-IEEE Press.

Yeh, J., & Hsu, P. (2010). H HUIF and MSICF - Novel algorithms for privacy preserving utility mining. *Expert Systems with Applications*, 37(7), 4779–4786. doi:10.1016/j.eswa.2009.12.038

KEY TERMS AND DEFINITIONS

Artificial Neural Networks: Computational models based on the structure and functions of biological neural networks.

Data Transformation: Modification of every point in a data set by a mathematical function to change data to the appropriate form for a particular statistical test or method.

Geometrical Data Transformation: A method for transforming data using the concepts of translation, scaling and rotation in such a way that similarities between data objects are maintained.

Linear Discriminant Analysis: A classification and dimension reduction method that uses the concept of searching for a linear combination of variables (predictors) that best separates two classes (targets).

Misclassification Error: A measure to calculate the percentage of legitimate data points that are not well classified in the distorted database.

Privacy Level: A measure to calculate the privacy provided by a perturbation technique as the variance between the actual and the perturbed values.

Privacy Preserving Clustering: Protection of the underlying attribute values of objects subjected to clustering analysis.

Chapter 12
Risk Prediction Model for Osteoporosis Disease Based on a Reduced Set of Factors

Walid Moudani
Lebanese University, Lebanon

Fadi Chakik
Lebanese University, Lebanon

Ahmad Shahin
Lebanese University, Lebanon

Dima Rajab
Lebanese University, Lebanon

ABSTRACT

The health industry collects huge amounts of health data, which, unfortunately, are not mined to discover hidden information. Information technologies can provide alternative approaches to the diagnosis of the osteoporosis disease. In this chapter, the authors examine the potential use of classification techniques on a huge volume of healthcare data, particularly in anticipation of patients who may have osteoporosis disease through a set of potential risk factors. An innovative solution approach based on dynamic reduced sets of risk factors using the promising Rough Set theory is proposed. An experimentation of several classification techniques have been performed leading to rank the suitable techniques. The reduction of potential risk factors contributes to enumerate dynamically optimal subsets of the potential risk factors of high interest leading to reduce the complexity of the classification problems. The performance of the model is analyzed and evaluated based on a set of benchmark techniques.

INTRODUCTION

Osteoporosis is a real public health problem because of its increasing frequency over the countries. It is considered as one of the major problems among women and older people. However, it becomes an essential index of health and economics in every country. Osteoporosis disease is a chronic complex health problem for

millions of women worldwide, 80% of whom are postmenopausal, unless prevented or treated, this silent disease will continue to limit both the quantity and the quality of many older women and significantly add to health care cost for this group (Taylor, Schreiner, Stone, 2004; Kanis, 2002). This disease infects 30% of women after 50 years and 70% after 80 years. Osteoporosis prevention is complicated but it holds promise as the best way

DOI: 10.4018/978-1-4666-6639-9.ch012

to decrease future fractures (Kanis, Johansson, Johnell, 2005). Looking around the world, we see that osteoporosis occurs in some areas much more than in others — just as the incidence of cancer, heart disease, and diabetes varies from one culture to another. This clarifies that the development of weak bones is not a natural artifact of aging. While the United States has one of the highest osteoporosis rates in the world, there are other areas where this disorder is relatively rare, even among the older segments of the population (Dawson-Hughes, Tosteson, Melton, et al., 2008). For example, the inhabitants of Singapore, Hong Kong, and certain sectors of former Yugoslavia, as well as the Bantu of South Africa have traditionally held extremely low rates of osteoporotic fracture. In Japan, vertebral compression fractures among women between ages 50 and 65 were so rare that many physicians doubt their existence, and the incidence of hip fractures among the elderly Japanese historically has been much less than half that of Western countries (Koh, Sendrine, Torralba, et al. 2001; Sen, Rives, Messina, et al., 2005). Africans and native peoples living traditional lifestyles have been classified as "almost immune" to osteoporosis (De Laet, Kanis, Oden, et al., 2005). Interestingly enough, as these less technologically advanced countries become more Westernized, their rates of osteoporotic fracture are steadily increasing (Taylor, Schreiner, Stone, 2004). We note that some Lebanese studies have showed that the mean BMD for the Lebanese female is lower than that of the European woman. Another Lebanese study showed that the hip fractures occur at a younger age in Lebanon (between 65 and 75) compared to western population (above 75) and that 60% of patients with hip fractures have osteopenia rather than osteoporosis (Taylor, Schreiner, Stone, 2004; Kanis, 2002). The social economic burden of osteoporosis is so large that its etiology, prevention and treatment have become an urgent issue that needs to be coped with worldwide.

The disease may continue its progress until even a slight twisting or bending motion may cause bones to fracture and break. Risk factors for developing osteoporosis include controllable factors such as nutrition, physical activity level, smoking, and consumption of alcohol, and uncontrollable factors like sex, family history, and ethnicity. Many people in any ages appear to be unaware of the risk factors and preventive behaviors. Preventing osteoporosis, and subsequent fractures, had become a goal of many health care practitioners.

Osteoporosis is a bone disease that commonly occurs among postmenopausal women. Recognizing population with high risks of osteoporosis remains a difficult challenge. Early detection and diagnosis is the key for prevention but are very difficult, without using costly diagnosing devices, due to complex factors involved and its gradual bone lose process with no obvious warning symptoms. Building an osteoporosis prediction system using data mining techniques based on analyzing postmenopausal risk factors is the aim of this study. By discovering the osteoporosis disease warehouses for Osteoporosis, significant patterns can be extracted in order to build a robust disease prediction models that aim to guide medical decision making (Harold, 2008) and provide an easier way to detect if a person can have the risk of an osteoporosis. The aim of this study is to examine the potential use of classification on a massive volume of healthcare data, particularly in prediction of patients that may have Osteoporosis Disease (OD), which unfortunately continues to increase postmenopausal in the whole world, then it will possible to prevent OD through modification of its risk factors. It enables significant knowledge, e.g. patterns, relationships between medical factors related to Osteoporosis disease, to be established.

The methodology used in this study to build the mining predictive model consists of several phases that start with medical-technical environment understanding, data understanding, data preparation, modeling, implementation and evaluation. The environment understanding phase focuses on illustrating the medical and technical parts of this research by defining the osteoporosis disease, introducing its major risk factors which will constitute the input parameters for the mining operation; and in the technical part, we will identify the role of data mining techniques and explain the classification algorithm chosen to be used in this work. Data understanding phase uses the raw of the data, proceeds to understand the data, identify its structure, gain preliminary insights, and detect interesting subsets. Data preparation phase constructs the final dataset that will be fed into the modeling tools. This includes table, record, and attribute selection as well as data cleaning and transformation. The modeling phase selects and applies various techniques, and calibrates their parameters to optimal values. The solution approach applied can predict the likelihood of patients getting with Osteoporosis risk disease while reducing the complexity of the classification process without affecting the solution quality. The implementation phase specifies the tasks that are needed to build and use the models. The results of this study should be helpful to the development of the computer-aided system in the other medical field. The performance of the proposed model is analyzed and evaluated based on set of benchmark techniques applied in classification problems.

The rest of this paper is organized as follows. Section 2 presents in details the osteoporosis disease and all related features such as: risk factors, symptoms, and prevention. Sections 3 and 4 discuss the works found in the literature related to this disease and also the computational techniques applied for solving this task. Section 5 describes how to build multi-way decision trees using a hierarchical clustering algorithm. In Section 5, we present some empirical results we have obtained by applying our alternative approach to build decision trees. Finally, some conclusions and

pointers to future work are given in Section 6. In (Kanis, 2002), we describe alternative similarity measures which can be used in our hierarchical clustering algorithm.

DESCRIPTION AND ANALYSIS OF OSTEOPOROSIS DISEASE

Definition

Osteoporosis, a skeletal disease characterized by low bone mass (BMD), micro-architectural deterioration of bone tissue and an increasing risk of fracture, represent an enormous public health burden in both economic costs and human suffering (Figure 1). Osteoporosis literally leads to abnormally porous bone that is compressible, like a sponge. This disorder of the skeleton weakens the bone and results in frequent fractures (breaks) in the bones.

According to the National Institute of Arthritis and Musculoskeletal and Skin Diseases, osteoporosis statistics show a greater burden for women in the following ways:

- 68 percent of the 44 million people with osteoporosis risk are women.
- One of every two women over age 50 will likely have an osteoporosis-related fracture in their lifetime. That's twice the rate of fractures in men — one in four.
- 75 percent of all cases of hip osteoporosis affect women.

Symptoms and Types of Osteoporosis

Osteoporosis can be present without any symptoms for decades because osteoporosis doesn't cause symptoms until bone fractures. Moreover, some osteoporotic fractures may escape detec-

Figure 1. Difference between normal bone and bone osteoporosis

 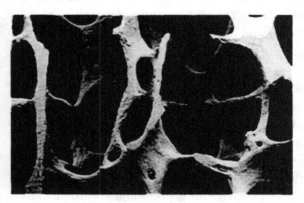

Normal Bone   **Osteoporosis**

tion for years when they do not cause symptoms. Therefore, patients may not be aware of their osteoporosis until they suffer a painful fracture (Kanis, 2002; Kanis, Johnell, Oden, Johansson, McCloskey, 2008). The symptoms of osteoporosis in men are similar to the symptoms of osteoporosis in women. As the disease progresses, it may have symptoms related to weakened bones, including:

- Back pain,
- Loss of height and stooped posture (Figure 2),
- A curved upper back (dowager's hump).

We distinguish three types related to this disease as stated:

- **Primary Type 1 or Postmenopausal Osteoporosis:** This form of osteoporosis is the most common in women after menopause.
- **Primary Type 2 Osteoporosis or Senile Osteoporosis:** Occurs after age 75 and is seen in both females and males at a ratio of 2:1.
- **Secondary Osteoporosis:** May arise at any age and affects men and women equally. It results from chronic predisposing medi-

cal problems or disease, or prolonged use of medications such as glucocorticoids, when the disease is called steroid-or glucocorticoid-induced osteoporosis (SIOP or GIOP).

Fractures and Risk Factors

Osteopenia is a condition of bone that is slightly less dense than normal bone but not to the degree of bone in osteoporosis. Normal bone is composed of protein, collagen, and calcium, all of which give bone its strength. Bones that are affected by osteoporosis can break (fracture) with relatively minor injury that normally would not cause a bone to fracture. The fracture can be either in the form of cracking (as in a hip fracture) or collapsing (as in a compression fracture of the vertebrae of the spine). The spine, hips, ribs, and wrists are common areas of bone fractures from osteoporosis although osteoporosis-related fractures can occur in almost any skeletal bone. Fragility fractures can affect many sites: Vertebral column, hip, rib and wrist. But the hip fractures are much more numerous, more severe and associated with greater mortality and morbidity.

Concerning the risk factors for osteoporotic fracture, it can be split between non-modifiable

Figure 2. Loss of height and stooped posture caused by osteoporosis

and modifiable. Each of them has a relative effect and importance. We can distinguish here two risk factors: Non-modifiable and modifiable factors (Taylor, Schreiner, Stone, 2004).

Non-Modifiable Factors

- Advanced age (in both men and women).
- Female gender.
- **Estrogen Deficiency and Early Menopause:** This deficiency is responsible for a speed increase bone remodeling (Bone remodeling (or bone metabolism) is a life-long process where mature bone tissue is removed from the skeleton (Resorption) and new bone tissue is formed (Formation) and induces an imbalance between resorption and formation, leading to net bone loss.
- Early menopause (before age 45) and any prolonged periods in which hormone levels

are low and menstrual periods are absent or infrequent can cause loss of bone mass.
- **Heredity:** Those with a family history of fracture or osteoporosis are at an increased risk; the heritability of the fracture as well as low bone mineral density are relatively high, ranging from 25 to 80 percent.
- **Previous Fracture:** Those who have already had a fracture are at least twice as likely to have another fracture compared to someone of the same age and sex.
- **Rheumatoid Disease:** Those affected by rheumatoid arthritis may also have an increased risk of developing osteoporosis, a condition in which the bones become less dense and more likely to fracture.

Modifiable Factors

- **Excess Alcohol:** Small amounts of alcohol do not increase osteoporosis risk but chronic heavy drinking (alcohol intake greater than 3 units/day), especially at a younger age, increases risk significantly (Kanis, Johansson, Johnell, 2005).

- **Tobacco Smoking:** Tobacco smoking inhibits the activity of osteoblasts (cells responsible of formation), and is an independent risk factor for osteoporosis (Kanis, Johnell, Oden, et al., 2005). Smoking also results in increased breakdown of exogenous estrogen, lower body weight and earlier menopause, all of which contribute to lower bone mineral density.
- **Vitamin D Deficiency:** Mild vitamin D insufficiency is associated with increased Parathyroid Hormone (PTH) production that increases bone resorption, leading to bone loss. Also Vitamin D is necessary to absorb calcium, while bodies can synthesize vitamin D from sunlight, in some regions where sunlight is not present for many months at a time, a supplement is necessary.
- **Calcium:** Calcium is the most abundant mineral in the body; the bones and teeth accounting for about 99% of the total body stores. The main function of calcium is the well-known building and renewal of the skeleton.
- **Glucocorticoids:** Glucocorticoids are important drugs in the treatment of variety diseases, but long-term period use can lead to various adverse effects, including osteoporosis by inhibition of osteoplastic bone formation, which results not only in decreased bone mineral density, but reduction of bone strength. The evidence suggests that daily oral glucocorticoid doses higher than 5 mg or equivalent increase the risk of fracture within 3–6 months after the start of therapy.

Osteoporosis Prevention

Effective prevention measures should include non-pharmacologic interventions and pharmacologic when necessary (Adinoff and Hollister, 1983; Melton, Kan, Wahner, Riggs, 1988; Yildirim, Çeken, Hassanpour, Esmelioglu, Tolun, 2011).

Non-Pharmacologic Methods

- **Reducing Fall Risk:** Fall prevention can help prevent osteoporosis complications. Older patients should be consistently counseled to modify the home environment to improve safety and reduce risk of fall (Removal of obstacles and loose carpets in the living environment, install railings along stairways, etc.). (Kanis, Johnell, Oden, Johansson, McCloskey, 2008).
- **Lifestyle:** Patients should be educated to minimize their use of alcohol, caffeine and tobacco (Kanis, Johnell, Oden, et al., 2005; Melton, Kan, Wahner, Riggs, 1988).
- **Nutrition:** Nutrition plays a critical role in reducing the risk of osteoporosis. An adequate calcium, vitamin D and protein intake resulted in reduced bone remodeling. Supplementation with calcium and vitamin D is a critical component of osteoporosis to improve BMD and to reduce fracture risk. The National osteoporosis foundation recommends that postmenopausal woman consume at least 1200 mg calcium per day (Adinoff and Hollister, 1983; Melton, Kan, Wahner, Riggs, 1988; Koh, Sendrine, Torralba, et al. 2001).
- **Physical Exercise:** A 2 year study showed that adding a physical exercise program to medication improved BMD significantly and is superior to medication alone (De Laet, Kanis, Oden, et al., 2005; Kanis, Oden, Johnell, et al., 2007).

Pharmacologic Methods

- Estrogen replacement therapy remains a good treatment for prevention of osteoporosis but, at this time, is not recommended unless there are other indications for its use as well. There is uncertainty and controversy about whether estrogen should be recommended in women in the first decade after the menopause (De Laet, Kanis, Oden, et al., 2005).

- Some bisphosphonates have been shown to reduce fracture risk after relatively a brief period of use. The scientists found that woman treated with Alendronate (5mg/day) had a lower relative risk for symptomatic vertebral and non-vertebral fractures within 1 year of treatment (Melton, Kan, Wahner, Riggs, 1988; Koh, Sendrine, Torralba, et al. 2001).

LITERATURE OVERVIEW

Description of the Methods Applied in Literature

Many approaches have been proposed for improving the selection of women at high risk and who should be treated for preventing hip fracture. They aimed either to increase the specificity and sensitivity of detection or to maintain the best possible sensitivity and specificity while decreasing the number of expensive or not easily available measurements required. Approaches have tested all possible combinations of clinical risk factors, DXA, QUS, and bone turnover assessed by biomarkers. Use of clinical risk factors for predicting bone mass with sufficient accuracy to avoid bone densitometry measurements in postmenopausal women has been studied. Conclusions are that clinical risk factors alone have a poor predictive

value in identifying women with low bone mass and that bone densitometry is necessary for assessing osteoporosis risk. However, when risk factors are combined into risk scores, they significantly predict hip fractures, even though combining risk factors with low BMD into risk score is associated with higher risk of hip fracture. Clinical risk factors are noninvasive and inexpensive to assess. Furthermore, some of them are potentially modifiable and sometimes reversible by a change in habits (i.e. physical activity, smoking, alcohol drinking, dietary calcium intake). Others are associated with falls and are not measurable by bone densitometry nor may their effect be directly reduced by anti-osteoporotic agents. Although when certain clinical risk factors were used to determine entry into a clinical treatment trial, the medication was ineffective at preventing fractures. It is important to recall that the choice of clinical risk factors is crucial because they don't have the same power in predicting a traumatic fracture. In the past, the osteoporosis risk was usually modeled from the predominance of one factor. Adinoff and Hollister (1983) show that the use of oral glucocorticoids is a major determinant of fractures, while Melton, Kan, Wahner, Riggs (1988) suggest that the bone mineral density (BMD) is the only factor responsible for increasing fracture risk. But recently, a great deal of research has taken place to identify factors other than BMD that contribute to fracture risk i.e. age, a previous fracture, heredity of fracture and lifestyle such as physical exercises, smoking and alcohol. In Koh, Sendrine, Torralba, et al. (2001), a study has been validated in Asia, Europe, the United States and Latin America. The results classified the risk level into high, moderate or low. This indexation is based only on two factors: age and body weight by a series of statistical calculations: 0.2 x [(body weight in kg) – (age in years). Sen, Rives, Messina, et al. (2005) have proposed one of the most important studies called the "Osteorisk" risk assessment tool. The sensitivity of this method reaches 94% and the specificity, 45%. Results given help doctors to identify patients who are at greater risk of low bone mass and request examinations of higher complexity, and even begin therapy if it is impossible to undertake such examinations or to avoid unnecessary tests for patients at low risk. A similar study on older woman (Chiu, Li, Yu, Wang, 2006) was based on 6252 women with 65 years or more, compares the value of FRAX models (FRAX®, 2008) that include BMD with that of parsimonious models based on age and BMD alone for prediction of fractures, also a comparison between FRAX models without BMD with simple models based on age and fracture history alone. The calculation uses the logistic regression to examine receiver operating characteristic (ROC) curves for each model across a range of sensitivities and specificities, then the area under the curve (AUC) statistics from (ROC) curve analysis were compared between FRAX tool and simple models. Since results show no difference between models and FRAX values, this suggests that both the FRAX models and simple models are limited in their ability to predict fracture in older women. To be noted that in the context of osteoporosis, there are two tools other than FRAX for fracture risk calculation, QFractur (www.qfracture.org) and the Garvan tool (www.garvan.org.au). In Quinlan (1993), the GLOW study shows the ability of predicting fractures using 3 algorithms: FRAX, Garvan and a simple model of age and fracture history. The analysis found that the estimation of fracture risk of postmenopausal women can be made using clinical risk factors alone, without BMD models incorporating multiple clinical risk factors including falls, were not superior to more parsimonious models in predicting future fracture in this population.

Hui, Xiaoy, Bone, Buyea, Ramanathan & Zhang (2012) developed and evaluated a novel 3D computational bone framework, in order to enable quantitative assessment of bone microarchitecture, bone mineral density and bone's deterioration. A simulation and analyze of the microstructure of human normal bone network and osteoporotic bone network with different bone loss rate had been performed. Bayesian models are applied to analyze bone fracture risk based on demographic characteristics and life styles. They found as a result that people might start to cease drinking alcohol and smoking to protect their bone health. Finally, they designed the measurements in biological, mechanical and geometrical domains to validate our model. The validation results clearly demonstrated that the proposed 3D bone model is robust to reflect the properties of the bone microstructure in the real world.

Hatamzadeh, Jalilian, Emdadi, Rezaei, Mirzaee, and Ramhormozi (2011) have described relationship health belief model components with the practice of osteoporosis-protective behaviors among a random sample of Iranian women. They performed a cross-sectional study among 400 women. Sampling was performed via random classification and data were collected by standard questionnaire. A questionnaire was developed to measure each of the expanded health belief model components. Data were analyzed by SPSS-13. The results show that perceived severity has a significant relationship with performing preventive behaviors. Also there was a significant relationship between having a person with osteoporosis in the family, age, education, occupation, knowledge and performing preventive behaviors. As it revealed by statistical analyzes perceived severity was the most effective factor between women for predicting osteoporosis-protective behaviors. The results show the need to train women, especially for women with lower education.

Tae, Sung, Deok, Joon, Wan, Ein & Eun-Cheol (2013) have developed and validated machine learning models with the aim of more accurately identifying the risk of osteoporosis in postmenopausal women compared to the ability of conventional clinical decision tools. The medical data, collected from Korean postmenopausal women, was used to construct models based on popular machine learning algorithms such as support vector machines (SVM), random forests, artificial neural networks (ANN), and logistic regression (LR). The machine learning models were compared to four conventional clinical decision tools: osteoporosis self-assessment tool (OST), osteoporosis risk assessment instrument (ORAI), simple calculated osteoporosis risk estimation (SCORE), and osteoporosis index of risk (OSIRIS). The results show that SVM had significantly better area under the curve (AUC) of the receiver operating characteristic than ANN, LR, OST, ORAI, SCORE, and OSIRIS for the training set. SVM predicted osteoporosis, risk with an AUC of 0.827, accuracy of 76.7%, sensitivity of 77.8%, and specificity of 76.0% at total hip, femoral neck, or lumbar spine for the testing set. The significant t factors selected by SVM were age, height, weight, body mass index, duration of menopause, duration of breast feeding, estrogen therapy, hyperlipidemia, hypertension, osteoarthritis, and diabetes mellitus. As conclusion, the machine learning methods may be effective tools for identifying postmenopausal women at high risk for osteoporosis.

Yildirim, Çeken, Hassanpour, Esmelioglu, Tolun (2011) present the importance of osteoporosis disease in terms of medical research and pharmaceutical industry. They introduce a knowledge discovery approach regarding the treatment of osteoporosis from a historical perspective. They propose to use a freely available biomedical search engine leveraging text-mining technology to extract the drug names used in the treatment of osteoporosis from MEDLINE articles. They conclude that alendronate (Fosamax) and raloxifene (Evista) have the highest number of articles in MEDLINE and seem the dominating drugs for the treatment of osteoporosis in the last decade.

Description of the Classification Techniques

Classification Based on Neural Network and Ensemble Data Mining Approach

Predicting osteoporosis in not limited on clinical factors but may be also based on intelligent models using several techniques of data mining such neural network by (Chiu, Li, Yu, Wang, 2006) where the model was developed and validated as an artificial neural network (ANN) to identify the osteoporotic subjects in the elderly. After training processes, the final best ANN was a multilayer perceptron network which determined seven input variables (gender, age, weight, height, body mass index, postmenopausal status, and coffee consumption) as significant features. The discriminatory power of ANN for test set (AUC) was excellent.

Wang and Rea (2005) present the research in developing an ensemble of data mining techniques for predicting the risk of osteoporosis prevalence in women. It consists to develop an intelligent decision support system based on data mining ensemble technology to assist General Practitioners in assessing patient's risk of developing osteoporosis (Hillbrand, 2007; Harold, 2008). It focuses on investigating the methodologies for constructing effective ensembles, specifically on the measurements of diversity between individual models induced by two types of machine learning techniques, i.e. neural networks and decision trees for predicting the risk of osteoporosis. The constructed ensembles as well as their member predictors are assessed in terms of reliability, diversity and accuracy of prediction. The results indicate that the intelligently hybridised ensembles have high-level diversities and thus are able to improve their performance.

Methods have been explored in attempting to build better ensembles by trying either to generate more accurate models or to create more diverse models or both ideally. Boosting (Schapire et al., 1997) and Adaboots (Freund & Schapire, 1996) are two useful techniques to manipulate the data set by adding more weight to so called "hard" data subsets to force the models to learn the aspects represented by these weighted training data subsets. In addition, the decision fusion strategies also play important role in determining the performance of an ensemble. Averaging and simple or weighted voting, are the tow commonly used ones, pending the type of machine learning algorithms employed. For one, such as neural networks, outputs continuous value, averaging seems naturally suitable but the diversity, if not carefully handled, may have some adverse effects on the final averaged result. Voting strategy is best suitable for the modeling algorithms with categorical outputs, such as decision trees for classification problems. However, the continuous outputs can be discretized; the voting can then be applied.

Classical Decision Trees

It is well-known that decision trees are probably the most popular classification model (Berzal, Cubero, Marın, Sanchez, 2001; Breiman, Friedman, Olshen, Stone, 1984; Quinlan, 1986; Kaiquan, Wang, Ren, Liu, Xu, and Liao, 2011; Fei-Long & Feng-Chia, 2010). The aim of the decision tree learning process is to build a decision tree which conveys interesting information in order to make predictions and classify previously unseen data. In order to apply classification tree, we should separate data into 2 groups: attributes (inputs or predictors) and class (output or response). Decision Trees algorithms usually assume the absence of noise in input data and they try to obtain a perfect description of data. This is usually counterproductive in real problems, where management of noisy data and uncertainty is required. The Decision Tree algorithm family includes classical algorithms, such as CLS (Concept Learning System), ID3 (Quinlan, 1986), C4.5 and CART (Classifica-

tion And Regression Trees) (Quinlan, 1993), as well as more recent ones, such ART (Quinlan, 1986) and RF (Brieman, 2001). Some of those algorithms build binary trees, while others induce multi-way decision trees. However, when working with numerical attributes, most Decision Trees algorithms choose a threshold value in order to perform binary tests. The particular tests which are used to branch the tree depend on the heuristics used to decide which ones will potentially yield better results. Every possible test which splits the training dataset into several subsets will eventually lead to the construction of a complete decision tree, provided that at least two of the generated subsets are not empty. Each possible test must be evaluated using heuristics and, as most Decision Trees algorithms perform a one-ply lookahead heuristic search without backtracking (i.e. they are greedy), the selected heuristics plays an essential role during the learning process. For instance, most Decision Trees algorithms decide how to branch the tree using some measure of node impurity. Such heuristics, splitting rules henceforth, are devised to try to obtain the "best" decision tree according to some criterion. The objective is usually to minimize the classification error, as well as the resulting tree complexity. Several splitting rules have been proposed in the literature. CART (Quinlan, 1993) uses Gini index to measure the class diversity in the nodes of a decision tree. ID3 method attempts to maximize the information gain achieved through the use of a given attribute to branch the tree. C4.5 (Quinlan, 1993) normalizes this information gain criterion in order to reduce the tree branching factor and adjusts C4.5 criterion to improve its performance with continuous attributes. (De Mantaras, 1991) proposed an alternative normalization based on a distance metrics. (Taylor and Silverman, 1993) proposed the mean posterior improvement criterion as an alternative to the Gini rule for binary trees. All the above-mentioned criteria are impurity-based functions, although there are measures which fall into other categories: some of them measure the difference among the split subsets using distances or angles, emphasizing the disparity of the subsets (on binary trees, typically), while others are statistical measures of independence between the class proportions and the split subsets, emphasizing the reliability of class predictions. Pruning techniques, used in C4.5, have proved to be really useful in order to avoid overfitting. Those branches with lower predictive power are usually pruned once the whole decision tree has been built.

Multi-Classifier Based on Decision Trees

Multi-classifiers are the result of combining several individual classifiers. When individual classifiers are combined appropriately, we usually obtain a better performance in terms of classification precision and/or speed to find a better solution. Multi-classifiers differ among themselves by their diverse characteristics: the number and the type of the individual classifiers; the characteristics of the subsets used by every classifiers of the set; the consideration of the decisions; and the size and the nature of the training sets for the classifiers. Segrera & Moreno (2005). divided the methods for building multi-classifiers in two groups: ensemble and hybrid methods. The first type, such as Bagging and Boosting, induces models that merge classifiers with the same learning algorithm, while introducing modifications in the training data set. The second, type such as Stacking, creates new hybrid learning techniques from different base learning algorithms. An ensemble uses the predictions of multiple base classifiers, typically through majority vote or averaged prediction, to produce a final ensemble-based decision. The ensemble-based predictions typically have lower generalization error rates than the ones obtained by a single model. The difference depends on the type of base-classifiers used, ensemble size, and the diversity or correlation between classifiers (Ahn, Moon, Fazzari, Lim, Chen and Kodell, 2007). They indicate that, over the last few years, three ensemble-voting approaches have received attention by researchers: boosting, bagging and random subspaces. Brieman (2001) defined RF as a classifiers composed by decision trees where every tree h_t has been generated from the set of data training and a vector θ_t of random numbers identically distributed and independent from the vectors θ_1, θ_2,..., θ_{t-1} used to generate the classifiers h_1, h_2, .., h_{t-1}. Each tree provides his unitary vote for the majority class given the entry. Examples of RF are: randomization, Forest-RI (Random Input selection) and Forest-RC (random combination), double-bagging. Hamza & Larocque (2005) conclude several elements such as: RFs are significantly better than Bagging, Boosting and a single tree; their error rate is smaller than the best one obtained by other methods; and they are more robust to noise than the other methods. Consequently, RF is a very good classification method with the following characteristics: it's easy to use; it does not require models, or parameters to select except for the number of predictors to choose at random at each node.

Description of Random Forest

Nowadays, numerous attempts in constructing ensemble of classifiers towards increasing the performance have been introduced (Brieman, 2001; Ho, 1998). Examples of such techniques are Adaboost, Bagging and RFs (Ho, 1998). RFs have been quite successful in classification and regression tasks (Breiman, 1996). RF is a class of ensemble methods specifically designed for decision tree classifiers (Brieman, 2001). It combines the predictions made by multiple decision trees, where each tree is generated based on the values of an independent set of random vectors and with the same distribution for all trees in the forest (Figure 3). Each decision tree is built from

Figure 3. Random Forest model

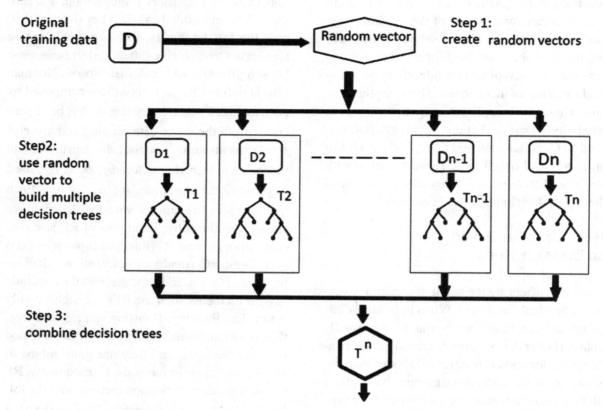

a random subset of the training dataset. It uses a random vector that is generated from some fixed probability distribution, where the probability distribution is varied to focus examples that are hard to classify. A random vector can be incorporated into the tree-growing process in many ways. The leaf nodes of each tree are labeled by estimates of the posterior distribution over the data class labels. Each internal node contains a test that best splits the space of data to be classified. A new, unseen instance is classified by sending it down every tree and aggregating the reached leaf distributions. There are three approaches for RFs such as: Forest-RI, Forest-RC, mixed of Forest-RI and Forest-RC. Forest-RI consists to randomly select F input features to split at each node of the decision tree. As a result, instead of examining all the available features, the decision to split a node is determined from

these selected F features. The tree is then grown to its entirety without any pruning. This may help reduce the bias present in the resulting tree. Once the trees have been constructed, the predictions are combined using a majority voting scheme. The strength and correlation of RFs may depend on the size of F. if F is sufficiently small, then the trees tend to become less correlated. On the other hand, the strength of the tree classifier tends to improve with a larger number of features, F. As a tradeoff, the number of features is commonly chosen to be $F = \log_2 d + 1$, where d is the number of input features. Since only a subset of the features needs to be examined at each node, this approach helps to significantly reduce the runtime of the algorithm.

Forest-RC is used to create combination of the input features. In case the number of original features d is too small, then it is difficult to choose an independent set of random features for building the decision trees. One way to increase the features space is to create linear combination of the input features. Specifically, at each node, a new feature is generated by randomly selecting L of the input features. The input features are linearly combined using coefficients generated from a uniform distribution in the range of [-1, +1]. At each node, F of such randomly combined new features are generated, and the best of them is subsequently selected to split the node.

A third approach for generating the random trees is to randomly select one of the F best splits at each node of the decision tree. This approach may potentially generate trees that are more correlated than Forest-RI and Forest–RC, unless F is sufficiently large. It also does not have the runtime savings of Forest-RI and Forest–RC because the algorithm must examine all the splitting features at each node of the decision tree.

The use of RFs technique has provides some desirable characteristics shown such as: it is unexcelled in accuracy among current algorithms, it runs efficiently on large databases, it is relatively robust to outliers and noise; it is simple and easily parallelized; it is faster than bagging or boosting; it can handle thousands of input variables without variable deletion; it gives estimates of what variables are important in the classification; it generates an internal unbiased estimate of the generalization error as the forest building progresses, it has an effective method for estimating missing data and maintains accuracy when a large proportion of the data are missing, it has methods for balancing error in class population unbalanced data sets, and it computes proximities between pairs of cases that can be used in clustering.

The generalization error of RFs classifiers depends on the strength of the individual trees in the forest and the correlation between them. However, it has theoretically proven that the upper bound for generalization error of RFs converges to the following expression, when the number of trees is sufficiently large.

$$Generalization\ error \leq \frac{\overline{\rho}\left(1-s^2\right)}{s^2} \qquad (1)$$

where $\overline{\rho}$ is the average correlation among the trees and s is a quantity that measures the strength of the tree classifiers. The strength of a set of classifiers refers to the average performance of the classifiers, where performance is measured probabilistically in terms of the classifier's margin:

$$m\arg in,\ M\left(X,Y\right) = $$
$$P\left(\hat{Y}_\theta = Y\right) - \max_{Z \neq Y} P\left(\hat{Y}_\theta = Z\right) \qquad (2)$$

where $\hat{Y}_\theta$ is the predicted class of X according to a classifier built from some random vector θ. The higher the margin is, the more likely it is that the classifier correctly predicts a given example X. As the trees become more correlated or the strength of the ensemble decreases, the generalization error bound tends to increase. Randomization helps to reduce the correlation among decision trees so that the generalization error of the ensemble can be improved.

Techniques Applied for Attributes Reduction

In the literature, much effort has been made to deal with the attribute reduction problem (Thangavel, Shen, Pethalakshmi, 2006; Moudani, Shahin, Chakik, Mora-Camino, 2011; Robnik-Sikonja, 2004). Some computational intelligence methods (GenRSAR, AntRSAR, SimRSAR, and TSAR) have been presented to solve the attribute reduction problem. GenRSAR is a genetic-algorithm-based method and its fitness function takes into account both the size of subset and its evaluated suitability. AntRSAR is an ant colony-based method in which the number of ants is set to the number of attributes, with each ant starting on a different attribute. Ants construct possible solutions until they reach a RS reduct. SimRSAR employs a simulated annealing based attribute selection mechanism. SimRSAR tries to update solutions, which are attribute subsets, by considering three attributes to be added to the current solution or to be removed from it. Optimizing the objective function attempts to maximize the RS dependency while minimizing the subset cardinality. The TSAR method proposed in Hedar, Wangy, & Fukushima (2008) is based on using the Tabu Search (TS) neighborhood search methodology for searching reducts of an information system. TS is a heuristic method originally proposed by (Glover & Laguna, 1997). It has primarily been proposed and developed for combinatorial optimization problems, and has shown its capability of dealing with various difficult problems. Moreover, there have been some attempts to develop TS for continuous optimization problems (Hedar & Fukushima, 2006). TS neighborhood search is based on two main concepts; avoiding return to a recently visited solution, and accepting downhill moves to escape from local maximum information. Some search history information is reserved to help the search process to behave more intelligently. Specifically, the best reducts found so far and the frequency of choosing each attribute are saved to provide the diversification and intensification schemes with more promising solutions. TSAR invokes three diversification and intensification schemes; diverse solution generation, best reduct shaking which attempts to reduce its cardinality, and elite reducts inspiration.

OSTEOPOROSIS SOLUTION APPROACH AND METHODOLOGY

In this section, we present an intelligent classification solution which is based on dynamic reduced sets of features while preserving the solution quality. This approach is validated by using RF decision tree classification technique to identify the osteoporosis cases (Figure 4). The study population is composed of 2845 adults.

Description of the Proposed Solution

The strategy reported here can be described as a KDD (Knowledge discovery in databases) experiment. Following a typical KDD framework, where Data Mining is the core in the overall process, the experiment went through several steps, starting from the stage of gaining profound knowledge of the domain till the actual use of discovered knowledge. A description of database, source of data, pre-processing steps (cleaning, transformation, and integration) is given here.

Figure 4. Solution approach based on roadmap of the KDD process

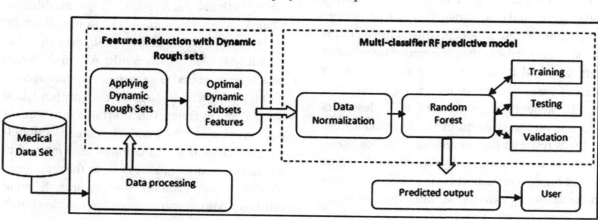

Data Source

During data collection process and after analysis based on experts' knowledge, a set of collected data related to osteoporosis information for about 2845 patients is established. All records gathered from the real cases are processed by using the FRAX tool (i.e. WHO Fracture Risk Assessment) in order to predict the appropriate risk level. FRAX is a major milestone towards helping health professionals worldwide to improve identification of patients at high risk of fracture. The FRAX algorithms give the 10-year probability of fracture. The output is a web-based calculation tool assesses the ten-year risk probability of hip fracture and the 10-year probability of a major osteoporotic fracture (clinical spine, forearm, hip or shoulder fracture). The FRAX models have been developed from studying population-based cohorts from Europe, North America, Asia and Australia.

The osteoporosis risk factors for each patient are defined and saved into a .csv file representing the target dataset for our study.

Data Description

The study is based on a set of relevant features collected and defined after discussion with experts. Table 1 lists the description of features that are significant to osteoporosis disease. The results provided by FRAX are presented as probability values which are normalized based on experts knowledge in order to determine the set of risk level classes (Table 2).

Data Processing

Data are transformed and normalized in order to fit with the requirements of the classification techniques used in our case. Moreover, some

Table 1. Osteoporosis factors including in study

Attribute	Type	Description
Age	Numeric	Between 40 and 90 years.
BMI= weight/(height)^2	Numeric	a.Weight:∈[34kg-110kg] / b.Height: ∈[139cm-185cm]
Previous fracture	Boolean	
Osteoporosis Heredity	Boolean	
Smoking	Boolean	
Glucocorticoids	Boolean	Treatment for more than 3 months at a dose of 5 mg daily or more.
Rheumatoids	Boolean	
Secondary osteoporosis	Boolean	Premature menopause (before 45 years), chronic malnutrition, or malabsorption & chronic liver disease.
Excess alcohol	Boolean	3 unit/day or more
Estrogene	Numeric	premenopausal: 30 to 400 pg/mL; postmenopausal: 0 to 30 pg/mL
Calcium	Numeric	[8.5mg/dl- 10.2 mg/dl].
Vitamin D	Numeric	[30.0 ng/ml - 74.0 ng/ml]
BMD value	Numeric	Normal bone: T-score better than -1 Osteopenia:T-score between -1 and -2.5 Osteoporosis: T-score less than 2.5
Excess caffeine	Boolean	
Immobilization	Boolean	Ex: long immobilization after a fracture

Table 2. Osteoporosis risk level

Class Name	Range
No risk	< 5%
Low risk	[5%-20%[
Moderate risk	[20%-40%[
High risk	[40%-50%[
Severe risk	>50%

data collected to build the database requests to be cleaned, integrated, and normalized to realize the process.

CLASSIFICATION USING RF BASED ON REDUCED SET OF FEATURES

In this section, we describe the proposed methodology which is based RF technique associated to reduced subsets of features in order to predict osteoporosis patients. The reduction of the features is processed by applying the optimal technique of Dynamic programming (DP), leading to generate dynamic equivalence subsets of features.

Dynamic Attribute Reduction Approach

An intelligent approach using DP is applied to deal with the generation of optimal subsets of features (Bellman, 1957). The results help to generate a suitable classification related to the considered problem where the constraints are involved in verifying the validity of the developed solution. In fact, as shown in the choice of the criterion, it is to maximize the dependence or the accuracy degree in our solution which in principle meets all the constraints level. Using DP technique leads to generate dynamic equivalence subsets of features or attributes. It becomes a problem of discrete combinatorial optimization and applying DP approach leads to get an exact solution. This can be effective for the treatment of combinatorial

optimization problems, in a static, dynamic or stochastic, but only if the level constraints are present in limited numbers (Moudani, Shahin, Chakik, Mora-Camino, 2011). Indeed, scaling constraints level lead to address every step of the optimization process exponentially growing number of states within the parameters sizing the problem, making it impossible to process numerically the problem of consequent dimensions. The proposed method, called Dynamic Attribute Reduction (DAR), shows promising and competitive performance compared with some other computational intelligence tools in terms of solution qualities since it produces optimistic reduced attribute subsets. To implement the DAR method, it is necessary to define two key elements: the states and the stages and the various possible levels of constraints associated with dynamic assignment. Solving the problem of DAR to build the minimal subsets of attributes by the proposed schema leads to the following mathematical formulation:

J : Is the number of stages which is associated to the number of attributes;

I : Is the number of states which is based on the super set of attributes;

E_j : Is the number of states associated to stage j;

X_j : Represents the decision vector taken at stage j;

$\sum_{j=1}^{J} p_{ij} x_{ij}$: Represents the sum of accuracies associated to a sequence of decisions $\tilde{x} = (\tilde{x}_1, \tilde{x}_2, \cdots \tilde{x}_j)$ which starts from the initial state e_0 to the current state e_j ;

$TR_{ij}(e_{i,j-1}, x_{ij}) = e_{ij}$: represents the state transition.

Therefore, solving this problem involves finding an optimal sequence $\hat{x} = (\hat{x}_1, \hat{x}_2, \cdots \hat{x}_J)$ that starts from the initial state e_0 brings us to the state e_J while maximizing the precision rate with a reduced number of attributes. The principle of optimality of DP shows that whatever the decision in stage J brings us from state $e_{j-1} \in E_{j-1}$ to state $e_j \in E_j$, the portion of the policy between e_0 and e_{j-1} must be optimal.

However, applying this principle of optimality, we can calculate step by step $F(J, e_J)$ using the following recurrence equation:

$$F(j, e_j) =$$
$$\underset{\{x_{ij} \in X_j / e_{ij} = TR_{ij}(e_{i,j-1}, x_{ij})\}}{MAX} \left\{ p_{ij} . x_{ij} + F(j-1, e_{j-1}) \right\}$$
(3)

with $F(0, e_0) = 0$

However, as the precisions p_{ij} is based on the dependence degree of the attributes, it seems that for each state of each stage it is necessary to reassess the precisions following the path leading to it.

The effectiveness of the algorithm described above is assessed by temporal and memory space complexity depending on the number of iterations needed to obtain the solution (s). The evaluation of the number of iterations is done in the worst case. Indeed, it is impossible in the general case to count the exact number of paths to build in order to solve the optimization problem. The temporal complexity associated while processing this problem is the order of:

$$\sim O\left(I^3 \times J^3\right)$$
(4)

However, the memory space required for the algorithm developed here depends on the number of states and the number of stages considered. Indeed, the number of states set the maximum number of vertices to be considered in one step.

This number multiplied by the number of stages defined here also helps to set the maximum number of vertices in the graph solutions. Thus, the number of variables to remember throughout the resolution process is the order of:

$$\sim O(I \times J)$$
(5)

Association of RF and DAR for Predicting the Osteoporosis Cases

The main concept of the proposed approach is the build optimally, step by step; the dynamic features subsets for constructing the effective RF decision tree. The use of DP permits to evaluate the accuracy of the proposed model reached at a given stage with defined features subsets. Therefore, the criterion to be optimized is related to the accuracy deduced from the considered dynamic subsets of features. The accuracy of the prediction can be improved gradually as the size of these subsets may develop. At the end of this process, the highest accuracy associated to an optimal reduced subset(s) is retained as solution.

RESULTS ANALYSIS AND DISCUSSION

The results of the classification techniques applied in this study are now processed and analyzed in order to compare the relative performance followed by an interpretation, validation and discussion. We have concluded some features stated as below:

- Age and BMI are the most effective attributes that lead to Osteoporosis prediction. The risk level is proportional to the age, inversely proportional to BMI;

- The influence of previous fracture and heredity is highly important, especially when both are available;
- Alcohol or smoking alone has no effects on this disease;
- The risk level 'No Risk' is not available when the age factor is above 80 years.

Moreover, the performance evaluation of the prediction system is based on some parameters such as: Attributes reduction, Misclassification rate, and Accuracy. The results issued by applying several decision trees techniques are summarized in Table 3 and Figure 5. The variation of misclassification rate between the different techniques shows that the rate of the incorrectly classified instance (0.0007%) is the lowest by using Forest-RC comparing to the other set of techniques presented. ID3 decision tree produces the highest rate of misclassification (0.1543). Therefore, the accuracy rate of Forest-RI is the best among the different techniques presented in Table 3. The classification results using RFs are obtained from ten-fold cross-validation. However, we conclude that the initial number of attributes has been reduced while using RFs multi-classifier technique from 16 to 9. The relevant features are only taken into consideration which leads to enhance the complexity of the proposed model by focusing the study based on reduced features. This number is somehow great when using ID3 and J48 techniques.

After analyzing the values of different parameter, the performance of the classification process generates a highly precision while using RF multi-classifier decision trees, especially, when using the variant Forest-RC which provides the highest accuracy rate. For this reason, the proposed Predictive Osteoporosis System (POS) is built based on RFs multi-classifier decision trees in order to build a high accuracy and robustness solution.

In Table 4, we show a prototype of instances as they are fed into the Predictive Osteoporosis System (POS). It displays the classification provided by both POS and FRAX tools. As mentioned in the Table 2, FRAX classification is normalized based on experts' knowledge in order to define the appropriate risk level. The obtained results show high accuracy prediction using POS. The data used in this study has been obtained while processing several patients' information that covers almost the whole cases validated by experts'. Also, all the results given by POS are validated by physicians, so the output of the model is reliable but this will not exclude some error maybe occur.

IMPLEMENTATION OF THE TOOL POS

In order to allow the non-technical persons or users of the system to utilize this tool, we have implemented an Osteoporosis Risk Prediction Web based system. It has been developed in such

Table 3. Results of classification techniques parameters

Classification Methods	Reduced # of Attributes (Initial, Reduced)	Incorrectly Classified Instances	Error Rate
J48	(16, 11)	15	0.0052
ID3	(16, 13)	439	0.1543
Forest-RC	(16, 9)	2	0.0007
Forest-RI	(16, 9)	4	0.0017

Figure 5. Accuracy of the classification techniques

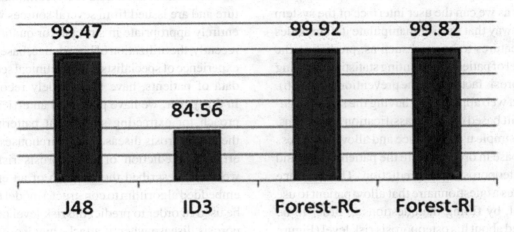

Table 4. Comparison of predicting level risk between POS and FRAX

Inst	Input	Output by POS	Output by FRAX	Match
1	48 23.8 0 0 0 0 1 0 0 ...	4	14%	Yes
2	55 19.5 1 1 0 0 0 0 0 ...	4	6.4%	Yes
3	79 18 1 1 1 0 0 1 0 ...	4	12%	Yes
4	82 41.3 0 0 1 0 1 0 1 ...	5	20%	Yes
5	42 34.2 0 1 0 1 1 1 0 ...	3	3.3%	Yes
6	90 23.6 0 0 1 0 0 0 1 ...	7	51%	Yes
7	56 21.3 1 1 1 1 0 1 0 ...	3	19%	No
8	86 18.9 0 0 1 0 1 1 1 ...	6	46%	Yes
9	63 33.5 0 1 1 0 0 1 0 ...	5	13%	No
10	40 21 0 0 1 1 1 0 1 ...	4	8.5%	Yes
11	77 15.8 1 0 0 0 1 0 0 ...	5	29%	Yes
12	45 23.2 0 0 0 0 1 1 1 ...	4	6.3%	Yes
13	87 21.6 0 0 0 0 1 1 1 ...	6	46%	Yes
14	76 29 0 0 1 1 1 1 1 ...	4	13%	Yes
15	51 17 0 1 0 1 0 1 1 ...	3	4.6%	Yes
16	78 19.8 0 0 1 1 1 1 1 ...	4	17%	Yes
17	60 23.7 0 0 0 0 0 0 0 ...	5	27%	Yes
18	66 28.3 1 1 0 0 0 0 0 ...	4	9.4%	Yes
19	42 20.9 0 1 1 1 1 0 0 ...	3	4.4%	Yes
20	81 24.1 0 0 0 1 1 1 1 ...	5	23%	Yes
...	....	...	...	...

a manner that it can be used easily and in comfortable way without the request to have the support of a technical person. In fact, we have simplified as most as we can the user interface of the system and the way that its user manipulate it. It includes some features to be used such as: predicting the risk level of patients, presenting statistics, showing osteoporosis factors and the prevention (Figure 6). POS is a web application, having the system's engine built based on RFs classification algorithms. It has a simple user interface and allows an access to database in order to store the patients' data and their osteoporosis risk prediction. The interface illustrates a questionnaire that allow patient to use this tool, by filling the questions in order to be informed about his osteoporosis risk level (Figure 7). This questionnaire resumes all necessary data including in our database.

CONCLUSION AND PERSPECTIVES

Data mining in health care management is not analogous to the other fields due to the reason that the data existing here are heterogeneous in nature and that a set of ethical, legal, and social limitations apply to private medical information. Osteoporosis related data are voluminous in nature and are issued from several sources with not entirely appropriate in structure or quality. Most recently, the utilization of knowledge, based on the experience of specialists and the clinical screening data of patients, have been widely recognized. In this paper, we have presented an efficient approach for extracting significant patterns from the osteoporosis disease data warehouses for the efficient prediction of osteoporosis risk. This work has described the research of an effective embedded algorithm to construct a model that can be used in order to predict the risk level of osteoporosis disease when it attacks any woman. The experimental results have illustrated the efficacy of the designed prediction system in predicting the osteoporosis disease. However, we can state the most important steps as:

- The results issued from POS has not focuses only on informing about the presence of a risk or not, but also it provides the level of the osteoporosis risk for the patient.

Figure 6. POS Home page interface

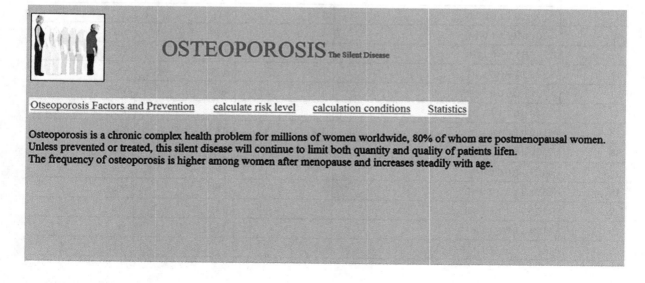

Figure 7. POS Interface for calculating Osteoporosis Risk Level

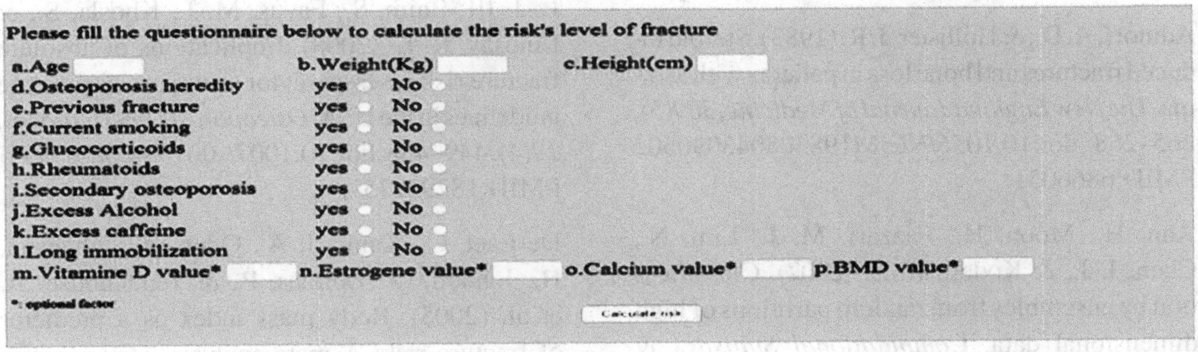

- The proposed tool, POS, contributes in managing osteoporosis by reducing the risk of fractures, identifying early the patients, assessing accurately the risk, and improving the patient's perception of that risk.
- The key step is the compilation of representative and expressive data that will cover the large number of cases in order to generalize and extract rules by determining the effect of each attribute.
- Enhancing the complexity by defining the optimal number of relevant attributes that can be used in order to build the model without affecting the solution quality.
- Building the model for prediction of the osteoporosis risk level using multi-classifier decision trees instead of one decision tree.
- Performing an evaluation of the performance of the proposed model based on set of benchmark techniques applied in classification problems such as: RFs and its variants, ID3, J48.

In perspective, we suggest to integrate a set of positive features in order to improve the knowledge quality services, such as:

- Studying the relation with the surrounding countries known as the highest osteoporosis rates in the world in order to compare it with the Lebanese population and to get relevant knowledge.
- Improving the quality of the prediction by applying new classification techniques (Time Series, Bayesian Relief Network).
- Applying Text Mining to mine the vast amount of unstructured data available in Osteoporosis databases.
- Providing greater accessibility in order to help physicians make informed about the treatment decisions. POS may become accessible as a real online questionnaire in clinical settings using the Internet.
- Ensuring that high-risk individuals are identified and ultimately leading to the more effective management of patients with osteoporosis.
- Providing fast and portable physician access to the risk evaluation by proposing an iPhone POS application aiming to make the diagnostic tool more accessible for patients.

ACKNOWLEDGMENT

Our thanks to the experts who have contributed towards development of the proposed intelligent osteoporosis prediction tool.

REFERENCES

Adinoff, A. D., & Hollister, J. R. (1983). Steroid induced fractures and bone loss in patients with asthma. *The New England Journal of Medicine, 309*(5), 265–268. doi:10.1056/NEJM198308043090502 PMID:6866051

Ahn, H., Moon, H., Fazzari, M. J., Lim, N., Chen, J. J., & Kodell, R. L. (2007). Classification by ensembles from random partitions of high dimensional data. *Computational Statistics & Data Analysis, 51*(12), 6166–6179. doi:10.1016/j.csda.2006.12.043

Bellman, R. E. (1957). *Dynamic programming.* Princeton University Press.

Berzal F, Cubero JC, Marın N, & Sanchez D. (2001). *Building multi-way decision trees with numerical attributes.* Technical report. Unpublished.

Breiman, L. (1996). Bagging predictors. *Machine Learning Journal, 26*(2), 123140.

Breiman, L., Friedman, J. H., Olshen, R. A., & Stone, C. J. (1984). *Classification and regression trees.* Wadsworth.

Brieman, L. (2001). Random forests. In Machine learning. Kluwer Academic Publisher.

Chen, F.-L., & Li, F.-C. (2010). Comparison of the hybrid credit scoring models based on various classifiers. *International Journal of Intelligent Information Technologies, 6*(3), 56–74.

Chiu, J. S., Li, Y. C., Yu, F. C., & Wang, Y. F. (2006). Applying an artificial neural network to predict osteoporosis in the elderly. *Osteoporosis International, 124*, 609–614. PMID:17108584

Dawson-Hughes, B., Tosteson, A. N., Melton, L. J. III, Baim, S., Favus, M. J., Khosla, S., & Lindsay, R. L. (2008). Implications of absolute fracture risk assessment for osteoporosis practice guidelines in the USA. *Osteoporosis International, 19*(4), 449–458. doi:10.1007/s00198-008-0559-5 PMID:18292975

De Laet, C., Kanis, J. A., Oden, A., Johanson, H., Johnell, O., Delmas, P., & Tenenhouse, A. et al. (2005). Body mass index as a predictor of fracture risk: A meta-analysis. *Osteoporosis International, 16*(11), 1330–1338. doi:10.1007/s00198-005-1863-y PMID:15928804

FRAX® WHO Fracture Risk Assessment Tool. (n.d.). Retrieved from http://www.shef.ac.uk/FRAX/

Freund, Y., & Schapire, R. E. (1996). Experiments with a new boosting algorithm. In L. Saitta (Ed.), *Machine Learning: Proceedings of the 13th National Conference.* Morgan Kaufmann.

Glover, F., & Laguna, M. (1997). *Tabu search.* Boston, MA: Kluwer Academic Publishers. doi:10.1007/978-1-4615-6089-0

Hamza, M., & Larocque, D. (2005). An empirical comparison of ensemble methods based on classification trees. *Statistical Computation & Simulation, 75*(8), 629–643. doi:10.1080/00949650410001729472

Hatamzadeh, N., Jalilian, F., Emdadi, S., Rezaei, R., & Mirzaee Ramhormozi, S. (2011). Application of health belief model for predicting osteoporosis-protective behaviors among Iranian women. In *Proceedings of First International & 4th National Congress on health Education & Promotion, 2011.* Academic Press.

Hedar, A., & Fukushima, M. (2006). Tabu search directed by direct search methods for nonlinear global optimization. *European Journal of Operational Research*, *170*(2), 329–349. doi:10.1016/j.ejor.2004.05.033

Hedar, A., Wangy, J., & Fukushima, M. (2008). Tabu search for attribute reduction in rough set theory. *Journal of Soft Computing*, *12*, 9.

Hillbrand, C. (2007). Towards stable model bases for causal strategic decision support systems. *International Journal of Intelligent Information Technologies*, *3*(4), 1–24. doi:10.4018/jiit.2007100101

Ho, T. K. (1998). The random subspace method for constructing decision forests. *IEEE Transactions on Pattern Analysis and Machine Intelligence*, *20*(8), 832844.

Hui, L., Xiaoy, L., Bone, L., Buyea, C., Ramanathan, M., & Zhang, A. (2012). 3D bone microarchitecture modeling and fracture risk prediction. In *Proceedings of ACM-BCB*. ACM.

Kaiquan, S. J. (2011). Classifying consumer comparison opinions to uncover product strengths and weaknesses. *International Journal of Intelligent Information Technologies*, *7*(1), 1–14. doi:10.4018/jiit.2011010101

Kanis, J. A. (2002). *Diagnosis of osteoporosis and assessment of fracture risk*. Academic Press.

Kanis, J. A., Johansson, H., Johnell, O., Oden, A., De Laet, C., Eisman, J. A., & Tenenhouse, A. et al. (2005). Alcohol intake as a risk factor for fracture. *Osteoporosis International*, *16*(7), 737–742. doi:10.1007/s00198-004-1734-y PMID:15455194

Kanis, J. A., Johnell, O., Oden, A., Johansson, H., De Laet, C., Eisman, J. A., & Tenenhouse, A. et al. (2005). Smoking and fracture risk: A meta-analysis. *Osteoporosis International*, *16*(2), 155–162. doi:10.1007/s00198-004-1640-3 PMID:15175845

Kanis, J. A., Johnell, O., Oden, A., Johansson, H., & McCloskey, E. (2008). FRAX and the assessment of fracture probability in men and women from the UK. *Osteoporosis International*, *19*(4), 385–397. doi:10.1007/s00198-007-0543-5 PMID:18292978

Kanis, J. A., Oden, A., Johnell, O., Johansson, H., De Laet, C., Brown, J., & Yoshimura, N. et al. (2007). The use of clinical risk factors enhances the performance of BMD in the prediction of hip and osteoporotic fractures in men and women. *Osteoporosis International*, *18*(8), 1033–1046. doi:10.1007/s00198-007-0343-y PMID:17323110

Koh, L. K., Sendrine, W. B., & Torralba, T. P. (2001). A simple tool to identify Asian women at increased risk of osteoporosis. *Osteoporosis International*, *12*(8), 699–705. doi:10.1007/s001980170070 PMID:11580084

Lagroue, H. J. III. (2008). Supporting structured group decision making through system-directed user guidance: An experimental study. *International Journal of Intelligent Information Technologies*, *4*(2), 57–74. doi:10.4018/jiit.2008040104

Lopez de Mantaras, R. (1991). A distance-based attribute selection measure for decision tree induction. *Machine Learning*, *6*.

Marko Robnik-Sikonja. (2004). *Improving random forests, machine learning, ECML, proceedings*. Berlin: Springer.

Melton, L. J., Kan, S. H., Wahner, H. W., & Riggs, B. L. (1988). Lifetime fracture risk: An approach to hip fracture risk assessment based on bone mineral density and age. *Journal of Clinical Epidemiology*, *41*, 985–994. doi:10.1016/0895-4356(88)90036-4 PMID:3193143

Moudani W, Shahin A, Chakik F, & Mora-Camino F. (2011). Dynamic rough sets features reduction. *International Journal of Computer Science and Information Security, 9*(4).

Quinlan, J. R. (1986). Learning decision tree classifiers. *ACM Computing Surveys*, 28(1).

Quinlan, J. R. (1993). *C4.5: Programs for machine learning*. Morgan Kaufmann.

Quinlan, J. R. (1996). Improved use of continuous attributes in C4.5. *Journal of Artificial Intelligence Research*, 4.

Schapire. (1997). Boosting the margin: A new explanation for the effectiveness of voting methods. In *Machine Learning: Proceedings of 14th Int. Conference*. Morgan Kaufmann.

Segrera, S., & Moreno, M. (2005). Multiclassifiers: Applications, methods and architectures. In *Proc. of International Workshop on Practical Applications of Agents and Multiagents Systems* (pp. 263–271). Academic Press.

Sen, S. S., Rives, V. P., Messina, O. D., Morales-Torres, J., Riera, G., Angulo-Solimano, J. M., & Ross, P. D. et al. (2005). A risk assessment tool (OsteoRisk) for identifying Latin American women with osteoporosis. *Journal of General Internal Medicine*, 20(3), 245–250. doi:10.1111/j.1525-1497.2005.40900.x PMID:15836528

Tae, K. Y., Sung, K., Deok, W. K., Joon, Y. C., Wan, H. L., Ein, O., & Eun-Cheol, P. (2013). Osteoporosis risk prediction for bone mineral density assessment of postmenopausal women using machine learning. *Yonsei Medical Journal*, 54(6), 1321–1330. doi:10.3349/ymj.2013.54.6.1321 PMID:24142634

Taylor, B. C., Schreiner, P. J., Stone, K. L., Fink, H. A., Cummings, S. R., Nevitt, M. C., & Ensrud, K. E. et al. (2004). Long-term prediction of incident hip fracture risk in elderly white women: Study of osteoporotic fractures. *Journal of the American Geriatrics Society*, 52(9), 1479–1486. doi:10.1111/j.1532-5415.2004.52410.x PMID:15341549

Taylor, P. C., & Silverman, B. W. (1993). Block diagrams and splitting criteria for classification trees. *Statistics and Computing*, 3(4), 147–161. doi:10.1007/BF00141771

Thangavel, K., Shen, Q., & Pethalakshmi, A. (2006). Application of clustering for feature selection based on rough set theory approach. *AIML Journal*, 6(1), 19–27.

Wang, W., & Rea, S. (2005). Intelligent ensemble system aids osteoporosis early detection. In *Proceedings of the 6th World Scientific and Engineering Academy and Society (WSEAS) International Conference on Evolutionary Computing*. WSEAS.

Yildirim, P., Çeken, Ç., Hassanpour, R., Esmelioglu, S., & Tolun, M. R. (2011). Mining MEDLINE for the treatment of osteoporosis. *Journal of Medical Systems*. doi:10.1007/s10916-011-9701-6 PMID:21494854

KEY TERMS AND DEFINITIONS

Data Mining: Data mining, called data or knowledge discovery, is the process of analyzing data from different perspectives and summarizing it into useful information. Data mining software is one of a number of analytical tools for analyzing data and finding correlations or patterns among dozens of fields in large relational databases.

Dynamic Programming: Dynamic programming is used for optimization. It is used for solving complex problems by breaking them down into simpler sub-problems. It allows examining all possible ways to solve the problem and will pick the best solution. It is applicable to problems exhibiting the properties of overlapping sub-problems and optimal sub-structure.

Features Reduction: Features reduction is a commonly used step in machine learning, especially when dealing with a high dimensional space of features. The original feature space is mapped onto a new, reduced dimension space. It is usually performed either by selecting a subset of the original features or/and by constructing some new features.

Osteoporosis: Osteoporosis is a disease of the bones. It happens when your bones become weak and may break from a minor fall or, in serious cases, even from simple actions. In other words, the bones have lost density or mass and its structure tissue has become abnormal.

Predictive Modeling: Predictive modeling is the process by which a model is created or chosen to try to best predict the probability of an outcome. In many cases the model is chosen on the basis of detection theory to try to guess the probability of an outcome given a set amount of input data.

Random Forests: Random forests are an ensemble learning method for classification (and regression) that operate by constructing a multitude of decision trees at training time and outputting the class that is the mode of the classes output by individual trees.

Rough Sets: A rough set is a formal approximation of a crisp set in terms of a pair of sets which give the lower and the upper approximation of the original set. The goal of the rough sets is to generate a set of rules that are high in dependency, discriminating index, and significance.

Compilation of References

Aarts, O., Schraagen, J. M., van Maanen, P.-P., & Ouboter, T. (2012). Online social behavior in Twitter: A literature review. In *Proceedings of 2013 IEEE 13th International Conference on Data Mining Workshops* (pp. 739–746). IEEE. doi:10.1109/ICDMW.2012.139

Ackerman, M., & Halverson, C. (1999). Organizational memory: Processes, boundary objects, and trajectories. In *Proceedings of 32nd Hawaiian International Conference on Systems Science*. Maui, HI: IEEE. Retrieved February 2, 2012 from: www.eecs.umich.edu/~ackerm/pub/99b26/hicss99.pdf

Ackert, L., & Deaves, R. (2009). *Behavioral finance psychology, decision-making, and markets*. Houston, TX: South-Western Educational Publishers.

Adinoff, A. D., & Hollister, J. R. (1983). Steroid induced fractures and bone loss in patients with asthma. *The New England Journal of Medicine*, 309(5), 265–268. doi:10.1056/NEJM198308043090502 PMID:6866051

Agarwal, M., & Cagan, J. (1998). A blend of different tastes: The language of coffeemakers. *Environment and Planning. B, Planning & Design*, 25(2), 205–226. doi:10.1068/b250205

Agarwal, R., & Srikant, R. (2000). Privacy-preserving data mining. In *Proc of the 2000 ACM SIGMOD International Conference on Management of Data* (pp. 439–450). ACM. doi:10.1145/342009.335438

Agrawal, R., Lin, K. I., Sawhney, H. S., & Shim, K. (1995). Fast similarity search in the presence of noise, scaling, and translation in times-series databases. In *Proceedings of the Twenty First International Conference on Very Large Data Bases* (pp. 490-510). Academic Press.

Aguirre-Rodriguez, A. (2014). Cultural factors that impact brand personification strategy effectiveness. *Psychology and Marketing*, 31(1), 70–83. doi:10.1002/mar.20676

Ahn, H., Moon, H., Fazzari, M. J., Lim, N., Chen, J. J., & Kodell, R. L. (2007). Classification by ensembles from random partitions of high dimensional data. *Computational Statistics & Data Analysis*, 51(12), 6166–6179. doi:10.1016/j.csda.2006.12.043

Ali, J. M. (2007). Content-based Image classification and retrieval: A rule-based system using rough sets framework. *International Journal of Intelligent Information Technologies*, 3(3), 41–58. doi:10.4018/jiit.2007070103

Amor, M., Fuentes, L., & Vallecillo, A. (2005). Bridging the gap between agent-oriented design and implementation using MDA*. In *Agent-Oriented Software Engineering V* (LNCS), (vol. 3382, pp. 93-108). Springer-Verlag GmbH.

Anbumani, K., & Nedunchezhian, R. (2006). Rapid privacy preserving algorithm for large databases. *International Journal of Intelligent Information Technologies*, 2(1), 68–81. doi:10.4018/jiit.2006010104

Anumba, C. J. Z., Ren, A., Thorpe, O., Ugwu, O., & Newnham, L. (2003). Negotiation within a multi-agent system for the collaborative design of light industrial buildings. *Advances in Engineering Software*, 34(7), 389–401. doi:10.1016/S0965-9978(03)00038-3

Arbore, A., & Busacca, B. (2009). Customer satisfaction and dissatisfaction in retail banking: Exploring the asymmetric impact of attribute performances. *Journal of Retailing and Consumer Services*, 16(4), 271–280. doi:10.1016/j.jretconser.2009.02.002

Arockiaraj, G., & Baranidharan, K. (2013). Impact of social media on brand awareness for fast moving consumer goods. *International Journal of Logistics & Supply Chain Management Perspectives.*, 2(4), 472–477.

Ashrafi, M. Z., Taniar, D., & Smith, K. (2005). PPDAM: Privacy-preserving distributed association-rule-mining algorithm. *International Journal of Intelligent Information Technologies, 1*(1), 49–69. doi:10.4018/jiit.2005010104

Assawamekin, N., Sunetnanta, T., & Pluempitiwiriyawej, C. (2009). Ontology based multiple respective requirements traceability framework. *Knowledge and Information Systems Journal, 25*(3), 493-522.

Asuncion, A., Welling, M., Smyth, P., & Teh, Y.-W. (2009). On smoothing and inference for topic models. *UAI.* Retrieved from http://www.ics.uci.edu/ asuncion/pubs/UAI_09.pdf

Athawale, V. M., & Chakraborty, S. (2010). Facility location selection using PROMETHEE II method. In *Proceedings of the 2010 International Conference on Industrial Engineering and Operations Management (IEOM 2010)* (pp. 59-64). Bangladesh Society of Mechanical Engineers Press.

Aydin, I., Karakose, M., & Akin, E. (2009). The prediction algorithm based on fuzzy logic using time series data mining method. *World Academy of Science, Engineering, and Technology, 51*(27), 91–98.

Azevedo, A., & Santos, M. F. (2008). KDD, SEMMA and CRISP-DM: A parallel overview. In Ajith Abraham (Ed.), *Proceedings of IADIS European Conference on Data Mining* (pp. 182–185). IADIS.

Azzam, U. A., Sadeeq, U. M., Ahmed, J., & Riaz-ul-Hasnain. (2009). Traffic responsive signal timing plan generation based on neural network. International Journal of Intelligent Information Technologies, 5(3), 84-101.

Bailey, J., & Pearson, S. (1983). Development of a tool for measuring and analyzing computer user satisfaction. *Management Science, 29*(5), 530–545. doi:10.1287/mnsc.29.5.530

Bannon, L., & Schmidt, L. (1989). CSCW: Four characters in search of a context. In *Proceedings of the First European Conference on Computer Supported Cooperative Work.* Retrieved February 2, 2012 from: http://www.it-c.dk/~schmidt/papers/cscw4chart.pdf

BARC. (2009). *Performance management – Aktuelle Herausforderungen und Perspektiven.* Retrieved from www.barc.de/marktforschung/.../performance-management.html

Bargiela, A., & Pedrycz, W. (2003). *Granular computing: An introduction.* Amsterdam: Kluwer Academic Publishers. doi:10.1007/978-1-4615-1033-8

Barnes, S. J., & Böhringer, M. (2011). Modeling Use continuance behavior in microblogging services: The case of Twitter. *Journal of Computer Information Systems, 51*(4), 1–13.

Barwise, J., & Seligman, J. (1997). The logic of distributed systems. *Cambridge Tracts in Theoretical Computer Science, 44.*

Basilsi, V. R., Caldiera, G., & Rombach, H. D. (1994). Experience factory. In Encyclopedia of software engineering (vol. 1, pp. 469-476). John Wiley & Sons.

Baskerville, R., & Pries-Heje, J. (2010). Erklärende Designtheorie. *Wirtschaftsinformatik, 5/2010*(5), 259–271. doi:10.1007/s11576-010-0237-z

Bateman, J.A. (2010). A linguistic ontology of space for natural language processing. *Journal of Artificial Intelligence, 174*(14), 1027-1071.

Beale, M. H., Hagan, M. T., & Demuth, H. B. (2011). *R2011b documentation -Matlab help pages of neural network toolbox.* Retrieved October 2011 from http: // www.mathworks.com/help/pdf_doc/nnet/nnet_ug.pdf

Beaubouef, T., Petry, F., & Yager, R. (2011). Attribute generalization with rough set hierarchies. In *Proceedings World Conference on Soft Computing* (pp. 222-227). New York: Springer.

Bellman, R. E. (1957). *Dynamic programming.* Princeton University Press.

Bemelmans, R., Gelderblom, G., Jonker, P., & de Witte, L. (2012). Socially assistive robots in elderly care: A systematic review into effects and effectiveness. *Journal of the American Medical Directors Association*, *13*(2), 114–120. doi:10.1016/j.jamda.2010.10.002 PMID:21450215

Benevenuto, F., Magno, G., Rodrigues, T., & Almeida, V. (2010). Detecting spammers on Twitter. In *Proceedings of Collaboration, Electronic Messaging, Anti-Abuse and Spam Conference (CEAS)*. Retrieved from http://ceas.cc/2010/papers/Paper%2021.pdf

Benoit, R., Pierre, M., & Jerome, S. (2011). An algorithm for calculi segmentation on ureteroscopic images. *International Journal of Computer Assisted Radiology and Surgery*, *6*(2), 237–246. doi:10.1007/s11548-010-0504-x PMID:20574798

Bermingham, A., & Smeaton, A. F. (2010). Classifying sentiment in microblogs: Is brevity an advantage? In ACM (Ed.), *Proceedings of the 19th ACM International Conference on Information and Knowledge Management* (pp. 1833–1836). New York: ACM. doi:10.1145/1871437.1871741

Berre, D. L. (2006). Monitoring and diagnosing software requirements. *Journal of Automated Software Engineering*, *16*(1), 3–35.

Bertino, E., Lin, D., & Jiang, W. (2008). A survey of quantification of privacy preserving data mining algorithms. In Privacy-preserving data mining. Springer. doi:10.1007/978-0-387-70992-5_8

Berzal F, Cubero JC, Marın N, & Sanchez D. (2001). *Building multi-way decision trees with numerical attributes*. Technical report. Unpublished.

Beyer, H., & Holtzblatt, K. (1998). *Contextual design: Defining customer-centered systems*. San Francisco, CA: Morgan Kaufmann.

Bi, B., Tian, Y., Sismanis, Y., Balmin, A., & Cho, J. (2014). Scalable topic-specific influence analysis on microblogs. In B. Carterette, F. Diaz, C. Castillo, & D. Metzler (Eds.), *Proceedings of the 7th ACM International Conference* (pp. 513–522). ACM. doi:10.1145/2556195.2556229

Bijker, W. (1995). *Of bicycles, bakelites, and bulbs: Toward a theory of sociotechnical change*. Cambridge, MA: MIT Press.

Bitici, U., Mendibil, K., Nudurupati, S., Turner, T., & Garengo, P. (2004). The interplay between performance measurement, organizational culture and management style. *Measuring Business Excellence*, *8*(3), 28–41. doi:10.1108/13683040410555591

Black, F. (1969). The capital asset pricing model: Some empirical tests. In *Studies in the theory of capital markets*. Academic Press.

Blackler, F. (1995). Knowledge, knowledge work and organizations: An overview and interpretation. *Organization Studies*, *16*(6), 1021–1046. doi:10.1177/017084069501600605

Blei, D. M., & Lafferty, J. D. (2006). Dynamic topic models. *ICML*. Retrieved from http://portal.acm.org/citation.cfm?id=1143859

Blei, D. M., & McAuliffe, J. D. (2007). Supervised topic models. *NIPS*. Retrieved from http://books.nips.cc/papers/files/nips20/NIPS2007_0893.pdf

Blei, D., & Lafferty, J. (2009). *Topic models*. Retrieved September 25, 2011 from http://www.cs.princeton.edu/~blei/papers/BleiLafferty2009.pdf

Blei, D. M., & Lafferty, J. D. (2007). A correlated topic model of science. *AAS*, *1*(1), 17–35.

Blei, D. M., Ng, A., & Jordan, M. (2003). Latent Dirichlet allocation. *JMLR*, *3*, 993–1022.

Blei, D., Ng, A., & Jordan, M. (2003). Latent Dirichlet allocation. *Journal of Machine Learning Research*, *3*, 933–1022.

Bodea, C., Dascalu, M., & Serbanati, L. D. (2012). An ontology-alignment based recommendation mechanism for improving the acquisition and implementation of managerial training services in project oriented organizations. In *Proceedings of IEEE International Conference and Workshops on Engineering of Computer Based Systems* (ECBS) (pp.257-266). Novi Sad, Serbia: ECBS. doi:10.1109/ECBS.2012.14

Boersch, C., & Elschen, R. (2007). *Die grenzenlose Unternehmung: Information, Organisation und Management*. Wiesbaden: Gabler.

Böhringer, M., & Gluchowski, P. (2009). Microblogging. *Informatik Spektrum*, *32*(6), 505–510. doi:10.1007/s00287-009-0383-0

Boisot, M. (1998). *Knowledge assets: Securing competitive advantage in the information economy*. New York: Oxford University Press.

Bommanna, R. K., Madheswaran, M., & Thyagarajah, K. (2006). A general segmentation scheme for contouring kidney region in ultrasound kidney images using improved higher order spline interpolation. *International Journal of Biological and Life Sciences*, *2*(2), 81–88.

Bommanna, R. K., Madheswaran, M., & Thyagarajah, K. (2010). Texture pattern analysis of kidney tissues for disorder identification and classification using dominant gabor wavelet. *Journal Machine Vision and Applications*, *21*(3), 287–300. doi:10.1007/s00138-008-0159-6

Bose, R. (2006). Understanding management data systems for enterprise performance management. *Industrial Management & Data Systems*, *106*(1), 43–59. doi:10.1108/02635570610640988

Bosilj-Vuksic, V., Milanovic, L., Skrinjar, R., & Indihar-Stemberger, M. (2008). Organizational performance measures for business process management: A performance measurement guideline. In *Proceedings of Tenth International Conference on Computer Modeling and Simulation (uksim 2008)*. IEEE. doi:10.1109/UKSIM.2008.114

Bradshaw, J. (1997). An introduction to software agents. In Software agents (pp. 3-46). Menlo Park, CA: AAAI Press.

Braz, R., Scavarda, L., & Martins, R. (2011). Reviewing and improving performance measurement systems: An action research. *International Journal of Production Economics*, *133*(2), 751–760. doi:10.1016/j.ijpe.2011.06.003

Breiman, L. (1996). Bagging predictors. *Machine Learning Journal*, *26*(2), 123140.

Breiman, L., Friedman, J. H., Olshen, R. A., & Stone, C. J. (1984). *Classification and regression trees*. Wadsworth.

Bresciani, P., Giorgini, P., Giunchiglia, F., Mylopoulos, J., & Perini, A. (2002). TROPOS: An agent-oriented software development methodology. *Journal of Autonomous Agents and Multi-Agent Systems*.

Brieman, L. (2001). Random forests. In Machine learning. Kluwer Academic Publisher.

Broadbent, J. (2007). *If you can't measure it how can you manage it*. Research Paper, School of Business and Social Sciences, Roehampton University.

Budny, D. D., & Paul, C. (2003). Working with students and parents to improve the freshman retention. *Journal of Science, Mathematics, Engineering, and Technology Education*, *4*(3&4), 45–53.

Burch, R. (2010). Deduction, induction, and abduction. In *The Stanford encyclopedia of philosophy*. Retrieved from http://plato.stanford.edu/archives/fall2010/entries/peirce/

Buytendijk, F. (2009). *Performance leadership: The next practices to motivate your people, align stakeholders, and lead your industry*. New York: McGraw-Hill.

Byrd, T., Thrasher, E., Lang, T., & Davidson, N. (2006). A process-oriented perspective of IS success: Examining the impact of IS on operational cost. *Omega*, *34*(5), 448–460. doi:10.1016/j.omega.2005.01.012

Caire, G., Chainho, P., Evans, R., Garijo, F., Gomez Sanz, J., Kearney, P., . . . Stark, J. (2001). *Agent Oriented Anlysis Using MESSAGE/UML*. Paper presented at the Second International Workshop on Agent-Oriented Software Engineering, Montreal, Canada.

Callon, M. (1986). Some elements of a sociology of translation: Domestication of the scallops and the fishermen of St Brieux Bay. In J. Law (Ed.), *Power, action and belief: A new sociology of knowledge?* (pp. 196–229). London: Routledge & Kegan Paul.

Cant, M. C., Wiid, J. A., & Hung, Y. T. (2013). The importance of branding for south african SMES: An exploratory study. *Corporate Ownership & Control*, *8*, 735–744.

Cao, L. (2003). Support vector machines experts for time series forecasting. *Neurocomputing*, *51*, 321–339. doi:10.1016/S0925-2312(02)00577-5

Carbonneau, R., Vahidov, R., & Laframboise, K. (2007). Machine learning-based demand forecasting in supply chains. *International Journal of Intelligent Information Technologies*, *3*(4), 40–57. doi:10.4018/jiit.2007100103

Caridi, M., Crippa, L., Perego, A., Sianesi, A., & Tumino, A. (2010). Measuring visibility to improve supply chain performance: A quantitative approach. *Benchmarking: An International Journal*, *17*(4), 593–615. doi:10.1108/14635771011060602

Carstensen, P., & Schmidt, K. (2002). Computer supported cooperative work: New challenges to systems design. In *Handbook of human factors*. Retrieved February 2, 2012 from: http://www.it-c.dk/people/schmidt/papers/cscw_intro.pdf

Carver, C. A., Howard, R. A., & Lane, W. D. (1999). Enhancing student learning through hypermedia courseware and incorporation of student learning styles. *IEEE Transactions on Education*, *42*(1), 33–38. doi:10.1109/13.746332

Cecconi, P., Franceschini, F., & Galetto, M. (2007). The conceptual link between measurements, evaluations, preferences and indicators, according to the representational theory. *European Journal of Operational Research*, *179*(1), 174–185. doi:10.1016/j.ejor.2006.03.018

Chang, C. C., Chen, P. L., Chiu, F. R., & Chen, Y. K. (2009). Application of neural networks and Kano's method to content recommendation in web personalization. Expert Systems with Applications, 36(3), 5310-5316.

Chang, J., Boyd-Graber, J., Wang, C., Gerrish, S., & Blei, D. M. (2009). Reading tea leaves: How humans interpret topic models. *NIPS*. Retrieved from http://books.nips.cc/papers/files/nips22/NIPS2009_0125.pdf

Chase, S. C. (2002). A model for user interaction in grammar-based design systems. *Automation in Construction*, *11*(2), 161–172. doi:10.1016/S0926-5805(00)00101-1

Chen, F., & Han, C. (2007). Time series forecasting based on wavelet KPCA and support vector machine. In *Proceedings of the IEEE International Conference on Automation and Logistics* (pp. 1487-1491). IEEE. doi:10.1109/ICAL.2007.4338806

Chen, F.-L., & Li, F.-C. (2010). Comparison of the hybrid credit scoring models based on various classifiers. *International Journal of Intelligent Information Technologies*, *6*(3), 56–74.

Chen, S. M., & Chang, Y. C. (2011). Weighted fuzzy rule interpolation based on GA-based weight-learning techniques. *IEEE Transactions on Fuzzy Systems*, *19*(4), 729–744. doi:10.1109/TFUZZ.2011.2142314

Chen, T. (2010). A fuzzy-neural approach with collaboration mechanisms for semiconductor yield forecasting. *International Journal of Intelligent Information Technologies*, *6*(3), 17–33. doi:10.4018/jiit.2010070102

Chen, T. (2011). A dynamically optimized fluctuation smoothing rule for scheduling jobs in a wafer fabrication factory. *International Journal of Intelligent Information Technologies*, *7*(4), 47–64. doi:10.4018/jiit.2011100103

Cherkassky, V. (2002). Model complexity control and statistical learning theory. *Natural Computing*, *1*(1), 109–133. doi:10.1023/A:1015007927558

Chiu, J. S., Li, Y. C., Yu, F. C., & Wang, Y. F. (2006). Applying an artificial neural network to predict osteoporosis in the elderly. *Osteoporosis International*, *124*, 609–614. PMID:17108584

Choi, N., Song, I.-Y., & Han, H. (2006). A survey on ontology mapping. *SIGMOD Record*, *35*(3), 34–41. doi:10.1145/1168092.1168097

Chung, J., & Mustafaraj, E. (2011). Can collective sentiment expressed on Twitter predict political elections? In Burgard W. Roth D. (Eds.), *Proceedings of the Twenty-Fifth AAAI Conference on Artificial Intelligence* (pp. 1770-1771). AAAI Press.

Cialdini, R. (2001). The science of persuasion. *Scientific American*, *2*(2), 76–81. doi:10.1038/scientificamerican0201-76

Cialdini, R. (2008). *Influence: Science and practice* (5th ed.). Boston, MA: Pearson Education.

Crawford, E. (2009). *Learning to improve negotiation in semi-cooperative agreement problem*. (PhD Thesis). School of Computer Science, Carnegie Melon University, Pittsburgh, PA.

Cristani, M. (2008). Ontologies and e-learning: How to teach a classification. *Intelligent Information Technologies: Concepts, Methodologies, Tools, and Applications*, *4*(2), 322–331. doi:10.4018/978-1-59904-941-0.ch017

Dahlem, N. (2011). OntoClippy: A user-friendly ontology design and creation methodology. *International Journal of Intelligent Information Technologies*, *7*(1), 15–32. doi:10.4018/jiit.2011010102

Daumé, H., III. (2009). Markov random topic fields. Academic Press.

Dave, K., Lawrence, S., & Pennock, D. (2003). Mining the peanut gallery: Opinion extraction and semantic classification of product reviews. In ACM (Ed.), *Proceedings of the 12th International Conference on World Wide Web* (pp. 519–528). New York: ACM. doi:10.1145/775224.775226

Davenport, T., Morison, R., & Harris, J. (2010). *Analytics at work: Smarter decisions, better results*. New York: Harvard Business Press.

David, G., Jenkins, J., & Joseph, F. (2006). Collaborative bibliography. *Information Processing & Management*, *42*(3), 805–825. doi:10.1016/j.ipm.2005.05.007

Davis, F. (1989). Perceived usefulness, perceived ease of use, and user acceptance of information technology. *Management Information Systems Quarterly*, *13*(3), 319–340. doi:10.2307/249008

Dawson-Hughes, B., Tosteson, A. N., Melton, L. J. III, Baim, S., Favus, M. J., Khosla, S., & Lindsay, R. L. (2008). Implications of absolute fracture risk assessment for osteoporosis practice guidelines in the USA. *Osteoporosis International*, *19*(4), 449–458. doi:10.1007/s00198-008-0559-5 PMID:18292975

De Laet, C., Kanis, J. A., Oden, A., Johanson, H., Johnell, O., Delmas, P., & Tenenhouse, A. et al. (2005). Body mass index as a predictor of fracture risk: A meta-analysis. *Osteoporosis International*, *16*(11), 1330–1338. doi:10.1007/s00198-005-1863-y PMID:15928804

De Marnee, M. C., & Manning, C. D. (2010). *Stanford typed dependencies manual*. Retrieved from http://www.mendeley.com/research/stanford-typed-dependencies-manual

Deborah, L. J., Baskaran, R., & Kannan, A. (2011). Ontology construction using computational linguistics for e-learning. In *Proceedings of the 2nd International Conference on Visual Informatics* (pp. 50-63). Kualalumpur, Malaysia: Springer.

DeLoach, S. A. (1999). Systems engineering: A methodology and language for designing agent systems. In Proceedings of Agent Oriented Information Systems (pp. 45-57). Academic Press.

DeLoach, S. A., Wood, M. F., & Sparkman, C. H. (2001). Multiagent system engineering. *International Journal of Software Engineering and Knowledge Engineering*, *11*(3), 231–258. doi:10.1142/S0218194001000542

Deloitte. (2004). *In the dark: What boards and executives don't know about the health of their businesses*. New York: Deloitte.

Deloitte. (2007). *In the dark II: What many boards and executives still don't know about the health of their businesses*. New York: Deloitte.

DeLone, W., & McLean, E. (1992). Information systems success: The quest for the dependent variable. *Information Systems Research*, *3*(1), 60–95. doi:10.1287/isre.3.1.60

DeLone, W., & McLean, E. (2003). The DeLone and McLean model of information systems success: A ten-year update. *Journal of Management Information Systems*, *19*(4), 9–30.

Deng, J. D., Purvis, M. K., & Purvis, M. A. (2011). Software effort estimation: Harmonizing algorithms and domain knowledge in an integrated data mining approach. *International Journal of Intelligent Information Technologies*, *7*(3), 41–53.

Denis, P., & Baldridge, J. (2007). A ranking approach to pronoun resolution. In *Proceedings of IJCAI 2007* (pp. 1588-1593). Hyderabad, India: IJCAI.

Denyer, D., & Tranfield, D. (2009). Producing a systematic review. In *The Sage handbook of organizational research methods* (pp. 671–689). Los Angeles, CA: Sage.

Ding, Y., & Foo, S. (2002). Ontology research and development. Part I - A review of ontology generation. *Journal of Information Science*, 123–136.

Doan, A., Madhavan, J., Dhamankar, R., Domingos, P., & Halevy, A. (2003). Learning to match ontologies on the semantic web. *The VLDB Journal, 12*(4), 303–319. doi:10.1007/s00778-003-0104-2

Dollmann, T., Loos, P., Fellmann, M., Thomas, O., Hoheisel, A., Katranuschkov, P., & Scherer, R. J. (2011). Design and usage of a process-centric collaboration methodology for virtual organizations in hybrid environments. *International Journal of Intelligent Information Technologies, 7*(1), 45–64. doi:10.4018/jiit.2011010104

Dorst, K. (2006). Design problems and design paradoxes. *Design Issues, 22*(3), 4–17. doi:10.1162/desi.2006.22.3.4

Dubois, J. P., & Adbellatif, O. (2005). Improved m-ary signal detection using support vector machine classifiers. In *Proceedings of the International Conference on Signal Processing*. Academic Press.

Dugan, M. & Smith, A. (2013). *Social media update 2013*. Academic Press.

Dunn, R. (1990). Understanding the Dunn and Dunn learning styles model and needs for individual diagnosis and prescription, reading. *Writing and Learning Disabilities, 6*(3), 233–247.

Durfee, E. (1987). *A unified approach to dynamic coordination: Planning actions and interactions in a distributed problem solving network.* (Ph.D. dissertation). Department of Computer and Information Science, University of Massachusetts.

Eberl, M. (2004). *Formative und reflektive Indikatoren im Forschungsprozess: Entscheidungsregeln und die Dominanz des reflektiven Modells.* Ludwig-Maximilians-Universität München, München. Retrieved from http://www.imm.bwl.uni-muenchen.de/forschung/schriftenefo/ap_efoplan_19.pdf

Edvinsson, L. (1997). Developing intellectual capital at Skandia. *Long Range Planning, 30*(3), 366–373. doi:10.1016/S0024-6301(97)90248-X

Efraim, T., Sharda, R., & Delen, D. (2010). Decision support and business intelligence systems. Pearson Publishing.

Ehrig, M., & Staab, S. (2004). Efficiency of ontology mapping approaches. In *Proceedings of the International Workshop on Semantic Intelligent Middleware for the Web and the Grid* (pp.64-71). Valencia, Spain: Institute of Applied Informatics and Formal Description Methods.

Elayeb, B., Bounhas, I., Khiroun, O. B., Evrard, F., & Bellamine-BenSaoud, N. (2011). Towards a possibilistic information retrieval system using semantic query expansion. *International Journal of Intelligent Information Technologies, 7*(4), 1–25. doi:10.4018/jiit.2011100101

Embley, D., Xu, L., & Ding, Y. (2004). Automatic direct and indirect schema mapping: Experiences and lessons learned. *SIGMOD Record, 33*(4), 14–19. doi:10.1145/1041410.1041413

Engeström, Y., Miettinen, R., & Punamaki, R. (1999). *Perspectives on activity theory.* Cambridge University Press. doi:10.1017/CBO9780511812774

Espinoza, M., Suykens, J. A. K., & Moor, B. D. (2006). Fixed-size least square support vector machines: A large scale application in electrical load forecasting. *Computational Management Science, 3*(2), 113–129. doi:10.1007/s10287-005-0003-7

Evfimievski, A., & Grandison, T. (2009). Privacy preserving data mining. In *Handbook of research on innovations in database technologies and applications: Current and future trends.* IGI Global.

Fayyad, U. M. (1996). *Advances in knowledge discovery and data mining.* Menlo Park, CA: AAAI Press.

Fayyad, U., Piatetsky-shapiro, G., & Smyth, P. (1996). From data mining to knowledge discovery in databases. *AI Magazine, 17*, 37–54.

Felder, R. M., & Silverman, L. K. (1988). Learning styles and teaching styles in engineering education. *English Education, 78*(7), 674–681.

Fischer, K. (2010). Why it is interesting to investigate how people talk to computers and robots. *Journal of Pragmatics, 42*(9), 2349–2354. doi:10.1016/j.pragma.2009.12.014

Fitzpatrick, G., Kaplan, S., & Mansfield, T. (1996). Physical spaces, virtual places and social worlds: A study of work in the virtual. In *Proceedings of the Conference on Computer Supported Cooperative Work*. ACM. doi:10.1145/240080.240322

Flaherty, D. (1989). *Protecting privacy in surveillance societies*. The University of North Carolina Press.

Fox, S. (2009). *Generative production systems for sustainable product creation*. VTT.

Franceschini, F., Galetto, M., Maisano, D., & Viticchiè, L. (2006). The condition of uniqueness in manufacturing process representation by performance/quality indicators. *Quality and Reliability Engineering International*, *22*(5), 567–580. doi:10.1002/qre.762

Franco-Santos, M., Kennerley, M., Micheli, P., Martinez, V., Mason, S., Marr, B., & Neely, A. et al. (2007). Towards a definition of a business performance measurement system. *International Journal of Operations & Production Management*, *27*(8), 784–801. doi:10.1108/01443570710763778

FRAX® WHO Fracture Risk Assessment Tool. (n.d.). Retrieved from http://www.shef.ac.uk/FRAX/

Freund, Y., & Schapire, R. E. (1996). Experiments with a new boosting algorithm. In L. Saitta (Ed.), *Machine Learning:Proceedings of the 13th National Conference*. Morgan Kaufmann.

Fried, A. (2010). Performance measurement systems and their relation to strategic learning: A case study in a software-developing organization. *Critical Perspectives on Accounting*, *21*(2), 118–133. doi:10.1016/j.cpa.2009.08.007

Fulcher, B.D., & Jones, N.S. (2014). *Highly comparative, feature-based time-series classification*. CoRR abs/1401.3531.

Fulcher, B. D., Little, M. A., & Jones, N. S. (2013). Highly comparative time-series analysis: The empirical structure of time series and their methods. *Journal of the Royal Society, Interface*, *10*(83), 20130048. doi:10.1098/rsif.2013.0048 PMID:23554344

Garengo, P., Nudurupati, S., & Bititci, U. (2007). Understanding the relationship between PMS and MIS in SMEs: An organizational life cycle perspective. *Computers in Industry*, *58*(7), 677–686. doi:10.1016/j.compind.2007.05.006

Garg, V. K., & Murty, M. N. (2009). Feature subspace SVMs (FS-SVMs) for high dimensional handwritten digit recognition. *International Journal of Data Mining, Modelling, and Management*, *1*(4), 411–436.

Gasmelseid, T. (2006). Multi agent web based DSS for global enterprises: An architectural blueprint. *Engineering Letters*, *13*(2), 173-184. Available online at: http://www.engineeringletters.com/issues_v13/issue_2/EL_13_2_16.pdf

Gasmelseid, T. (2008). Modern design dimensions in multi agent computer supported collaborative work systems (CSCW). In *Handbook on modern system analysis and design Applications and technologies*. Academic Press.

Gasmelseid, T. (2014). On the orchestration of stakeholder concerns in large scale information systems. In Agent oriented analysis using MESSAGE/UML. Konradin Verlag.

Gasmelseid, T. (2007, July-September). From operational dashboards to effective e-business: Multi-agent formulation and negotiation of electronic contracts. *International Journal of E-Business Research*, *3*(3), 77–97. doi:10.4018/jebr.2007070106

Gasmelseid, T. (2009). Intelligent collaboration: The paradox of "ethical agency" and "corporate governance". *Journal of Electronic Commerce in Organizations*, *2009*(1), 50–58. doi:10.4018/jeco.2009010104

Gatian, A. (1994). Is user satisfaction a valid measure of system effectiveness? *Information & Management*, *26*(3), 119–131. doi:10.1016/0378-7206(94)90036-1

Geesaman, P. L., Cordy, J. R., & Zouaq, A. (2013). Light-weight ontology alignment using best-match clone detection. In *Proceedings of International Workshop on Software Clones* (pp.1-7). Antwerp, Belgium: IWSC. doi:10.1109/IWSC.2013.6613032

Geng, X., & Chu, X. (2012). A new importance–Performance analysis approach for customer satisfaction evaluation supporting PSS design. *Expert Systems with Applications*, *39*(1), 1492–1502. doi:10.1016/j.eswa.2011.08.038

Gharipour, A., Jazi, A. Y., & Sameti, M. (2011). Forecast combination with optimized SVM based on quantum-inspired hybrid evolutionary method for complex systems prediction. In *Proceedings of the IEEE Symposium on Computational Intelligence for Financial Engineering and Economics* (pp. 15-20). IEEE. doi:10.1109/CIFER.2011.5953562

Ghazvinian, A., Noy, N. F., & Musen, M. A. (2011). *From mappings to modules: Using mappings to identify domain-specific modules in large ontologies.* Paper presented at the K-CAP'11, Banff, Canada. doi:10.1145/1999676.1999684

Gilbert, J. E., & Han, C. Y. (1999). Adapting instruction in search of a significant difference. *Journal of Network and Computer Applications*, *22*(3), 149–160. doi:10.1006/jnca.1999.0088

Ginsberg, M. (1987). *Readings in nonmonotonic reasoning.* Los Altos, CA: Morgan Kaufmann.

Giunchiglia, F., Autayeu, A., & Pane, J. (2010). *S-match: An open source framework for matching lightweight ontologies* (Technical Report # DISI-10-043). University of Trento.

Giunchiglia, F., Perini, A., & Sannicol, F. (2001). Knowledge level software engineering. In Intelligent Agents VIII (LNCS), (vol. 2333, pp. 6-20). Seattle, WA: Springer-Verlag.

Giunchiglia, F., Shvaiko, P., & Yatskevich, M. (2004). S-match: An algorithm and an implementation of semantic matching. *Semantic Web: Research and Applications*, 61-75.

Giunchiglia, F., Perini, A., & Mylopoulus, J. (2002). The Tropos software development methodology: Processes, models and diagrams. In *Proceedings of the First International Joint Conference on Autonomous Agents and Multiagent Systems* (pp. 63-74). Bologna, Italy: ACM Press. doi:10.1145/544743.544748

Giunchiglia, F., Yatskevich, M., & Shvaiko, P. (2007). Semantic matching – Algorithms and implementation. *Journal on Data Semantics IX*, *4601*, 1–38. doi:10.1007/978-3-540-74987-5_1

Glaser, B., & Strauss, A. (1967). *The discovery of grounded theory: Strategies for qualitative research.* Chicago: Aldine Publishing Company.

Glaser, B., Strauss, A., & Paul, A. (2010). *Grounded theory: Strategien qualitativer Forschung.* Bern: Huber.

Gleich, R. (2011). *Performance measurement: Konzepte, Fallstudien und Grundschema für die Praxis.* Munich: Vahlen. doi:10.15358/9783800639151

Glover, F., & Laguna, M. (1997). *Tabu search.* Boston, MA: Kluwer Academic Publishers. doi:10.1007/978-1-4615-6089-0

Godin, F., Slavkovikj, V., Neve, W. D., Schrauwen, B., & van de Walle, R. (2013). Using topic models for Twitter hashtag recommendation. In *Proceedings of International World Wide Web Conferences Steering Committee* (pp. 593–596). ACM. Retrieved from http://dblp.uni-trier.de/db/conf/www/www2013c.html#GodinSNSW13

Golder, S. A., & Macy, M. W. (2011). Diurnal and seasonal mood vary with work, sleep, and daylength across diverse cultures. *Science*, *333*(6051), 1878–1881. doi:10.1126/science.1202775 PMID:21960633

Gomez-Perez, A., Fernadez-Lopez, M., & Corcho, O. (2004). *Ontological engineering with examples from the areas of knowledge management, e-commerce and the semantic web.* Berlin: Springer-Verlag.

Goodhue, D., & Thompson, R. (1995). Task-technology fit and individual performance. *Management Information Systems Quarterly*, *19*(2), 213. doi:10.2307/249689

Goth, G. (2011). I, domestic robot. *Communications of the ACM*, *54*(5), 16–17. doi:10.1145/1941487.1941494

Gottgtroy, P., Kasabov, N., & MacDonell, S. (2008). *An ontology driven approach for knowledge discovery in biomedicine.* Paper presented at the Trends in Artificial Intelligence.

Grando, N., Centeno, T. M., Botelho, S. S. C., & Fontoura, F. M. (2010). Forecasting electric energy demand using a predictor model based on liquid state machine. *International Journal of Artificial Intelligence and Expert Systems*, *1*(2), 40–53.

Grant, C. E., George, C. P., Jenneisch, C., & Wilson, J. N. (2011). Online topic modeling for real-time Twitter search. In *TREC, National Institute of Standards and Technology NIST*. Retrieved from http://dblp.uni-trier.de/db/conf/trec/trec2011.html#GrantGJW11

Grant, R. (1996). Toward a knowledge-based theory of the firm. *Strategic Management Journal*, *17*(S2), 109–122. doi:10.1002/smj.4250171110

Greenbaum, J., & Kyng, M. (1991). *Design at work: Cooperative design of computer systems*. Hillsdale, NJ: Lawrence Erlbaum.

Gregor, S., & Jones, D. (2007). The anatomy of a design theory. *Journal of the Association for Information Systems*, *8*(5), 312–335.

Gruber, T. (1995). Toward principles for the design of ontologies used for knowledge sharing. *International Journal of Human-Computer Studies*, *43*(5-6), 907–928. doi:10.1006/ijhc.1995.1081

Grüning, M. (2002). *Performance-Measurement-Systeme: Messung und Steuerung von Unternehmensleistung*. Wiesbaden: Deutscher Universitätsverlag. doi:10.1007/978-3-663-08089-3

Gupta, A., Gosain, B., & Kaushal, S. (2010). A comparison of two algorithms for automated stone detection in clinical b-mode ultrasound images of the abdomen. *Journal of Clinical Monitoring and Computing*, *24*(5), 341–362. doi:10.1007/s10877-010-9254-0 PMID:20714793

Guyet, T., Garbay, C., & Dojat, M. (2007). Knowledge construction from time series data using a collaborative exploration system. *Journal of Biomedical Informatics*, *40*(6), 672–687. doi:10.1016/j.jbi.2007.09.006 PMID:17988953

Ha Thuc, V. (2011). Topic modeling and applications in web 2.0. Iowa City, IA: Academic Press.

Halford, S., & Leonard, P. (2005). Place, space and time: Contextualizing workplace subjectivities organization. *Studies*, *27*(5), 657–676.

Hamza, M., & Larocque, D. (2005). An empirical comparison of ensemble methods based on classification trees. *Statistical Computation & Simulation*, *75*(8), 629–643. doi:10.1080/00949650410001729472

Han, J. (1995). Mining knowledge at multiple concept levels. In *Proceedings 4th International Conference on Information and Knowledge Management* (pp. 19-24). New York: ACM Press.

Han, J., Cai, Y., & Cercone, N. (1992). Knowledge discovery in databases: An attribute-oriented approach. In *Proceedings of 18th Very Large Database Conference* (pp. 547-559). Los Altos, CA: Morgan Kaufmann.

Harland, Z. (2002). Using support vector machines to trade aluminum on the LME. *Market Technician*, *44*, 9–12.

Harraway, D. (1991). *Simians, cyborgs and women: The reinvention of nature*. New York: Routledge.

Hatamzadeh, N., Jalilian, F., Emdadi, S., Rezaei, R., & Mirzaee Ramhormozi, S. (2011). Application of health belief model for predicting osteoporosis-protective behaviors among Iranian women. In *Proceedings of First International & 4th National Congress on health Education & Promotion, 2011*. Academic Press.

Havemann, S. (2005). *Generative mesh modeling*. (PhD Thesis). Technical University Braunschweig.

He, J. Y., Deng, S. P., & Ouyang, J. M. (2010). Morphology, particle size distribution, aggregation, and crystal phase of nanocrystallites in the urine of healthy persons and lithogenic patients. *IEEE Transactions on Nanobioscience*, *9*(2), 156-163. doi:10.10.1109/TNB.2010.2045510

Hedar, A., & Fukushima, M. (2006). Tabu search directed by direct search methods for nonlinear global optimization. *European Journal of Operational Research*, *170*(2), 329–349. doi:10.1016/j.ejor.2004.05.033

Hedar, A., Wangy, J., & Fukushima, M. (2008). Tabu search for attribute reduction in rough set theory. *Journal of Soft Computing*, *12*, 9.

Heinrich, K. (2011). Influence potential framework: Eine Methode zur Bestimmung des Referenzpotenzials in Microblogs. In P. Gluchowski, A. Lorenz, C. Schieder, & J. Stietzel (Eds.), Tagungsband zum 14: Interuniversitären Doktorandenseminar Wirtschaftsinformatik (pp. 26–36). Chemnitz: Universitätsverlag Chemnitz. Retrieved from http://nbn-resolving.de/urn:nbn:de:bsz:ch1-qucosa-70640

Henk, A., & Paul, B. (2004). Travail, transparency and trust: A case study of computer-supported collaborative supply chain planning in high-tech electronics. *European Journal of Operational Research*, *153*(2), 445–456. doi:10.1016/S0377-2217(03)00164-4

Hevner, A., March, S., Park, J., & Ram, S. (2004). Design science in information systems research. *Management Information Systems Quarterly*, *28*(1), 75–105.

He, Y., Lin, C., Gao, W., & Wong, K.-F. (2012). (in press). Dynamic joint sentiment-topic model. *ACM Transactions on Intelligent Systems and Technology*. Retrieved from http://oro.open.ac.uk/36255/

Hildebrand, K., Gebauer, M., Hinrichs, H., & Mielke, M. (2011). Informationsqualität – Definitionen, Dimensionen und Begriffe. Wiesbaden: Vieweg+Teubner.

Hilgers, D. (2008). *Performance Management. Leistungserfassung und Leistungssteuerung in Unternehmen und öffentlichen Verwaltungen*. Wiesbaden: Gabler.

Hillbrand, C. (2007). Towards stable model bases for causal strategic decision support systems. *International Journal of Intelligent Information Technologies*, *3*(4), 1–24. doi:10.4018/jiit.2007100101

Hoffman, M., Blei, D. M., & Bach, F. (2010). *Online learning for latent Dirichlet allocation*. NIPS.

Hofmann, T. (1999). Probabilistic latent semantic indexing. In F. Gey, M. Hearst, & R. Tong (Eds.), *Proceedings of the 22nd Annual International ACM SIGIR Conference* (pp. 50–57). ACM. doi:10.1145/312624.312649

Hohmann, B., Havemann, S., Krispel, U., & Fellner, D. (2010). A GML shape grammar for semantically enriched 3D building models. *Computers & Graphics*, *34*(4), 322–334. doi:10.1016/j.cag.2010.05.007

Hong, L., & Davison, B. D. (2010). Empirical study of topic modeling in Twitter. In Proceedings of the First Workshop on Social Media Analytics (pp. 80–88). New York: ACM. Retrieved from http://doi.acm.org/10.1145/1964858.1964870 doi:10.1145/1964858.1964870

Hong, L., Dom, B., Gurumurthy, S., & Tsioutsiouliklis, K. (2011). A time-dependent topic model for multiple text streams. In C. Apte, J. Ghosh, & P. Smyth (Eds.), *Proceedings of the 17th ACM SIGKDD International Conference* (p. 832). ACM. doi:10.1145/2020408.2020551

Horvarth & Partners. (2008). *Balanced Scorecard Studie 2008: Ergebnisbericht*. Stuttgart: Horvarth&Partners.

Ho, T. K. (1998). The random subspace method for constructing decision forests. *IEEE Transactions on Pattern Analysis and Machine Intelligence*, *20*(8), 832844.

Hui, L., Xiaoy, L., Bone, L., Buyea, C., Ramanathan, M., & Zhang, A. (2012). 3D bone microarchitecture modeling and fracture risk prediction. In *Proceedings of ACM-BCB*. ACM.

Hyacinth, S. (1996). Software agents: An over view. *The Knowledge Engineering Review*, *11*(3), 1–40.

Iglesias, C., Garrijo, M., & Gonzalez, J. (1998). A survey of agent-oriented methodologies. In *Intelligent Agents V – Proceedings of the 1998 Workshop on Agent Theories, Architectures and Languages*. Academic Press.

Indumathi, J., & Uma, G.V. (2009). A novel framework for optimised privacy preserving data mining using the innovative desultory technique. *International Journal of Computer Applications in Technology*, *35*(2/3/4), 194 - 203.

Isaac, A., Van der Meij, L., Schlobach, S., & Wang, S. (2007). *An empirical study of instance-based ontology matching*. Paper presented at the ISWC/ASWC. doi:10.1007/978-3-540-76298-0_19

Ittner, C., & Larcker, D. (2003, November). Coming up short on nonfinancial performance measurement. *Harvard Business Review*, 1–9.

Jacobs, T., & Graf, B. (2012). Practical evaluation of service robots for support and routine tasks in an elderly care facility. In *Proceedings of IEEE Workshop on Advanced Robotics and its Social Impacts* (pp 46-49). Hoboken, NJ: Wiley-IEEE Press. doi:10.1109/ARSO.2012.6213397

Jäger, U., & Reinecke, S. (2009). Expertengespräch. In C. Baumgarth (Ed.), *Empirische Mastertechniken: Eine anwendungsorientierte Einführung für die Marketing- und Managementforschung* (pp. 29–66). Wiesbaden: Gabler.

Jan, S., Li, M., Al-Raweshidy, H., Mousavi, A., & Qi, M. (2012). Dealing With uncertain entities in ontology alignment using rough sets. *IEEE Transactions on Systems, Man and Cybernetics. Part C, Applications and Reviews*, 42(6), 1600–1612. doi:10.1109/TSMCC.2012.2209869

Jansen, B. J., Zhang, M., Sobel, K., & Chowdury, A. (2009). Twitter power: Tweets as electronic word of mouth. *Journal of the American Society for Information Science and Technology*, 60(11), 2169–2188. doi:10.1002/asi.21149

Java, A., Song, X., Finin, T., & Tseng, B. (2007). Why we twitter. In H. Zhang, B. Mobasher, L. Giles, A. McCallum, O. Nasraoui, & M. Spiliopoulou (Eds.), *Proceedings of the 9th WebKDD and 1st SNA-KDD 2007 Workshop* (pp. 56–65). ACM. doi:10.1145/1348549.1348556

Jean-Mary, Y. R., & Kabuka, M. R. (2007). ASMOV: Results for OAEI 2008. In *Proceedings of ISWC 2007 Ontology Matching Workshop* (pp. 132-139). Busan, Korea: OAEI.

Jeyalakshmi, R., & Kadarkarai, R. (2010). Segmentation and feature extraction of fluid-filled uterine fibroid-A knowledge-based approach. *Maejo International Journal of Science and Technology*, 4(3), 405–416.

Jones, M. R. (1998). Information systems and the double mangle: Steering a course between the scylla of embedded structure and the charybdis of strong symmetry. In *Proceedings of the IFIP WG 8.2 and 8.6 Joint Working Conference on Information Systems*. Academic Press. doi:10.1007/3-540-49057-4_21

Josephson, J., & Josephson, S. (Eds.). (1995). *Abductive inference: Computation, philosophy, technology*. Cambridge, UK: Cambridge University Press.

Jouannot, E., Huyen, J. P. D. V., Bourahla, K., Laugier, P., Pegorier, M. L., & Bridal, L. (2004). Comparison and validation of high frequency ultrasound detection techniques in a mouse model for renal tumors. In *Proceedings of IEEE International Ultrasonic Symposium* (Vol. 1, pp. 748-751). IEEE. doi:10.1109/ULTSYM.2004.1417832

Jung, K., & Lee, C. (2000). Dimension expansion of neural networks. In *Proc of the Geoscience and Remote Sensing Symposium* (Vol. 2, pp. 678-680). Academic Press.

Jungherr, A., Jurgens, P., & Schoen, H. (2012). Why the pirate party won the German election of 2009 or the trouble with predictions: A response to Tumasjan, A., Sprenger, T. O., Sander, P. G., & Welpe, I. M. "Predicting Elections With Twitter: What 140 Characters Reveal About Political Sentiment". *Social Science Computer Review*, 30(2), 229–234. doi:10.1177/0894439311404119

Jungj, C. R., & Scharcanski, J. (2005). Robust watershed segmentation using the wavelet transform. *Image and Vision Computing*, 23(7), 661–669. doi:10.1016/j.imavis.2005.03.001

Kalb, H. (2009). *Design Science bei der Schwester der Wirtschaftsinformatik – Teil 1*. Retrieved from http://lswiim.wordpress.com/2009/02/13/design-science-bei-der-schwester-der-wirtschaftsinformatik-teil-1/

Kalfoglou, Y., & Schorlemmer, M. (2003). *IF-map: An ontology-mapping method based on information-flow theory*. Springer.

Kalfoglou, Y., & Schorlemmer, M. (2003). Ontology mapping: The state of the art. *The Knowledge Engineering Review*, 18(1), 1–31. doi:10.1017/S0269888903000651

Kallinikos, J. (2006). *The consequences of information: Institutional implications of technological change*. Cheltenham, UK: Edward Elgar Publishing. doi:10.4337/9781847204301

Kanda, T., Nabe, S., Hiraki, K., Ishiguro, H., & Hagita, N. (2008). Human friendship estimation model for communication robots. *Autonomous Robots*, 24(2), 135–145. doi:10.1007/s10514-007-9052-9

Kanis, J. A. (2002). *Diagnosis of osteoporosis and assessment of fracture risk*. Academic Press.

Kanis, J. A., Johansson, H., Johnell, O., Oden, A., De Laet, C., Eisman, J. A., & Tenenhouse, A. et al. (2005). Alcohol intake as a risk factor for fracture. *Osteoporosis International, 16*(7), 737–742. doi:10.1007/s00198-004-1734-y PMID:15455194

Kanis, J. A., Johnell, O., Oden, A., Johansson, H., De Laet, C., Eisman, J. A., & Tenenhouse, A. et al. (2005). Smoking and fracture risk: A meta-analysis. *Osteoporosis International, 16*(2), 155–162. doi:10.1007/s00198-004-1640-3 PMID:15175845

Kanis, J. A., Johnell, O., Oden, A., Johansson, H., & McCloskey, E. (2008). FRAX and the assessment of fracture probability in men and women from the UK. *Osteoporosis International, 19*(4), 385–397. doi:10.1007/s00198-007-0543-5 PMID:18292978

Kanis, J. A., Oden, A., Johnell, O., Johansson, H., De Laet, C., Brown, J., & Yoshimura, N. et al. (2007). The use of clinical risk factors enhances the performance of BMD in the prediction of hip and osteoporotic fractures in men and women. *Osteoporosis International, 18*(8), 1033–1046. doi:10.1007/s00198-007-0343-y PMID:17323110

Kano, N., Seraku, N., Takahaashi, F., & Tsuji, S. (1984). Attractive quality and must-be quality. *Hinshitsu: The Journal of the Japanese Society for Quality Control, 14*(2), 39–48.

Kantz, H., & Schreiber, T. (2003). *Nonlinear time series analysis.* Cambridge University Press. doi:10.1017/CBO9780511755798

Kaplan, R., & Norton, D. (1996). Using the balanced scorecard as a strategic management system. *Harvard Business Review,* (January-February), 150–161.

Kaufmann, M. (2010). *Syntactic normalization of Twitter messages.* Retrieved October 17, 2011 from http://www.cs.uccs.edu/~kalita/work/reu/REUFinalPapers2010/Kaufmann.pdf

Kaza, S., & Chen, H. (2008). Evaluating ontology mapping techniques: An experiment in public safety information sharing. *Decision Support Systems, 45*(4), 714–728. doi:10.1016/j.dss.2007.12.007

Keerthi, S. S., & Lin, C. J. (2003). Asymptotic behaviors of support vector machines with Gaussian kernel. *Neural Computation, 15*(7), 1667–1689. doi:10.1162/089976603321891855 PMID:12816571

Kendall, E. (1999). Role modeling for agent system analysis, design, and implementation. In *Proceedings of Third International Symposium on Mobile Agents* (MA'99). Palm Springs, FL: Academic Press.

Kenrick, D., Goldstein, N., & Braver, S. (2012). *Six degrees of social influence.* New York, NY: Oxford University Press.

Keogh, E., Chakrabarti, K., Pazzani, M., & Mehrotra, S. (2000). Dimensionality reduction for fast similarity search in large time series databases. *Knowledge and Information Systems, 3*(3), 263–286. doi:10.1007/PL00011669

Keogh, E., Lin, K., & Fu, A. (2005). HOT SAX: Finding the most unusual time series subsequence: Algorithms and applications. In *Proceedings of the Fifth IEEE International Conference on Data Mining* (pp. 226-233). IEEE. doi:10.1109/ICDM.2005.79

Kevin, L. M. (2003). Computer-supported cooperative work. In Encyclopedia of library and information science (pp. 666-677). Academic Press.

Khashei, M., & Bijari, M. (2011). Which methodology is better for combining linear and nonlinear models for time series forecasting? *Journal of Industrial and Systems Engineering, 4*(4), 265–285.

Kim, J., & Storey, V. (2011). Construction of domain ontologies: Sourcing the world wide web. *International Journal of Intelligent Information Technologies, 7*(2), 1–24. doi:10.4018/jiit.2011040101

Kitchenham, B., Pearl Brereton, O., Budgen, D., Turner, M., Bailey, J., & Linkman, S. (2009). Systematic literature reviews in software engineering - A systematic literature review. *Information and Software Technology, 51*(1), 7–15. doi:10.1016/j.infsof.2008.09.009

Klein, B., Gaedt, L., & Cook, G. (2013). Emotional robots: Principles and experiences with Paro in Denmark, Germany, and the UK. *GeroPsych: The Journal of Gerontopsychology and Geriatric Psychiatry, 26*(2), 89–99.

Klosgen, W. (1995). Anonymization techniques for knowledge discovery in databases. In *Proc of the First International Conference on Knowledge Discovery and Data Mining Montreal* (pp. 186-191). Academic Press.

Koh, L. K., Sendrine, W. B., & Torralba, T. P. (2001). A simple tool to identify Asian women at increased risk of osteoporosis. *Osteoporosis International, 12*(8), 699–705. doi:10.1007/s001980170070 PMID:11580084

Kotter, J. P., Schlesinger, L. A., & Sathe, V. (1986). *Organization: Text, cases, and readings on the management of organizational design and change.* Homewood: Irwin.

Krishnamurthy, B., Gill, P., & Arlitt, M. (2008). A few chirps about twitter. In C. Faloutsos, T. Karagiannis, & P. Rodriguez (Eds.), *Proceedings of the First Workshop on Online Social Networks* (p. 19). Academic Press. doi:10.1145/1397735.1397741

Krish, S. (2011). A practical generative design method. *Computer Aided Design, 43*(1), 88–100. doi:10.1016/j.cad.2010.09.009

Küpper, H. (2005). *Controlling: Konzeption, Aufgaben, Instrumente.* Stuttgart: Schäffer-Poeschel.

Lagroue, H. J. III. (2008). Supporting structured group decision making through system-directed user guidance: An experimental study. *International Journal of Intelligent Information Technologies, 4*(2), 57–74. doi:10.4018/jiit.2008040104

Lambrix, P., & Tan, H. (2006). SAMBO - A system for aligning and merging biomedical ontologies. *Journal of Web Semantics, 4*(3), 196–206. doi:10.1016/j.websem.2006.05.003

Larcker, D. (2004). *Performance measures: Insights and challenges, management accounting research group.* Retrieved from www.cimaglobal.com

Latham, R., & Sassen, S. (2005). *Digital formations: It and new architectures in the global realm.* Princeton, NJ: Princeton University Press.

Latour, B. (1987). *Science in action.* Cambridge, MA: Harvard University Press.

Latour, B. (2005). *Reassembling the social: An introduction to actor-network theory.* Oxford, UK: Oxford University Press.

Lau, J. H., Collier, N., & Baldwin, T. (2012). On-line trend analysis with topic models: \#twitter trends detection topic model online. In Martin Kay & Christian Boitet (Eds.), *COLING 2012, 24th International Conference on Computational Linguistics, Proceedings of the Conference: Technical Papers* (pp. 1519–1534). Indian Institute of Technology Bombay.

Law, J. (2004). *After method: Mess in social science research.* Routledge.

Lee, D., Jeong, O.-R., & Lee, S.-G. (2008). Opinion mining of customer feedback data on the web. In ACM (Ed.), *Proceedings of the 2nd International Conference on Ubiquitous Information Management and Communication* (pp. 230-235). New York: ACM. doi:10.1145/1352793.1352842

Lee, D., & Kim, M. (1997). Database summarization using fuzzy ISA hierarchies. *IEEE Transactions on Systems, Man, and Cybernetics. Part B, Cybernetics, 27*(1), 68–78. doi:10.1109/3477.552186 PMID:18255840

Lee, H. C. (2011). Engineering design analysis using evolutionary grammars with Kano's model to refine product design strategies. *Communications in Computer and Information Science, 180*(6), 627–641. doi:10.1007/978-3-642-22191-0_54

Lee, H. C., & Tang, M. X. (2008). Evolving product form designs using parametric shape grammars integrated with genetic programming. *Artificial Intelligence for Engineering Design, Analysis and Manufacturing, 23*(02), 131–158. doi:10.1017/S0890060409000031

Lee, T. B., Hendler, J., & Lassila, O. (2001). The semantic web. *Scientific American, 284*(5), 34–43. doi:10.1038/scientificamerican0501-34 PMID:11396337

Leonardi, P. M., & Barley, S. R. (2008). Materiality and change: Challenges to building better theory about technology and organizing. *Information and Organization, 18*(3), 159–176. doi:10.1016/j.infoandorg.2008.03.001

Lester, S., & Rada, R. (1987). A method of medical knowledge base augmentation. *Methods of Information in Medicine, 26*(1), 31–39. PMID:3550379

Lind, J. (1999). *A review of multiagent systems development methods: Technical report.* Martlesham Heath, UK: British Telecom, Adastral Park Labs.

Lin, J., Keogh, E., Lonardi, S., & Chiu, B. (2003). A symbolic representation of time series, with implications for streaming algorithms. In *Proceedings of the Eighth ACM SIGMOD Workshop on Research Issues in Data Mining and Knowledge Discovery*. San Diego, CA: ACM. doi:10.1145/882082.882086

Lin, R., & Kraus, S. (2010). Can automated agents proficiently negotiate with humans? *Communications of the ACM, 53*(1), 78–88. doi:10.1145/1629175.1629199

Liu, Y., Niculescu-Mizil, A., & Gryc, W. (2009). Topic-link LDA. In A. Danyluk, L. Bottou, & M. Littman (Eds.), *ICML '09 Proceedings of the 26th Annual International Conference on Machine Learning* (pp. 1–8). ICML. doi:10.1145/1553374.1553460

Liu, B. (2007). *Web data mining: Exploring hyperlinks, contents, and usage data*. Berlin: Springer.

Liu, B., Hu, M., & Cheng, J. (2005). Opinion observer: Analyzing and comparing opinions on the web. In ACM (Ed.), *Proceedings of the 14th International Conference on World Wide Web* (pp. 342–351). New York: ACM. doi:10.1145/1060745.1060797

Liu, K., Kargupta, H., & Ryan, J. (2006). Random projection-based multiplicative data perturbation for privacy preserving distributed data mining. *IEEE Transactions on Knowledge and Data Engineering, 18*(1), 92–106. doi:10.1109/TKDE.2006.14

Li, W., & McCallum, A. (2006). *Pachinko allocation: DAG-structured mixture models of topic correlations*. ICML. doi:10.1145/1143844.1143917

Lo, R. T.-W., He, B., & Ounis, I. (2005). Automatically Building a stopword list for an information retrieval system. In *Proceedings of the Fifth Dutch-Belgian Information Retrieval Workshop* (pp. 17-24). Academic Press.

Loizou, C. P., Christodoulou, C., Pattischis, C. S., Istepanian, R. S. H., Pantziaris, M., & Nicolaides, A. (2002). Speckle reduction in ultrasound images of atherosclerotic carotid plaque. In *Proceedings of IEEE International Conference on Digital Signal Processing* (Vol. 2, pp. 525-528). IEEE. doi:10.1109/ICDSP.2002.1028143

Loizou, C. P., Pattischis, C. S., Istepanian, R. S. H., Pantziaris, M., Tyllis, T., & Nicolaides, A. (2004). Quality evaluation of ultrasound imaging in the carotid artery. In *Proceedings of IEEE Mediterranean Electro technical Conference* (Vol. 1, pp. 395 – 398). IEEE. doi:10.1109/MELCON.2004.1346891

Lomuscio, A.R., & Sergot, M.J. (2003). Deontic interpreted systems. *The Dynamics of Knowledge, 75*(1), 63-92.

Lopes, I. S., Sousa, S. D., & Nunes, E. (2013). Quantification of uncertainty of performance measures using graph theory. In *Proceedings of the XI Congreso Galego de Estatística e Investigación de Operacións*, (pp. 264-269). Universidade da Coruña Press.

Lopez de Mantaras, R. (1991). A distance-based attribute selection measure for decision tree induction. *Machine Learning, 6*.

Lucas, H. (1978). Empirical evidence for a descriptive model of implementation. *Management Information Systems Quarterly, 2*(2), 27–42. doi:10.2307/248939

Lynch, R., & Cross, K. (1992). *Measure up!: The essential guide to measuring business performance*. London: Mandarin.

Machanavajjhala, A., Gehrke, J., Kifer, D., & Venkitasubramaniam, M. (2006). l-Diversity: Privacy beyond k-anonymity. In *Proceedings of the 22th International Conference on Data Engineering*. Academic Press.

Maes, P. (1995). Artificial life meets entertainment: Life like autonomous agents. *Communications of the ACM, 38*(11), 108–114. doi:10.1145/219717.219808

Mandal, U. K., & Sarkar, B. (2012). An exploratory analysis of intelligent manufacturing system (Ims) under fuzzy utopian environment. *IOSR Journal of Engineering, 2*(8), 129–140. doi:10.9790/3021-0281129140

Manousakas, I., Lai, C. C., & Chang, W. Y. (2010). A 3D ultrasound renal calculi fragmentation image analysis system for extracorporeal shock wave lithotripsy. In *Proceedings of the International Symposium on Computer, Communication, Control and Automation* (Vol. 1, pp. 303-306). Academic Press. doi:10.1109/3CA.2010.5533823

Manousakas, I., Pu, Y. R., Chang, C. C., & Liang, S. M. (2006). Ultrasound image analysis for renal stone tracking during extracorporeal shock wave lithotripsy. In *Proceedings of the IEEE EMBS Annual International Conference* (pp. 2746-2749). IEEE.

March, S., & Smith, G. (1995). Design and natural science research on information technology. *Decision Support Systems*, *15*(4), 251–266. doi:10.1016/0167-9236(94)00041-2

Marjit, U., & Mandal, M. (2012). Multiobjective particle swarm optimization based ontology alignment. In *Proceedings of 2nd IEEE International Conference on Parallel Distributed and Grid Computing* (pp. 368-373). Himachal Pradesh, India: PDGC. doi:10.1109/PDGC.2012.6449848

Markert, K., & Nissim, M. (2005). Comparing knowledge sources for nominal anaphora resolution. *Association for Computational Linguistics*, *31*(3), 367–402. doi:10.1162/089120105774321064

Marko Robnik-Sikonja. (2004). *Improving random forests, machine learning, ECML, proceedings*. Berlin: Springer.

Markus, M. L. & Silver, M. S. (2008). A foundation for the study of IT effects: A new look at DeSanctis and Poole's concepts of structural features and spirit. *Journal of the Association for Information Systems, 9*(10/11), 609-632.

Marr, B. (2005). Corporate performance measurement - State of the art. *Controlling*, *11*(11), 645–652. doi:10.15358/0935-0381-2005-11-645

Martin, J. (1992). *Cultures in organizations: Three perspectives*. New York: Oxford University Press.

Matatov, N., Rokach, L., & Maimon, O. (2010). Privacy-preserving data mining: A feature set partitioning approach. *Information Sciences*, *80*(14), 2696–2720. doi:10.1016/j.ins.2010.03.011

Matsusaka, Y., Tojo, T., & Kobayashi, T. (2003). Conversation robot participating in group conversation. *IEICE Transactions on Information and Systems, E86*(1), 23–36.

Mattern, F., & Naghshineh, M. (2002). *Modeling context information in pervasive computing systems*. Berlin: Springer.

Maulik, U. (2009). Medical image segmentation using genetic algorithms. *IEEE Transactions on Information Technology in Biomedicine*, *13*(2), 166–173. doi:10.1109/TITB.2008.2007301 PMID:19272859

McCallum, A. K. (2002). *MALLET: A machine learning for language toolkit*. Retrieved from http://mallet.cs.umass.edu

McCormack, J. P., & Cagan, J. (2002). Designing inner hood panels through a shape grammar based framework. *AI EDAM, 16*(4), 273–290.

McKinsey Global Institute. (2011). *Big data: The next frontier for innovation, competition, and productivity*. Retrieved from http://www.mckinsey.com/.../Big%20Data/MGI_big_data

McMath, C., Tamaru, B., & Rada, R. (1989). Graphical interface to thesaurus-based information retrieval system. *International Journal of Man-Machine Studies*, *31*(2), 121–147. doi:10.1016/0020-7373(89)90024-2

Meekings, A. (1995). Unlocking the potential of performance measurement: A practical implementation guide. *Public Money & Management*, *15*(4), 5–12. doi:10.1080/09540969509387888

Melton, L. J., Kan, S. H., Wahner, H. W., & Riggs, B. L. (1988). Lifetime fracture risk: An approach to hip fracture risk assessment based on bone mineral density and age. *Journal of Clinical Epidemiology*, *41*, 985–994. doi:10.1016/0895-4356(88)90036-4 PMID:3193143

Meng, S. K., & Chatwin, C. R. (2010). Ontology-based shopping agent for e-marketing. *International Journal of Intelligent Information Technologies*, *6*(2), 21–43. doi:10.4018/jiit.2010040102

Michalewicz, Z. (1996). *Genetic algorithms + data structures = evolution programs*. London: Springer-Verlag. doi:10.1007/978-3-662-03315-9

Mili, H., & Rada, R. (1988). Merging thesauri: Principles and evaluation. *IEEE Transactions on Pattern Analysis and Machine Intelligence*, *10*(2), 204–220. doi:10.1109/34.3883

Mili, H., & Rada, R. (1992). A model of hierarchies based on graph homomorphisms. *Computers & Mathematics with Applications (Oxford, England)*, *23*(2), 343–361. doi:10.1016/0898-1221(92)90147-A

Mili, H., Rada, R., Wang, W., Strickland, K., Bolydreff, C., Olsen, L., & Elzer, P. et al. (1994). Practitioner and SoftClass: A comparative study of two software reuse research projects. *Journal of Systems and Software*, *25*(2), 147–170. doi:10.1016/0164-1212(94)90003-5

Miller, G. A. (1995). WordNet: A lexical database for English. *Communications of the ACM*, *38*(11), 39–41. doi:10.1145/219717.219748

Mimno, D., & McCallum, A. (2008). Topic models conditioned on arbitrary features with Dirichlet-multinomial regression. *UAI*. Retrieved from http://www.cs.umass.edu/ mimno/papers/dmr-uai.pdf

Minh, H., Tran, G., Raikundalia, K., & Yun Yang, S. (2006). An experimental study to develop group awareness support for real-time distributed collaborative writing. *Information and Software Technology*, *48*(11), 1006–1024. doi:10.1016/j.infsof.2005.12.009

Mitra, P., Wiederhold, G., & Decker, S. (2001). *A scalable framework for interoperation of information sources.* Paper presented at the 1st International Semantic Web Working Symposium (SWWS'01), Stanford, CA.

Mkwelo, S., Jager, D. G., & Nicolls, F. (2003). Watershed-based segmentation of rock scenes and proximity-based classification of watershed regions under uncontrolled lighting conditions. In *Proceedings of the Fourteenth Annual Symposium of the Pattern Recognition Association* (pp. 107-112). Academic Press.

Mohr, L. (1982). *Explaining organizational behavior.* San Francisco: Jossey-Bass.

Monteiro, E., & Hanseth, O. (1995). Social shaping of information infrastructure: On being specific about the technology. In Information technology and changes in organizational work. Chapman & Hall.

Moudani W, Shahin A, Chakik F, & Mora-Camino F. (2011). Dynamic rough sets features reduction. *International Journal of Computer Science and Information Security, 9*(4).

Mukherjea, S. (2005). Information retrieval and knowledge discovery utilizing a biomedical semantic web. *Briefings in Bioinformatics*, *6*(3), 252–262. doi:10.1093/bib/6.3.252 PMID:16212773

Mukherjee, I., & Blei, D. (2008). Relative performance guarantees for approximate inference in latent Dirichlet allocation. *NIPS*. Retrieved from http://books.nips.cc/papers/files/nips21/NIPS2008_0434.pdf

Mukhopadhyay, S., & Parzen, E. (2013). *Nonlinear time series modeling by LPTime, non-parametric empirical learning.* arXiv:1308.0642.

Müller, B., & Olbrich, S. (2012). Developing theories in information systems research: The Grounded theory method applied. In Information systems theory: Explaining and predicting our digital society (vol. 2, pp. 323-347). Berlin: Springer. doi:10.1007/978-1-4419-9707-4_16

Müller-Merbach, H. (2004). Organisationelle Intelligenz - ein historischer Überblick von 1967 bis heute. In P. Chamoni (Ed.), *Multikonferenz Wirtschaftsinformatik (MKWI) 2004* (pp. 287–300). Berlin: AKA.

Musat, C., Velcin, J., Trausan-Matu, S., & Rizoiu, M.-A. (2011). *Improving topic evaluation using conceptual knowledge.* IJCAI.

Myles, J. (2008). *Discovering critical success factors for implementing an automated performance measurement system: A case study approach.* (Doctoral Dissertation). School of Management, Edith Cowan University.

Nagi, J., Yap, K. S., Nagi, F., Tiong, S. K., & Ahmed, S. K. (2011). A computational intelligence scheme for the prediction of the daily peak load. *Applied Soft Computing*, *11*(8), 4773–4788. doi:10.1016/j.asoc.2011.07.005

Neely, A., Adams, C., & Kennerley, M. (2002). *The performance prism: The scorecard for measuring and managing business success.* London: Prentice Hall Financial Times.

Neely, A., Richards, H., Mills, J., Platts, K., & Bourne, M. (1997). Designing performance measures: A structured approach. *International Journal of Operations & Production Management*, *17*(11), 1131–1152. doi:10.1108/01443579710177888

Neumann, G., Backofen, R., Baur, J., Becker, M., & Braun, C. (1997). *An information extraction core system for real world German text processing*. Paper presented at the Fifth Conference on Applied Natural Language Processing, Washington, DC. doi:10.3115/974557.974588

Newman, D., Karimi, S., & Cavedon, L. (2009). External evaluation of topic models. In *Proceedings of Australasian Document Computing Symposium* (pp. 11–18). Sydney: Academic Press.

Newman, D., Lau, J. H., Grieser, K., & Baldwin, T. (2010). Automatic evaluation of topic coherence. In *Proceedings of Human Language Technologies. The 2010 Annual Conference of the North American Chapter of the Association for Computational Linguistics* (pp. 100-108). ACL.

Newman, D., Han Lau, J., Grieser, K., & Baldwin, T. (2010). *Automatic evaluation of topic coherence*. NAACL.

Nicolini, D. (2007). Stretching out and expanding work practices in time and space: The case of telemedicine. *Human Relations*, *60*(6), 889–920. doi:10.1177/0018726707080080

Nicolini, D., & Gherardi, S. (2003). *Knowing in organizations: A practice-based approach*. Armonk, NY: M.E. Sharpe Inc.

Niculescu, A., van Dijk, B., Nijholt, A., Li, H., & See, S. (2013). Making social robots more attractive: The effects of voice pitch, humor and empathy. *International Journal of Social Robotics*, *5*(2), 171–191. doi:10.1007/s12369-012-0171-x

Noble, A., & Boukerroui, D. (2006). Ultrasound image segmentation: A survey. *IEEE Transactions on Medical Imaging*, *25*(8), 987–1010. doi:10.1109/TMI.2006.877092 PMID:16894993

Nonaka, I. (1994). A dynamic theory of organizational knowledge creation. *Organization Science*, *5*(1), 14–37. doi:10.1287/orsc.5.1.14

North, K. (2011). Wissensmanagement implementieren. In *Wissensorientierte Unternehmensführung* (pp. 265–339). Wiesbaden: Gabler. doi:10.1007/978-3-8349-6427-4_8

Noy, N. F., & Klein, M. (2004). Ontology evolution: Not the same as schema evolution. *Knowledge and Information Systems*, *6*(4), 428–440. doi:10.1007/s10115-003-0137-2

Noy, N. F., & Musen, M. A. (2003). The PROMPT suite: Interactive tools for ontology merging and mapping. *International Journal of Human-Computer Studies*, *59*(6), 983–1024. doi:10.1016/j.ijhcs.2003.08.002

Nudurupati, S., Bititci, U., Kumar, V., & Chan, F. (2011). State of the art literature review on performance measurement. *Computers & Industrial Engineering*, *60*(2), 279–290. doi:10.1016/j.cie.2010.11.010

O'Connor, B., Balasubramanyan, R., Routledge, B. R., & Smith, N. A. (2010). From Tweets to polls: Linking text sentiment to public opinion time series. In W. Cohen & S. Gosling (Eds.), *Proceedings of the Fourth International AAAI Conference on Weblogs and Social Media* (pp. 122–129). The AAAI Press.

Odell, J., Parunak, V. D., & Bauer, B. (2000). Extending UML for agents. In *Proc. of the Agent-Oriented Information Systems Workshop at the 17th National Conference on Artificial Intelligence*. Academic Press.

Oliveira, S. R. M., & Zaiane, O. R. (2010). Privacy preserving clustering by data transformation. *Journal of Information and Data Management*, *1*(1), 37–51.

Onn, Y. (2005). Privacy in the digital environment. Haifa Center of Law and Technology, 1-12.

Orlikowski, W. (2007). Sociomaterial practices: Exploring technology at work. *Organization Studies*, *28*(9), 1435.

Orlikowski, W., & Scott, S. V. (2008). Sociomateriality: Challenging the separation of technology, work and organization. The Academy of Management Annals, *2*(1), 433-474.

Orlikowski, W. (2002). Knowing in practice: Enacting a collective capability in distributed organizing. *Organization Science*, *13*(3), 249–273. doi:10.1287/orsc.13.3.249.2776

Orlikowski, W. (2006). Material knowing: The scaffolding of human knowledgeability. *European Journal of Information Systems*, *15*(5), 460–466. doi:10.1057/palgrave.ejis.3000639

Orlikowski, W., & Iacono, C. (2001). Research commentary: Desperately seeking the "it" in IT research-A call to theorizing the IT artifact. *Information Systems Research*, *12*(2), 2. doi:10.1287/isre.12.2.121.9700

Orsborn, S., Cagan, J., Pawlicki, R., & Smith, R. C. (2006). Creating cross-over vehicles: Defining and combining vehicle cases using shape grammars. *AIEDAM, 20*(03), 217–246. doi:10.1017/S0890060406060185

Oulasvirta, A., Lehtonen, E., Kurvinen, E., & Raento, M. (2010). Making the ordinary visible in microblogs. *Personal and Ubiquitous Computing, 14*(3), 237–249. doi:10.1007/s00779-009-0259-y

Padgham, L., & Winiko, M. (2002a). Prometheus: A pragmatic methodology for engineering intelligent agents. In *Proceedings of the OOPSLA 2002 Workshop on Agent-Oriented Methodologies* (pp. 97-108). Seattle, WA: OOPSLA.

Padgham, L., & Winiko, M. (2002b). *Prometheus: Engineering intelligent agents*. Tutorial notes. Unpublished.

Pak, A., & Paroubek, P. (2010). Twitter as a corpus for sentiment analysis and opinion mining. In *Proceedings of the Seventh International Conference on Language Resources and Evaluation (LREC'10)*. Valletta, Malta: European Language Resources Association (ELRA).

Pantel, P., Philpot, A., & Hovy, E. (2005). Data alignment and integration. *Computer, 38*(12), 43–50. doi:10.1109/MC.2005.406

Papanikolaou, K. A., Grigoriadou, M., Magoulas, G. D., & Kornilakis, H. (2002). Towards new forms of knowledge communication: The adaptive dimension of a Web-based learning environment. *Computers & Education, 39*(4), 333–360. doi:10.1016/S0360-1315(02)00067-2

Paredes, P., & Rodriguez, P. (2002). Considering sensing-intuitive dimension to exposition-exemplification in adaptive sequencing. In *Proceedings of AH2002 Conference* (pp. 556–559). Malaga, Spain: Adaptive Hypermedia and Adaptive Web-Based Systems. doi:10.1007/3-540-47952-X_83

Parikh, R., & Movassate, M. (2009). *Sentiment analysis of user-generated Twitter updates using various classification techniques*. Retrieved October 17, 2011 from http://nlp.stanford.edu/courses/cs224n/2009/fp/19.pdf

Partyka, J., Alipanah, N., Khan, L., Thuraisingham, B., & Shekhar, S. (2008). Content-based ontology matching for GIS datasets. In *Proceedings of the International Conference on Advances in Geographic Information Systems* (pp.407-410). New York: Academic Press.

Patel, C., Supekar, K., Lee, Y., & Park, E. K. (2003). OntoKhoj: A semantic web portal for ontology searching, ranking and classification. In *Proceedings of the 5th ACM CIKM International Workshop on Web Information and Data Management* (pp. 58-61). ACM. doi:10.1145/956708.956712

Peirce, C. (1991). Deduktion, Induktion und Hypothese. In C. Peirce & K. Apel (Eds.), *Schriften zum Pragmatismus und Pragmatizismus* (pp. 229–250). Frankfurt: Suhrkamp.

Perez, A. G., Lopez, M. F., & Corcho, O. (2003). *Ontological engineering*. Retrieved from http://www.imamu.edu.sa/topics/IT/IT%206/Ontological%20/Engineering.pdf

Perini, A., Bresciani, P., Giorgini, P., Giunchiglia, F., & Mylopoulos, J. (2001). Towards an agent oriented approach to software engineering. In A. Omicini & M. Viroli (Eds.), *WOA 2001 Dagli oggetti agli agenti: tendenze evolutive dei sistemi software*. Modena, Italy: Pitagora Editrice Bologna.

Perini, A., Bresciani, P., Giunchiglia, F., Giorgini, P., & Mylopoulos, J. (2001). A knowledge level software engineering methodology for agent oriented programming. In J. P. M®uller, E. Andre, S. Sen, & C. Frasson (Eds.), *Proceedings of the Fifth International Conference on Autonomous Agents* (pp. 648-655). Montreal, Canada: Academic Press.

Perkiö, J., Buntine, W. L., & Sami Perttu, S. (2004). Exploring independent trends in a topic-based search engine. In Proceedings of Web Intelligence (pp. 664–668). Academic Press. doi:10.1109/WI.2004.10053

Petry, F., & Yager, R. (2008). Evidence resolution using concept hierarchies. *IEEE Transactions on Fuzzy Systems, 16*(2), 299–308. doi:10.1109/TFUZZ.2007.895966

Petry, F., & Yager, R. (2010). Negotiation as creative social interaction using concept hierarchies. In *Proceedings of International Conference on Informaion Processing and Management of Uncertainty* (pp. 281-289). New York, NY: Springer. doi:10.1007/978-3-642-14049-5_29

Petry, F., & Zhao, L. (2009). Data mining by attribute generalization with fuzzy hierarchies in fuzzy databases. *Fuzzy Sets and Systems*, *160*(15), 2206–2223. doi:10.1016/j.fss.2009.02.014

Pickering. (1995). *The mangle of practice: Time, agency, and science*. The University of Chicago.

Pidun, T., Buder, J., & Felden, C. (2011). Optimizing process performance visibility through additional descriptive features in performance measurement. In *Proceedings of the 2011 IEEE 15th International Enterprise Distributed Object Computing Conference Workshops*. IEEE. doi:10.1109/EDOCW.2011.17

Pidun, T., & Felden, C. (2011). On the restriction to numeric indicators in performance measurement systems. In *Proceedings of the 2011 IEEE 15th International Enterprise Distributed Object Computing Conference Workshops*. IEEE. doi:10.1109/EDOCW.2011.16

Pidun, T., & Felden, C. (2012). On improving the visibility of hard-measurable process performance. *International Journal of Intelligent Information Technologies*, *8*(2), 59–74. doi:10.4018/jiit.2012040104

Pidun, T., & Felden, C. (2013). The role of performance measurement systems between assessment tool and knowledge repository. In *Proceedings of the 46th Hawaii International Conference on System Science (HICSS)*. IEEE. doi:10.1109/HICSS.2013.539

Pinto, H., Gomez-Perez, A., & Martins, J. (1999). *Some issues on ontology integration*. Paper presented at the IJCAI99 Conference on Ontologies and Problem Solving Methods: Lessons Learned and Future Trends.

Poernomo, I., Umarov, T., & Hajiyev, F. (2011). Formal ontologies for data-centric business process management. In *Proceedings of International Conference on Application of Information and Communication Technologies* (pp. 1-8). AICT. doi:10.1109/ICAICT.2011.6110897

Popescu, A.-M., & Etzioni, O. (2007). Extracting product features and opinions from reviews. In A. Kao & S. R. Poteet (Eds.), *Natural language processing and text mining* (pp. 9–28). London: Springer. doi:10.1007/978-1-84628-754-1_2

Power, M. (1999). *The audit society: rituals of verification*. Oxford, UK: Oxford University Press. doi:10.1093/acprof:oso/9780198296034.001.0001

Pugliese, M. J., & Cagan, J. (2002). Capturing a rebel: Modelling the Harley-Davidson brand through a motorcycle shape grammar. *Research in Engineering Design: Theory Applications and Concurrent Engineering*, *13*(3), 139–156.

Qi, Y., Song, M., Yoon, S. C., & Watrous-deVersterre, L. (2011). Combining supervised learning techniques to key-phrase extraction for biomedical full-text. *International Journal of Intelligent Information Technologies*, *7*(1), 33–44. doi:10.4018/jiit.2011010103

Quanquan, Z., Yingjie, L., & Weiliang, Z. (2013). Uterine calcifications segmentation and extraction from ultrasound images based on level set. In *Proceedings of International Conference on Information Management, Innovation Management and Industrial Engineering* (vol. 2, pp. 591–594). Academic Press. doi:10.1109/ICIII.2013.6703222

Quinlan, J. R. (1986). Learning decision tree classifiers. *ACM Computing Surveys*, *28*(1).

Quinlan, J. R. (1993). *C4.5: Programs for machine learning*. Morgan Kaufmann.

Quinlan, J. R. (1996). Improved use of continuous attributes in C4.5. *Journal of Artificial Intelligence Research*, *4*.

Rahman, N., Burkhardt, P. W., & Hibray, K. W. (2010). Object migration tool for data warehouses. *International Journal of Strategic Information Technology and Applications*, *1*(4), 55–73. doi:10.4018/jsita.2010100104

Rahm, E., & Bernstein, P. A. (2001). A survey of approaches to automatic schema matching. *The VLDB Journal*, *10*(4), 334–350. doi:10.1007/s007780100057

Rainer, R., & Watson, H. (1995). The keys to executive information system success. *Journal of Management Information Systems, 12*(2), 83.

Rajalakshmi, M., Purusothaman, T., & Pratheeba, S. (2010). Collusion-free privacy preserving data mining. *International Journal of Intelligent Information Technologies, 6*(4), 30–45. doi:10.4018/jiit.2010100103

Raj, P., & Raj, K. (2011). Comparison of stock using different neural network types. *International Journal of Advanced Engineering & Application, 2*(1), 158–160.

Ramachandran, L., & Alagumurthi, N. (2013). Appraisal of equipments for lean manufacturing environment - A MCDA approach. *International Journal of Recent Technology and Engineering, 2*(1), 44–47.

Ramage, D., & Rosen, E. (2009). *Stanford topic modeling toolbox*. Retrieved from http://nlp.stanford.edu/software/tmt/tmt-0.3/

Ramage, D., Dumais, S., & Liebling, D. (2010). Characterizing microblogs with topic models. In W. Cohen & S. Gosling (Eds.), *Proceedings of the Fourth International AAAI Conference on Weblogs and Social Media* (pp. 130–137). The AAAI Press.

Ramage, D., Rosen, E., Chuang, J., Manning, C. D., & McFarland, D. A. (2009). Topic modeling for the social sciences. In *Proceedings of NIPS 2009 Workshop on Applications for Topic Models: Text and Beyond*. Whistler, Canada: NIPS. Retrieved from http://www.brokenurl#pubs/tmt-nips09.pdf

Ramage, D., Hall, D., Nallapati, R., & Manning, C. D. (2009). Labeled LDA: A supervised topic model for credit attribution in multi-labeled corpora.EMNLP. doi:10.3115/1699510.1699543

Rani, C., & Deepa, S. N. (2011). An intelligent operator for genetic fuzzy rule based system. *International Journal of Intelligent Information Technologies, 7*(3), 28–40. doi:10.4018/jiit.2011070103

Rao, R. V. (2013). *Decision making in the manufacturing environment using graph theory and fuzzy multiple attribute decision making methods* (Vol. 2). London: Springer Verlag. doi:10.1007/978-1-4471-4375-8

Rao, R. V., & Patel, B. K. (2011). Material selection using a novel multiple attribute decision making method. *International Journal of Manufacturing, Materials, and Mechanical Engineering, 1*(1), 43–56. doi:10.4018/ijmmme.2011010104

Reiter, R. (1980). A logic for default reasoning. *Artificial Intelligence, 13*(1-2), 81–132. doi:10.1016/0004-3702(80)90014-4

Rendon, E., Abundez, I. M., Gutierrez, C., Díaz, S., Zagal, Arizmendi, A., ... Arzate, H. E. (2011). A comparison of internal and external cluster validation indexes. In *Proceedings of the Fifth WSEAS International Conference on Computer Engineering and Applications* (pp. 158-163). WSEAS.

Rezaee, M. R., Zwet, P. M. J., Lelieveldt, B. P. F., Geest, R. J., & Reiber, J. H. C. (2000). A multiresolution image segmentation technique based on pyramidal segmentation and fuzzy clustering. *IEEE Transactions on Image Processing, 9*(7), 1238–1248. doi:10.1109/83.847836 PMID:18262961

Richard, P., Devinney, T., Yip, G., & Johnson, G. (2009). Measuring organizational performance: Towards methodological best practice. *Journal of Management, 35*(3), 718–804. doi:10.1177/0149206308330560

Richter, A., Koch, M., & Krisch, J. (2007). *Social commerce - Eine Analyse des Wandels im E-Commerce (technical report no. 2007-03)*. Munich: Faculty Informatics, Bundeswehr University Munich.

Rigi, M. A., & Khoshalhan, F. (2011). Eliciting user preferences in multi-agent meeting scheduling problem. *International Journal of Intelligent Information Technologies, 7*(2), 45–62. doi:10.4018/jiit.2011040103

Robertson, D. (2006). Airbus will lose €4.8bn because of A380 delays. *The Times (UK)*. Retrieved December 30, 2011, from http://www.thetimes.co.uk/tto/business/industries/engineering/article2170403.ece

Rosemann, M., Recker, J., & Flender, C. (2008). Contextualisation of business processes. *International Journal of Business Process Integration and Management, 3*(1), 47. doi:10.1504/IJBPIM.2008.019347

Roshni, V. S., & Raju, G. (2011). Image segmentation using multiresolution texture gradient and watershed algorithm. *International Journal of Computers and Applications*, *22*(6), 21–28. doi:10.5120/2588-3579

Saart, P., Gao, J., & Kim, N. H. (2014). Semiparametric methods in nonlinear time series analysis: A selective review. *Journal of Nonparametric Statistics*, *26*(1), 141–169. doi:10.1080/10485252.2013.840724

Safari, H., & Jafarzadeh, A. H., Khanmohammadi, E., & Fathi, M. R. (2013). Applying interval GTMA method for technology selection in the presence of both cardinal and ordinal data. *World Applied Programming*, *3*(4), 142–149.

Sahay, S. (1997). Implementation of information technology: A time-space perspective. *Organization Studies*, *18*(2), 229–260. doi:10.1177/017084069701800203

Salman, N. (2006). Image segmentation based on watershed and edge detection techniques. *The International Arab Journal of Information Technology*, *3*(2), 104–110.

Salton, G., & McGill, M. (1983). *Introduction to modern information retrieval*. New York: McGraw-Hill.

Sanders, D. A., & Suso, J. B. (2010). Inferring learning style from the way students interact with a computer user interface and the WWW. *IEEE Transactions on Education*, *53*(4), 613–620. doi:10.1109/TE.2009.2038611

Sang, Y., Shen, H., & Tian, H. (2009). Privacy-preserving tuple matching in distributed databases. *IEEE Transactions on Knowledge and Data Engineering*, *21*(12), 1767–1782. doi:10.1109/TKDE.2009.39

Santos, I. J. G., & Madeira, E. R. M. (2010). A semantic-enabled middleware for citizen centric e-government services. *International Journal of Intelligent Information Technologies*, *6*(3), 34–55. doi:10.4018/jiit.2010070103

Sapankevych, N. I., & Sankar, R. (2009). Time series prediction using support vector machines a survey. *IEEE Computational Intelligence Magazine*, *4*(2), 25–38. doi:10.1109/MCI.2009.932254

Saunders, C., & Kim, J. (2007). Perspectives on time. *Management Information Systems Quarterly*, *31*(4), iii–xi.

Sawyer, S., & Southwick, R. (2002). Temporal issues in information and communication technology-enabled organizational change. *The Information Society*, *18*(4), 263–280. doi:10.1080/01972240290075110

Scaffidi, C., Bierhoff, K., Chang, E., Felker, M., Ng, H., & Chun, K. (2007). Red Opal: Product-feature scoring from reviews. In ACM (Ed.), *Proceedings of the 8th ACM Conference on Electronic Commerce* (pp. 182–191). New York: ACM.

Schäffer, U., & Matlachowsky, P. (2008). Warum die Balanced Scorecard nur selten als strategisches Managementsystem genutzt wird. *Zeitschrift für Planung & Unternehmenssteuerung*, *19*(2), 207–232. doi:10.1007/s00187-008-0055-2

Schapire. (1997). Boosting the margin: A new explanation for the effectiveness of voting methods. In *Machine Learning: Proceedings of 14th Int. Conference*. Morgan Kaufmann.

Schatzki, T. R. (2006). On organizations as they happen. *Organization Studies*, *27*(12), 1863–1873. doi:10.1177/0170840606071942

Schiff, L., Van House, N., & Butler, M. (1997). Understanding complex information environments: A social analysis of watershed planning. In *Proceedings of the Conference on Digital Libraries* (pp. 161-168). Academic Press.

Segrera, S., & Moreno, M. (2005). Multiclassifiers: Applications, methods and architectures. In *Proc. of International Workshop on Practical Applications of Agents and Multiagents Systems* (pp. 263–271). Academic Press.

Sen, S. S., Rives, V. P., Messina, O. D., Morales-Torres, J., Riera, G., Angulo-Solimano, J. M., & Ross, P. D. et al. (2005). A risk assessment tool (OsteoRisk) for identifying Latin American women with osteoporosis. *Journal of General Internal Medicine*, *20*(3), 245–250. doi:10.1111/j.1525-1497.2005.40900.x PMID:15836528

Severinson-Eklundh, K., Green, A., & Huutenrauch, H. (2003). Social / collaborative aspects of interaction with a service robot. *Robotics and Autonomous Systems*, *42*(3-4), 223–234. doi:10.1016/S0921-8890(02)00377-9

Shah, S. R., Desai, M. D., & Panchal, L. (2010). Identification of content descriptive parameters for classification of renal calculi. *International Journal of Signal and Image Processing*, *1*(4), 255–259.

Shapiro, D. (1994). *The limits of ethnography: Combining social sciences for CSCW*. Chapel Hill, NC: ACM. doi:10.1145/192844.193064

Sharif Ullah, A. M. M., & Tamaki, J. (2011). Analysis of Kano-model-based customer needs for product development. *Systems Engineering*, *14*(2), 154–172. doi:10.1002/sys.20168

Sharma, A., & Ojha, V. (2010). Implementation of cryptography for privacy preserving data mining. *International Journal of Database Management Systems*, *2*(3), 57–65. doi:10.5121/ijdms.2010.2306

Shea, K., Ertelt, C., Gmeiner, T., & Ameri, F. (2010). Design-to-fabrication automation for the cognitive machine shop. *Advanced Engineering Informatics*, *24*(3), 251–268. doi:10.1016/j.aei.2010.05.017

Silvia, D., Saskia, B., Wim, J., & Nick, J. (2007). Students' experiences with collaborative learning in asynchronous computer-supported collaborative learning environments. *Computers in Human Behavior*, *23*(1), 496–514. doi:10.1016/j.chb.2004.10.021

Simon, H. (1959). Theories of decision-making in economics and behavioral science. *The American Economic Review*, *49*(3), 253–283.

Simon, H. A. (1984). The structure of ill-structured problems. In C. Nigel (Ed.), *Developments in design methodology*. New York: John Wiley & Sons.

Simon, H. A. (1990). *The sciences of the artificial* (2nd ed.). Cambridge, MA: The MIT Press.

Singh, K., Malik, D., & Sharma, N. (2011). Evolving limitations in k-means algorithm in data mining and their removal. *International Journal of Computational Engineering & Management*, *12*, 105–109.

Singh, R. (2007). A multi-agent decision support architecture for knowledge representation and exchange. *International Journal of Intelligent Information Technologies*, *3*(1), 37–59. doi:10.4018/jiit.2007010103

Siriwan, S., & Peter, H. (2006). A Bayesian approach to generating tutorial hints in a collaborative medical problem-based learning system. *Artificial Intelligence in Medicine*, *38*(1), 5–24. doi:10.1016/j.artmed.2005.04.003 PMID:16183267

Slife, B. (2004). Taking practice seriously: Toward a relational ontology. *Journal of Theoretical and Philosophical Psy.*, *24*, 2.

Slim, C. (2006). Neuro-fuzzy network based on extended Kalman filtering for financial time series. *World Academy of Science. Engineering and Technology*, *22*, 134–139.

Smith, A. & Brenner, J. (2012). *Twitter use 2012*. Academic Press.

Sommer, S., Schieber, A., Heinrich, K., & Hilbert, A. (2012). What is the conversation about? A topic-model-based approach for analyzing customer sentiments in Twitter. *International Journal of Intelligent Information Technologies*, *8*(1), 10–25. doi:10.4018/jiit.2012010102

Spender, J.-C. (1998). Pluralist epistemology and the knowledge-based theory of the firm. *Organization*, *5*(2), 233–256. doi:10.1177/135050849852005

Sridevi, U. K., & Nagaveni, N. (2011). An ontology based model for document clustering. *International Journal of Intelligent Information Technologies*, *7*(3), 54–69. doi:10.4018/jiit.2011070105

Sridhar, S., & Kumaravel, N. (2001). Automatic segmentation of medical images for renal calculi and analysis. *Medical Informatics and the Internet in Medicine*, *37*, 405–409. PMID:11347425

Sridhar, S., Kumaravel, N., & Easwarakumar, K. S. (2002). Segmentation of renal calculi in ultrasound images. *Medical Informatics and the Internet in Medicine*, *27*(4), 229–236. doi:10.1080/1463923021000054217 PMID:12745904

Steele-Johnson, D., Beauregard, R., Hoover, P., & Schmidt, A. (2000). Goal orientation and task demand effects on motivation, affect, and performance. *The Journal of Applied Psychology*, *85*(5), 724–738. doi:10.1037/0021-9010.85.5.724 PMID:11055145

Stephen, A., & Toubia, O. (2010). Deriving value from social commerce networks. *Networks Journal of Marketing Research, 67*(2), 215–228. doi:10.1509/jmkr.47.2.215

Steve, G., & Phebe, M. (2003). Interdisciplinary: Perceptions of the value of computer-supported collaborative work in design for the built environment. *Automation in Construction, 12*(5), 495–499. doi:10.1016/S0926-5805(03)00035-9

Steyvers, M., & Griffiths, T. (2005). *Matlab topic modeling toolbox.* Retrieved from http://psiexp.ss.uci.edu/research/programs_data/toolbox.htm

Stieglitz, S., Krüger, N., & Eschmeier, A. (2011). Themenmonitoring in Twitter aus der Perspektive des Issue Managements. In K. Meißner & M. Engelien (Eds.), Virtual enterprises, communities & social networks (pp. 69–78). Dresden: TUDpress.

Stiny, G. (2006). *Shape, talking about seeing and doing.* Cambridge, MA: The MIT Press.

Stoutenburg, S. (2008). *Acquiring advanced properties in ontology mapping.* Paper presented at the PIKM'08, Napa Valley, CA. doi:10.1145/1458550.1458553

Strauss, A. L., & Corbin, J. M. (1998). *Basics of qualitative research: Techniques and procedures for developing grounded theory.* Sage Publications.

Strecker, S., Frank, U., Heise, D. and Kattenstroth, H. (2012). MetricM: A modeling method in support of the reflective design and use of performance measurement systems. *Information Systems and e-Business Management, 10*(2), 241–276.

Strübing, J. (2008). *Grounded Theory: Zur sozialtheoretischen und epistemologischen Fundierung des Verfahrens der empirisch begründeten Theoriebildung.* Wiesbaden: Verlag für Sozialwissenschaften. doi:10.1007/978-3-531-91968-3

Stumme, G., & Maedche, A. (2001). *FCA-merge: Bottom-up merging of ontologies.* Paper presented at the International Joint Conference on Artificial Intelligence.

Suchman, L.A. (1989). *Notes on computer support for cooperative work.* Department of Computer Science, University of Jyvaskyla.

Suso, J. B., Sanders, D. A., & Tewkesbury, G. E. (2005). Intelligent browser-based systems to assist Internet users. *IEEE Transactions on Education, 48*(4), 580–585. doi:10.1109/TE.2005.854570

Sycara, K. P. (1998). Multi-agent systems. *AI Magazine, 19*(2), 79–92.

Systems Engineering Fundamentals. (2001). Defense Acquisition University Press.

Tae, K. Y., Sung, K., Deok, W. K., Joon, Y. C., Wan, H. L., Ein, O., & Eun-Cheol, P. (2013). Osteoporosis risk prediction for bone mineral density assessment of postmenopausal women using machine learning. *Yonsei Medical Journal, 54*(6), 1321–1330. doi:10.3349/ymj.2013.54.6.1321 PMID:24142634

Tamilselvi & Thangaraj. (2011). An efficient segmentation of calculi from us renal calculi images using anfis system. *European Journal of Scientific Research, 55*(2), 323–333.

Tamilselvi & Thangaraj. (2011). Computer aided diagnosis system for stone detection and early detection of kidney stones. *Journal of Computer Science, 7*(2), 250-254. doi:10.3844/jcssp.2011.250.254

Tamiselvi, P. R. (2013). Segmentation of renal calculi using squared euclidean distance method. *International Journal of Scientific Engineering and Technology, 2*(7), 651–655.

Tan, H., & Lambrix, P. (2007). *A method for recommending ontology alignment strategies.* Paper presented at the ISWC/ASWC 2007. doi:10.1007/978-3-540-76298-0_36

Tang, J., Li, J., Liang, B., Huang, X., Li, Y., & Wang, K. (2006). Using Bayesian decision for ontology mapping. *Journal of Web Semantics: Science, Services and Agents on the World Wide Web, 4*(4), 243-262.

Tay, F. E. H., & Cao, L. J. (2002). E-descending support vector machines for financial time series forecasting. *Neural Processing Letters*, 15(1-4), 179–195. doi:10.1023/A:1015249103876

Taylor, B. C., Schreiner, P. J., Stone, K. L., Fink, H. A., Cummings, S. R., Nevitt, M. C., & Ensrud, K. E. et al. (2004). Long-term prediction of incident hip fracture risk in elderly white women: Study of osteoporotic fractures. *Journal of the American Geriatrics Society*, 52(9), 1479–1486. doi:10.1111/j.1532-5415.2004.52410.x PMID:15341549

Taylor, P. C., & Silverman, B. W. (1993). Block diagrams and splitting criteria for classification trees. *Statistics and Computing*, 3(4), 147–161. doi:10.1007/BF00141771

Thanasis, D., Alejandra, M., & Fatos, X. (2006). A layered framework for evaluating on-line collaborative learning interactions. *International Journal of Human-Computer Studies*, 64(7), 622–635. doi:10.1016/j.ijhcs.2006.02.001

Thangamani, M., & Thangaraj, P. (2011). Effective fuzzy ontology based distributed document using non-dominated ranked genetic algorithm. *International Journal of Intelligent Information Technologies*, 7(4), 26–46. doi:10.4018/jiit.2011100102

Thangavel, K., Shen, Q., & Pethalakshmi, A. (2006). Application of clustering for feature selection based on rough set theory approach. *AIML Journal*, 6(1), 19–27.

Thomas, J., Sussman, S., & Henderson, J. (2001). Understanding "strategic learning": Linking organizational learning, knowledge management, and sensemaking. *Organization Science*, 12(3), 331–345. doi:10.1287/orsc.12.3.331.10105

Thomas, M., Redmond, R., & Yoon, V. (2009). Using ontological reasoning for an adoptive e-commerce experience. *International Journal of Intelligent Information Technologies*, 5(4), 41–52. doi:10.4018/jiit.2009080703

Tian, H., & Zhang, W. (2011). Extending l-diversity to generalize sensitive data. *Data & Knowledge Engineering*, 70(1), 101–126. doi:10.1016/j.datak.2010.09.001

Tipping, M. E. (2000). The relevance vector machine. *Advances in Neural Information Processing Systems*, 12, 652–658.

Toutanova, K., & Johnson, M. (2007). A Bayesian LDA-based model for semi-supervised part-of-speech tagging. NIPS. Retrieved from http://books.nips.cc/papers/files/nips20/NIPS2007_0964.pdf

Triantafillou, E., Pomportsis, A., & Georgiadou, E. (2002). AES-CS: Adaptive educational system based on cognitive styles. In *Proceeding of AH2002 Workshop on Recommendation and Personalization in Ecommerce* (pp. 10–20). Malaga, Spain: Universidad de Málaga, Departamento de Lenguajes y Ciencias de la Computación.

Tripathi, A., Gupta, P., Trivedi, A., & Kala, R. (2011). Wireless sensor node placement using hybrid genetic programming and genetic algorithms. *International Journal of Intelligent Information Technologies*, 7(2), 63–83. doi:10.4018/jiit.2011040104

Tsoukas, H. (1996). The firm as a distributed knowledge system: A constructivist perspective. *Strategic Management Journal*, 17(S2), 11–25. doi:10.1002/smj.4250171104

Tumasjan, A., Sprenger, T. O., Sandner, P. G., & Welpe, I. M. (2010). Predicting elections with Twitter: What 140 characters reveal about political sentiment. In W. Cohen & S. Gosling (Eds.), *Proceedings of the Fourth International AAAI Conference on Weblogs and Social Media* (pp. 178–185). The AAAI Press.

Twopcharts. (2014). *Twitter activity monitor*. Retrieved March 06, 2014, from http://twopcharts.com/twitteractivitymonitor

Urquhart, C., Lehmann, H., & Myers, M. (2009). Putting the 'theory' back into grounded theory: Guidelines for grounded theory studies in information systems. *Information Systems Journal*, 20(4), 357–381. doi:10.1111/j.1365-2575.2009.00328.x

Veeramalai, S., & Kannan, A. (2011). Intelligent information retrieval using fuzzy association rule classifier. *International Journal of Intelligent Information Technologies*, 7(3), 14–27. doi:10.4018/jiit.2011070102

Vidya Banu, R., & Nagaveni, N. (2013). Evaluation of a perturbation-based technique for privacy preservation in a multi-party clustering scenario. *Information Sciences*, 232, 437–448. doi:10.1016/j.ins.2012.02.045

VidyaBanu, R., & Nagaveni, N. (2009). Preservation of data privacy using PCA based transformation. In *Proc of the IEEE International Conference on Advances in Recent Technologies in Communication and Computing* (pp. 439-443). IEEE.

VidyaBanu, R., & Nagaveni, N. (2012). Low dimensional data privacy preservation using multi layer artificial neural network. *International Journal of Intelligent Information Technologies, 8*(3), 17–31. doi:10.4018/jiit.2012070102

Villarreal, P., Alesso, M., Rocco, S., Galli, M. R., & Chiotti, O. (2003). Approaches for the analysis and design of multi-agent systems. *Inteligencia Artificial, Revista Iberoamericana de Inteligencia Artificial, 21*, 73-81. Retrieved from http://www.aepia.org/revista

Vincent, L., & Dougherty, E. R. (1994). Morphological segmentation for textures and particles. In E. Dougherty (Ed.), *Digital image processing: Fundamentals and applications* (pp. 43–102). New York, NY: Marcel-Dekker.

Vorakulpipat, C., & Rezgui, Y. (2008). An evolutionary and interpretive perspective to knowledge management. *Journal of Knowledge Management, 12*(3), 17–34. doi:10.1108/13673270810875831

Vyas Gayatri, S., & Misal Chetan, S. (2013). Comparative study of different multi-criteria decision-making methods. *International Journal on Advanced Computer Theory and Engineering, 2*(4), 2319–2526.

Wagatsuma, K., Goto, Y., & Cheng, J. (2012). Formal analysis of cryptographic protocols by reasoning based on deontic relevant logic: A case study in Needham-Schroeder shared-key protocol. In *Proceedings of International Conference on Machine Learning and Cybernetics* (ICMLC) (pp. 1866-1871). ICMLC. doi:10.1109/ICMLC.2012.6359660

Wallach, H. M., Murray, I., Salakhutdinov, R., & Mimno, D. (2009). Evaluation methods for topic models. In *Proceedings of the 26th International Conference on Machine Learning* (pp. 1-8). ACM Press.

Wang, A. H. (2010). Don't follow me - Spam detection in Twitter. In *Security and Cryptography (SECRYPT), Proceedings of the 2010 International Conference on* (pp. 142–151). Retrieved from http://dblp.uni-trier.de/db/conf/secrypt/secrypt2010.html#Wang10

Wang, C., Blei, D. M., & Heckerman, D. (2008). Continuous time dynamic topic models. *UAI.* Retrieved from http://uai2008.cs.helsinki.fi/UAI_camera_ready/wang.pdf

Wang, W., & Rea, S. (2005). Intelligent ensemble system aids osteoporosis early detection. In *Proceedings of the 6th World Scientific and Engineering Academy and Society (WSEAS) International Conference on Evolutionary Computing.* WSEAS.

Wang, P., & Xu, B. (2007). LILY: The results for the ontology alignment contest OAEI 2007. In *Proceedings of ISWC 2007 Ontology Matching Workshop* (pp. 167-175), Busan, Korea: OAEI.

Wang, X., & McCallum, A. (2006). Topics over time: A non-Markov continuous-time model of topical trends. KDD. doi:10.1145/1150402.1150450

White, J. (1997). Mobile agents. In *Software agents.* AAAI Press.

Wikipedia. (n.d.). *Statistical measures.* Retrieved from http://en.wikipedia.org/wiki/Sensitivity_and_specificity

Wikipedia. (n.d.a). *Decision support system.* Retrieved from http://en.wikipedia.org/wiki/Decision_support_system

Wikipedia. (n.d.b). *Pattern recognition.* Retrieved from http://en.wikipedia.org/wiki/Pattern_recognition

Wikipedia. (n.d.c). *Statistical learning theory.* Retrieved from http://en.wikipedia.org/wiki/Statistical_learning_theory

Wikipedia. (n.d.d). *Structural risk minimization.* Retrieved from http://en.wikipedia.org/wiki/Structural_risk_minimization

Wikipedia. (n.d.e). *Support vector machine.* Retrieved from http://en.wikipedia.org/wiki/Support_vector_machine

Wilson, P. (1991). *Computer supported cooperative work: An introduction.* Kluwer Academic Publishers.

Wimmer, H., & Zhou, L. (Eds.). (2013). AMCIS. Chicago, IL: Academic Press.

Winograd, T. (1972). *Understanding natural language.* New York, NY: Academic Press.

Wooldridge, M. (1997). Agent based software engineering. *IEEE Proceedings of Software Engineering, 144*(1), 26–37.

Wooldridge, M., Jennings, N. R., & Kinny, D. (2000). The gaia methodology for agent-oriented analysis and design. *Journal of Autonomous Agents and Multi-Agent Systems, 3*(3), 285–312. doi:10.1023/A:1010071910869

Wright, D., Gutwirth, S., Friedewald, M., Hert, P. D., Langheinrich, M., & Moscibroda, A. (2009). Privacy, trust and policy-making: Challenges and responses. *Computer Law & Security Report, 25*(1), 69–83. doi:10.1016/j.clsr.2008.11.004

Wu, H., Salzberg, B., & Sharp, G. C. (2005). Subsequence matching on structured time series data. In *Proceedings of the ACM International Conference on Management of Data* (pp. 682-693). ACM. doi:10.1145/1066157.1066235

Wu, Y., Chen, Y., & Chang, R. (2011). Mining negative generalized knowledge from relational databases. *Knowledge-Based Systems, 24*(1), 134–145. doi:10.1016/j.knosys.2010.07.013

XAP. (n.d.). *Time series with real time analytics.* Retrieved from http://docs.gigaspaces.com/sbp/time-series.html

Xie, J., Jiang, Y., & Tsui, H. (2005). Segmentation of kidney from ultrasound images based on texture and shape priors. *IEEE Transactions on Medical Imaging, 24*(1), 45–56. doi:10.1109/TMI.2004.837792 PMID:15638185

Xue-shen, S., Zhong-ying, Q., Da-ren, Y., Qing-hua, H., & Hui, Z. (2007). A novel feature selection approach using classification complexity for SVM of stock market trend prediction. In *Proceedings of the Fourteenth International Conference on Management Science & Engineering* (pp. 1655-1659). Academic Press.

Xu, K., Wang, W., Ren, J. S. J., Xu, J., Liu, L., & Liao, S. S. Y. (2011). Classifying consumer comparison opinions to uncover product strengths and weaknesses. *International Journal of Intelligent Information Technologies, 7*(1), 1–14. doi:10.4018/jiit.2011010101

Yager, R. (2004). On the retranslation process in Zadeh's paradigm of computing with words. *IEEE Transactions on Systems, Man and Cybernetics, A, 34*(2), 1184-95,

Yager, R., & Petry, F. (2013). Intuitive decision-making using hyper similarity matching. In *Proceedings IFSA-NAFIPS'13* (pp. 386-389). Hoboken, NJ: Wiley-IEEE Press.

Yager, R. (1988). A generalized view of non-monotonic knowledge: A set theoretic perspective. *International Journal of General Systems, 14*(3), 251–265. doi:10.1080/03081078808935007

Yager, R. (1990). A model of participatory learning. *IEEE Transactions on Systems, Man, and Cybernetics, 20*(5), 1229–1234. doi:10.1109/21.59986

Yager, R. (2009). Participatory learning with granular observations. *IEEE Transactions on Fuzzy Systems, 17*(1), 1–13. doi:10.1109/TFUZZ.2008.2005690

Yager, R., & Petry, F. (2012). A linguistic approach to influencing decision behavior. *IEEE Transactions on Fuzzy Systems, 20*(2), 249–261.

Yager, R., & Petry, F. (2014). Hyper matching: Similarity matching with extreme values. *IEEE Transactions on Fuzzy Systems, 22*(4), 949–957. doi:10.1109/TFUZZ.2013.2278988

Yamazaki, A., Yamazaki, K., Burdelski, M., Kuno, D., & Fukushima, M. (2010). Coordination of verbal and non-verbal actions in human-robot interaction at museums and exhibitions. *Journal of Pragmatics, 42*(9), 2398–2414. doi:10.1016/j.pragma.2009.12.023

Yan, F., Xu, N., & Qi, Y. (2009). Parallel inference for latent Dirichlet allocation on graphics processing units. *NIPS.* Retrieved from http://books.nips.cc/papers/files/nips22/NIPS2009_0546.pdf

Yang, W., & Qiao, S. (2010). A novel anonymization algorithm: Privacy protection and knowledge preservation. *Expert Systems with Applications, 37*(1), 756–766. doi:10.1016/j.eswa.2009.05.097

Yan, X., & Jacob, F. S. (2007). Emergent CSCW systems: The resolution and bandwidth of workplaces. *International Journal of Medical Informatics, 76*(1), S261–S266. PMID:16822715

Yao, L., Mimno, D., & McCallum, A. (2009). Efficient methods for topic model inference on streaming document collections. *KDD.* Retrieved from http://www.cs.umass.edu/ mimno/papers/fast-topic-model.pdf

Yeh, J., & Hsu, P. (2010). H HUIF and MSICF - Novel algorithms for privacy preserving utility mining. *Expert Systems with Applications*, *37*(7), 4779–4786. doi:10.1016/j.eswa.2009.12.038

Ye, J., & Ji, S. (2010). Discriminant analysis for dimensionality reduction: An overview of recent developments. In *Biometrics: Theory, methods, and applications*. New York: Wiley-IEEE Press.

Yi, J., & Niblack, W. (2005). Sentiment mining in webfountain. In *Proceedings of the 21st International Conference on Data Engineering* (pp. 1073-1083). IEEE Computer Society.

Yildirim, P., Çeken, Ç., Hassanpour, R., Esmelioglu, S., & Tolun, M. R. (2011). Mining MEDLINE for the treatment of osteoporosis. *Journal of Medical Systems*. doi:10.1007/s10916-011-9701-6 PMID:21494854

Yin, R. (2003). Applied social research methods series:*Case study research: Design and methods* (3rd ed.; vol. 5). Thousand Oaks, CA: Sage Publications.

Yoshikawa, S., Satou, K., & Konagaya, A. (2004). Drug interaction ontology (DIO) for inferences of possible drug-drug interactions. *Studies in Health Technology and Informatics*, *107*(1), 454–458. PMID:15360854

Yu, A. C. (2006). Methods in biomedical ontology. *Journal of Biomedical Informatics*, *39*(3), 252–266. doi:10.1016/j.jbi.2005.11.006 PMID:16387553

Zadeh, L. (1975). The concept of a linguistic variable and its application to approximate reasoning. *Information Sciences*, *8*(3), 199–249. doi:10.1016/0020-0255(75)90036-5

Zadeh, L. (1996). Fuzzy logic = computing with words. *IEEE Transactions on Fuzzy Systems*, *4*(2), 103–111. doi:10.1109/91.493904

Zambonelli, F., Jennings, N. R., & Wooldridge, M. (2001). Organizational rules as an abstraction for the analysis and design of multi agent systems. *International Journal of Software Engineering and Knowledge Engineering*, *11*(3), 303–308. doi:10.1142/S0218194001000505

Zammuto, R. F., Griffith, T. L., Majchrzak, A., Dougherty, D. J., & Faraj, S. (2007). Information technology and the changing fabric of organization. *Organization Science*, *18*(5), 749–762. doi:10.1287/orsc.1070.0307

Zhang, J., Song, Y., Zhang, C., & Liu, S. (2010). Evolutionary hierarchical Dirichlet processes for multiple correlated time-varying corpora. *KDD*. Retrieved from http://research.microsoft.com/en-us/um/people/shliu/p1079-zhang.pdf

Zhang, J., Gou, Q., Liang, L., & He, X. (2013). Ingredient branding strategies in an assembly supply chain: Models and analysis. *International Journal of Production Research*, *51*(23–24), 6923–6949. doi:10.1080/00207543.2013.825747

Zhang, L., Dong, W., Zhang, D., & Shi, G. (2010). Two-stage image denoising by principal component analysis with local pixel grouping. *Pattern Recognition*, *43*(4), 1531–1549. doi:10.1016/j.patcog.2009.09.023

Zhao, W., Jiang, J., Weng, J., He, J., Lim, E.-P., Yan, H., & Li, X. (2011). Comparing Twitter and traditional media using topic models. In P. Clough, C. Foley, C. Gurrin, G. Jones, W. Kraaij, H. Lee, & V. Mudoch (Eds.), *Advances in information retrieval* (pp. 338–349). Berlin: Springer. doi:10.1007/978-3-642-20161-5_34

Zhou, J., Bai, T., Zhang, A., & Tian, J. (2008). The integrated methodology of wavelet transform and GA based-SVM for forecasting share price. In *Proceedings of the International Conference on Information and Automation* (pp. 729-733). Academic Press.

Zhu, J., Ahmed, A., & Xing, E. P. (2009). *MedLDA: Maximum margin supervised topic models for regression and classification*. ICML. doi:10.1145/1553374.1553535

Zhu, J., & Xing, E. P. (2010). *Conditional topic random fields*. ICML.

About the Contributors

Vijayan Sugumaran is Professor of Management Information Systems in the department of Decision and Information Sciences at Oakland University, Rochester, Michigan, USA. He is also WCU Professor of Global Service Management at Sogang University, Seoul, South Korea. He received his Ph.D in Information Technology from George Mason University, Fairfax, VA. His research interests are in the areas of Service Science, Ontologies and Semantic Web, Intelligent Agent and Multi-Agent Systems, Component Based Software Development, and Knowledge-Based Systems. He has published more than 150 articles in journals, conferences, and books. His most recent publications have appeared in *Information systems Research, ACM Transactions on Database Systems, IEEE Transactions on Education, IEEE Transactions on Engineering Management, Communications of the ACM, Healthcare Management Science*, and *Data and Knowledge Engineering*. He has edited twelve books and two journal special issues. He is the editor-in-chief of the *International Journal of Intelligent Information Technologies* and also serves on the editorial board of seven other journals. He was the program co-chair for the International Conference on Applications of Natural Language to Information Systems (NLDB 2008 and NLDB 2013). In addition, he has served as the chair of the Intelligent Agent and Multi-Agent Systems mini-track for Americas Conference on Information Systems (AMCIS 1999 - 2014) and Intelligent Information Systems track for the Information Resources Management Association International Conference (IRMA 2001, 2002, 2005 - 2007). He served as Chair of the E-Commerce track for Decision Science Institute's Annual Conference, 2004. He was the Information Technology Coordinator for the Decision Sciences Institute (2007-2009). He also regularly serves as a program committee member for numerous national and international conferences.

* * *

Noraziah Ahmad received Ph.D in Distributed Database from University Malaysia Terengganu (UMT) in 2007. She has published more than 200 papers (including International and national journals, conference papers, book chapters and articles). Currently, she is an Associate Professor at Faculty of Computer Systems & Software Engineering, University Malaysia Pahang. She serves as 270 committee members in conferences and reviewer of proceedings and journal; editorial board members for various journals; members in professional societies include IEEE, IAENG, IACSIT, MNCC and SDIWC. She has received more than 80 awards and recognitions including the Best FRGS Project 2010 Award in

2014; Diploma and Gold Medal in Moscow International Salon of Inventions and Innovation Technologies (ARCHIMEDES 2013); Special Awards - The Best Excellence, Grand Prix Archimedes Moskova 2013; Gold Medal and Special Award - Asia Invention Creativity Association in European Exhibition of Creativity and Innovation (EUROINVENT 2012), Romania. Her current research interests are distributed systems, data grid, Cloud Computing, modeling and simulation, and biofeedback.

Kannan Arputharaj received MSc degree from Annamalai University-Tamil Nadu in 1986, ME and PhD degrees from Anna University, Chennai, Tamil Nadu-India in 1991 and 2000, respectively. He is currently working as a Professor in the Department of Information Science and Technology, Anna University, Chennai, Tamil Nadu. His areas of interest include Database Systems, Data Mining and Artificial Intelligence.

Fadi Chakik has received his undergraduate degree from the Lebanese University and Master degree from Toulon and Var University in France. From 1995 till 1998, he pursued his PhD studies in Cognitive Science at the "Institut National Polytechnique de Grenoble" (INPG) in France inside the LEIBNIZ Laboratory. He joined the Lebanese-French University as full-time professor and led the computer science department from 1998 till 2007. He is actually an Associate Professor at the Lebanese University since 2008. His research areas focus on the conception and development of new algorithms for intelligent and robust object tracking in video sequences derived from the artificial intelligence domain mainly using Support Vector Machines and Neural Networks. Dr. Chakik published more than 20 scientific papers in the areas of support vector machines and neural networks, image recognition, object tracking, virtual advertisement and its applications. He is currently with the Group of Bioinformatics and Modeling in the research center of AZM for research in biotechnology and its applications in the Lebanese University.

Tagelsir Mohamed Gasmelseid holds BSc, MSc, postgraduate diploma, MPhil, and PhD in Information Systems. He published some articles in referred journal and contributed to some international conferences. His research interests include multi-agent, mobile and context aware systems, agent oriented software engineering and simulation, service oriented architectures, and the use of software agents in management and decision support systems for electronic commerce and electronic government. He edited two books on "Hydroinformatics" and "Pharmacoinformatics", and organized international workshops in these areas. He acted as head department, information systems in higher education institutions in Sudan and is currently teaching for the Department of Information Systems, College of Computer Sciences and Information Technology, King Faisal University in Saudi Arabia.

Kai Heinrich is a PhD student at Dresden University of Technology. He studied business informatics at Dresden University of Technology, focusing on statistical and econometric methods as well as business intelligence and information systems. His research interests include data mining, especially web mining and social network analysis in the domain of microblogs and virtual social networks. He is a teaching and research assistant within the Business Intelligence Research (BIR) competence center at Dresden University of Technology.

Tutut Herawan received PhD degree in computer science in 2010 from Universiti Tun Hussein Onn Malaysia. He is currently a senior lecturer at Department of Information System, University of Malaya. His research area includes rough and soft set theory, DMKDD, and decision support in information system. He has successfully co-supervised two PhD students and published more than 110 articles in various international journals and conference proceedings. He is an editorial board and act as a reviewer for various journals. He has also served as a program committee member and co-organizer for numerous international conferences/workshops.

Andreas Hilbert is Chair of Business Information Systems and Business Intelligence at the Technische Universität Dresden. He studied mathematics and economics at the University of Kaiserslautern and Karlsruhe (TH) and received his doctoral degree in 1998 at the Chair of mathematical methods in economics at the University of Augsburg. Since 2004, he is university professor at TU Dresden. Since then, Prof. Dr. Hilbert has worked as lecturer and consultant in the areas of market research, statistical data analysis, data mining and data model development. Prof. Dr. Hilbert authored numerous publications and is a frequent speaker on scientific and practical issues. He is also Chairman of the Business Intelligence Research e.V. (Dresden) and member of the Executive Committee of the Division of Business Intelligence within the Gesellschaft für Informatik e.V.

Jegatha Deborah Lazarus is currently working as an Assistant Professor in University College of Engineering Tindivanam affiliated to Anna University of Technology Chennai. She completed her Bachelor's degree in the Department of Computer Science and Engineering under Madurai Kamarajar University, Madurai during the year 2002. Following that, she pursued her Masters degree in the same discipline under Anna University Chennai during 2003-2005. She completed her doctoral program in the area of Artificial Intelligence under Anna University Chennai in the faculty of Information and Communication Engineering. Her areas of expertise are Artificial Intelligence, Knowledge Engineering, Data Mining, and Natural Language Processing.

Ho Cheong Lee received Ph.D in Computing, Product and Engineering Design from the Hong Kong Polytechnic University in 2007. He worked as an engineer in design, manufacturing, and installation of structural steelworks, and electrical and mechanical products. After gaining ten years professional experiences in industry, he then started his teaching and research career in the Design Technology Research Centre (DTRC) in the School of Design of the Hong Kong Polytechnic University. He has participated in professional society activities and has memberships of ACM, ASME, BCS, IEEE, and IET, and an associate member of ACS and IMechE. His research interests include computational design, finite element analysis, and particularly shape grammars and evolutionary design technology, their implementation, and their applications to engineering and product designs.

Tom Miller works as a Business Intelligence Consultant in the field of Reporting & Analytics at T-Systems Multimedia Solutions GmbH in Dresden, Germany. He designs and implements Business Intelligence Solutions mainly on the BI Stacks of Microsoft, MicroStrategy and SAS. On top of those solutions, he also develops individual software-components to solve analytical challenges. Tom Miller studied Business Informatics with a focus on Business Intelligence at the Technische Universität Dresden.

Walid Moudani received his Master diploma degree and Doctorate degree in computer science from Institut National Polytechnique of Toulouse (INPT) and Laboratory for Analysis and Architecture of Systems LAAS-CNRS in 1997 and 2001, respectively. Associate Professor at the Lebanese University since 2001. Member of the International Society on Multi-Criteria Decision-Making (MCDM). Main research subjects: Air transportation operations planning, decision making for revenue management, Data Compression, Image Recognition, Fuzzy logic and Data mining in Medical prediction. Publication of more than 30 papers in the areas of optimization, image recognition, compression and analysis, data warehouse, data mining and its applications. Member of the Group of Bioinformatics and Modeling in the research center of AZM for research in biotechnology and its applications at the Lebanese University. Director of Centre National des Arts et Métiers-CNAM, Tripoli-Lebanon Center, from 2005 until 2009.

N. Nagaveni received B.Sc and M.Sc degrees in Mathematics from Bharathiar University, India, in 1985, 1987 and 1988, respectively. She received her M.Phil degree from Avinashilingam University, India in 1989, M.Ed degree from Annamalai University, India in 1992 and PhD in the area of Topology in Mathematics from Bharathiar University, India in 2000. Since 1992, she has been with the Department of Mathematics, Coimbatore Institute of Technology, Coimbatore, Tamil Nadu, India, where she is working as an Associate Professor. She is a research supervisor and her research interests include Topology, Fuzzy sets and Continuous Functions, Distributed Computing, Web mining and Privacy Preserving Data Mining. She is a member of the Indian Science Congress Association (ICSA). She has presented research papers in the annual conference of ICSA. She has published papers in several National and International journals.

Frederick E. Petry (M'76–SM'81–F'96) received BS and MS degrees in physics and a PhD in computer and information science from The Ohio State University in 1975. He is currently a computer scientist in the Naval Research Laboratory at the Stennis Space Center Mississippi. He has been on the faculty of the University of Alabama in Huntsville, the Ohio State University and at Tulane University for 27 years until the EECS Department was eliminated after hurricane Katrina. His recent research interests include representation of imprecision via fuzzy sets and rough sets in databases, GIS and other information systems, semantic web systems and artificial intelligence including genetic algorithms. His research has been funded by NSF, NASA, DOE, NIH, and various DOD agencies and industry and by his affiliation with the Naval Research Laboratory. He has directed 22 PhD students in these areas in the past 15 years. Dr. Petry has over 350 scientific publications including 150 journal articles/book chapters and 9 books written or edited. His monograph on fuzzy databases has been widely recognized as the definitive volume on this topic. He is currently an associate editor of IEEE Transactions on Fuzzy Systems, Neural Processing Letters, International Journal of Intelligent Systems, etc., and area editor of information systems for Fuzzy Sets and Systems and has been general chairperson of several international conferences. He was selected as an IEEE Fellow in 1996 for his research on the use of fuzzy sets for modeling imprecision in databases in 2003 Fellow of the International Fuzzy Systems Association and an ACM Distinguished Scientist in 2008. In 2002 he was chosen as the outstanding researcher of the year in the Tulane University School of Engineering and received the Naval Research Laboratory's Berman Research Publication awards in 2004, 2008 and 2010.

Tim Pidun works as research consultant at the Project office for Institutional Strategy of the Dresden University of Technology. He is also currently doing a doctorate at the Chair of Business Intelligence Research of the Faculty of Business and Economics. His main research interest is the application and adaptation of Management systems in practice. Prior to this, he was working as scientific assistant, engineer and analyst in Germany. He is an independent engineering consultant and serves as lecturer at the Leipzig University of Applied Science, which also awarded a Diplom-Ingenieur (FH) degree to Mr. Pidun. He also holds a Master of Business Administration from the Danube University Krems in Austria.

Roy Rada, M.D., PhD, has a B.A. in Psychology from Yale Univ., a M.D. from Baylor College of Medicine, and a Ph.D. in Computer Science from Univ. Illinois in Urbana. He was in the mid-1980s the Editor of Index Medicus at the National Library of Medicine, in the early 1990s a Prof. of Computer Science at the Univ. of Liverpool, and in the late 1990's the Boeing Distinguished Prof. of Software Engineering at Washington State Univ. Currently he is a Prof. of Information Systems at the Univ. of Maryland Baltimore County. Roy founded the Many Using and Creating Hypermedia research group that earned millions of dollars worth of funding. Later, he was a prominent consultant on the topic of HIPAA for health care information systems. Roy is a Fellow of the Association for Computing Machinery and has authored two hundred journal articles and twenty books. His main current research interest is evolutionary computation applied to finance and health care.

Dima Rajab is a PhD. student in BioInformatics and Modeling at the Doctorate School of Sciences and Technologies. She received her Master diploma degree from Doctorate School of Sciences and Technologies at the Lebanese University in 2010.

Baskaran Ramachandran received ME degree from University of Madras in the year 2011 and PhD degree from Anna University, Chennai-600 025, Tamil Nadu-India in the year 2007. He is currently working as an Assistant Professor in the Department of Computer Science and Engineering, College of Engineering Guindy, Anna University, Chennai, Tamil Nadu, India. His areas of interest include Database Systems, Data Mining, Artificial Intelligence and Multimedia.

Ahmad Shahin has a BSc degree in Mathematics and Computer Science, a Master Degree in Automatic and Computer Engineering, a PhD in Computer Science (Fuzzy Modeling of Natural Objects in Computer Vision). He has worked on Doppler Color aliasing correction with the Research Center of Poitiers Hospital in France from 1994 to 1996. Since 1999, he is lecturing at the Lebanese University. During the last fifteen years, Dr. Ahmad Shahin has participated to several research activities and has more than 40 papers. Actually, he is part of the Laboratory of Mathematics and their Applications (LaMA-Lebanon) and the Group of Bioinformatics and Modeling at the Lebanese University. He is also the Head of the CIS Department at the Lebanese University – Faculty of Business Administration and the Chairman of the IT Association in Lebanon. Dr. Shahin has also a good experience in Multimedia Systems within the research he is doing and the Multimedia System Courses he gives in the MS programs. Dr. Shahin's research is focusing now on Image and Data Processing and more precisely on Compression in Image and Video, Face and Hand Identification for Biometrics, Classification in Hyper-Spectral Imaging, and Data Mining in Medical Predictions.

Stefan Sommer is Senior Manager Data Driven Advertising at Deutsche Telekom AG specialized in the fields of business intelligence and data analytics in the online business. Prior to joining Deutsche Telekom, he worked as Head of Business Intelligence – Reporting & Analytics at T-Systems Multimedia Solutions GmbH. Next to his professional life, Stefan Sommer is an external PhD student at the Technische Universität Dresden. Since 2009 he is member of the board of the Business Intelligence Research Association. Stefan Sommer studied business informatics and East Asia studies at the Technische Universität Dresden.

J. Suganthi is with Hindusthan college of Engineering and Technology since August 2008. She obtained her B.E degree in CSE from Madurai Kamaraj University, PG degree in M.E CSE from Bharathiar University, Coimbatore. & further did her PhD in Anna University, Chennai. She has 8 years of experience in Industry and 14 years of teaching experience. She has published several research papers in both International and National Journals and also She has published 2 books. She has organized several conferences, seminars, workshops in National Level. She is a life member of professional bodies like ISTE, IEI, and CSI.

P. R. Tamilselvi is an Assistant Professor(Senior Grade) in School of Computer Technology and Applications, Kongu Engineering College, Perundurai, Erode, India. She received the Master of Science in Computer Science in 1996 from Bharathiar University. She has completed M.Phil in Computer Science in the year 2001 from Bharathiar University and Ph.D degree in the year 2013 from Anna University, Chennai. She has guided 20 M.Phil research scholars from various universities. She has presented and published many papers in national and international conferences and journals. She has organized many Staff development Programmes, national Conferences, workshops and Hand-On Training Programmes. She completed and involved in many consultancy works. Her areas of interest are Medical Image Processing, Artificial Intelligence, Algorithm Design and Java Programming. As an eminent scholar she has guided many projects funded by different funding agencies.

S. Uma is Professor and Head of the PG Department of Computer Science and Engineering at Hindusthan Institute of Technology, Coimbatore, Tamil Nadu, India. She received her B.E., degree in Computer Science and Engineering from P.SG. College of Technology and the M.S., degree from Anna University, Chennai, Tamil Nadu, India. She received her Ph.D., in Computer Science and Engineering from Anna University, Chennai, Tamil Nadu, India. She has nearly 23 years of academic experience. She has organized many National Level events like seminars, workshops and conferences. She is a potential reviewer of International Journals and life member of the ISTE professional body. Her research interests are pattern recognition and analysis of nonlinear time series data.

R. VidyaBanu received her Bachelor's degree in Computer Science and Applications from Avinashilingam University, Coimbatore, India and her Masters degree in Computer Applications from Bharathidasan University, Trichy, India, during 1998 and 2001, respectively. In 2005, she completed her M.Phil (Computer Science) from Bharathiar University, Coimbatore, India and Ph.D (Computer Applications) from Anna University, Chennai, India in 2013. She has over 12 years of experience in teaching, and her areas of interest include Databases, Distributed Computing and Privacy Preserving Data Mining. She is currently Assistant Professor in the Department of Computer Applications, Sri Krishna College of Engineering and Technology, Coimbatore, India. She has presented research papers in National and International conferences and published papers in reputed International journals.

Hayden Wimmer is an Assistant Professor of Information Technology Management at Bloomsburg University. He holds a Ph.D. from the University of Maryland Baltimore County in Information Systems based in data mining and artificial intelligence applied to financial data supervised by Drs. Roy Rada (UMBC) and Victoria Yoon (VCU). He has a M.S. in Information Systems also from UMBC based in artificial intelligence and knowledge management. Additionally Dr. Wimmer holds an M.B.A. from the Pennsylvania State University Harrisburg campus focusing in Information Systems and a B.S. in Information Systems from York College of PA. Prior to academia, he worked in industry for over 10 years in different capacities in Information Technology performing programming, web design and administration, server administration, network configuration, database administration, and of course technical support on all levels.

Ronald R. Yager (S'66-M'68–SM'93–F'97) has worked in the area of fuzzy sets and related disciplines of computational intelligence for over twenty-five years. He has published over 500papers and fifteen books. He is considered one the world's leading experts in fuzzy sets technology. He was the recipient of the IEEE Computational Intelligence Society Pioneer award in Fuzzy Systems. Dr. Yager is a fellow of the IEEE, the New York Academy of Sciences and the Fuzzy Systems Association. He was recently given an award by the Polish Academy of Sciences for his contributions. He served at the National Science Foundation as program director in the Information Sciences program. He was a NASA/Stanford visiting fellow and a research associate at the University of California, Berkeley. He has been a lecturer at NATO Advanced Study Institutes. He received his undergraduate degree from the City College of New York and his PhD from the Polytechnic University of New York. Currently, he is Director of the Machine Intelligence Institute and Professor of Information and Decision Technologies at Iona College. He is Editor-in-Chief of the International Journal of Intelligent Systems. He serves on the editorial board of a number of journals including the *IEEE Transactions on Fuzzy Systems, Neural Networks, Data Mining and Knowledge Discovery, IEEE Intelligent Systems, Fuzzy Sets and Systems, the Journal of Approximate Reasoning,* and the *International Journal of General Systems.* In addition to his pioneering work in the area of fuzzy logic he has made fundamental contributions in decision making under uncertainty and the fusion of information. Among his current interests is the development of intelligent semantic web technology, communication for cooperating autonomous systems, information aggregation and decision making in adversarial and uncertain environments.

Victoria Yoon is Professor in the Department of Information Systems at Virginia Commonwealth University. She received her M.S. from the University of Pittsburgh and her Ph.D. from the University of Texas at Arlington. Her primary research interests have been in the application of Artificial Intelligence (AI) to business decision making in organizations and the managerial issues of such technology. She has published many articles in leading journals such as *MIS Quarterly, Decision Support Systems, Communications of the ACM, Journal of Management Information Systems, Information and Management,* and *Journal of Operation Research Society.*

Index